FORCES FOR GOOD

FORCES FOR GOOD

The Six Practices of High-Impact Nonprofits

Revised and Updated Edition

Leslie R. Crutchfield and

Heather McLeod Grant

Foreword by J. Gregory Dees

A project of the Center for the Advancement of
Social Entrepreneurship at Duke University's
Fuqua School of Business

JOSSEY-BASS
A Wiley Imprint
www.josseybass.com

Published by Jossey-Bass
A Wiley Imprint
One Montgomery Street, Suite 1200, San Francisco, CA 94104-4594—www.josseybass.com

Jossey-Bass books and products are available through most bookstores. To contact Jossey-Bass directly call our Customer Care Department within the U.S. at 800-956-7739, outside the U.S. at 317-572-3986, or fax 317-572-4002.

Wiley publishes in a variety of print and electronic formats and by print-on-demand. Some material included with standard print versions of this book may not be included in e-books or in print-on-demand. If this book refers to media such as a CD or DVD that is not included in the version you purchased, you may download this material at http://booksupport.wiley.com. For more information about Wiley products, visit www.wiley.com.

Library of Congress Cataloging-in-Publication Data

Crutchfield, Leslie R.
    Forces for good: the six practices of high-impact nonprofits / Leslie R. Crutchfield and Heather McLeod Grant; foreword by J. Gregory Dees. —Revised and updated
        p. cm.
    Includes bibliographical references and index.
    ISBN 978-1-118-11880-1 (hardback); ISBN 978-1-118-22457-1 (ebk); ISBN 978-1-118-23793-9 (ebk); ISBN 978-1-118-26269-6 (ebk)
        1. Nonprofit organizations—Management. 2. Leadership. 3. Organizational effectiveness.
I. Grant, Heather McLeod. II. Title.
HD62.6.C78 2012
658'.048—dc23
                                                                                    2012008074

Printed in the United States of America
revised and updated edition

HB Printing 10 9 8 7 6

CONTENTS

For Somerset
For Caleigh and Quinn

Foreword to the Revised and Updated Edition

Back in 2004, when Leslie Crutchfield and Heather McLeod Grant first teamed up to conduct the research for what became *Forces for Good*, I was excited about the project. I saw the potential for creating a popular research-based book that could help reframe the discussion of scale in the nonprofit sector, moving it away from organizational growth and replication toward a focus on broader strategies for magnifying impact on the world—which should be the goal of any nonprofit. This has been a major theme of my academic research over the past twenty years, as I've taught social entrepreneurship on the faculties of Duke's, Stanford's, and Harvard's schools of business. And it is now a major focus of the Center for the Advancement of Social Entrepreneurship (CASE) here at Duke University's Fuqua School of Business, where I currently teach.

By sponsoring Leslie and Heather's project and advising them on the original research, CASE had a chance to further an important agenda. The focus for any nonprofit organization that cares about improving social conditions must be on cost-effective ways to magnify its impact on the world. Sure, we need more people and more money to do this work. But more important, we need greater impact per person, per dollar—and we need resources to be directed to their highest and best use. That lesson is even more evident in today's turbulent environment. So the opportunity to partner on the original research for this book was one that CASE could not pass up. The end result surpassed our initial expectations. *Forces for Good* has become an instant classic, receiving great reviews and awards. It has made major strides in reorienting the discussion of scaling toward impact, just as we had hoped. And the book has sold very well, and continues to do so.

So you might wonder: Why bother with a revised and updated edition? The authors' answer was compelling, but it also made me nervous: they wanted to revisit the original twelve organizations to see how they were doing five years later. The first edition of this book was published in late 2007, just before one of the worst economic downturns in U.S. history, and we're not out of the recession yet. Was *now* the right time to revisit these nonprofits? In tough times like these, even the best organizations can struggle.

After all, I was at McKinsey & Company in the early 1980s when two partners, Tom Peters and Bob Waterman, published the management best seller *In Search of Excellence,* which also became an instant classic. And I recall the awkwardness when *Business Week* published a cover story a few years later titled "Oops," which showed that many of the "excellent" companies featured in the book were struggling, and no longer appeared so great.[1] As I recall, there were good explanations, but to many, these just sounded defensive.

Nonetheless, even with that memory lingering in my mind, I knew that any new edition of *Forces for Good* would have to consider how the original twelve high-impact groups fared during the downturn. If they struggled, there would be lessons. If they thrived, again there would be lessons. Fortunately, it was the latter, as you will see in Chapter Ten. They remained strong forces for good, despite the difficult financial times. This suggests, among other things, that nonprofits which do not focus just on growth to increase their impact can be more effective in down times. It is somewhat paradoxical that an organization might actually grow more when growth per se is not the goal. The high-impact strategies of these organizations—the six practices—have served them well, even in difficult times, as Leslie and Heather highlight in Chapter Eleven.

The other reason Leslie and Heather wanted to update the first edition made more immediate sense to me. They wanted to help leaders see more clearly how to apply the six practices to their organizations, especially local and regional nonprofits that may not have the means—or the desire—to scale up. In particular, Leslie and Heather wanted to illustrate how these practices can be applied to smaller organizations that might not identify with the large national or global nonprofits profiled in the original edition. This alone seemed like a good reason to pursue additional research. And the new edition does an excellent job of illustrating this, as you will see in Chapter Twelve.

If you want to know how to apply the six practices locally or in a smaller nonprofit, then this revised and updated edition will be very helpful to you. If you want to learn more about how the twelve high-impact nonprofits featured in the first edition have fared through the Great Recession, and how they have deepened their impact, then the new material in this book will surprise and intrigue you. Even if you've already read the original version of *Forces for Good,* you will still want to read these updates. And if you have not read the original, you have in your hands a richer, deeper, and even more practical version of the book—one that will help you immensely in your work.

As much as the findings in *Forces for Good* have helped move the social sector conversation away from scale and toward impact, we still have much to learn about how to accelerate social change and more effectively solve the complex problems facing our world. Research continues in that arena among other academics and practitioners, including our work at CASE.[2] Meanwhile, my own focus has shifted to what leaders in society (business, government, philanthropy, and so on) can do to create an external environment that allows us to yield the greatest impact from the work being done by social entrepreneurs all over the world. This includes creating a supportive policy environment, appropriate funding structures, reasonable performance measures, and more. For without the right ecosystem and infrastructure, many "forces for good" meet too much resistance. That's why I am currently working on a new book to promote the idea of a society that maximizes the benefits of social entrepreneurship. God willing, that book will be out in 2012.

On a personal level, writing this Foreword gave me the opportunity to reflect back on the many adventures I've had working with Heather and Leslie over the past twenty years. I first met them when they had just graduated from Harvard and were launching *Who Cares* magazine—a publication about social entrepreneurs and young activists seeking positive social change. We have remained friends and colleagues ever since. Both went off to earn MBAs after their experiences at *Who Cares.* Heather became a student of mine at Stanford, where I was teaching at the time. Leslie went to Harvard, a few years after I had left. After business school, Leslie went to work at Ashoka, a great place to learn more about social entrepreneurship; Heather went to McKinsey & Company, a fabulous environment for honing research and analytic skills. Each developed a set of complementary strengths. So it was a real pleasure to collaborate again on the research that led to *Forces for Good,* and to see this revised and updated edition come to fruition. In both the original content and the new chapters, you will find great lessons that can help you become a high-impact nonprofit.

November 2, 2011

J. GREGORY DEES
Center for the Advancement of
Social Entrepreneurship
Duke University's Fuqua School of Business

PART ONE

INTRODUCTION

Introduction to the Revised and Updated Edition

What makes great nonprofits great?

That was driving question we attempted to answer as we wrote the original edition of *Forces for Good: The Six Practices of High-Impact Nonprofits*. Since then, the entire world has changed.

When we set out to study the twelve high-impact nonprofits featured in the first edition, it was the mid-2000s. The U.S. economy had recovered from the dot-com bust of 2001 and was humming along, fueled by consumer demand, housing price inflation, and rampant technological and social innovation. At that exuberant moment in time, the social sector was obsessed with growth, scale, and organizational effectiveness. As they ramped up their private foundations and shifted their energy to the business of catalyzing social change, new "philanthrocapitalists," such as Bill Gates, Jeff Skoll, Pierre Omidyar, and Steve Case, were channeling funding to enterprising nonprofits.[1] And more individual donors than ever were giving at record levels, fueling rapid growth in the number of nonprofits.

In short, it was a boom time for the nonprofit world. Until, suddenly, it wasn't.

About a year after *Forces for Good* was released in fall 2007, the global economy ground to a halt. Lehman Brothers collapsed in September 2008; the housing bubble burst; financial markets melted down; unemployment spiked; and the U.S. economy fell into recession. Billions of dollars were ploughed into the financial sector, but nonprofits were left unmoored. In the social sector, the collapse not only affected individual people and organizations but also impacted us *collectively* as well. The fear is that this might be the "new normal."

Many individuals—including the wealthy and the simply generous—have cut back on their philanthropy. Overall U.S. giving declined in 2008 for the first time in more than two decades; toward the end of 2011, a majority of U.S. nonprofits had reported decreased or flat levels of charitable gifts, and researchers were predicting mixed fundraising prospects for most nonprofits in 2012, given the unpredictable economy and rising demand for critical nonprofit programs and services.[2] As foundation endowments have dropped, some funders have refocused on pressing social needs, leaving "nice to haves," such as arts groups, to fend for themselves. Many businesses have cut back on their charitable giving, despite record corporate profits for some. Everywhere, local, state, and federal governments today are struggling to balance budgets and reduce deficits by any means necessary—and social spending is usually first on the chopping block. In short, it has been a perfect storm for nonprofits these past five years: greater needs, fewer resources. Talk about having to do more with less.

So as we approached the fifth anniversary of the first edition of *Forces for Good,* we were acutely aware that the last few years have been challenging for the nonprofit sector. It was against this backdrop that we decided to revisit our initial work and update it to reflect a new, more austere reality—and once again see what we might learn from some of the best nonprofits about how to survive, and even thrive, in difficult times.

CAN WE THRIVE IN TUMULTUOUS TIMES?

This sense of crisis prompted us to write an update to *Forces for Good.* We were deeply curious to learn how these enormous economic, social, and political changes were playing out in the social sector: How were they impacting the original twelve organizations we studied? How had these trends affected smaller nonprofits struggling to do more with less in local communities? And closer to home and the point of this book, *Do the six practices we uncovered still hold up in a dramatically different context?*

Nothing we found caused us to reject the six practices as described in the first edition. In fact, as we have toured the country these past few years speaking to nonprofits and philanthropic groups, leading workshops, and advising organizations in the sector, our belief in the fundamental effectiveness of the six practices for scaling social impact has been reinforced. Everywhere we've been, we've seen examples of nonprofits large and small deploying some or all of the practices to increase their impact. Most important, our findings were reinforced by feedback from our readers, who told us they'd found a new language and framework to describe what some of them had been doing all along.

When we embarked on our initial research for *Forces for Good,* we did so with the investigative lens of organizational effectiveness and nonprofit management. We were writing in the genre of business management books like *Good to Great* and *Built to Last,* and we therefore anticipated uncovering internal *management* practices that caused these twelve nonprofits to be great. The counterintuitive insight we uncovered and presented in the first edition was that building a good organization was necessary, but not sufficient. In fact, the twelve high-impact nonprofits we studied were all managed quite differently and had varying cultures, wide-ranging budgets and brands, extremely diverse boards, and very few patterns around their internal operations.

What was the same across them all—and what ultimately led us to uncover the six practices—was that they focused very clearly on the outside world, on engaging all the sectors, and on influencing others to become advocates for their cause. As we expressed it then, they spent as much time focused externally on changing systems—by influencing government policies, shaping markets, building fields of practice, and nurturing social and organizational networks—as they did on their own operations. They cared less about management practices per se than they did about their ability to influence others and to build entire movements to create more lasting change.

It was a fresh way of looking at the work of nonprofits—and this framework seemed to resonate in the field. Over the past five years, we've observed a change in the language and mind-set of many of the nonprofits we've met—not just because of our work, but because others have begun to write and talk about these ideas as well. There has been a shift from the previous two decades, which were more focused on the role of individuals (social entrepreneurs) and organizations; now the focus is on larger networks, ecosystems, and collective impact. We didn't invent the six practices—after all, advocacy, corporate partnerships, movement building, grassroots organizing, and innovation are all concepts that have been around for years—but they had perhaps not been getting as much attention. What we did was shine a spotlight on these practices and put them in context, with clear examples of how they were being used by twelve nonprofits as different pathways for scaling impact.

Many readers intuitively understood that the six practices weren't actually about nonprofit management as much as a different approach to increasing an organization's impact on the world, using the power of influence and movement building. They welcomed a framework that would help them shift from an organizational mind-set to a relational mind-set; from a more industrial-era model of production, where the nonprofit produces goods and services for customers, to a network model, where the *nonprofit's raison d'être is to catalyze social change by inspiring action in others.* Although this model is most relevant for social change organizations that aspire to lasting impact, rather than pure charities such as schools, hospitals, or churches, it speaks to many nonprofits in our sector.

The difference is subtle, but important. And it has real implications for how we define success in the social sector: Is success about building an efficient and effective organization to meet immediate short-term needs—or it is about achieving the mission and sustaining significant impact over the long term? Most nonprofits *say* it is about the latter, but many of them primarily *act* in pursuit of the former. Ultimately it's "both-and": it is important to have effective and efficient nonprofits, not as ends in themselves, but as means to achieving social impact; and it's important to meet short-term needs, even as we aspire to longer-term social change. And that view is becoming more widespread in our sector. It's as if the best thinking about social movements and advocacy from the 1960s and 1970s is being combined with what we've learned in the 1980s and 1990s about building strong organizations—and now taken to a new level with the addition of systems thinking, online tools, and new understanding about networks and collective action.

Nonprofit leaders increasingly realize that their real power lies in the ability to build platforms for connections; to share ideas and information; to influence others to spread innovative models; to connect the dots across issues, industries, and sectors even as they provide services for their clients and help meet immediate needs. This is the power of what the Monitor Institute (where Heather now works) refers to as working with and through networks—or networked approaches to social change. To achieve the highest levels of impact, the best nonprofits and funders realize they can't act unilaterally, but instead must collaborate and leverage the power of individual and organizational networks. They can enhance relationships with their nonprofit peers as well as with other actors—engaging private and governmental entities, and mobilizing individual citizens—so that they can align action to solve at the scale of the problem.

To put it another way, success is found when nonprofits strive to create *collective impact* rather than work in isolation focused only on shoring up their own organizations—a concept that Leslie and her FSG colleagues John Kania and Mark Kramer wrote about in their book, *Do More Than Give: The Six Practices of Donors Who Change the World* (which builds on the best practices articulated in *Forces for Good* and draws on Kania and Kramer's *Stanford Social Innovation Review* article).[3] Collective impact requires organizations to adopt a systemic approach to social change, one in which nonprofits, governments, businesses, and the public come together around a common agenda and use shared metrics to track progress. The focus of collective impact is on the relationships *between* the organizations and their progress toward *shared* objectives. The point is that organizations aiming to solve some of the complex problems facing our world shouldn't dwell only on scaling up or spreading any single social innovation; the best organizations are *networked nonprofits* that drive collective impact and thus are able to achieve greater results than any one player could achieve alone.

Indeed, in our more recent work as advisers and consultants in the social sector, both of us have focused on this theme, exploring what it means for nonprofit and philanthropic leaders to collaborate more effectively to achieve results. What does it take to fundamentally change systems? What does it mean to focus on scaling *impact* rather than just on scaling a *program or an organization*? And perhaps most important, how can smaller, local nonprofits maximize their effectiveness in this networked world, given that they receive the lion's share of resources and collectively touch more lives than any single national nonprofit?

After all, according to a study by the Urban Institute, more than 80 percent of all American charities operate on less than $1 million annually.[4] For every one of the large nonprofits featured in our initial research, there are literally hundreds of thousands of organizations that are serving local communities and aspiring to have outsized impact with fewer resources. Although our initial research looked at how nonprofits can scale their social impact, by the time we studied the twelve high-impact groups, most were between twenty and thirty years old and operating on very substantial budgets, averaging around $40 million. (One of our selection criteria was that they had to have national or international scale of impact.) This was a far cry from the reality facing many local organizations trying to have deep impact in one place. In sum, as we prepared to write this revised and updated edition, what we wanted to know was, *How are the six practices applied in a different economic context, and how are they being applied by smaller nonprofits?*

We followed two parallel tracks to answer these questions. First, we contacted each of the original twelve high-impact nonprofits, interviewed all but one of their CEOs, and spoke with other senior leaders in select cases, to understand what had changed, how these groups had adapted to the new economic reality, and what, if anything, they were doing differently in applying the six practices. Second, we searched for leading examples of local or smaller nonprofits that were using one or more of the practices to deepen their community impact, and we studied them as well. What we found might surprise you—as it did us.

WHAT'S NEW IN THIS EDITION

This edition includes three completely new chapters based on new research, and a diagnostic tool to help leaders of organizations of all types, sizes, and ages understand their starting point and strengthen their application of the six practices. In addition, we have restructured the book to clarify the purposes of the different parts.

Part One includes this new Introduction, which reflects the more recent context for our work—a time of economic austerity. It also includes the original Introduction from 2007, which has been updated for accuracy, but still reflects the context at the time of our initial research—a period of economic growth and expansion for nonprofits and philanthropy.

Part Two describes our original findings in detail, exploring each of the six practices of high-impact nonprofits. (These chapters reflect our initial research, which concluded in 2006.) It also includes the two original chapters focused on how to implement and sustain the six practices.

Part Three includes several completely new chapters, in which we present our most recent research to show how the six practices have been employed by the original twelve high-impact nonprofits to both widen and deepen impact in the social sector; we also examine how local and smaller organizations use the six practices to achieve greater impact in one geographical region or issue area. Part Four includes all our appendixes and research data—details about our methodology for the original research as well as this updated edition—and original "front matter" to the first edition; it also includes our author bios and acknowledgments. If you're already familiar with *Forces for Good,* you may want to turn immediately to Part Three after reading this new Introduction.

Chapter Ten tackles our first new research question: How did our original twelve high-impact nonprofits survive the Great Recession? The most striking and surprising trend we uncovered when we reached out to these twelve groups was that most of them had *grown* in the past five years, even as they continued to scale their impact. The news was heartening. It affirmed that these were truly extraordinary organizations, not just groups that got lucky during a boom time. In this chapter, you'll learn just how these nonprofits managed to thrive during a downturn, and additional lessons you can apply to your organization.

Chapter Eleven revisits the original twelve nonprofits through the lens of the six practices we uncovered in the first edition. How have these groups continued to apply the six practices as levers for increasing impact—and what else have they learned along the way? Are all the practices relevant during a downturn, or are some more important than others? We share new stories and examples of how the original twelve nonprofits have continued to apply the six practices with remarkable success.

Then in Chapter Twelve we reveal what we learned from our recent research on local and smaller nonprofits. After all, the nonprofits we examined for the first edition were national in scale and scope, but they represent a very small percentage of the whole sector. Our big finding was that local and smaller groups can use some or all of the practices to great effect, and we share their lessons here.

In Chapter Thirteen, we offer a simple diagnostic tool to help nonprofits of all sizes and stripes understand their current organizational capabilities and how they can begin to apply the six practices. This tool was developed in collaboration with leaders of nonprofits large and small, as we prepared materials for workshops and conferences.

In Part Four, Appendixes A through D give more detail on our research methods and sources for the first edition. Appendix E provides updated profiles of the original twelve nonprofits, reflecting current data as a supplement to the moment-in-time data presented in the original chapters on the six practices. Appendix F describes our research methodology and sources for the new material. We've also moved the original Preface from the first edition back here (Appendix G); it felt more specific to the moment in time when we first wrote this book.

WE CAN'T AFFORD TO WAIT

Ultimately, we hope this new edition will help nonprofits cross the chasm between the current scale of our solutions and the increasing complexity of social and environmental problems. At times it feels as though these problems are growing faster than our ability to solve them—and, in fact, sometimes they are. Issues of global population explosion, extreme poverty, climate change, failing or nonexistent health care, pandemics, archaic K–12 education, volatile economies that create greater rich-poor divides—all are increasingly interconnected, complex, and systemic. And we are realizing that attempting to solve these problems through the efforts of any single organization or social entrepreneur acting alone is a fool's errand. Although we need innovative models, entrepreneurial individuals, and courageous leadership—and although we rely on strong and healthy organizations to provide critical services—we also need these isolated actors to work in more aligned ways and influence larger systems in order to make lasting collective impact.[5]

So what are you waiting for? Once again, we hope this book will serve both as a rallying cry and as a map into this unknown territory. Whether you're picking it up for the first time and just discovering the six practices, or revisiting them through new stories; or whether you're working globally, locally, or somewhere in between—we hope you find something in here to inspire you to become a greater *force for good.*

INTRODUCTION TO THE
FIRST EDITION

During the last several decades, a new cadre of entrepreneurial nonprofits has created extraordinary levels of social impact. These pioneering "change makers" are the vanguard of a growing civic sector—a segment of the U.S. economy now valued at more than $1 trillion. Operating at the interstices of government and the market—a broad and ill-defined "grey space"—these organizations play an increasingly important role in shaping our world.

That's why we set out nearly a decade ago to research and write about some of the most successful nonprofits of our era. We surveyed thousands of nonprofit CEOs and conducted more than sixty interviews just to select the twelve exemplary organizations featured in this book. (See Table I.1.)

Then we spent two years studying these organizations intensively and uncovering their secrets to success. *We wanted to know what enabled them to have such high levels of impact.* What we learned along the way truly surprised us.

In the course of our research, we discovered six practices that help great nonprofits achieve significant results. Our findings were nothing like the conventional wisdom about nonprofit management we had read before. You'll learn in this book—just as we learned—that we need new frameworks for understanding what makes great nonprofits great, and new ways of thinking about creating social change. Fortunately, these twelve organizations can help show us the way.

TABLE I.1. TWELVE EXEMPLARY ORGANIZATIONS.

Organization	Issue Areas
Center on Budget and Policy Priorities	Federal and state budget analysis
City Year	National service, youth leadership
Environmental Defense Fund	Environment
Exploratorium	Museums, science education
Feeding America (formerly America's Second Harvest—The Nation's Food Bank Network)	Hunger relief
Habitat for Humanity	Housing
The Heritage Foundation	Conservative public policy
National Council of La Raza	Hispanic interests
Self-Help	Housing and economic development
Share Our Strength	Hunger relief
Teach For America	Education reform
YouthBuild USA	Youth leadership, housing, job training

WHY THIS BOOK, AND WHY NOW?

Our research on high-impact nonprofits arrives at a key inflection point in the development of the global social sector. Indeed, we believe the rise of this sector is one of the great untold stories of our time.

When we started writing the first edition of this book, 1.5 million nonprofits in the United States alone accounted for more than $1 trillion in revenues annually of the nation's economy.[1] During the preceding fifteen years, nonprofits had grown faster than the overall economy, with thirty thousand new organizations created each year. In fact, nonprofits were the third-largest industry in the United States, behind retail and wholesale trade, but ahead of construction, banking, and telecommunications.[2]

Although terminology varies—the industry has been alternately called civil society, the citizen sector, the social sector, the non-profit sector, or the third sector—its importance is undeniable.

Internationally, similar trends are reflected in the growth of a global civil society. "Few developments on the global scene over the past three decades have been as momentous as the recent upsurge in private, nonprofit, voluntary, or civil society organizations," notes scholar Lester Salamon, writing in 1999. "We are in the midst of a 'global associational revolution.'"[3] Worldwide expenditures in this sector accounted for nearly 5 percent of combined global gross domestic product, or $1.1 trillion in economic activity.[4]

Several forces have propelled this growth. First is the unprecedented amount of wealth flowing to charitable organizations from corporate foundations, private philanthropists, and individual donors. American grantmaking foundations alone had nearly $500 billion in assets under management as of 2006.[5] And the estimated amount of money predicted to be transferred between generations by 2050 was *$43 trillion,* some of which would ultimately go to charitable institutions.[6] Even more important has been the new emphasis on "giving while living"—with more donors taking an active role in their philanthropy during their lifetimes. Because nonprofits operate at the interstices of the market and the state, they increasingly act as intermediaries, channeling private wealth to help solve public problems.

At the same time, political pressures and economic realities are forcing many governments to retrench. As the social welfare state scales back at all levels, nonprofits are filling the gaps and providing services that were historically the domain of the state. In the United States, federal cutbacks in social spending, and pressures to devolve services to the local level, have resulted in more outsourcing to community-based groups. The trend is similar in other developed nations around the world.

Simultaneously, new technologies and instantaneous global communications have created a heightened awareness of the problems facing our fragile planet: climate change; natural disasters; ethnic and cultural conflict; nuclear proliferation; AIDS and pandemics; and hunger, homelessness, and persistent poverty. All these issues are compounded by a surging global population that is quickly depleting the earth's resources. There's a sense of urgency to solving these problems, as well as a growing awareness that our other institutions are failing us.

In response, leading social sector organizations are rising to the challenge, finding ways to address the world's problems by working with, and through, government and business to launch innovative solutions. The best are run by social entrepreneurs—highly adaptive, innovative leaders who see new ways to solve old problems and who find points of leverage to create large-scale systemic change. These organizations—including the twelve profiled in this book—are the vanguard of the social sector. Like their equivalents in the for-profit sector, these nonprofits aren't content merely to plod along with incremental change or let conventional wisdom stand in the way of their success. They are collectively creating new models for social change.

And the global power elite is taking notice. Today, no Davos World Economic Forum gathering of leaders would be complete without a coterie of social entrepreneurs.[7] These leaders are the social sector equivalents of successful business entrepreneurs, only they are creating innovative new solutions to the world's most pressing social and environmental problems. So it's not surprising that the two groups are teaming up. Philanthropy has been rediscovered, with a new twist.

Today's corporate titans aren't content to merely accrue wealth; they now want to have a more meaningful impact *in their lifetimes*. High-tech leaders such as Bill Gates of Microsoft, Pierre Omidyar and Jeff Skoll of eBay, Steve Case of America Online, and newcomers such as Sergey Brin and Larry Page of Google are giving while living. The global philanthropy game is no longer about making money and passing it on to heirs or donating it to traditional charities such as an alma mater, local opera company, or United Way. The new philanthropy is all about leveraging financial resources by investing in the most entrepreneurial agents of change—those that have figured out how to scale their impact exponentially. It's the end of charity as we know it, and the beginning of high-impact philanthropy.

Given all these converging trends, it's not surprising that leading social entrepreneurs and their organizations have outgrown the conventional tools of the trade. Merely building a great board or delivering adequate services or even running an efficient non-profit is no longer enough. In order to be true forces for good, they must learn new ways of thinking and acting. Today's social entrepreneurs, nonprofit leaders, board members, and philanthropists are hungrier than ever for concise, well-researched information that can help them achieve greater social change.

But if you were to study the existing nonprofit management literature, you'd be no closer to understanding how to achieve meaningful impact in this new fast-paced, global environment. Most early research on nonprofit scale focused on *program replication* as a means of expanding social impact.[8] In the for-profit world, this is the equivalent of studying product development and distribution: a necessary function, but overall, only a small part of what makes great companies successful. In fact, because the sector was still emerging back then, studying nonprofits was a new discipline. These early thinkers paid little attention to the nonprofit organizations themselves and more to the sector as a whole.

Then, in the past two decades, the focus shifted to building *organizational capacity* in order to deliver programs more efficiently.[9] Scholars looked at how nonprofit leaders could build effective organizations and manage them well to magnify their impact. Many practitioners welcomed the attention to developing their organizations, because it had been long neglected and represented a necessary step forward. Yet this insight has still not penetrated the conventional wisdom in the field. Too few funders and donors pay attention to building solid organizational foundations.

More recently, nonprofits have been told to look to the private sector for models of success, in part because of the increasing cross-fertilization between the sectors. "Nonprofits need to be run more like business" is the common refrain. Although we agree that nonprofits can learn proven practices from their for-profit counterparts, this still isn't enough. *Better management practices can create only incremental, not breakthrough, social change.* And even the best businesses cannot tell us how to change the world, because that is not their primary purpose.

Only the best nonprofit organizations—those that have achieved real impact—can show us the way. That's why we chose to study the best nonprofits themselves, rather than take management practices derived from businesses and try to translate them to the social sector, as others have done.

A New Way of Thinking About Nonprofits

If the 1980s and early 1990s were all about replicating programs and the subsequent decade was about building effective organizations, we believe the next leap is to see nonprofits as *catalytic agents of change*. We must begin to study and understand nonprofits not merely as organizations housed within four walls but as catalysts that work within, and change, entire systems. The most effective of these groups employ a strategy of leverage, using government, business, the public, and other nonprofits as *forces for good,* helping them deliver even greater social change than they could possibly achieve alone.

As we learned in the course of our research, great nonprofits follow six practices to achieve more impact. We describe these practices in more detail in the following chapters. In a nutshell, organizations seeking greater impact must learn how to do the following:

- Work with government and advocate for policy change, in addition to providing services
- Harness market forces and see business as a powerful partner, not as an enemy to be disdained or ignored
- Create meaningful experiences for individual supporters and convert them into evangelists for the cause
- Build and nurture nonprofit networks, treating other groups not as competitors for scarce resources but as allies instead
- Adapt to the changing environment and be as innovative and nimble as they are strategic
- Share leadership, empowering others to be forces for good

These things may sound simple or obvious, but they're not. It has taken us, and the groups we studied, years of trial and error to distill these practices—and to make them explicit. We can all learn a great deal from them.

Yet even if nonprofits do all these things, they will still fall short unless the other sectors of society meet them halfway. Business, government, and concerned citizens must be open to working with these nonprofit institutions—and to becoming forces for good themselves. And donors should change their definition of what it means to be great, eschewing less meaningful metrics like overhead ratios and instead funneling resources to those groups that have the most impact. This is what separates the best from the rest.

Without heeding this call to action, we are doomed to plod along with slow, incremental change. We'll barely make a dent in climate change. We'll meagerly fund programs that only perpetuate the cycle of poverty. We'll continue to allow millions of children to go to bed hungry or without health care. We'll let global pandemics wipe out entire populations because we can't figure out how to distribute cheap medications. And we'll continue to make the mistake of focusing too much on inputs and processes rather than on outcomes and results.

We don't have time for incremental change—we need dramatic change if we are to solve the complex global problems that plague us today. The stakes are high on all sides, and we must rise to the challenge. Doing anything less would squander this momentous opportunity to advance the greater good. Fortunately, these great nonprofits—and the lessons we can learn from them—can show us a new way.

Why *You* Should Read This Book

Anyone who is interested in creating social change—or in the nonprofit sector more broadly—should read this book. Although there's something for anyone who cares about social impact, our findings have critical implications if you are . . .

A leader of a national or international organization. If you lead a large nonprofit, you'll see how applying the six practices of high-impact nonprofits can help you dramatically increase your own results. In fact, you're probably already putting some of these practices to work. But like many of the great groups we studied, you may need to learn how to do all of them, or how to do some better. This book provides a starting point for thinking about *what* to do to increase your impact. Later, in Chapter Nine, we'll help you understand *how* to begin implementing these practices to achieve greater good.

A *leader of a local nonprofit*. Although we limited our initial study to organizations that have achieved significant national or international impact, in Chapter Twelve we show that these practices are also applicable to local contexts. If you're not already advocating for policy reform and partnering with businesses, you'll learn why you should consider doing so. You'll learn how to engage more individuals through meaningful experiences and convert them to evangelists for your cause. And you'll come to understand the power that can be gained from collaboration with your fellow nonprofits. By harnessing these forces, you can create deeper local impact, without necessarily growing your organization to a larger scale.

A *donor, board member, or volunteer*. Whether you're independently wealthy, an average wage earner, or one of the nation's millions of working poor, the vast majority of you give something to charity each year, including your valuable time and money. When you consider which groups most deserve your attention, we hope you'll consider those great nonprofits that most effectively convert resources into results. This book can help you understand how to get more bang for your charitable buck, the same way you would with your for-profit investments. Understanding the six practices of high-impact nonprofits can help serve as a screen for your social investments and help you too become a stronger force for good.

A *foundation leader or philanthropist*. Foundation leaders and philanthropists have a unique and important role to play in creating social change. You control important resources in the sector and can signal smart investments to government, businesses, and individuals by virtue of where you make your grants. You also have an important leadership role in supporting effective practices, encouraging innovation, disseminating knowledge, and convening and coordinating others to focus on the highest priorities. And as leaders of nonprofits yourselves, you can also apply many of these six practices to your own organizations and become catalytic agents of change. (This is a theme that Leslie Crutchfield and her coauthors explore in greater depth in their recent book, inspired by *Forces for Good,* called *Do More Than Give: The Six Practices of Donors Who Change the World* [Jossey-Bass, 2010].)

A business leader. Nonprofits are learning how to leverage market forces and to work with business to advance their causes. Now more than ever, businesses need to understand their nonprofit counterparts. Whether they are activist opponents, pragmatic allies, or catalysts for social responsibility, nonprofits can no longer be ignored. This book helps you get inside the minds of top nonprofits and understand what to look for in a social sector partner. It can also give you insights as you consider more broadly your approach to social responsibility and your commitment to the community. Your future hangs in the balance, too. You have vast power and resources, and these groups can help you learn how to do well while doing good.

An elected official or policymaker. If you are a political leader, we hope you'll see that nonprofits are not just a convenient place to outsource government programs and services. They are an excellent *source* of policy ideas and social innovation as well. At their best, nonprofits can be government's partner in solving social problems and can also bring business and citizens to the table. But they need government resources to achieve their goals. Government has the money, political power, and distribution might; nonprofits have the talent, networks, knowledge, and entrepreneurial energy needed to create social change. Together they are more powerful.

A nonprofit consultant or adviser. If you consult with nonprofits on any subject—strategy, operations, fundraising, human resources—this book has important implications for your work. Once you've read *Forces for Good,* we challenge you to step out of the traditional management silos and to expand your focus beyond the nonprofit itself as you consider its place in the larger system. Building a strong organization is necessary, but not sufficient, for achieving great impact. We hope this book provokes you to think differently about the work of nonprofits.

An academic. Those who study the social sector have a special charge. Although we realize that our methodology was inductive and grounded in applied research, we believe that our findings highlight areas of academic study that are ripe for further exploration, testing, and refinement. We have just begun to scratch the surface of learning about what makes great nonprofits great and how they use leverage to maximize impact. We hope you will see our findings as a springboard for future research—and we welcome your feedback.

HOW TO READ PART TWO OF THIS BOOK

Chapter One provides a more detailed overview of our findings in the first edition of *Forces for Good,* including discussion of the six practices we discovered and the myths of nonprofit management that fell by the wayside in the course of our research. It also introduces the organizations we studied in a summary table and briefly describes our research methodology. *It's important to read the next chapter first in order to understand the rest of this book.* Chapter One is also a great way to get a quick summary of our work if you have limited time. You can then read the more detailed chapters as needed.

Chapters Two through Seven focus in depth on each one of the practices that highly effective nonprofits use to create greater social impact. To bring the concepts to life, each chapter includes stories and lessons from the social entrepreneurs and organizations we studied, as well as powerful frameworks that can help you apply these practices to your work. At the end of these chapters, we've provided a brief summary of the main ideas to serve as a quick reference guide. You can either read these six chapters sequentially or dip into those that seem the most interesting or relevant to your particular work.

Chapter Eight highlights the critical elements necessary for nonprofits to sustain their impact going forward—things such as exceptional people, sufficient capital, and solid infrastructure. Great nonprofits master the six practices to create maximum impact, *and* they build an effective organization to sustain that impact. Organizations that try to do the former without the latter risk being unable to deliver on their promises. But organizations that focus only on their own management risk having less impact.

Chapter Nine addresses how the six practices fit together and how pursuing them simultaneously creates compound good. It also addresses what you might consider doing differently once you've read this book, and the larger implications for the field.

This chapter can help you put what you've learned into practice. Finally, readers who are interested in learning more about the twelve organizations or our methodology should dive into the appendixes. These include organizational "facts at a glance" and a much more detailed account of our research methodology. Our endnotes and additional resources offer more sources of information.

Whether you're a nonprofit leader, a philanthropist, a business executive, a donor, a volunteer, or a board member—or simply interested in learning how to change the world—we hope this book inspires *you* to become a high-impact nonprofit.

ACHIEVING IMPACT

CHAPTER ONE

FORCES FOR GOOD

What makes great nonprofits great?

It's a simple-sounding question, but, like a riddle, one with a not-so-simple answer. Our attempt at answering this question is the book you're holding in your hands.

Forces for Good is about the six practices that high-impact nonprofits use to maximize social change. These practices can be applied by any organization seeking to make a difference in the world. Our findings are grounded in several years of research on twelve of the most successful nonprofits founded in recent U.S. history—groups that we selected and studied precisely because they have achieved significant levels of impact.

This book is not about America's most well-managed nonprofits. It's not about the best-marketed organizations with the most recognized brands. And it's not about the groups with the highest revenues or the lowest overhead ratios—those misleading metrics too often used as a proxy for real accomplishment in the social sector.

We chose to study these dozen organizations because they have created real social change. They have come up with innovative solutions to pressing social problems, and they have spread these ideas nationally or internationally. They have produced significant and sustained results, and created large-scale systemic change in just a few decades. In the business world, these organizations would be akin to companies such as Google or eBay, which catapulted onto the Fortune 500 list of biggest companies in a matter of years.

One group we studied has housed more than a million poor people; another has sharply reduced acid rain and created new models for addressing climate change; and one has helped hundreds of thousands of young people volunteer through national service programs. Collectively, they have influenced important legislation on issues ranging from immigration to welfare reform, pressured corporations to adopt sustainable business practices, and mobilized citizens to act on such issues as hunger, education reform, and the environment.

Founded and led by social entrepreneurs—whether they call themselves that or not—these nonprofits have truly become forces for good.

THE TWELVE HIGH-IMPACT NONPROFITS

Teach For America is one of these high-impact groups. Launched by Princeton senior Wendy Kopp in 1989 on a shoestring budget in a borrowed office, it now has forty-four hundred corps members and more than twelve thousand alumni. Many of the country's best and brightest college grads now spend two years teaching in America's toughest public schools, in exchange for a modest salary. Within the past two decades, Teach For America has shown extraordinary growth: from $10 million in 1995 to $70 million by 2007 and reaching $240 million by 2011. In that same time period, the number of teachers in the classroom went from five hundred to nearly five thousand.[1]

But rapid growth is only part of the story. More important, Teach For America has succeeded in doing what was once considered impossible: it has changed how we think about teacher credentialing, made teaching in public schools "cool," and created a vanguard for education reform among America's future leaders. It is now the recruiter of choice on Ivy League campuses, out-competing elite firms such as Goldman Sachs and McKinsey & Company—with forty-eight thousand applicants in 2010.[2] And graduates who went through the program in the 1990s and 2000s are now launching charter schools, running for elected office, managing education foundations, and working as school principals. Teach For America's audacious goal is to one day have a U.S. president who is an alumnus of the program.

Habitat for Humanity is another extraordinary nonprofit. Founder Millard Fuller was a successful businessman who gave away his fortune and launched Habitat in 1976 with the outrageous goal of "eliminating poverty housing and homelessness from the face of the earth." Today, hundreds of thousands of Habitat volunteers around the world build houses with low-income families, who take part in the construction and pay for their homes with no-interest loans. At the time we were writing the first edition of *Forces for Good,* more than twenty-one hundred Habitat affiliates were operating in nearly one hundred countries, and Habitat ranked among the *Chronicle of Philanthropy*'s top twenty-five nonprofits in revenues, with a combined budget approaching the $1 billion mark.[3] It since has doubled in size to more than $2 billion globally.

But even more impressive than these statistics is Habitat's ever-expanding community of evangelists for housing reform. Fuller never set out to build an organization—instead, he wanted to start a *movement* that put poverty and housing "on the hearts and minds" of millions of volunteers. In just the past few years, the group has begun to turn its hammers into votes, seeking to influence the larger economic and political systems that create poverty and homelessness in the first place.

Then there's the Environmental Defense Fund (EDF). Founded in the late 1960s, this groundbreaking nonprofit was the brainchild of scientists who wanted to ban the pesticide DDT, which was killing endangered birds of prey. Although EDF has achieved enormous legal victories on behalf of the environment, today it is best known for introducing market-based strategies that help change corporate behavior. EDF's cap-and-trade program was a key component of the Clean Air Act; the pollution credit–trading system has helped reduce sulfur dioxide emissions that cause acid rain and now serves as an important model in the fight to reverse climate change.

Under the leadership of president Fred Krupp, EDF has also forged innovative partnerships with such companies as McDonald's, Federal Express, and Walmart, despite initial cries from other groups that it was selling out. In the early 1990s, the organization helped McDonald's eliminate more than 150,000 tons of packaging waste, and it has helped FedEx convert its midsize truck fleet to hybrid vehicles.[4] Over the past decade, the nonprofit has been working with Walmart to help the company become more environmentally sustainable.

With a staff of more than three hundred, a membership base of seven hundred thousand, and an annual budget of $100 million by the time this updated research was completed, EDF has had an extraordinary growth trajectory. Although its original founders knew little about nonprofit management, the organization has become a model of social innovation that other groups now copy. By daring to "find the ways that work," EDF has influenced not only other green groups but also government policy and business practices.

Three nonprofits, three extraordinary stories. This book tells the stories of twelve great organizations, which we studied over two years to understand the secrets to their success. We provide a quick snapshot of who they are and what they do—along with the impact they've achieved—in Exhibit 1.1 (this data is from 2005). Updated organization profiles are available in Appendix E, and their stories are woven throughout the book. Later in this chapter, we explain how we selected these organizations and the method behind our research.

SHATTERING THE MYTHS OF NONPROFIT MANAGEMENT

When we delved into our initial research at each organization in 2005, we donned our MBA hats, examining traditional silos of nonprofit management: leadership, governance, strategy, programs, development, and marketing. In the spirit of best-selling business books, we thought we would find that great nonprofits had time-tested habits that conferred a competitive advantage—things such as brilliant marketing, perfect operations, or rigorously developed strategic plans. We imagined that there was a "secret sauce" involved in building the organization, and that if you could just get the recipe right and then scale up—presto!—you'd have more impact.

But what we found surprised us—and flew in the face of the perceived wisdom in the field. Achieving large-scale social change is *not* just about building an organization and then scaling it up

EXHIBIT 1.1. ORGANIZATION PROFILES.

Organization, Year Founded, Location	Revenues, FY2005	What It Does	Examples of Impact
Center on Budget and Policy Priorities 1981, Washington, D.C.	$13 M	Performs research and analysis on state and federal budget and fiscal policy; advocates on behalf of low-income individuals	Protected billions of dollars in federal benefits and allocations to programs for the poor; works with about thirty state affiliates and six thousand local nonprofits; established state and international budget projects
City Year 1988, Boston, Mass.	$42 M	Builds democracy through citizen service, leadership, and social entrepreneurship; advocates for national service policy	Youth corps now in seventeen U.S. cities and in South Africa, with eight thousand alumni; influenced adoption of AmeriCorps, enabling seventy thousand volunteers to serve annually; helped build the fields of youth service and social entrepreneurship
Environmental Defense Fund 1967, New York, N.Y.	$69 M	Creates innovative solutions to environmental problems through research, advocacy, and creative use of market tools and partnerships	Influenced critical environmental policies including the Clean Air Act and Kyoto Protocol; engages five hundred thousand active members; helps such companies as McDonald's, FedEx, and Walmart become more sustainable
Exploratorium 1969, San Francisco, Calif.	$ 4 M	Museum of science, art, and human perception designed as a model for new forms of education	Receives five hundred thousand visitors annually; reaches twenty million people through exhibits at 124 partner museums and Web site; has influenced the global movement for interactive science centers and museums

(continued)

EXHIBIT 1.1. ORGANIZATION PROFILES (*continued*).

Organization, Year Founded, Location	Revenues, FY2005	What It Does	Examples of Impact
Feeding America (formerly America's Second Harvest—The Nation's Food Bank Network) 1979, Chicago, Ill.	$543 M (includes value of in-kind donations)	Distributes donated food and grocery products to grassroots nonprofits; advocates for hunger policy	More than two hundred food banks in network distribute two billion pounds of food to more than fifty thousand local nonprofits, feeding twenty-five million hungry Americans each year
Habitat for Humanity International 1976, Americus, Ga.	$1 B (includes global affiliates)	Seeks to eliminate poverty housing and homelessness by building houses, raising awareness, and advocating for change	Through twenty-one hundred global affiliates in one hundred countries, has built 275,000 homes, housing one million people; engages millions of volunteers in the United States and abroad
The Heritage Foundation 1973, Washington, D.C.	$40 M	Formulates and promotes conservative policy based on principles of free enterprise, freedom, traditional values, limited government, and a strong defense	Formulated policy agenda for Reagan administration; helped lead conservative revolution in Congress in 1990s; works with twenty-five hundred state affiliates; engages 275,000 individual members
National Council of La Raza 1968, Washington, D.C.	$29 M	Hispanic civil rights and advocacy organization; works to improve opportunities for all Latinos	Helped build field of more than three hundred local grassroots affiliates; implemented program innovation in education, health, and civil rights for Hispanics; influenced critical legislation on immigration

Organization	Budget	Description	Accomplishments
Self-Help 1980, Durham, N.C.	$75 M	Works on economic development through lending, asset development, and research and advocacy	Provided more than $4.5 billion in loans to fifty thousand small businesses and low-income individuals through corporate partnerships; led national anti-predatory lending campaign and legislative reform in twenty-two states
Share Our Strength 1984, Washington, D.C.	$24 M	Inspires and engages individuals and businesses to share their strengths to end childhood hunger	Raised $200 million in twenty years for hunger relief groups through Taste of the Nation events in sixty cities; engages one million volunteers through Great America Bake Sale; known for innovative cross-sector partnerships
Teach For America 1990, New York, N.Y.	$41 M	National teaching corps of recent college graduates who spend two years in needy schools and become leaders for education reform	Twelve thousand corps members engaged since inception have reached 2.5 million students and created a vanguard for education reform; has influenced teacher training and credentialing systems
YouthBuild USA 1988, Boston, Mass.	$18 M	Low-income youths ages sixteen to twenty-four learn job and leadership skills by building affordable community housing while earning a GED	Engaged more than sixty thousand youths to produce fifteen thousand units of housing since inception; works with 226 affiliates; influenced national legislation to create $645 million in federal funding

site by site. Many of these groups are not perfectly managed. Nor are they all well marketed. And at least half don't score well on conventional charity ratings, because they care more about having impact than having low-overhead budgets. They do what it takes to get results.

As we got further into our research, we saw that many beliefs about what makes great nonprofits great were falling by the wayside. In fact, the vast majority of social sector management books focus on things that don't always lead to greater impact. We found little evidence to support common myths of nonprofit excellence.

Myth 1: Perfect management. Some of the organizations we studied are not particularly well managed in the traditional sense of the term. Although some treat their systems, processes, and strategic plans as high priorities, others are more chaotic, and regard "plan" as a four-letter word. Some management is necessary (as you'll see in Chapter Eight), but it is not *sufficient* to explain how these organizations achieve such high levels of impact.

Myth 2: Brand-name awareness. Although a handful of groups we studied are household names, we were surprised to learn that a few hardly focus on marketing at all. For some of them, traditional mass marketing is a critical part of their impact strategy; for others, it's unimportant.

Myth 3: A breakthrough new idea. Although some groups came up with radical innovations, others took old ideas and tweaked them until they achieved success. As we will explore later, their success often depends more on how they implement a new idea or innovate as they execute than it does on the idea or model itself.

Myth 4: Textbook mission statements. All these nonprofits are guided by compelling missions, visions, and shared values. In fact, it is their obsession with impact that creates internal alignment, despite the lack of perfect management. But only a few of these groups spend time fine-tuning their mission statement on paper— most of them are too busy living it.

Myth 5: High ratings on conventional metrics. When we looked at traditional measures of nonprofit efficiency, which use metrics such as "overhead ratios," many of these groups didn't score so well. A few garnered only one or two stars out of four (in 2005).

Popular ratings Web sites can tell you which groups have the lowest ratio of overhead to program spending, but they can't always tell you which have had the most impact.

Myth 6: Large budgets. We discovered that size doesn't matter much when it comes to making an impact. Some of these nonprofits have achieved great impact with large budgets; others have achieved great impact with relatively small budgets. And all of them have different fundraising strategies.

As we dismissed the conventional wisdom about what makes great nonprofits great, we began to realize that there was a flawed assumption underlying our initial research question. When we began this project, we assumed there was something inherent to these *organizations* that made them great. Instead, we learned that becoming a great nonprofit is not about building a great organization and then expanding it to reach more people. In fact, growing too quickly without adequate investment can cause an organization to falter or implode. Although growing an organization can be one strategy for increasing impact, it is not the only way these groups achieve success.

THE SIX PRACTICES OF HIGH-IMPACT NONPROFITS

What we learned about these nonprofits astonished us, and intrigued others with long experience in the field. We believe that the framework we've discovered offers a new lens for understanding the social sector and what it takes to create extraordinary levels of social change. Any organization seeking to increase its social impact can emulate the six practices that we describe in detail below.

The secret to success lies in how great organizations mobilize every sector of society—government, business, nonprofits, and the public—to be a force for good. In other words, *greatness has more to do with how nonprofits work outside the boundaries of their organizations than how they manage their own internal operations.* Textbook strategies such as relentless fundraising, well-connected boards, and effective management are necessary, of course, but they are hardly sufficient. The high-impact nonprofits we studied are satisfied with building a "good enough" organization and then spending their time and energy focused externally on catalyzing large-scale systemic change. Great organizations work *with and through others* to create more impact than they could ever achieve alone.

"Give me a lever long enough, and I alone can move the world" is the common paraphrase of Archimedes. These twelve groups use the power of leverage to create tremendous change. In physics, leverage is defined as the mechanical advantage gained from using a lever. In the social sciences, it translates into the ability to influence people, events, and decisions. In business, it means using a proportionately small initial investment to gain a high return. Whatever the definition, we think the concept of leverage captures exactly what great nonprofits do. Like a man lifting a boulder three times his weight with a lever and fulcrum, they have far more impact than their mere size or structure would suggest (see Figure 1.1). *They influence and transform others in order to do more with less.*

FIGURE 1.1.   LEVERAGE INCREASES IMPACT.

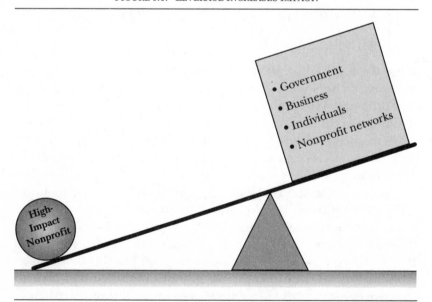

The organizations in this book seed social movements and help build entire fields. They shape government policy, and change the way companies do business. They engage and mobilize millions of individuals and, in so doing, help change public attitudes and behaviors. They nurture larger networks of nonprofits and collaborate rather than compete with their peers. They spend as much time managing external relationships and influencing other groups as they do worrying about building their own organizations. These high-impact nonprofits are not only focused on themselves but also on the relentless pursuit of results.

After a long process of studying these organizations, of reflection and writing, of testing and retesting our thinking, we began to see patterns in the ways they work. In the end, six of these patterns crystallized into the form presented here—the *six practices* that high-impact nonprofits use to achieve extraordinary impact. Although they didn't all use every single practice, at least ten of the twelve groups applied each one, or else we didn't consider it significant enough to constitute a "pattern."

The first four practices are more external; they represent how these groups dramatically expand their impact outside the borders of their own organizations. Each of these practices influences an external stakeholder group with which the nonprofit works, so as to do more with less. In observing this external focus, we also realized that working *outside* the organization entails special practices *inside* that help these nonprofits relate more effectively to their environment. This led us to discern two additional internal practices that enable high-impact nonprofits to operate successfully in the outside world and bridge boundaries.

More specifically, we learned that great social sector organizations do these six things:

1. **Advocate *and* serve.** High-impact organizations don't just focus on doing one thing well. They may start out providing great programs, but eventually they realize that they cannot achieve systemic change through service delivery alone. So they add policy advocacy to access government resources or to change legislation, thus expanding their impact. Other nonprofits start out doing advocacy and later add grassroots programs to supercharge their strategy. Ultimately, all of them

bridge the divide between service and advocacy, and become good at doing both. And the more they advocate *and* serve, the greater the impact they achieve.

2. **Make markets work.** Tapping into the power of self-interest and the laws of economics is far more effective than appealing to pure altruism. No longer content to rely on traditional notions of charity or to see the private sector as the enemy, great nonprofits find ways to work with markets and help business "do well while doing good." They influence business practices, build corporate partnerships, and develop earned-income ventures—all ways of leveraging market forces to achieve social change on a grander scale.

3. **Inspire evangelists.** Great nonprofits see volunteers as much more than a source of free labor or membership dues. They create meaningful ways to engage individuals in emotional experiences that help them connect to the group's mission and core values. They see volunteers, donors, and advisers not only for what they can contribute to the organization in terms of time, money, and guidance but also for what they can do as evangelists for their cause. They build and sustain strong communities to help them achieve their larger goals.

4. **Nurture nonprofit networks.** Although most groups pay lip service to collaboration, many of them really see other non-profits as competition for scarce resources. But high-impact organizations help the competition succeed, building networks of nonprofit allies and devoting remarkable time and energy to advancing their larger field. They freely share wealth, expertise, talent, and power with their peers, not because they are saints, but because it's in their self-interest to do so.

5. **Master the art of adaptation.** All the organizations in this book are exceptionally adaptive, modifying their tactics as needed to increase their success. They have responded to changing circumstances with one innovation after another. Along the way, they've made mistakes and have even produced some flops. But unlike many nonprofits, they have also mastered the ability to listen, learn, and modify their approach in response to external cues—allowing them to sustain their impact and stay relevant.

6. **Share leadership.** We witnessed much charisma among the leaders in this book, but that doesn't mean they have oversize egos. These CEOs are exceptionally strategic and gifted entrepreneurs, but they also know they must share power in order to be a stronger force for good. They distribute leadership throughout their organization and their nonprofit network—empowering others to lead. And they cultivate a strong second-in-command, build enduring executive teams with long tenure, and develop highly engaged boards in order to have more impact.

These organizations employ all, or a majority, of these six practices. But they didn't all start out doing so; some initially incorporated only a few practices and added others over time. Some focus more on certain levers than others and apply them to different degrees. The key point is that they all use more of these practices, not fewer. Rather than becoming mired in bureaucracy or doing what they've always done, they continuously move in new directions and then build the capacities they need to be effective. They have found "levers long enough" to exponentially increase their impact by working with and through others. Figure 1.2 illustrates these six critical practices and how they fit together.

When a nonprofit applies all these forces simultaneously, it creates momentum that fuels further success. "It's like pushing a snowball down a hill," says one Habitat for Humanity volunteer. "At first you have to work at it, and it takes a lot of energy. But once it gets going, momentum builds and it starts rolling on its own." It's a concept similar to what Jim Collins calls the "Flywheel."

Once we identified the six practices and studied them closely, we began to see that each of them can interact with the others in mutually reinforcing ways. Like a complex organism with interdependent components, the whole is greater than the sum of its parts. For example, building a network of nonprofits and inspiring evangelists give organizations even more force to influence government policy or business practices. Through shared leadership, these organizations empower others to act on their behalf. Through adaptation, they remain relevant in an ever-changing environment. In Chapter Nine, we will revisit how these practices

FIGURE 1.2. ORGANIZING FRAMEWORK.

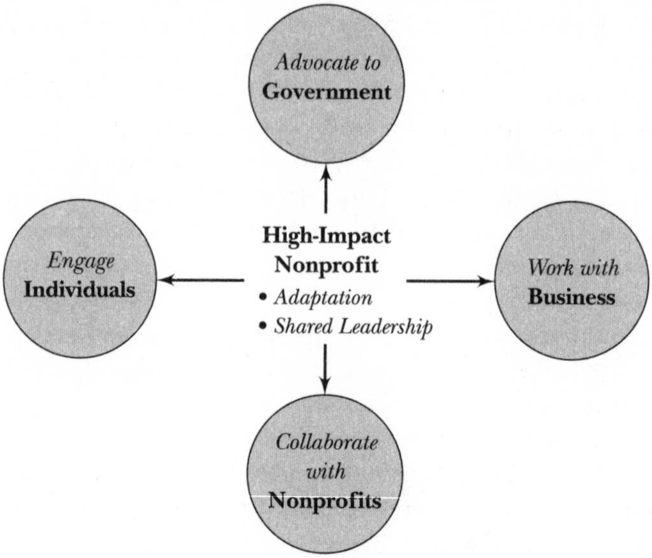

can reinforce each other, once we've examined how each of them independently creates greater impact.

MAXIMIZING SOCIAL CHANGE

As we reached the final stage of our research, we asked ourselves, Why do these nonprofits harness multiple forces for good, when it would be easier to focus on growing and perfecting their own organizations? The explanation lies in their unwavering commitment to creating real impact. These organizations, and the extraordinary individuals who lead them, want to solve many of the biggest problems plaguing our world: hunger, poverty, failing education, climate change. They aspire to change the world.

Just as they are driven to achieve *broad* social change, they have an unstoppable desire to create *lasting* impact as well. They don't want simply to apply social Band-Aids, but rather to attack and eliminate the root causes of social ills. It's not enough for Teach For America to raise the test scores of students in its classrooms; it seeks to transform the entire educational system. It's not

enough for Habitat to build houses; it aspires to eliminate poverty housing and homelessness from the face of the earth. It's not
enough for City Year to build a few successful youth corps; it wants
every young person to spend a year serving his or her community
through national service.

It is this relentless pursuit of results in the face of almost insurmountable odds that characterizes social entrepreneurship—as
opposed to nonprofit management. As Bill Drayton, the founder
of Ashoka, says, "Social entrepreneurs are not content to merely
give a man a fish, or even teach him how to fish; these entrepreneurs won't stop until they have revolutionized the entire fishing industry."[5] At its core, social entrepreneurship is an externally
focused act. *It's all about results, not processes.* And that's why it sometimes looks so messy and chaotic from the outside.

Whether these leaders agree with the label or not, their
underlying mind-set typifies the outlook of social entrepreneurs
as defined by academic Greg Dees: they create social value; they
relentlessly pursue new opportunities; they act boldly without
being constrained by current resources; they innovate and adapt;
and they are obsessed with results.[6] As Self-Help founder Martin
Eakes says, "I need to have impact more than I need to be right."
If that means checking their egos at the door, or even putting
their individual or organizational needs second, these social entrepreneurs will do whatever it takes.

"We are extremely pragmatic," says Gwen Ruta, now vice president for corporate partnerships at EDF. "We're all about results. It
doesn't matter whom we work with if we can get credible results.
And we'll use whatever tool it takes to make progress: we will sue
people, we will partner with business, we will lobby on the Hill or
educate the public. Every one of these tools is in our tool kit, and
we deploy the one most likely to get us to our goal."

This shared mind-set—an obsession with impact, a pragmatic
idealism—is what ultimately drives these entrepreneurs to create
greater social change. And it was their extraordinary impact that
led us to select their organizations in the first place. We didn't
want to study "perfect" nonprofits; instead we looked for organizations that had achieved the greatest results. But before we could
even begin to understand *how* they have done this, we first had to
devise a methodology for selecting and studying them.

Our Methodology

When we began our journey in 2004, our first challenge was to develop a working definition of what it means to be "high impact" in a sector that has no agreed-on metric of success. Defining and measuring impact in the business world is a lot simpler. When business writers set out to identify great corporations, they can measure bottom-line results or stock performance in relation to the S&P 500 index of leading companies. With nonprofits, it's different. Although the goal is social impact, there is no universal definition of what that means, no clear metrics for measuring it, and great variation in mission and goals from organization to organization. (See Appendix A for more details on metrics and our methodology.)

So when we set out to select these organizations, we defined impact relatively, because it is so contextual. We created a two-part definition. One part was a measurement of concrete outputs, such as the number of people served or products produced. We asked, *Did the organization achieve substantial and sustained results at the national or international level?* The second part of our definition was more qualitative. We chose organizations that had impacted a larger system, such as government policies or common practices in their fields. We asked, *Did the organization have an impact on an entire system?*

One important distinction in our methodology was that we did not equate *scale of impact* with traditional definitions of nonprofit *growth,* which focus on an organization's presence in multiple communities or its total budget. A nonprofit can achieve large-scale social impact without expanding beyond a single site, a phenomenon we observed in several organizations in this book, such as The Heritage Foundation and the Exploratorium. Further, we didn't want to use budget size as an indicator of success, because that would be measuring an input (funding), not an output (results), as Jim Collins writes in *Good to Great and the Social Sectors.*[7]

At the same time, we chose not to focus on organizations that had achieved impact only in their immediate community. (This was the subject of our new research, in Chapter Twelve.) There are countless groups, such as hospitals, schools, and soup kitchens, that are making a difference locally or providing necessary services, but their goals are not the same as those seeking to achieve social impact more broadly. Similarly, we eliminated international organizations that had been founded outside the United States, as the social, political, and economic context in which they began was markedly different. This doesn't mean that local groups or international nongovernmental organizations can't apply our findings to their contexts—they too can learn a great deal from these high-impact nonprofits (as noted in Chapter Twelve).

Because we were also interested in studying organizations that had achieved significant impact relatively quickly, we focused on nonprofits founded between 1965 and 1994. These organizations have grown from "zero to great" in a short time vis-à-vis their peers, and have faced similar social, economic, and political conditions. We excluded organizations younger than ten years old when our research began, as there was not enough proof that they would sustain their impact. (As a note to our updated edition, this meant that we missed many high-impact nonprofits founded since 1994, such as Kiva or MoveOn.org, which have used the Internet and online tools to scale.) Nor did we focus on age-old giants such as the American Red Cross, which were founded in the last century and have grown over time.

Finally, we only considered nonprofits with 501(c)(3) status that exist primarily to serve the broader public interest. We excluded religious organizations, such as churches, and we excluded membership organizations that serve a single group, such as fraternities. Last, we eliminated grantmaking foundations, as they do not face the same capital constraints as most nonprofits, and we were interested in groups that struggle with similar growth challenges. Table 1.1 summarizes the criteria we used to determine which organizations to include and exclude.

Once we had defined the parameters of our research, we pursued a four-phase process, over three years of research, to select and study the organizations that fit our criteria. Please see Appendix A for more details on these phases.

Phase 1: National peer survey (2004). In the absence of universal metrics, we turned to other nonprofit leaders to help us select those organizations that have had the most impact. We borrowed from the playbook of *Built to Last,* in which Jim Collins and Jerry Porras surveyed Fortune 500 CEOs and Inc. 100 entrepreneurs

TABLE 1.1.   CRITERIA FOR SELECTION.

	Baseline Criteria	Excluded
Type of organization	• 501(c)(3) nonprofit • Founded in the United States	• Churches, membership organizations • Organizations founded abroad • Grantmaking foundations
Definition of impact	• Has achieved substantial, sustained results • Has created larger systemic change	• Impact at both levels not substantiated or sustained
Scale	• National or international impact	• Only local impact
Time frame	• Founded 1965–1994	• Founded before 1965 or after 1994
Final sample	• Deliberately selected a diverse sample in terms of issue area, geographical location, size, and business model	• Some organizations that met all other criteria were not included

to nominate the "most visionary" companies.[8] Similarly, we surveyed nearly twenty-eight hundred executive directors of nonprofits, including the leaders of the largest nonprofits listed in the Chronicle of Philanthropy 400, making sure this sample was representative of the sector in terms of organization size, geographical location, and diversity of issue areas. We asked these leaders to nominate up to five nonprofits that "have had the most significant impact at the national or international level in the last thirty-five years," and to tell us why. We received more than five hundred responses and hundreds of nominations from our online survey.

Phase 2: Field-expert interviews (2004). We then vetted the nominations with more than sixty experts from various fields of the social sector, such as education, the environment, and so on. (See Appendix B.) We selected experts on the basis of their deep knowledge of a particular area and because they represented a relatively objective point of view as journalists, academics, foundation staff, or thought-leaders. Our field experts participated in two rounds of interviews, during which they analyzed, discussed, and helped us rank the nominated organizations. They also suggested organizations that had substantial impact but that are less broadly known or didn't come up in the peer survey.

Combining the peer survey results, the field-expert interviews, and additional data culled from public sources, we narrowed down the list to about thirty-five nonprofits that had demonstrated the most significant impact. From that group, we selected twelve organizations that represented a broad cross-section of the nonprofit world. We deliberately selected a diverse portfolio of nonprofits for further study, picking those with varying funding mixes, organizational structures, program offerings, issue areas, and geographical locations. We felt that the patterns of success that emerged across a diverse group would be more robust and more useful to the sector as a whole.

Phase 3: Case study research and analysis (2005 and 2006). We then studied these twelve organizations in depth over the course of two years in order to understand how they achieved great impact. For each nonprofit, we compiled all the available public information we could find (articles, books, case studies, information on Web sites); interviewed on average twelve senior managers, board members, and the founder or CEO (see Appendix D for a list of all interviewees by organization); and conducted site visits to the headquarters, and to affiliate sites when possible. We also asked for, and studied, volumes of internal information, such as annual reports, high-level financial statements going back to the founding year, compensation levels, and organizational charts. In the interviews, we asked a broad range of questions, touching on management, marketing, strategy, governance, leadership, operations and programs, and fundraising. (See Appendix C for a list of sample interview questions.) We also asked open-ended questions about how the nonprofits achieve impact. Next, we summarized the data from each organization, noting themes within each case.

Phase 4: Pattern identification and testing (2006). Finally, we analyzed all the case study data to identify patterns, or practices, that cut *across* the organizations and that we believed had contributed to their phenomenal impact. As patterns emerged, we engaged in an iterative process, testing themes against the data, referring back to our conversations with field experts, and drawing on our knowledge of nonprofit management practices and literature. We also field tested our hypotheses through working sessions with practitioners and thought-leaders. We wanted to confirm that the patterns we saw differentiated these nonprofits from the average organization. We also looked for new insights and deliberately avoided focusing on the obvious, such as "diversify your funding." This iterative process helped refine our thinking, and often led us to go back to collect more data or to test hypotheses. From these patterns, we eventually distilled the six practices that we present here.

In the next chapter, we introduce the first of these six practices and explore how high-impact nonprofits use the power of policy advocacy to dramatically increase social change. We invite you to dive in. We believe you'll be as intrigued by these findings—and these extraordinary nonprofits—as we were.

CHAPTER TWO

ADVOCATE *AND* SERVE

A school bus driver walked into Self-Help's offices in Durham, North Carolina, one day in 1998 looking for some advice on refinancing his mortgage. A recent widower, the man was raising his only daughter in a house he had built with his now-deceased wife. But with only one modest income, he was struggling to make his payments and was only a month away from losing his home.

Several Self-Help staff members examined the man's financial documents. They were puzzled: he had a $44,000 mortgage, financed at a fairly high interest rate of 14 percent.[1] But that wasn't all. When they looked closer, they discovered that his actual loan amount was only $29,000. The lender had tacked on $10,000 in "credit insurance" and $5,000 in fees—a 50 percent increase in the mortgage.

Self-Help's staff had never seen anything like this in their fifteen years of making loans to low-income families. Founder Martin Eakes recalls meeting the man: "He was a big, African American guy, and he looked at me and said, 'I can't lose this house because I helped build it with my own hands—it's the only connection my nine-year-old daughter has with her mother who passed.'" Eakes was outraged: "These lenders were able to do what a criminal in the dead of night could not do with a gun—steal his home."

Eakes and Self-Help agreed to help the bus driver. When the nonprofit's efforts to speak with the lender failed, it helped him sue the company instead. Eventually the bus driver won the suit and was able to keep his home. Although the legal victory was encouraging, the encounter had uncovered a disturbing trend.

Self-Help learned that approximately ten thousand North Carolinians were losing their homes to predatory lenders each year. These lenders targeted low-income borrowers—poorly educated, minority, or elderly people who were most vulnerable to deception—overloading loans with excessive fees and high rates. These extra charges virtually ensured that the borrowers would default.

"Their practices made a mockery of everything we had worked for in the last twenty years," says Eakes, who founded Self-Help to build the wealth of low-income residents in North Carolina. Eakes vowed that Self-Help would aggressively fight predatory lending. He quickly realized that educating thousands of borrowers would never work, so he decided instead to advocate for stronger industry regulation.

Self-Help first lobbied Congress to close loopholes in the Home Ownership Protection Act. When it became clear that changing federal law would be difficult, the nonprofit went back to its home turf in North Carolina, where the organization had regional relationships and influence, as well as local lobbying experience from its work in the areas of charter school and housing financing.

Self-Help mobilized a statewide coalition of seventy allies that included credit unions, churches, and local affiliates of the American Association of Retired Persons and the National Association for the Advancement of Colored People. It pitched stories about the campaign to the regional press. And Eakes convinced several of North Carolina's most powerful banks that it was their moral responsibility to support new legislation.

The organization's advocacy efforts paid off in 1999, when the state enacted the landmark North Carolina Anti–Predatory Lending Law, which curtailed abusive lending without limiting the amount of credit available to low-income borrowers. Soon groups around the country contacted Self-Help for assistance in passing similar legislation in their states. Eakes realized that if Self-Help wanted to stop predatory lending nationally, it would need to actively assist groups in other states. In 2002, Self-Help launched the Center for Responsible Lending (CRL), a national subsidiary that conducts research, advocates for policy reform at both the state and federal levels, and helps state-based groups change lending laws. What started over thirty years ago as a local effort to build home ownership among North Carolina's neediest citizens has since grown into a formidable force for national policy reform. Through its direct programs, Self-Help had by 2006 provided more than $4.5 billion in loans to fifty thousand families, and another three thousand loans to small businesses and community facilities. And through its advocacy efforts, it had helped pass anti–predatory lending laws in twenty-two states, leading to the protection of billions in assets belonging to the nation's most vulnerable citizens at the time. Self-Help has combined service *and* advocacy to achieve extraordinary social change.

SERVICE MEETS ADVOCACY

Most organizations in the social sector can be divided into two camps: direct service organizations that run programs in local communities, and advocacy organizations that raise public awareness and push for policy reform. In the field of women's issues, it's the difference between Junior League volunteers serving in shelters for battered women and the National Organization for Women fighting for equal pay and abortion rights. Both organizations aim to improve the lives of women, but they go about achieving that goal in markedly different ways.

Over the course of our research, however, we found something surprising and counterintuitive: high-impact nonprofits engage in both direct service *and* advocacy. They bridge the divide. The organizations we studied conduct programs on the ground and simultaneously advocate for policy change at the local, state, or national level. Providing services helps meet immediate needs, such as feeding the hungry or housing the poor; advocacy helps reform larger systems by changing public behavior or creating governmental solutions.

In its broadest sense, the term *advocacy* refers to activism around an issue like the environment or education reform. It can involve many activities, from mobilizing voters to pitching media stories to influencing elected officials and the political process. Sometimes the goal is to change laws or public policy; other times it is to change public behavior. *Policy advocacy*, also known as *lobbying*, refers to specific efforts to change public policy or obtain government funding for a social program, and it is the focus of this chapter.

Lobbying can have negative associations, evoking images of fat-cat power brokers lunching in fancy restaurants with policymakers on Capitol Hill. What constitutes lobbying in the social sector can be confusing, but a law passed by Congress in 1976 recognized lobbying as an "entirely proper function of nonprofits." It generally expanded nonprofits' ability to lobby without jeopardizing their tax-exempt status, while also imposing clear limits. (For a comprehensive overview of nonprofit lobbying, see INDEPENDENT SECTOR's *The Nonprofit Lobbying Guide.*[2])

Even though policy advocacy can be an incredibly powerful tool for large-scale social change, many nonprofits shy away from it. Sometimes they are unclear about the regulations that enable them to advocate, or they fear becoming too politicized and alienating critical supporters. Advocacy is difficult to manage and requires different organizational skills than those needed to provide direct services. Further, it is challenging to measure results. Many leaders fear that engaging in both service and advocacy can lead to mission-creep, and conventional wisdom dictates that nonprofits should focus on one or the other.

Thus it's even more surprising that *all the organizations in our book have engaged in both.* Although most groups started out as direct service providers, at some point they all realized that if they wanted to create more significant systemic change, they needed to influence the political process.

A VIRTUOUS CYCLE

As we examined more closely how and why organizations engaged in both policy advocacy and direct service, we discovered that simultaneously doing both creates a virtuous cycle. Rather than causing the organization to lose focus or decreasing its impact, the two together can create impact that is greater than the sum of the parts.

By operating programs, organizations gain a firsthand view of the problems facing their constituents, enabling them to see their impact directly. They are "close to their customer." Nonprofits that provide services create local solutions, which can then inform their policy positions. They can see what's working on the ground and what's not, modifying their approach as necessary. In the process of developing a large network of affiliates, working in coalitions, and engaging individuals through direct programs, organizations also gain a constituency of members and allies that they can mobilize—as we'll see in Chapters Four and Five. They have the real power of votes behind their political positions.

On the flip side, when engaging in advocacy, nonprofits sometimes discover new policy solutions that can be implemented through their programs. When they are successful in passing new legislation, groups gain the credibility that comes with having the government support their positions. And sometimes, by advocating for federal or state funding, they receive additional resources to support the replication of their programs.

When their policy is informed by direct service and their programs are informed by policy work, these organizations are more effective at both. (See Figure 2.1.)

FIGURE 2.1. COMBINING ADVOCACY AND SERVICE INCREASES IMPACT.

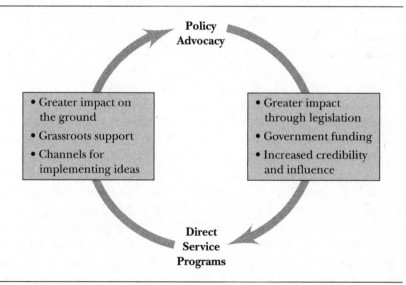

To take one example of how programs inform policy, the National Council of La Raza (NCLR) based its federally funded NCLR Homeownership Network on an innovative pilot project that NCLR and a few of its Arizona affiliates had developed. The original program, which offered financial counseling to Latinos before they purchased their first home, significantly increased home ownership and reduced loan delinquency and foreclosures.[3] So NCLR decided to scale up the model by lobbying the Department of Housing and Urban Development (HUD) for funding to implement the program nationally. Today, forty affiliates in fifteen states receive HUD grants and technical assistance from NCLR to implement the model. Thousands of Latino home owners have been created nationwide as a direct result of the Homeownership Network. The resulting federal funding was used to support similar programs sponsored by other nonprofits, such as ACORN, Catholic Charities, and the National Urban League.

The synergy also flows in the other direction when policy research or advocacy leads to the creation of new programs. When NCLR's policy analysis shed light on deficiencies in Latinos' education, for instance, the work led to the creation of Project EXCEL (Excellence in Community Education Leadership), which offered bilingual civics, math, and science curricula for after-school programs in twenty Hispanic communities. The EXCEL program ultimately led to the creation of NCLR's national charter school network, which focuses on creating educational opportunities for Latino students. If NCLR hadn't been engaged in education policy research, it might not have seen the gap that this program addressed—and which ultimately formed the base for a much larger project.

NCLR's decision to take on both activities from the outset went against conventional wisdom. "There was this audacious vision: to do policy advocacy and try to have a program footprint that speaks to the community directly," says Charles Kamasaki, NCLR senior vice president. "It's contrary to most management texts, and it has had its costs. But when they work in sync and come together, it allows us to get more done."

Unfortunately, such combined policy-program approaches are not common in the nonprofit sector. More typically, policy analysis and program implementation are decoupled. In one scenario, a think tank publishes research on an issue, which advocacy groups then market to the public and politicians, who in turn create leg-islation. Once a law is passed, the government then contracts with community-based groups to deliver the service.

Sound complicated? It is—and it's often less effective. "The idea generators and implementers end up separated by sev-eral layers of public policymaking," explain the authors of *High Performance Nonprofit Organizations*.[4] Often, public interest groups or think tanks will conduct research on an issue, but because they have no experience running programs on the ground, their hypotheses remain theoretical. These organizations also lack ways to translate the insights gained from project implementation into legislative changes.

In Self-Help's case, its experience making direct loans unearthed the first signs of lending abuse. It quickly realized that predatory lending could undermine its efforts to build wealth among low-income populations, and it saw the market failures as they arose. Because Self-Help was in the business of making loans, it gained credibility among other financial industry play-ers whom it could engage as evangelists for legal reform. Large banks and politicians saw that the organization understood the marketplace. It also had enormous political influence in North Carolina, because it engaged thousands of individuals through a vast network of nonprofit allies.

Self-Help could have maintained its original focus on providing services in the form of loans to low-income clients, and in the pro-cess it would have slowly chipped away at the ten-to-one wealth gap between American minorities and whites, one home at a time. But the worst elements of the lending industry were destined to eventu-ally undermine its best efforts, as the 2008 housing crisis and ensuing recession unfolded. Ultimately, Self-Help had to turn to politics to regulate the industry if it wanted to become a greater force for good.

THREE WAYS TO BRIDGE THE DIVIDE

Like Self-Help, many of the organizations we studied started out primarily providing direct services, and only ramped up their advocacy initiatives later. A few, such as The Heritage Foundation and the Center on Budget and Policy Priorities, did the reverse:

they started out pushing for national policy reform, and later added programs in order to reach the state and local levels. Organizations such as City Year and NCLR combined direct service and policy advocacy from the start. They believed early on in the wisdom of doing both, even when the strategy contradicted notions widely held in the nonprofit world.

The larger point is that each of these twelve nonprofits, at some stage in its evolution, realized that engaging in both service *and* advocacy could expand its impact. Each, however, followed one of three general paths to get there. (See Figure 2.2.)

START WITH SERVICE, ADD ADVOCACY

The largest cluster of organizations in this book began with direct service, or programs, and adopted policy advocacy well after they

FIGURE 2.2. ADVOCACY-SERVICE EVOLUTION.

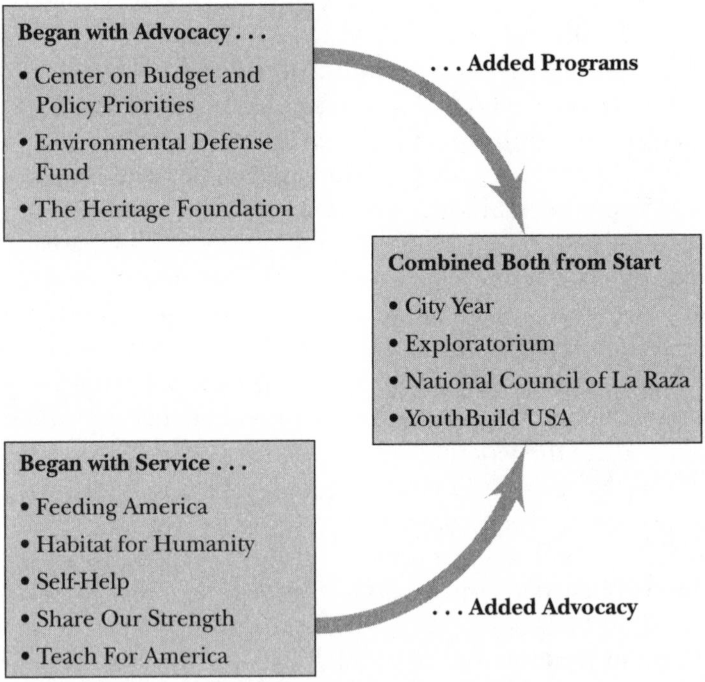

Began with Advocacy . . .
- Center on Budget and Policy Priorities
- Environmental Defense Fund
- The Heritage Foundation

. . . Added Programs

Combined Both from Start
- City Year
- Exploratorium
- National Council of La Raza
- YouthBuild USA

Began with Service . . .
- Feeding America
- Habitat for Humanity
- Self-Help
- Share Our Strength
- Teach For America

. . . Added Advocacy

TABLE 2.1. ADVOCACY CAN START AT ANY TIME.

Organization, Year Founded	When Formal Policy Advocacy Operation Began
Feeding America (formerly America's Second Harvest—The Nation's Food Bank Network) 1979	Government Relations and Public Policy Department created after the 1996 Welfare Reform Act
Habitat for Humanity 1976	Advocacy Task Force established in 2005
Self-Help 1980	Director of policy hired in 1995; the Center for Responsible Lending launched in 2002
Share Our Strength 1984	End Childhood Hunger campaign launched in 2004
Teach For America 1990	Research and Public Policy Department created in 2002

were founded. They all reached a point at which they realized the limitations of operating programs alone, although the events that triggered the shift varied from organization to organization. (See Table 2.1.) However, the underlying reason they decided to engage in advocacy was the same: to have more impact on the problems they were trying to solve.

For Feeding America (called America's Second Harvest at the time of our initial research), the defining moment came when a crucial federal program was threatened with extinction.[5] After the Republicans gained control of both the House and Senate in 1994, the legislative branch was gridlocked in its effort to balance the budget and reduce the federal deficit. The Temporary Emergency Food Assistance Program (TEFAP)—a $40 million federal food assistance program, which channeled funding to local food banks and shelters—was on the short list to be cut completely. Sister Christine Vladimiroff, then president and CEO of Feeding America, knew that she had to do something quickly to protect the program.

Feeding America was originally founded as a network of food banks that facilitated the donation and distribution of food to churches, soup kitchens, shelters, and local charities that help the poor. For years, many of its local directors felt uncomfortable getting involved in public policy advocacy. Some food bank members were restricted by their boards, others weren't familiar with federal guidelines, and some thought "public policy was unseemly," says Eleanor Thompson, director of government relations for Feeding America. "They saw themselves as direct service providers," she says of the local food banks.

Sister Christine changed all that. She knew that if she didn't do something to save federal programs such as TEFAP, her network would be inundated with even more hungry people. She went straight to the top, hiring Doug O'Brien, a key staff member on the Senate Committee on Agriculture, Nutrition, and Forestry with deep experience on food and poverty issues, to lead the defense of the federal food program. O'Brien assisted Sister Christine in preparing testimony, developing a legislative strategy, and speaking before members of Congress. He later helped draft legislation to protect TEFAP, and shepherded it through the Congress.

In 1996, the nonprofit played another critical advocacy role by shaping the proposed welfare reform legislation. The original version of the legislation would have drastically reduced funding for the Food Stamp Program and eliminated funding for other important programs feeding the poor (which are now currently part of the Supplemental Nutrition Assistance Program, or SNAP). Ultimately, lobbying efforts by Feeding America and others helped make TEFAP a mandatory part of the budget through funding under the former Food Stamp Program, helped secure food donations for food banks, and helped low-income people transition off welfare.

Changes proposed by Feeding America to the welfare reform legislation also led to an expanded role for local nonprofit agencies in distributing government-sponsored food donations. Prior to welfare reform, many states distributed TEFAP commodities directly—often out of the back of trucks, with people lining up in parking lots for free "government cheese." Under the new policy, Feeding America food banks, pantries, soup kitchens, and shelters replaced the government's rudimentary food distribution system. The nonprofit also was able to use the government food to augment private food donations, which were at times uneven, so that hungry people had more consistent access to food.

Since Feeding America began its advocacy efforts, an estimated $400 million more in federally sponsored commodities was flowing to the needy each year by 2007, or more than ten times the amount that was originally threatened in 1994. After the Welfare Reform Act of 1996, Feeding America and its food banks played a seminal role in preventing any further cuts to the nation's food stamp or child nutrition programs. In fact, the 2002 farm bill and the 2004 child nutrition reauthorization bill both provided billions in *new* money for food assistance programs. "Nineteen ninety-six was a watershed year," says O'Brien. "It showed the anti-hunger community that we have to be united, speak effectively with one voice, and we have to vigorously fight these things."

Of course, Feeding America can't claim sole credit for all these legislative wins. Other antihunger advocates, such as the Center on Budget and Policy Priorities and the Food Research and Action Center (FRAC), were also pushing for similar legislation. But 1996 was a critical victory, due in large part to the leadership and advocacy efforts of Feeding America.

The group attributes much of its success in advocacy to the size and power of its food bank network, combined with its direct services, such as local programs and research. The fact that there is a food bank in every congressional district in the country is not lost on elected officials, either. "Recently, President Bush recommended cutting food stamps in the Budget Act. I was in Minnesota with Senator Norm Coleman, and he and other Republican senators said they would not support the president's position on cutting food stamps, and that their position was not negotiable," explains O'Brien. "He had heard from food banks back home in Minnesota. They were adamant: there can be no food stamp cuts as part of budget reconciliation."

As for the formerly resistant food banks in the Feeding America network, they changed their view of advocacy when they saw the direct impact it could have on their bottom lines—more food to feed needy people in their communities.

Since its initial welfare reform victories, the group's advocacy efforts have grown ever stronger. Under the leadership of Bob Forney, who was CEO from 2001 to 2006, the public policy division of Feeding America expanded to include five full-time staff members in Washington, D.C., and three in Chicago. "Initially, we thought we should stick to what we know best—finding and distributing food," explains Forney. "Then over twenty-five years we shifted dramatically, and now everybody understands that we can't solve hunger in America without the government playing a role."

START WITH ADVOCACY, ADD SERVICE OR PROGRAMS

A few of the organizations in this book—Environmental Defense Fund (EDF), The Heritage Foundation, and the Center on Budget and Policy Priorities—started out primarily advocating for policy change, and only later added direct service or programs. For all three organizations, policy advocacy is a critical component of how they achieve social impact, and not just a means of obtaining government funding.

When EDF's founding scientists wanted to stop the use of the pesticide DDT, they sued companies and government agencies to end the practice, and they lobbied for new federal regulations.[6] Although the organization's approach of "Sue the Bastards" (its informal motto for the first few years) was effective, EDF realized that it could have even more impact if it helped create model environmental programs at the state and local levels to inform its advocacy efforts.

It started experimenting with trading permits for water in California, creating incentives for utilities to promote conservation instead of new generation, and later developed cap-and-trade programs to reduce air pollution. (See Chapter Three for more details.) The organization uses these local experiments to test its policy ideas on the ground and perfect them. For instance, EDF designed a cap-and-trade program for U.S. industries geared to eliminate acid rain in the Northeast by reducing sulfur dioxide emissions. It has since parlayed this regional experience into advocacy efforts at the international level. Sharply reducing acid rain proved to be the platform on which EDF could build its international advocacy efforts to address climate change.

Starting out with policy advocacy is particularly effective when an organization is relatively small in relation to the level of impact it seeks to achieve. The Center on Budget and Policy Priorities, for example, operated on an annual budget of less than $15 million in 2007—one of the lowest of the groups we studied—but it has influenced federal and state policies and budget decisions that have affected the lives of millions of low-income Americans. It's a great example of getting more bang for your buck.

In the beginning, the Center focused exclusively on analyzing how federal legislation and budget decisions affected low-income and working poor populations. One of its earliest achievements was its pivotal behind-the-scenes role in expanding the Earned Income Tax Credit (EITC) in 1984 and again in 1986. The Center has also had substantial impact on food stamp policy. For example, 90 percent of the policy provisions included in the 2002 legislation reauthorizing the Food Stamp Program were the ones that the Center helped design; these changes have boosted participation significantly.[7]

Although the Center was incredibly effective with policy research and advocacy at the federal level, it soon realized that the intended beneficiaries of its reform efforts would still suffer if these programs were not implemented correctly at the state and local levels. So the Center also developed outreach programs to inform and train local partners on how to implement the policies it helped pass. It now operates several major outreach campaigns to help working poor families receive two key public benefits: low-income tax credits and children's health insurance.

For instance, the 1986 Tax Reform Act increased EITC benefits and made more working people eligible for the credit, among other changes. The catch? Beneficiaries of the program had to do more to access these benefits, such as file a special form to get the EITC. The Center realized that many EITC benefits would go unclaimed because the intended recipients either wouldn't realize they were eligible and thus would not file an income tax return, or wouldn't know how to claim the benefits. This would result in an enormous missed opportunity to help low-income and working poor people.

So the Center took action. It mobilized its network of state-based policy and service groups to participate in a massive grass-roots education campaign, targeting America's most needy populations. More than six thousand nonprofits, government agencies, and businesses have joined this nearly two-decade effort, which the Center describes as "the nation's largest sustained private campaign to promote a public benefit." Participants include governors, mayors, labor unions, trade associations, day-care centers, and community development corporations. The result of this coordinated program has been that millions more low-income and working poor people are now aware of, and know how to access, this critical tax benefit designed to help them.

The success of this campaign confirmed for the Center the importance of combining programs on the ground with national policy research and advocacy. Even though the Center did not originally set out to provide grassroots programs, it realized that all its policy advocacy efforts would be for naught if they failed to put federal benefits within reach of America's most disadvantaged populations. "If nobody stepped up to the plate to do this, the ramifications would be huge. If no one else was going to, then we had to," says Bob Greenstein, founder and director of the Center.

COMBINE SERVICE AND ADVOCACY FROM THE OUTSET

Four of the organizations we studied employed service and advocacy from the outset, or early on in their evolution. The Exploratorium and YouthBuild USA both approached the government early for funding to expand their programs or models. City Year and National Council of La Raza have adopted policy advocacy as a means of both obtaining funding *and* influencing larger policy decisions that affect young people or Latinos. Regardless of their motives, these four nonprofits were enlightened enough to recognize the power of engaging in both advocacy and service, and resisted the pressure to specialize.

Within these organizations, we observed two main patterns. Leaders knew that replicating programs site by site, with private funding, would never propel them to the level of change they were seeking. So they focused on influencing national policy while building their organizations, or in some cases, as a *means* of expanding their organizations with federal funding. These leaders also shared a common philosophical belief that government should be a part of the solution. Policy reform sends a signal to the nation that the changes these organizations propose are important enough for society as a whole to adopt.

The National Council of La Raza (NCLR) demonstrates elements of both patterns. NCLR was formed in 1968, in the wake of the civil rights movement, to provide grassroots services such as health care, education, and housing assistance to Latinos. The nonprofit also advocated for Hispanic civil rights by promoting laws to ensure them equal access to housing and jobs, and to reduce racial discrimination. From the outset, its founders had a vision of both strengthening communities and advocating for larger policy change.

With early Ford Foundation funding, NCLR helped launch and support seven affiliate organizations in three southwestern states. It subgranted funds to these organizations to build local Latino leadership capacity and to support such activities as voter registration drives, economic empowerment programs, and local advocacy. But when Congress passed tax reform in 1969, it created a hostile climate for foundations that funded advocacy nonprofits. Ford withdrew its support for all NCLR activities except direct programs.

Raul Yzaguirre, hired as NCLR's director a few years later (his title later shifted to president and CEO), knew he had to find a way to continue this advocacy work. He helped NCLR diversify its funding base by cultivating corporate partners and charging for events, such as its annual conference. By 1975, NCLR had established an Office of Research and Policy Analysis to focus on the "Hispanic data gap." (Little was known at the time about the Latino population; 1980 was the first year that "Hispanic" was even included as a category in the U.S. Census.) NCLR broke new ground in policy research, which it used to influence critical legislation over the next two decades in the areas of housing, immigration, job training, and foreign trade. For example, NCLR produced influential studies that shaped such legislation as the National Affordable Housing Act of 1990 to include benefits for Latinos.

But by the 1980s, the pendulum had swung back. NCLR had become so effective at policy analysis and advocacy that some members of its board pushed the organization to eliminate affiliate and other programs. "First, getting the board to approve our public policy approach was hard—we won by one vote," recalls Yzaguirre. "Then five years later, there was a move to remove programs. So we had to fight with our board to keep both."

Despite external and internal pressures to specialize, NCLR's senior leaders stood their ground. "My thought was, you couldn't be good at either one of them if you couldn't see them both," says Yzaguirre. "Programs inform your public policy and give you the means to change it; and if you didn't have policy, you make your programs less potent."

Today NCLR is the nation's leading voice for the Hispanic community, recognized for both its successful advocacy initiatives and its direct service programs. It earned its stripes by conducting unparalleled policy advocacy efforts at the federal level, while also building and serving a national network of three hundred affiliated community-based organizations. NCLR also delivers programs on the ground and through its network, in such areas as education, workforce development, public health, legal and immigration services, and more. By refusing to choose between advocacy and service, NCLR has become a formidable force for social change.

WHAT'S HOLDING NONPROFITS BACK?

For every nonprofit that combines advocacy and service, there are many more that don't. Organizations that have traditionally focused on providing direct programs and services can find that the leap into advocacy requires significant change. There are real risks, as well. They face the possibility of losing key volunteers or donors. "The fear is that people who will pick up a hammer will not transition to voting on an issue," says Stephen Seidel, a member of Habitat for Humanity's advocacy task force. "People don't like politics. We wonder, if we go down that road, will we lose folks?"

Some leaders also worry that they will lose corporate support if they become too political. After all, many corporations are wary of being associated with any group that takes a polarizing position on an issue. To address this challenge, NCLR manages the expectations of its corporate partners: "Any time we sign on with a company, we tell them, 'We only take positions that make sense for the Latino community,'" says Emily Gantz McCay, former senior vice president. "We are always clear about being an advocacy group first."

An organization also has to walk a tightrope of building the skills necessary to engage in advocacy, while continuing to provide services (or vice versa). "Advocacy is very difficult to manage," admits Eric Stein, Self-Help chief operating officer. "If you are managing a loan program, there are very discrete, quantifiable parts to the process. It's very clear where everybody plugs in, and it's clear what the goal is—to make a good loan." But advocacy is a less cut-and-dried activity that entails pursuing multiple goals, playing different roles in competing arenas, and taking substantial risks, he says.

Precisely because advocacy often requires work in coalitions with others, it can become difficult to claim credit for success. And it's hard to quantify—which has indirect implications for fundraising. "Advocacy creates challenges for us in terms of measuring impact," says Habitat's Seidel. "It's easier to count houses than measure the impact of anyone's advocacy."

Given all these obstacles, it's not surprising that many leaders decide to stay focused on providing services or growing their own organizations. But when an organization's attention to perfecting its own programs overwhelms its focus on achieving long-term social change, it enters the "social entrepreneur's trap." This is when a nonprofit "seeks to improve or expand its own programs at the expense of not leveraging the organization's expertise and other capabilities for field-building, policy-making and broader societal change," writes Michael Brown, cofounder of City Year.[8]

Although there are times in every organization's life cycle when it must build internal capacity or shore up its programs, nonprofit leaders should not do so at the expense of engaging in other activities that advance their larger cause. The social entrepreneurs who run these twelve organizations avoid this trap; they understand that they must do more than scale out their own programs if they are to have more impact. They accept the fact that engaging in advocacy may not always yield direct benefits for their own organization—but nevertheless advances their larger cause.

FIVE PRINCIPLES FOR SUCCESSFUL POLICY CHANGE

As we've seen in this chapter, organizations have adopted policy advocacy in multiple ways and for many reasons. Tactically, however, they share a number of traits that we believe have made them extraordinarily successful at combining both approaches.[9]

Balance Pragmatism with Idealism

All the organizations we studied embody the paradoxical concept of "practical idealism." They are all guided by strong ideals, but few of them are ideological purists. They would rather win than be right. Unlike radical socialists in the 1930s or New Left activists in the 1960s, who protested "the system," these nonprofits temper their idealism with pragmatism. Yet they won't go so far as to completely sell their souls—they are able to strike a balance between achieving results and maintaining their integrity. It's a delicate and never-ending dance.

They are pragmatic above all because they are focused on creating solutions rather than on simply drawing attention to problems. None of the high-impact nonprofits that we studied use extremist tactics to achieve social change. "We offer a solution to significant problems that people want to solve," says Dorothy Stoneman, president of YouthBuild USA. "Rather than protest the way things are, our strategy was to offer solutions and work in a sophisticated way to influence Congress."

These groups have figured out how to work within the system to change the system, and have found ways to create answers to social problems that appeal to the political center. EDF, for example, finds "the ways that work" in order to make progress toward its larger goals. Historically, some prominent environmental organizations have used more radical, oppositional tactics to highlight problems, such as Greenpeace seizing whaling ships or Earth First! activists chaining themselves to trees. Whereas these activists stand outside the system, criticizing global capitalism or the current political administration, EDF and the organizations we studied make a point of working *within* the current economic and political reality.

"We are literally finding the ways that work, against a background of the environmental movement that has lost its way with mainstream America," says David Yarnold, former executive vice president. "The Greenpeaces of the world are the face of the environmental movement, but they don't represent who we are—we're a well-kept secret."

Our point is not that more radical approaches don't lead to social change. They absolutely do, by attracting media attention and raising public awareness of a problem. But these tactics can sometimes limit the long-term effectiveness of radical groups—a theme that came up often in our field-expert interviews when we were selecting organizations to study. To achieve maximum influence with a majority, as measured by the number of supporters alone, you must appeal to a broad political center rather than take a polarizing position. Put another way, the circle of supporters for a radical group will usually be smaller than for a centrist group that appeals to both sides of a debate. Stray too far in one direction, and a nonprofit risks alienating individual volunteers, donors, or corporate supporters, thereby diminishing the long-term impact it can achieve.

PRACTICE PRINCIPLED BIPARTISANSHIP

Just as these groups are able to work within the system, they are also adept at remaining bipartisan in their advocacy efforts—not just in rhetoric, but in reality. They put their issue above party politics and will work with whoever can help them achieve their goals. "We take the requirement to be bipartisan seriously, because we are required to do it, but also because it is necessary to do it," says Cecilia Muñoz, former vice president at NCLR.

To navigate America's two-party political system successfully, most of these organizations work closely with both Republicans and Democrats on crafting legislation or public policy. "If you contrast us to [some other green groups], they think the best way to protect the environment is a change of [political] administration," says Gwen Ruta, now vice president for corporate partnerships at EDF. "They may be right, but our goals are much more practical. We'll work with whoever is in power."

When major green groups widely criticized the George W. Bush administration for its stance on environmental issues, EDF president Fred Krupp praised the White House in one of our interviews for adopting a 2005 regulation, the Clean Air Interstate Rule that will reduce sulfur and nitrogen emissions. "I am not sure today in 2005 you will find another head of an environmental group who would acknowledge that maybe President Bush has been the worst environmental president ever, but also tell you that there have been stunning successes like a new 70 percent cut in [these] emissions," says Krupp. "We will give credit where credit is due to people in both parties."

NCLR also has a long history of bipartisanship. "The organization was built around Raul Yzaguirre and his ability to stay on point about the Hispanic community," says Tom Espinoza, CEO of the Raza Development Fund, the community development lending arm of NCLR. "NCLR was able to speak out when the Republicans were in and when the Democrats were in. Raul's strongest position as a leader was that he was always on point and never got co-opted by either party."

These nonprofits take pains to put their cause above party politics—even when that means diplomatically distancing the organization from potential supporters. For example, The Heritage Foundation clearly advocates on behalf of conservative values and policies, yet it makes an effort to differentiate itself from the Republican party. "We've chosen and publicized times when we have criticized the administration," says Stuart Butler, then vice president for domestic and economic policy. Heritage denounced the Bush prescription drug plan under the 2005 Medicare Modernization Act as "bad public policy," for instance. "We want to make sure we are not seen as an organization that is an extension of any White House," he says.

The Congressional Black Caucus motto, "no permanent friends, no permanent enemies, just permanent interests," captures this bipartisan mentality. As Krupp of EDF puts it, "There is a power to being evenhanded and being able to cross the [political] aisle. We are never going to win if these issues are owned by one party. These issues have to be above partisanship; they have to be above polarization."

Preserve Credibility and Integrity

There's a fine line between being pragmatic and maintaining integrity. The nonprofits we studied are able to walk this line, knowing when to compromise on their ideals for a pragmatic win and knowing when compromise might actually undermine their credibility. For some of the organizations—particularly those that focus on policy analysis, research, and advocacy—credibility is paramount to their success. They must remain true to the data and the facts, rather than bend information to support their case. Otherwise, they may win a short-term battle but lose the larger war.

EDF was founded by a group of scientists, and emphasizes highly technical research as the basis of its policy platforms. "We put science at the core of everything we do and stay true to that no matter what," explains Jane Preyer, now director of the southeast office. "It's about credibility. Even if what the science says is unpopular, we stay true to it."

The Center on Budget and Policy Priorities and The Heritage Foundation also stake their reputation on quality policy research and analysis. Although their interpretation of the solutions to social problems may differ, both aim to provide a rigorous analysis of the facts. "We set the bar really, really high for accuracy, timeliness, and quality," says Ellen Nissenbaum, now senior vice president for government affairs for the Center. And although The Heritage Foundation advocates for conservative policies and is perceived by outsiders as more biased than the Center, CEO Feulner and Heritage's senior policy analysts defend their interpretation of the data.

HIRE POLICY EXPERIENCE

When these nonprofits decide to engage in advocacy, they have to build—or buy—the skills to carry out those activities. Often this means cultivating relationships in Congress or state legislatures, and hiring staff or consultants who have deep backgrounds in advocacy and lobbying. Indeed, eleven of the twelve organizations we studied have a strong D.C. presence. Three of the organizations were founded in Washington, D.C. (Center on Budget and Policy Priorities, The Heritage Foundation, and Share Our Strength), one moved its headquarters to the capital from Phoenix, Arizona (NCLR), and seven opened D.C. offices as they became more involved with policy advocacy at the federal level.

Not surprisingly, these Washington offices are staffed by professionals who have significant political experience. Although Dorothy Stoneman was remarkably successful in creating a new federal YouthBuild program through grassroots advocacy, she realized that she needed professional help to obtain an appropriation for the program. So she engaged a Washington lobbying firm,

Rapoza Associates, to help her navigate the halls of Congress. Self-Help employed North Carolina lobbyist Mike Calhoun, who now runs the group's research and public policy affiliate. EDF's second-largest office is in D.C., with a substantial staff who work on policy as well as grassroots advocacy. And the list goes on.

But these organizations don't rely solely on professional lobbyists and media experts to advocate on their behalf. In each case, top leaders are highly engaged in policy reform as well. City Year cofounders Alan Khazei and Michael Brown flew from Boston to D.C. to lobby Congress every week at the height of threatened cuts to AmeriCorps funding in the 1990s. Dorothy Stoneman orchestrates the strategy for YouthBuild's policy advocacy on the Hill, and she has cultivated influential friends on both sides of the political aisle. And Self-Help's Martin Eakes regularly testifies before Congress on issues related to financial industry regulations and community lending; more recently, Eakes and his fellow Self-Help policy experts acted as chief behind-the-scenes architects of the Dodd-Frank Act of 2010. (For an update on how Self-Help advocated for this landmark federal legislation, see Chapters Ten and Eleven.)

Find Funding for Advocacy

One of the biggest challenges for many organizations is developing a reliable revenue stream to fund their advocacy work. Individual funders may withdraw their support if they don't agree with a policy position. And it's often difficult to convince donors to underwrite extensive research and policy analysis or nebulous collective action. The legislative process is often slow, and the outcomes are difficult to attribute to individual organizations.

But each of these organizations developed sustainable revenue streams—without strings attached—to support their advocacy work. NCLR has pursued a number of different funding strategies over the course of its almost four-decade history. When its federal funding was first slashed under the Nixon administration, NCLR turned to private foundations, which sustained the organization's policy work until new federal regulations put the funders "on notice."[10] When both federal and foundation support was cut, NCLR had to support advocacy with revenue from other activities, such as its annual conference. The income generated from this event currently totals more than $1 million—nearly double the average amount it spends on lobbying activities each year. It also built corporate partnerships to provide additional non-earmarked income.

Other organizations, such as The Heritage Foundation and EDF, have put a priority on building broad grassroots support to ensure strategic flexibility. By 2007, they boasted donor bases of 275,000 and 500,000 individuals, respectively, whose $25 checks could be allocated however the organization wished (within legal lobbying limits). This afforded them the freedom to say "no thanks" to large donors who wanted to unduly influence their policy positions.

Some groups are fortunate to have substantial sources of earned revenue due to the unique nature of their business models. A large part of Self-Help's income has come from home loan repayments, as has Habitat's. Share Our Strength taps individual donors through ticket sales to events. Although Self-Help and Share Our Strength raise additional funds from private foundations—and two-thirds of the $6.5 million budget of Self-Help's Center for Responsible Lending was funded by foundations as of 2006—they don't need to dip into core support to fund advocacy, given these relatively large grassroots streams.

COMBINING SERVICE AND ADVOCACY

Successfully engaging in policy advocacy is difficult—particularly for organizations that historically have only run programs or provided direct services. Advocacy touches on the myriad activities with which a nonprofit is involved. It necessarily entails greater risk and uncertainty, and requires a high level of adaptability on the part of the organization's leaders—a theme we explore further in Chapter Six. And lobbying has implications for everything from how a group raises money to how it works with other nonprofits in its field.

In addition to the basic principles we've outlined in this chapter, there are two other practices we discuss later in this book that lend additional force to nonprofit advocacy: engaging and mobilizing groups of individuals and building nonprofit networks. In

Chapter Four, we'll demonstrate how great nonprofits involve individuals not only as volunteers and donors but as evangelists for their cause. They build strong communities of supporters that can lend the power of votes and the conviction of public voices to their advocacy efforts. And they reach out to powerful leaders in business and government who can exert their influence on behalf of the nonprofit's cause. In Chapter Five, we illustrate how great nonprofits employ a network strategy, working with and through other nonprofits—either formal or informal affiliates—to build their larger field. Instead of seeing other groups as competition, these nonprofits share resources, knowledge, and talent with their peers, building strong alliances. They then mobilize these networks to participate in grassroots advocacy campaigns and push for legislative reform.

Though it can be more complicated to manage both service and advocacy, and though policy advocacy does entail some risks, the rewards can be significant. As we said earlier, simultaneously running programs and pursuing policy change create a reinforcing cycle for most organizations. The more they do of both, the greater the impact they can achieve.

Nearly every organization in this book has embraced policy advocacy as central to its vision for change—if not at the outset, then at some point along the way. Self-Help ramped up its advocacy when it realized that providing services in the form of loans was never going to stop predatory lending practices. The Center on Budget and Policy Priorities realized that it had to add programs in order to ensure implementation of the policies it had worked so hard to help pass. And groups such as City Year and NCLR embraced the wisdom of engaging in both from the outset.

Regardless of when they reached the decision to pursue both service and advocacy, high-impact nonprofits leverage the power of government, wielding it as a force for greater good.

CHAPTER TWO HIGHLIGHTS

- **Policy advocacy is a powerful force for social change.** High-impact nonprofits understand that they cannot achieve maximum results without advocating for policy reform or without accessing the power and resources of government. To achieve large-scale change, government needs to be part of the solution.

- **The best nonprofits both advocate and serve.** They couple policy reform with programs or direct services to create more impact. By operating programs on the ground, they gain a firsthand view of the problems facing their constituents and can test new models to inform their proposed policy solutions. And by engaging in policy research, analysis, and reform, organizations can influence legislation and identify new opportunities for programs. Ultimately the two activities reinforce each other.
- **Don't be afraid to jump into the political fray.** Many direct service organizations are hesitant to engage in policy reform. They fear that funders will stop supporting them, that advocacy impact is hard to measure, or that they don't have the skills to manage lobbying. But great nonprofits overcome these challenges.
- **It's never too late to advocate.** At least half of the twelve organizations in this book started out mainly providing programs or direct services, and added advocacy later. Some introduced it early on; one organization waited nearly three decades.
- **Follow a few principles for success.** Although these organizations advocate for widely divergent causes, they go about their work in strikingly similar ways. They all follow these basic principles:
  - *Balance pragmatism with idealism.* They work *within* the political system by focusing on centrist solutions that appeal to the broad majority of the American people, rather than advocate for extreme positions.
  - *Practice principled bipartisanship.* They will work with—and publicly credit—both sides of the political aisle for policy victory, but they also maintain their integrity around the interests they represent.
  - *Preserve credibility and integrity.* They take care not to compromise basic data, scientific facts, or analysis. Organizations that exaggerate claims to garner attention may win short-term battles, but lose the larger war.

- *Hire policy experience.* All but one of these groups have an office in Washington, D.C., and they hire skilled lobbyists with access to key decision makers on Capitol Hill.
- *Find funding for advocacy.* Not all funders want to support advocacy, so it's good to find flexible sources, such as earned income or individual donations.

CHAPTER THREE

MAKE MARKETS WORK

In the late 1980s, garbage was in the news. Nowhere was the problem more visible than in New York City. Landfills overflowed with trash, garbage barges floated offshore, and debris regularly washed up on nearby beaches. Many people blamed corporations for the problem, especially fast-food purveyors such as McDonald's. Every one of its "billions and billions served" generated throwaway packaging. All told, the nation's ravenous appetite for fast food was creating hundreds of thousands of tons of waste each year.[1]

Fred Krupp, president of Environmental Defense Fund (EDF), was personally confronted with the issue one day in 1987 as he sat in a Manhattan McDonald's enjoying a Happy Meal with his three children. At the end of the meal, Krupp looked around at the Styrofoam, plastic wrappers, and brightly colored, nonrecycled paper that formed a trash heap on the table. "I think we can help them do better," he said. That night, Krupp and his son composed a letter to the CEO of McDonald's proposing that the company work with EDF on a plan to reduce its solid waste.

One year and many meetings later, Krupp's idea turned into a groundbreaking partnership between the two organizations— much to the surprise of the public. After all, for the first few years of its existence, EDF's informal motto was "Sue the Bastards." Like many early environmental groups, it usually carried a big stick when it dealt with polluters, in the form of lawsuits combined with aggressive advocacy. And its methods worked, helping the government ban DDT, limit asbestos and lead, and pass such laws as the Safe Drinking Water Act.

Still, Krupp knew EDF needed a more pragmatic approach to be successful in the future. He began talking about "third wave" environmentalism, which he summed up in a *Wall Street Journal* article in 1986: "The American public does not want conflict between improving our economic well-being and preserving our health and natural resources. The early experience suggests it can have both."[2] In the future, EDF would focus less on lawsuits and more on market-based tools and "new coalitions, even coalitions of former enemies."

This strategy wasn't exactly popular with hard-core environmentalists. Many of them denounced the McDonald's partnership, accusing EDF of doing a deal with the devil. Sierra Club leader David Brower complained, "There is too much movement away from the ideals and too much emphasis on bottom lines. The MBAs are taking over from the people who have the dreams."[3]

But EDF proved its critics wrong. The work of the six-month cooperative task force with McDonald's resulted in the company's decision to phase out polystyrene "clamshell" containers and use more environmentally friendly packaging, such as paper bags, boxes, and napkins made with recycled fiber.[4] McDonald's would go on to reduce its packaging waste by 150,000 tons over a ten-year period. And, in turn, a number of other fast-food chains copied this industry leader, resulting in even greater waste reduction.

Building on this success, EDF advised FedEx in the 1990s, helping make its packaging more environmentally friendly and then revolutionizing the company's truck fleet. In 2003, FedEx announced it would test twenty hybrid electric trucks that would reduce emissions by up to 90 percent and go 50 percent farther on a gallon of gas.[5] The company's goal in 2007 was to replace thirty thousand trucks with hybrids over the next decade, as it retired conventional trucks from its fleet. Most recently, EDF has been advising Walmart and helping the company become more sustainable.

Unlike many nonprofits that partner with corporations as a funding strategy, EDF doesn't take money from its partners. Rather, it retains rights to any innovation that comes out of the partnership. "The innovation can't belong to the company," says Gwen Ruta, now vice president for corporate partnerships. "Whatever comes out of this, we're going to knock on the competitor's door and ask them to do the same thing." She cites recent tests of hybrid truck fleets by United Parcel Service, the U.S. Postal Service, and Frito-Lay, who are all now following the FedEx model, just as other burger chains copied McDonald's packaging.

In this way, EDF has even greater impact. It is strategic about partnering with high-profile corporations that can serve as early adopters of a new social innovation—which it can then replicate throughout an entire industry, creating even more positive social change.

EDF's innovative approach doesn't stop with corporate partnerships: the group helps create *new markets* to change corporate behavior on an even larger scale. For example, it developed a proposal for the first Bush Administration to pass amendments to the Clean Air Act in 1990, which created a market for trading pollution permits, combined with emissions caps—a system known as "cap and trade." Those utilities—such as coal-fired power plants—that reduce emissions by more than the required amount earn credits to bank for future need or to sell to companies unable to meet their reduction targets.

The system created a market for pollution and in the process created economic incentives for businesses to willingly reduce their damage to the environment. Ultimately the new legislation reduced sulfur dioxide in the air by 50 percent, helping curtail acid rain in the Northeast at a fraction of the cost projected. The cap-and-trade system became a key example in the framework of the 1996 international Kyoto Protocol and, more recently, of California's Global Warming Solutions Act (AB 32), the first statewide cap imposing significant limits on greenhouse gas emissions.

But if EDF thought it took criticism for collaborating with big companies, hard-core environmentalists were even more critical initially of its market-based approach. They charged the nonprofit with letting companies "pay to pollute." Yet today EDF is seen more as a pioneer of innovative solutions than as a traitor to the movement. Even the more radical Greenpeace has come around. "We now believe that [tradable permits] are the most straightforward system of reducing emissions and creating the incentives necessary for massive reductions," said Kert Davies, research director for Greenpeace, in the *Wall Street Journal*.[6] By the turn of the century, it was clear to EDF that it had evolved significantly from its early "Sue the Bastards" days. So it came up with a new slogan to capture its more pragmatic market-based approach: "Finding the Ways That Work."

DOING WELL AND DOING GOOD

The experience of EDF highlights a striking pattern we found among the organizations in our study. These nonprofits harness market forces and leverage the resources and power of business to have more impact than they could alone. They understand that business is a powerful institution in society—one that can sometimes be a force for evil, but that can also become a force for good. And they recognize what economists have long known: tapping into the power of self-interest is more effective than appealing to altruism. These nonprofits are finding ways to help companies do well while doing good, and are proving that social responsibility and profit aren't mutually exclusive. In fact, one can even enhance the other.

This finding surprised us. Though we both have MBAs, we understand that many nonprofits are still deeply skeptical about corporations and capitalism. Historically, the "left" has dominated activist social change. And within the social sector as a whole, a debate is raging about whether or not nonprofits should partner with business or even act more like businesses.

Many leaders still regard the private sector with skepticism—an attitude inherited from the old "New Left." They fear that they might lose focus or be co-opted if they partner with corporations. Some nonprofits play a corporate watchdog role and protest the excesses of capitalism and globalization—often for good reason. And a recent spate of corporate scandals hasn't helped improve the image of business. "Among many nonprofits, there is a view that business is the enemy," says Mike McCurry, who is on the board of Share Our Strength.

On the other side of this debate, more pragmatic members of the social entrepreneurship and corporate social responsibility movements have long touted the benefits of cross-sector partnerships and of harnessing market forces for social change. They argue that companies' bottom lines can benefit from social responsibility, while nonprofits can increase their impact when they harness the power of business to solve social problems. "A new, pro-business zeitgeist has made for-profit initiatives more acceptable," Greg Dees, professor and social entrepreneurship proponent, has written.[7]

Moreover, as nonprofits have been forced to become more accountable and more professional in recent years, many of them have borrowed management tools and practices from their for-profit counterparts. Some nonprofits, including many of those we studied, have hired talent from the corporate world. And a number of them have teamed up with corporate partners.

The high-impact nonprofits we studied are at the forefront of this larger trend sweeping both sectors—and blurring the boundaries between them. "This new paradigm pairs visionary companies that see how the social context in which they operate affects their bottom lines with a new breed of social entrepreneurs who understand how business principles can enable them to fulfill their social missions more effectively," wrote Shirley Sagawa and Eli Segal in their book on corporate-nonprofit partnerships, *Common Interest, Common Good.*[8]

Some groups, such as City Year, Share Our Strength, and the National Council of La Raza (NCLR), began working with companies back in the 1980s or early 1990s, when it was still uncommon. Others such as YouthBuild USA and the Exploratorium initially regarded the private sector with either indifference or disdain. Over time, however, they slowly realized that working with businesses could help them achieve their social change goals. The majority of these twelve organizations now embrace the power of the private sector through some combination of influencing business behavior, partnering with corporations to leverage the power of business, or running earned-income business ventures. In fact, only one—the Center on Budget and Policy Priorities—has made no attempt to leverage market forces or partner with business.

What's impressive about these high-impact nonprofits is that they go far beyond traditional models for working with business—while retaining their distinct missions and values. *They don't seek to act like a business so much as leverage the power of business.* In so doing, they have reframed the way others in the field think about the value of corporate partnerships and the application of market forces to social problem solving. By working with and through business, these nonprofits substantially increase their collective social impact. The whole is greater than the sum of its parts. These organizations are able to harness the best of both the social sector and the private sector to become a more powerful force for good.

Three Ways to Leverage Business

These twelve organizations we studied have found three distinct ways to work with and through businesses to achieve more social impact, and they often use more than one method simultaneously. We explore each of these strategies in more detail in later sections, but the following is a quick overview:

1. **Change business practices.** In some cases, these nonprofits change business practices to make companies more socially responsible, and in so doing, they often *change entire industries.* They might help transform how a business operates, in order to reduce pollution, influence the company's labor practices, or help it move into underserved markets. Often the company benefits just as much as the nonprofit's cause. Most of these nonprofits make a compelling business case, not just a moral case, about how changes can bolster the bottom line.
2. **Partner with business.** Partnerships can mean everything from simply accessing corporate donations and volunteers to creating more strategic corporate sponsorships or even operational alliances. These partnerships usually represent the easiest starting point for nonprofits seeking to leverage market forces. As they develop more corporate partnerships, they can become increasingly strategic in these alliances over time.
3. **Run a business.** Nonprofits also serve markets by running earned-income business ventures. They charge for a product or service, and that income is then channeled back into the charitable mission of the organization, increasing its own financial stability. For example, corporate partnerships led Share Our Strength to create Community Wealth Ventures, a for-profit consulting subsidiary that teaches other nonprofits how to build cause-marketing partnerships and generate

earned income. This effort in turn has helped build the entire social enterprise field.

These three pathways are not mutually exclusive, nor are the boundaries between them hard and fast. An organization could use all three strategies or focus on only one or two. Several of the nonprofits we studied leverage traditional corporate partnerships while also generating earned income through business ventures. In fact, there may be synergies in using multiple strategies. But because implementing them often entails different capabilities, most of the groups focus on only one or two at a time. And in some cases, such as EDF, the nonprofit works with corporate partners to change their practices, but without taking any money, as they believe it could create a conflict of interest.

CHANGE BUSINESS PRACTICES

Businesses don't make significant changes without a compelling bottom-line reason to do so. That's why many high-impact nonprofits have convinced companies to change their practices by making a business case, not just a moral appeal, for change. This strategy uses powerful financial incentives to help companies do the right thing. It changes how they operate, and in the process can alter the course of entire industries. Nonprofits can take two approaches: they can work to minimize a company's negative impact, such as on the environment or workers (what economists would call reducing "negative externalities"); and they can help companies become a force for good, helping them reach underserved markets or create economic assets for low-income populations. In either case, the nonprofit helps make markets work more effectively for everyone.

EDF, for example, partners with corporations such as McDonald's and Walmart in order to *decrease* their negative impact on the environment. It corrects for larger market failures with a relatively small investment of time and money. The nonprofit has worked with dozens of different corporate partners over the last two decades—creating many social innovations that have positively helped change standards in the fast-food, retail, packaging, and other industries.

Self-Help, by contrast, has helped companies serve low-income and minority markets that were historically neglected, and in the process it helped expand the U.S. mortgage industry. The North Carolina organization initially made home loans to minorities, single mothers, and the poor, who frequently didn't qualify for traditional mortgages. It carefully screened applicants and took calculated risks on people who it believed would repay their loans. The nonprofit soon discovered that its low-income borrowers were excellent credit risks, with a default rate similar to the middle class.[9]

But as successful as these loans were, founder Martin Eakes knew that his organization's assets were insignificant in comparison to those of the major financial institutions. He had to convince larger players to serve these long-neglected markets. "If we were going to reach more people, it was going to have to be through the large banks," says Eric Stein, chief operating officer. "Their distribution network is what we envied the most."

After years of effort, Martin Eakes got a meeting with Leslie M. Baker Jr., the CEO of Wachovia Bank. Eakes told him that Wachovia was missing an important business opportunity: serving single mothers. At first, Eakes didn't have the evidence to make his case, but once Self-Help proved this market could be profitable, Baker was willing to listen. "'Martin, if you will just leave me alone, we'll do a demonstration project," he said. "I'll allocate $10 million as a test just to get you out of my hair."

Six months later, the portfolio was performing so well that Wachovia upped its investment to $40 million, then $80 million, and finally $500 million to target primarily low-income, single-parent, and minority families. Both organizations benefited. The bank made a profit in a new market and met the federal community reinvestment requirements for banks; Self-Help helped build millions of dollars in home equity for low-income communities.

But there was a limit to how much risk Wachovia could assume. Like most commercial institutions, the bank faced a self-imposed cap that allowed nontraditional loans to make up no more than a certain percentage of its portfolio. Self-Help had no such limits, however, given its nonprofit status. And it believed—based on rigorous analysis and prior experience in the market—that it could safely manage the interest-rate and default risks.

The group soon found itself in the position of *buying* loans from Wachovia, so that the company could continue to issue more mortgages to the low-income market. And in an even more unusual move, Self-Help convinced Wachovia to *lend* it the $18 million it needed to buy these loans. Self-Help realized that there needed to be a secondary market for the loans, so that banks could recycle capital and continue lending to low-income families, just as Fannie Mae and Freddie Mac have done for home owners with greater income. So with this complicated move, Self-Help created the nation's largest secondary market solely for loans to low-income home owners.

(In light of the secondary mortgage market collapse in 2008, it's worth noting that Self-Help practiced responsible subprime lending, making sure its borrowers were well screened and had adequate support to prevent foreclosures. For more details on how Self-Help has responded since the real estate market crisis, see Chapters Ten and Eleven.)

Self-Help had stumbled on an extraordinarily powerful tool: using a small amount of collateral, it could take on debt to buy loans from financial services companies, allowing them to continue expanding into underserved markets. In this case, financial leverage also created strategic leverage. Eakes quickly worked to spread this innovation among other large financial players.

In 1998, the national mortgage powerhouse Fannie Mae was eager to buy loans for low-income families in order to meet its regulatory requirements. At the same time, Self-Help had reached its low-income loan purchasing capacity. Fannie Mae offered to buy Self-Help's existing portfolio of $100 million in mortgages to low-income families, allowing Self-Help to recycle its financing capacity and purchase more low-income loans from partner banks. Most nonprofits would have been thrilled at this offer, which would have doubled its impact (although Self-Help continued to hold the credit risk). But Eakes was already hatching bigger plans. He knew that one of Self-Help's earlier supporters, the Ford Foundation, was looking for a few large-scale investments. Eakes asked the foundation to make a $50 million grant to serve as risk reserve, boosting Self-Help's risk-taking capacity exponentially. He then parlayed the combined capital from Fannie Mae and Ford into collateral on *$2 billion* in loans to low-income home buyers.

By 2007, Self-Help's loan program operated in forty-nine states, through nearly forty large commercial lenders, including Bank of America, CitiBank, Wachovia, SunTrust, BB&T, and others. All told, Self-Help had by then financed $4.5 billion in loans—a total of fifty thousand mortgages—to low-income people whom large banks couldn't have served without Self-Help's intervention. "That's our model—we lend, innovate, do more lending, then go advocate to large financial institutions," says Randy Chambers, who was then chief financial officer of Self-Help (and currently serves as president of Self-Help Credit Union). Powerful companies went along, not because they believed in social justice goals, but because Self-Help proved it could also be *profitable*. (In hindsight, many of these companies did not adhere to the responsible lending practices advocated by Self-Help.)

The strategy has also proved to be a vital tool for financing Self-Help's own operation. Self-Help covers all its operating expenses with income from financial loans that it buys on secondary markets and other earned-income programs. This gives the organization enormous financial freedom and generates enough capital to sustain its growth. In many ways, Self-Help is running a double-bottom-line business—one with both financial and social returns—despite its nonprofit tax status.

"We have an advocacy and civil rights mission statement, but we have used the tools of business and law to further those goals," says Eakes. He likens this approach to a bicycle: "The front wheel of the bicycle is our mission—it's what comes first, what you keep your hands on, what steers you. The back wheel is our financial strength. The two together create impact with a scale that we couldn't obtain with only one or the other."

PARTNER WITH BUSINESS

Corporate partnerships are the most common way nonprofits work with businesses. Although companies have long played a philanthropic role in their communities, the trend began to accelerate in the 1980s and 1990s. Not only did corporate philanthropy increase, but firms also became more strategic about their partnerships, seeking alliances with nonprofits that would further their business goals. Simultaneously, nonprofits sought to deepen these partnerships for their own strategic benefit.[10]

These corporate-nonprofit partnerships follow many models, and other authors have written about these in more detail.[11] The most basic partnership is usually framed in traditional charitable terms. Typically, an organization approaches a corporation to support its work through a donation of money, volunteer time, or in-kind products. A few of the organizations we studied had not progressed beyond this early stage. YouthBuild and the Exploratorium had only a handful of corporate partners that acted mainly as donors or basic sponsors at the time we were concluding our initial research; since that time, they have moved to develop more of these partnerships. (For additional details, see Chapter Eleven.)

Sometimes the relationship progresses to greater commitment or strategic integration between the two organizations, through cause-marketing or sponsorship agreements, or operational alliances. Most of the organizations we examined have moved far beyond traditional "checkbook" philanthropy and into more strategic relationships, which we'll focus on in this chapter.

In these working arrangements, nonprofits can access a wide range of resources, and corporate partners can also help them achieve broader distribution of their ideas and services. The business may achieve measurable financial benefits, as well, through reduced operating costs, improved employee productivity, or even increased sales. Organizations often learn from each other, too, as they apply the best tools of the social and private sectors to solve social problems.[12]

Further, both partners usually benefit from a marketing perspective. The nonprofit often gains increased visibility for its cause and greater brand awareness. The business improves its corporate image; builds a stronger brand; generates greater loyalty among consumers, staff, retailers, and other stakeholders; and ultimately can generate more sales and higher profits.[13] But equally important, these organizations substantially increase their *collective social impact* by working together to solve social problems. More resources are channeled toward the cause, and public awareness is boosted. Not surprisingly, these cause-marketing partnerships have increased dramatically in the last fifteen years, reaching billions of dollars in value.[14]

One of the clearest examples of this win-win dynamic is Feeding America, known as America's Second Harvest—The Nation's Food Bank Network at the time of our original research. The nonprofit has not only significantly alleviated hunger in America but also transformed the food industry, creating a secondary market for food redistribution in the United States and generating enormous value for its corporate partners.[15]

Before Feeding America and food banking started in the late 1960s, there was no market for channeling excess food to the hungry. Back then, many businesses threw away excess or slightly damaged, but still edible, food. If they made donations, they did so only on a small, local scale. For its part, the U.S. government kept agricultural commodities off the market in order to bolster farm prices. Any farm product that wasn't sold through conventional markets became waste—while millions went hungry.

Jon Van Hengel, founder of Feeding America, saw a clear opportunity to distribute this excess food to people in need, and built the first food bank in America outside Phoenix, Arizona, to make his vision tangible. His idea began to catch on, as other communities built refrigerated warehouses to store food at a regional level and then redistribute it to community-based organizations.

It was a classic case of "If you build it, they will come." Without building a network of regional food banks, there would have been no way to make a national food distribution market work. But without corporate partnerships, the market wouldn't have worked either—corporations are the main source of the food that Feeding America redistributes.

It wasn't always a given that large corporations would work with food banks or make the sizable donations they do today. "The companies had seen many unprofessional charities handling their donated food," says Al Brislain, who at the time was senior vice president for member services at Feeding America and currently is executive director of Ft. Myers' Harry Chapin Food Bank. "Everyone could tell some horror story, and the companies were worried about liability. There were no standards at the local food banks. We got push-back from corporations saying, 'We need to know that you know how to handle our food.'"

Because of this push-back, Feeding America turned its attention to managing corporate partnerships and setting standards for the industry. "Our main services are food solicitation and setting standards," says Brislain. "[We are] the Good Housekeeping Seal of Approval. The food industry can now donate with confidence. We set the standards, and we get the food by building ties with national companies."

With standards in place, by the late 1970s the organization started receiving large donations from major companies such as Kraft, Nabisco, and Kellogg's. "There's a big difference in getting a pickup truck full of bread from Safeway and getting a *semi-trailer* load of cereal boxes from Kellogg's," says Brislain. These large corporate donations compelled Feeding America to scale up its operations. "The first year we started, Feeding America distributed five million pounds of food to fifteen food banks," says Brislain. "That's one small food bank's average today."

By 2007, Feeding America was moving more than *two billion* pounds of donated food a year, feeding more than twenty-five million people through its network of more than two hundred food banks and fifty thousand community agencies. Today it moves more than three billion pounds per year as demand has soared since the onset of the recession in 2008. In many ways, the group resembles a national grocery store chain more than a typical nonprofit.

At the same time that the nonprofit is helping end hunger, Feeding America is also helping solve a business problem for large corporations, which can now write off their excess production as a donation to charity. And the government can donate surplus commodities to the needy, rather than affect the market prices that farmers depend on. "We represent a solution to both business and government," says David Prendergast, senior vice president for technology and planning. "We're very good at pulling together disparate parties. We kind of represent a hub for all the organizations concerned about hunger."

The twelve organizations in this book collectively engage hundreds of corporate partners. (See Table 3.1.) City Year is another great example of a nonprofit that has built strong corporate partnerships to increase its social impact. In this case, City Year leverages its partnerships to garner more resources for its cause and simultaneously to engage the business community in strengthening local democracy.

TABLE 3.1. Exemplary Corporate Partnerships (as of 2007).

Organization	Leading Corporate Partners
City Year	Bank of America, Comcast, CSX, Timberland, T-Mobile
Environmental Defense Fund	Walmart, FedEx, McDonald's
Exploratorium	Amgen, Sony, IBM
Feeding America	ConAgra Foods, Kraft, Pampered Chef, Kroger, Walmart
Habitat for Humanity	Thrivent, Citigroup, Whirlpool, Home Depot
National Council of La Raza	PepsiCo, State Farm, General Motors, Bank of America, Citi, Johnson & Johnson
Self-Help	Fannie Mae, Bank of America, Wachovia
Share Our Strength	American Express, Sysco, Timberland, Tyson Foods, PARADE
Teach For America	Wachovia, Amgen
YouthBuild USA	Home Depot, Bank of America

When Alan Khazei and Michael Brown first founded the youth corps as a demonstration project for national service in 1988, they deliberately engaged the private sector.[16] Whereas many youth corps relied primarily on government funding, Khazei and Brown believed in harnessing the tremendous resources of the private sector, along with the entrepreneurial power of business. They also felt that companies had a moral responsibility to give back, and that doing so could be good for their bottom lines. They looked to the 1984 Olympics as a model for new forms of corporate sponsorships, where both the cause and the participating companies benefited. "Self-interest and the common good—you can't separate them," said Brown in an early article about City Year in *Inc.* magazine.[17]

City Year's corporate partners financially support the organization and frequently sponsor a local team with whom they build a strong relationship. Corps members wear the company's logo on their uniforms, give presentations to boards of directors, and work with company employees on community service days. Company leaders mentor young people and in some cases give them career advice and coaching. These alliances have always been strategic and symbiotic: City Year receives funding, skills, marketing, and in-kind support from local businesses; the companies receive marketing exposure, a boost in employee morale, and even an employee-recruiting pool. And both organizations learn from the other in the process of working together on common problems in their communities.

"The idea of leveraging the strengths of the City Year model with the skills of corporations—that goes beyond checkbook phi-lanthropy," says Jim Balfanz, who was chief operating officer at the time and now serves as president of City Year. "There's a com-pound factor of goodness that comes out of engaging corpora-tions in our work. It goes beyond a fundraising strategy, and has become part of our mission."

By 2007, City Year had more than 350 corporate sponsors, including local companies in the seventeen cities where it oper-ates. At the most elite level, its six National Leadership Sponsors invested a minimum of $1 million over two years and pledged employee time and ideas to support the program. These included Bank of America, Comcast, CSX, Pepperidge Farm, T-Mobile, and the Timberland Company, which at the time had contributed more than $12 million since first donating boots to City Year's pilot summer youth corps.

City Year also has helped pioneer a more strategic approach to partnerships. In a significant step, it has tried to take a com-pany's interests into consideration, rather than simply see itself as the recipient of a grant. "We're looking for highly leveraged partnerships, which takes connecting to the goals and strategy of the company," says Nancy Routh, senior vice president at City Year. "With a lot of new team [corporate] sponsors, when we start ask-ing about their corporate goals, along with their philanthropic goals, they are pleasantly surprised. They are not often asked these questions."

Companies donate to City Year, and in return, City Year helps them achieve their business goals. For example, when cable company Comcast was first entering Boston (through acquiring AT&T), City Year hosted a public reception with local officials, community members, and opinion leaders at its Boston headquarters. In effect, it used its local relationships to help ease the company's entry into a new market. Comcast was donating well over $1 million to City Year annually by 2007—and donated more than $18 million in free television advertising.

In another case, T-Mobile donated BlackBerry smartphones (with free service) to staff and cell phones with service to corps members—in return, it gets marketing exposure among youth and other critical communities. T-Mobile also provided Internet access for local nonprofits and schools where it works with City Year's Care Force program; City Year serves as the intermediary and broker. It's not just City Year that benefits, but the larger community as well. "The key thing here is that we are the glue between the corporate partners and the community partners," says Balfanz. "We can find a way to share those resources."

In a partnership with Pepperidge Farms, City Year cobranded a "Starfish" product modeled on the company's Goldfish crackers. On the back of the packaging was a favorite City Year story about how saving one starfish can make a difference. (See Chapter Four for the starfish story.) It's a classic City Year message of hope, optimism, and empowerment for children that dovetails with the Pepperidge Farms brand. "They started thinking about how to make a difference in the world and how they could use their brand to do that," says Routh. "That brought them to City Year as a partner of choice."

For City Year, these connections create an impact that spreads beyond the borders of its own organization: "City Year looks at it as part of our mission to engage corporate America and to shift resources into communities," says Balfanz. "But we do it in a way that is adding value to the company, because that allows them to justify to their shareholders what they are doing."

RUN A BUSINESS

Many nonprofits generate extra income running businesses; that is, they create markets for their own products and services. The only difference between these nonprofit businesses and a for-profit company is that any profits must be returned to serving their social purpose. In many of these cases, the business is not an organization's core focus and makes up only a small percentage of its total revenue.

These groups have discovered the benefits of having a no-strings-attached income stream that they can use to cover operating costs. Unlike foundation or government grants, or large individual donations—many of which are earmarked for specific programs—income earned through a legitimate business can be allocated any way the organization sees fit. Not surprisingly, many nonprofits have experimented with launching businesses to strengthen their financial sustainability.

Historically, some entities have had business models that intrinsically make it easier to charge for their products or services. For example, universities charge tuition, museums charge admission, and nonprofit hospitals bill for care. But even organizations that don't have obvious revenue streams have learned to play the earned-income game. The Girl Scouts' cookie sales and Goodwill's thrift stores are two well-known examples.

Among the organizations we studied, a few have business models that naturally lend themselves to mission-related earned-income ventures. (See Table 3.2.) The affordable-housing nonprofits such as Self-Help have a built-in revenue stream in the form of loan repayments and interest from community development

TABLE 3.2. PROGRAMS THAT GENERATE REVENUE.

Organization	Program
City Year	Care Force
Exploratorium	Ticket sales, gift shop, publications, leased ExNet rotating exhibits
National Council of La Raza	Raza Development Fund; annual conference
Self-Help	Secondary mortgage market income; housing and child-care lending; ventures fund
Share Our Strength	Community Wealth Ventures; cause-marketing alliances
YouthBuild USA	Housing sales and rentals (through affiliates)

Note: Habitat for Humanity does not classify its loan repayments as "earned income" but as a voluntary tithing program.

loans, as well as other financial tools that they leverage in the housing and lending markets. YouthBuild USA and the National Council of La Raza have also begun to develop similar financial tools through their respective housing and lending programs.

Other organizations don't have business models that inherently lend themselves to generating earned income. These non-profits have had to be more creative in their efforts to launch small businesses. City Year, for example, launched a small consulting business called Care Force, which leverages its community service expertise to help corporations lead volunteer events. The Exploratorium has long been able to charge admission to its museum, but it has also sold a number of publications designed to help children learn about science, and it charges other museums to lease exhibits. And the National Council of La Raza seeks corporate sponsorships and advertising income for its national conference and its ALMA (Spanish for "soul") Awards, a media awards ceremony.

Of all the organizations we studied, Share Our Strength is perhaps the most well known for advancing "social enterprise," a movement that capitalizes on earned income for social causes. The nonprofit started with basic corporate partnerships, which then progressed into much more integrated cause-marketing alliances. Then Share Our Strength began to focus on creating substantial earned income ventures for itself—and for other nonprofits in the sector—by preaching the virtues of community wealth.[18]

Share Our Strength was started in 1984 by Bill Shore and his sister, Debbie, with the goal of mobilizing the food and restaurant industry to help end hunger. Through early corporation-sponsored events, such as Taste of the Nation, the group raised millions of dollars for hunger relief. These first sponsorships soon developed into more strategic partnerships.

The nonprofit's big breakthrough came in 1993, when American Express sponsored a national campaign with Share Our Strength called The Charge Against Hunger, which ultimately raised $21 million over three years. Share Our Strength contributed its cause and its connections in the restaurant community; in return, American Express invested millions of marketing dollars into the campaign. Share Our Strength raised millions more for hunger relief than it could have alone, and American Express generated more card usage and greater profits. It was an experience that has been widely studied and copied.

Share Our Strength had discovered a powerful tool, now known as *social cause-marketing*. By the late 1990s, the group had formed nearly one hundred of these cause-marketing partnerships with such companies as Calphalon, Barnes & Noble, and Evian.[19] It continues to run many corporation-sponsored fundraising events, including the Great American Bake Sale, Taste of the Nation, Restaurants for Relief, and A Tasteful Pursuit. The organization is a cause-marketing machine.

Perhaps Share Our Strength's greatest insight was that nonprofits needed to move away from seeking charitable contributions and toward building *strategic partnerships* with companies' marketing departments. By working with a company's marketing arm to raise money for hunger, the nonprofit could increase its impact while helping the company boost profits. It was structured more like a business-to-business alliance than a philanthropic donation. For example, Share Our Strength licenses its logo to use on bottles of California wine. "It's no different than Disney licensing *Lion King* merchandise to Burger King," Shore has said.[20]

Share Our Strength grew so good at forging these cause-marketing deals that corporations were calling the organization for advice on how to generate more value from their nonprofit partnerships. "Six years ago I was making corporate outreach calls all day long," says Ashley Graham, director of leadership development. "Now they're calling us, and they're also asking us how we do what we do."[21] Other nonprofits also approached Share Our Strength to learn how they could leverage their assets to earn income or create cause-marketing alliances with companies.

In response to this demand, Share Our Strength launched a for-profit company in 1998. Community Wealth Ventures (CWV) is a social enterprise consulting firm that helps nonprofit organizations generate revenue through business ventures and cause-marketing partnerships, and helps corporations improve their bottom lines through more strategic philanthropy. The goal is to help both nonprofits and corporations think differently about market-based approaches to social change.

Underlying Share Our Strength's work is Bill Shore's vision of a world in which nonprofits don't have to depend on the crumbs of charity, but rather can create economic value *while* creating social change. "We began [CWV] for one simple reason: Our commitment to social change demands and depends on creating new resources to support those programs that are already proven to work but don't have the capacity to grow to scale," wrote Shore in one of his books, *The Cathedral Within*.[22] Although this larger vision has yet to be realized on a grand scale, there's no doubt that CWV has made an impact.

In its first eight years of operation, CWV had returned $1 million in profit to Share Our Strength. Although that was only 5 percent of Share Our Strength's operating budget, CWV had even greater impact by promoting the idea of social enterprise within the nonprofit sector. It has worked with hundreds of businesses and nonprofits on earned-income ventures and partnerships, and in the process has helped build the field of social enterprise. "We have the potential to transform the role that the civic sector plays in our society, and to transform the way the nonprofit and corporate communities work together to create change," Shore has said.[23]

MANAGING THE RISKS

By now it should be apparent that nonprofit organizations can harness the private sector as a force for good, whether it's through changing business behavior, creating corporate-nonprofit partnerships, or generating earned income. All but one of the groups we studied, the Center on Budget and Policy Priorities, have pursued at least one of these paths in the effort to expand their social impact.

Yet many nonprofits are still reluctant to follow any of these strategies—sometimes for good reason. The challenges and risks can seem formidable, and those seeking to leverage market forces should proceed with caution. Following are some general risks that come with the territory of working with business, as well as tips on managing them. Many others have written about each of these in more depth, so we list some general resources at the end of the book that can help you navigate these murky waters.

FEAR OF MISSION-DRIFT

For any nonprofit seeking to partner with business or run its own earned-income operation, perhaps the biggest risk is that it will be distracted from its charitable mission. The fear is that the organization will start to act more like a business or become consumed with running a business, and lose sight of its social purpose. "Are we at risk of selling out our values and losing our soul if we begin to engage in commerce?" a CWV report asks.[24] It's an important question, and for some groups, the answer might mean not partnering with business or running an earned-income venture.

But among the high-impact nonprofits we studied, mission-drift did not appear to be a problem: all of them are able to work with and through business while staying true to their values and focused on their social goals. If anything, a desire to have more impact propels them into these partnerships. But even though they are all pragmatic, they will draw the line if their social purpose is at risk of becoming compromised.

When the technology company Cisco Systems proposed that City Year corps members run technology training centers in high schools, for instance, City Year had to walk away from the deal because it wasn't the best use of its corps members' skills or time. "The training of corps members was taking too much time away from direct service hours. So we ended up saying no to Cisco. It was a hard decision, but we had to say, 'This isn't us,'" says Nancy Routh, senior vice president. The organization has found other ways to partner with Cisco, but this particular program would have taken it too far from its primary work. Nonprofits that pursue corporate partnerships or run earned-income ventures must constantly guard against this kind of mission-drift.

PERCEPTION OF SELLING OUT

Key stakeholders can also see a nonprofit as selling out or as being less needy because of its partnerships with for-profits. The fear is that partnerships could result in the withdrawal of individual, foundation, or other forms of financial support. But when other green groups thought EDF had sold out because of its early corporate partnerships, it didn't experience a loss of support from its board, staff, or donors. Now many environmentalists work with businesses—in fact, it has become almost trendy to do so. "Almost all the major environmental groups are now engaged in some way with corporations," says Gwen Ruta, now vice president for corporate partnerships at EDF. "That just wasn't the case fifteen years ago."

As the social sector becomes more comfortable with the idea of corporate relationships, and as donors realize that business partnerships can magnify their own donations, this risk will likely diminish. Now nonprofits are teaming up with companies on numerous issues, as the groups we studied illustrate—and proving that working with business and cultivating other donors don't have to be mutually exclusive.

Nevertheless, nonprofits should be cautious about whom they partner with—and in particular, their partner's motives—so that they can't be accused of being manipulated for PR benefit. For example, EDF initially turned down a partnership with Walmart when it was first approached, out of concern that the company wanted to use the nonprofit for "greenwashing," or to appear more environmental than it really is. It wasn't until EDF was convinced of Walmart's genuine intent to change its business practices—and Walmart committed to specific, measurable goals—that it formally announced that it would open an office in Bentonville and help the retailer become more environmentally sustainable.

Finding the Right Partner

Partnerships require trust, whether the alliance is more philanthropic, marketing oriented, or operational. Both parties must be sure that the partnership is a good fit and that their goals and motives are aligned. A single instance of corruption on either the corporate or nonprofit side can damage hard-earned brand integrity and credibility. There have been cases of organizations entering into a joint cause-marketing alliance, only to have their corporate partner exposed for unethical behavior. Though none of the groups we studied have been involved in this kind of scandal, they were all aware of the importance of protecting their integrity in the partnership.

For example, leaders at the National Council of La Raza (NCLR) cited the time they discovered that a major corporate partner (which they declined to name) was exploiting Hispanic migrant laborers in its workforce. At first NCLR tried to use its influence to help the company change its labor practices. But when those efforts went unheeded, NCLR had to walk away from the partnership, leaving money on the table to preserve its integrity.

Organizations should perform due diligence on potential corporate partners, doing as much research as they can to make sure their motives, goals, and integrity are aligned, rather than rushing in when a company dangles a grant. And this takes time. "It takes dogged persistence; we have to have seventeen thousand conversations first," says Ruta. "We do go out on a lot of first dates with potential partners. You have to do that before you find the right fit."

TENSIONS WITH OTHER PROGRAMS

There may be a tension between corporate partnerships and a nonprofit's other activities—policy advocacy in particular. A potential conflict of interest can develop if a group advocates in favor of a political issue on which its corporate partner has taken the opposite stance. The organizations we studied were all careful to manage expectations around these potential conflicts, as we discussed in Chapter Two. NCLR, for example, is always up front about its position on policy issues related to the Hispanic community, including immigration policy, so that it won't take its corporate partners by surprise.

At Feeding America, the organization ensures that making policy decisions is a function of the president and program staff—not of the board, on which many corporate partners serve. "We do not want the food industry to have undue influence on our public policy," says Doug O'Brien, vice president for public policy. "Initially, the board was overwhelmingly occupied by the food industry, and it was a prudent way to make sure that our operations wouldn't be viewed as an arm for any company's public relations team."

Further, the group takes a clear stand on policy issues related to hunger, but does not stray into larger areas like welfare reform, where there might be more conflict with corporate supporters. "The further we go from our mission, that's when we come into conflict," says O'Brien. "A lot of companies support food stamps. But advocating for [a higher] minimum wage might have been a problem."

THE LIMITS OF EARNED INCOME

Despite the promise of social enterprise, this approach hasn't proven to be the silver bullet for nonprofits that some hoped. Many nonprofits that lack an obvious mission-related income stream have found it difficult to build and sustain small businesses. Sometimes the revenue just isn't worth the amount of time and energy they must invest; other times, the business idea isn't profitable, or the organization doesn't have the skills to pull it off. It's hard enough for businesses to make a profit, let alone for nonprofits to do so.

For instance, City Year tried to launch a business selling City Year Gear, cobranded with Timberland. The retail line never took off, and City Year quietly shut down the effort. The group's Care Force business has been more successful, as it leverages the core skills of the organization to organize company volunteer events, but even that generates only a small percentage of the total budget. And even Share Our Strength's subsidiary, Community Wealth Ventures, has been far less successful as a business—in pure monetary terms—than its many corporate cause-marketing partnerships.

Earned income should not be held up as a potential source of large infusions of financial capital to most struggling nonprofits. Although the appeal of having unrestricted funding is great, if a nonprofit isn't careful, it can find itself drifting too far from its charitable mission, or even losing money in a failed business venture. Revenue generation is most successful for those groups that have a business model already conducive to making a profit— such as investments in real estate or such financial tools as loans and mortgages. For those that are in a pure service or advocacy business, it becomes much more difficult to find mission-related ventures that can return a real profit, once all costs are taken into consideration.

PRAGMATIC ACTIVISM

Where there's risk, there's also opportunity. All the stories told here illustrate the increased impact that results when groups leverage the power and resources of the private sector and of market dynamics for the purpose of creating social change.

As the various examples illustrate, the easiest place to start is with basic corporate partnerships, in which the company donates volunteer time, money, or in-kind products. Often these alliances progress to greater integration, as in Share Our Strength's many strategic cause-marketing partnerships, City Year's work connecting companies to their communities, and Feeding America's operational alliances with large food retailers.

A more complicated approach is for a nonprofit to start a business itself, as a few of these groups have done. This is particularly successful for those nonprofits that work in the housing markets—such as Self-Help and NCLR's Raza Development Fund. Other organizations we studied rely on earned income mainly to supplement their fundraising.

Finally, a few of these nonprofits work with corporate partners to change the corporations' operations: either decreasing their negative impact on society, as EDF has done, or increasing their positive reach to underserved markets, as in Self-Help's case. These nonprofits leverage markets, helping create economic incentives for companies to do the right thing. Although this last path is difficult, it is also powerful.

Regardless of which path an organization pursues, these high-impact nonprofits have demonstrated that businesses and nonprofits working together can have more impact. They are pragmatic idealists who combine their social values with more practical tactics—in keeping with the times. "Our goal has been to take civil rights and the women's movement into the economic arena," says Martin Eakes, founder of Self-Help. "The battles of the 1960s have largely been won, but if they are not translated into *economics,* it won't amount to much."

EDF began harnessing market forces and working with business when this was still anathema to many nonprofits. Now, many major green groups are getting into the corporate sponsorship game, but in teaming up with Walmart, EDF is going further. Where others saw bad behavior, EDF saw opportunity and opened an office in Bentonville, Arkansas. "Every week, 175 million customers shop at Walmart. If [we] can nudge them in the right direction on the environment, we can have huge impact," says David Yarnold, then executive vice president. "Walmart can have a ripple effect through the whole economy by demanding better environmental performance from its suppliers."

It's this pragmatic approach that has allowed great nonprofits such as EDF to ultimately have more impact on the issues they care about. And, as we'll see in Chapters Four and Five, following other practices we discovered—such as engaging individuals and working through nonprofit networks—can add even greater power to this approach. Because a number of these nonprofits have broad reach into many markets and have powerful alliances, businesses want to work with them in return.

"We believe that if you want to change America, you've got to change American business," says Ruta of EDF.[25] As these nonprofits have shown, it's possible, and even necessary, to engage corporate America in a constructive dialogue. Although there are certainly risks, the strategy has the potential to change the world.

CHAPTER THREE HIGHLIGHTS

- **It's hard to change the world without changing business.** High-impact nonprofits recognize that the private sector has substantial resources and wields enormous power. These groups see business as an ally, not an enemy, and they help companies become forces for good.
- **There are three ways to harness market forces.** Great non-profits figure out how to leverage free-market systems for social impact.
  - They work with business to change corporate practices and make companies more socially responsible.
  - They partner with business to access more resources for their cause, in the form of donations, volunteers, or cause-marketing.
  - Some organizations run their own businesses to generate earned income.
- **Nonprofits bring valuable assets to the table.** The best groups understand that they have as much to offer business as companies have to offer them. And effective cross-sector alliances create wins for both partners.
- **Manage the real risks.** It's difficult to work effectively with business. Risks include the potential to be co-opted by corporate interests, the perception of "selling out" among

peers or the public, and all the dangers inherent in any joint venture or effort to run a business. But high-impact nonprofits see more opportunities than obstacles.

- **Earned income can be a boon, but it's not a silver bullet.** Many of the groups we studied have found ways to run businesses. The fortunate ones benefit from robust revenue streams; others are unusually creative about finding ways to generate income. However, earned income is not for every nonprofit. Some models don't lend themselves to generating revenue.

CHAPTER FOUR

INSPIRE EVANGELISTS

Habitat for Humanity International is one of the most successful nonprofits of our time—although not necessarily for the reasons people might think. Founded in the 1970s in rural Georgia,
Habitat by 2007 had a total budget of nearly $1 billion, several
thousand affiliates, and hundreds of thousands of volunteers
worldwide.[1] It had built more than two hundred thousand houses
in nearly one hundred countries, and its brand name has been
rated in the same league as that of Starbucks.[2] Habitat is the only
nonprofit founded since 1960 to make it onto the top twenty-five
of the Chronicle of Philanthropy 400, a ranking by budget size. So
it's no surprise to find Habitat in a book about how leading social
sector organizations have scaled their social impact.

Still, if you were to evaluate Habitat *only* by the number of
houses it has built, you might be underwhelmed. Habitat's
numbers pale in comparison to those of real estate developers
(for-profit or nonprofit) that have built millions of low-income,
multiunit housing complexes. But if you look instead at the larger
community that Habitat has created, its impact becomes more
evident.

Habitat doesn't aspire merely to build houses for the poor,
but rather to mobilize communities to solve the problems of poverty housing. They inspire hundreds of thousands of middle-class
volunteers to help build Habitat houses—to change how they
think, how they act, and how they vote. "The goal of Habitat for
Humanity International is to eliminate poverty housing and homelessness from the face of the earth by building adequate and basic
housing," reads its mission statement. "Furthermore, all of our

words and actions are for the *ultimate purpose of putting shelter on the hearts and minds of people* in such a powerful way that poverty housing and homelessness become socially, politically, and religiously unacceptable in our nations and the world." Habitat seeks nothing less than to transform the relationship between the world's haves and have-nots. It's the ultimate example of a movement for grassroots change.

Despite its audacious goals, Habitat for Humanity has humble roots. It was founded by successful, self-made businessman Millard Fuller and his wife, Linda, in the late 1970s. Following marital troubles, they renounced their wealth and moved to Koinonia, a small Christian community in rural Georgia, where the idea of a "housing ministry" took root. After testing the Habitat model in Africa, the Fullers traveled the world, recruiting Christian volunteers to assist them in building houses for the poor. They used church networks to reach and engage individuals. "The largest organization in the world is the church, in all its manifestations," says Fuller (who passed away after publication of this initial research). "[Habitat] tapped into that huge existing organization to be its support base—it has been phenomenal."

The group's big breakthrough came in 1984, when Fuller persuaded former president Jimmy Carter—then living in nearby Plains, Georgia—to become an ambassador for Habitat. Carter agreed to serve on the board, act as a spokesman, and sign fundraising letters. His involvement propelled Habitat from a small group to a global organization with enormous fundraising capabilities. A decade later, revenues had gone from around $3 million to nearly $100 million, thanks largely to Carter's role as its premier evangelist. Today the nonprofit's combined budget has grown at an astonishing annual rate of 30 percent over two decades.[3]

Habitat's business model is stunning in its simplicity: volunteers build houses, working side-by-side with the recipients, who are required to commit hundreds of hours of sweat equity to obtain a home at below-market rates. Because Habitat relies on volunteer labor and donated materials, costs are relatively low. Further, new home owners are required to pay a no-interest mortgage, creating revenue that the local Habitat affiliate reinvests in building more homes. This combination of low costs and a steady income stream allows the group to keep expanding its work.

Habitat's results are so concrete—a house that people can see and touch—that engaging new volunteers and donors is extremely easy. "We have one thing that many other nonprofits do not have: a hands-on approach in which a person can actually participate in a project and see the beginning and end," says Sybil Carter, director of corporate partnerships and Jimmy Carter's sister-in-law. "You can be there for the dedication; you can ride by it a year later and say, 'We helped build that house.' That is one of the main draws."

From the outset, Habitat discovered the Holy Grail of the nonprofit world: a virtuous cycle in which one element of the model reinforces the other. It started out engaging individuals around the strong values of a faith-based organization. People gave time and money to support Habitat's work—and they built the houses. As Habitat grew, it turned volunteers and donors into evangelists for the housing cause, transforming their lives in the process. These evangelists recruited more people to the organization, who gave time and money in an ever-expanding circle of impact.

"The elements we rely on to grow—funding, volunteers, capacity, construction materials—all of that we have had in abundance," says Stephen Seidel, now director of U.S. urban programs. "Year after year, I kept thinking this will be the year in which funding or volunteers dissipate. It never happened. Every year there are new groups that want to participate and existing groups that want to increase their involvement."

Ultimately, Habitat has built much more than homes. It has created a global community committed to ending poverty housing, and has come closer than any organization we studied to building a movement. "I was more interested in building a movement than an organization," says Fuller. "The key ingredient of a movement is abandon—you don't hold back. It takes passion, commitment, dedication. But you can only have a movement if you attract a lot of people. That's what Habitat did—it attracted a huge following of hundreds of thousands of people."

TURNING OUTSIDERS INTO INSIDERS

Groups such as Habitat excel at engaging individuals from outside their organizations—as volunteers, donors, advisers, supporters, and evangelists. They go beyond building a community among their internal staff and clients: they actively mobilize the public for greater social change. As they grow, they continually expand the boundaries of their organization outward, drawing new individuals into their community or network of "change makers."

We have already seen how high-impact organizations mobilize other sectors of society to magnify their impact: lobbying government for policy change and working with business. These groups are similarly adept at engaging individuals and the larger public in their work. The approach has always been an important function of nonprofits, providing a voice for public concerns, a vehicle for civic engagement, and the bedrock of participatory democracy. But these groups don't actively involve individuals just because it's the right thing to do. It is in their strategic interest as well. They gain something in return: as they mobilize individuals and social networks, they magnify their impact.

Engaging individuals can be central to a group's resource strategy. People provide volunteer labor, as in Habitat's case, that allows a nonprofit to accomplish more work with lower costs. More important, volunteers and members often give money. Large numbers of individual donors can provide a relatively stable, sustainable, and flexible funding base, unlike such sources as the government or grants from foundations and businesses, which usually come with restrictions. A large base of individual donors allows the financial freedom to invest in capacity and to remain innovative and adaptive, because funding is not all committed to specific programs.

Individuals also help nonprofits increase their power and influence. Individuals, en masse, represent both voters and consumers, with the power to move governments and markets. Whether they engage the Hispanic community, religious conservatives, or liberal environmentalists, organizations often have a built-in base they can use to exert pressure on their elected representatives. As we illustrate in Chapter Five, City Year successfully mobilized thousands of supporters—individuals and other nonprofits—in its Save AmeriCorps campaign, resulting in renewed support for the federal program.

Many of the other groups we've studied, such as Environmental Defense Fund (EDF) and The Heritage Foundation, draw on their hundreds of thousands of supporters to influence public policy.

And Habitat has recently established an advocacy task force to figure out how to influence politics. "The task force is about leveraging the untapped resources of thousands of volunteers in local communities," says Seidel. "These are voters who by virtue of showing up with a hammer on the work site are connected to housing as an issue."

In addition to being *citizens* in the sphere of civil society, individuals are *consumers* in the marketplace. When an organization collaborates with a business—either to change its practices or to engage it in a partnership—it has more leverage at the negotiating table if it represents a lot of people in critical markets. It can mobilize supporters in a consumer boycott to protest poor business practices, or encourage members to purchase products from companies that support a cause. In the case of American Express and Share Our Strength (discussed in Chapter Three), the group's ability to reach tens of thousands of well-heeled event participants and supporters gave it added power in partnering for social change.

Citizens not only have power in numbers but also have influence in their local communities or society at large. Some of these influencers donate their expertise as board members or advisers. A few of them are "super-evangelists"—powerful leaders such as Jimmy Carter, who use their influence nationally or internationally to help a nonprofit accomplish more. As CEOs of corporations, they help broker partnerships; as politicians, they support legislative or policy changes; as celebrities or prominent social figures, they draw media attention and inspire others to act. Support from super-evangelists can help create tipping points, propelling organizations to achieve much greater impact.

These individuals also receive something in return: *they are connected, inspired, and transformed in the process of working for a cause.* The nonprofit helps reinforce their innermost values and convert their beliefs into action, whether this means voting, volunteering, donating, demonstrating, or attending a civic function. People are no longer passive consumers, but instead are cocreators of community.

"Believing is belonging," writes Patrick Hanlon in his book *Primal Branding*.[4] "When you are able to create brands that people believe in, you also create groups of people who feel that they belong. This sense of community is at the center of psychologist

Abraham Maslow's famous hierarchy of human needs. . . . It is an essential human truth that we all want to belong to something that is larger than ourselves." Although Hanlon applies this logic to businesses, the theory is even more applicable to nonprofits. As they engage others, these *purpose-driven* organizations meet an individual's need for belief and belonging—and they help create healthier communities in which to live and work.

Recent research suggests that people will help more if they are not seen merely as a means to an end, but as empowered equals. "Outsiders are much more likely to help a nonprofit achieve its larger goals if they are not just treated as free labor or deep pockets, but as valued members of a community," said scholar Joel Podolny in a speech at the Skoll World Forum. "Ultimately, the community should be treated as an end in itself."[5]

There are substantial network effects to this process of building a community. As more members join and become evangelists for a cause, they tap into their own social networks, recruiting friends to the organization. The circle keeps expanding outward. Large-scale involvement brings media attention to the organization, increasing its brand recognition, which leads to even more recruits. Ultimately, the ever-expanding cycle of conversion and engagement can create larger ripple effects on society as a whole.

THE RULES OF ENGAGEMENT

When we started closely examining these high-impact organizations, we found that most of them have a superior ability to involve outsiders in their mission and create committed networks of evangelists. Although some of these communities are larger than others, most number in the tens of thousands or hundreds of thousands of supporters. Even more important than the quantity of these relationships is the quality. In marketing parlance, they are "sticky" relationships.

Once it became apparent to us that individual engagement is a powerful lever for greater social impact, we were curious to know what successful groups do that distinguishes them from organizations that are not as effective. After all, the concept of individuals contributing to nonprofits is not new—it is the very essence of the

Figure 4.1. Ripples of Impact.

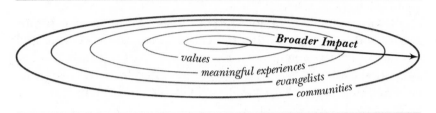

social sector. Volunteers donate time. Donors give money. Board members donate both time and money, ideally in large quantities.

The twelve groups in this book go beyond traditional notions of volunteerism. It's not that they don't ask donors to attend dinners and ask volunteers to help with mailings as everyone else does. But they transcend these more mundane tactics and create opportunities for people *to actively participate and to experience* what the nonprofits do. They make it an organizational priority, carefully crafting a strategy of engagement and deliberately committing the time and resources to create meaningful relationships. And they invest in sustaining these large communities of supporters who share their values and advocate for their cause.

We have discovered a few guiding principles that have enabled the most successful nonprofits to build large communities—or networks of evangelists—engaged on their behalf. We call these "the Rules of Engagement." Each of the four rules builds on the other, creating a series of ripples expanding outward. (See Figure 4.1.) Although not every organization applies all four equally well, most of them follow this framework, and they have all found a way to create deep and lasting relationships with their supporters.

Communicate Your Mission, Vision, and Values

Engagement of individuals starts with something obvious, but not at all simple: a clear and compelling expression of an organization's mission, vision, and values. As they articulate their mission and values to outsiders—and inspire others to act on their vision—these organizations are able to appeal to people's emotions at an almost unconscious level. Such connections inspire others to engage with the organization to express their own beliefs and values.

This is certainly true for Habitat. "After you strip away Jimmy Carter's impact, the fact that people keep coming back time and again to pick up a hammer or write a check is because Habitat really does have a dramatic impact on people's lives," says Stephen Seidel, director of U.S. urban programs. "They are living out their values by working with Habitat."

Communicating values goes beyond traditional marketing as it is commonly understood. It's not just about having compelling marketing materials, a snazzy Web site, sophisticated databases, or successful direct-mail campaigns. Some great nonprofits have all of these, but many don't. Rather, communicating values is more about telling a story, connecting your work with the beliefs of supporters, and inspiring others to join the tribe. Whether they employ the CEO, other executives, or even other evangelists in this visionary role, these groups inspire outsiders to move from belief to action, and they give them opportunities to participate. "[Millard Fuller] had a great ability to inspire people and make them feel they could make a difference," says Jill Claflin, now senior director of U.S. communications at Habitat. "He was a fine storyteller and a brilliant communicator."

Despite the passion of its founder, Habitat didn't initially have the trappings of a well-marketed organization, such as a compelling logo or a well-known brand. Habitat built a community around its beliefs, and its brand followed. "The brand has been built at the grassroots level by engaging people in our work," says Chris Clarke, senior vice president of communications.

Over and over again, we heard this theme: it's not about marketing per se; it's about the message. The network itself—and the opportunity to participate and make a difference—becomes the draw. People want to belong to a community that shares their values, and where they have an opportunity to give back.

Another way these nonprofits defy conventional marketing wisdom is that they don't necessarily narrow their audiences. "Habitat has such a broad appeal we haven't had to be too finely focused on whom we target, and that's why the program has grown to the size it has," says Tim Daugherty, senior director of direct marketing. "The ease of message has played a key role. Everyone has a roof over their heads and knows the importance of a home. It's an easy concept to grasp."

The experience of City Year echoes Habitat's—and flies in the face of most marketing textbooks. "What marketing tells you is that it's all about segmentation," says Jim Balfanz, chief operating officer at the time of our interview, now president of City Year. "But in the social sector we have to create common ground. We're trying to build a field and work toward something that needs to be part of the fabric of democracy."

Groups such as City Year and Habitat seek to connect people across society's divides. They work for fundamental beliefs about the greater good, such as social justice, democracy, freedom, or diversity. As we saw in Chapter Two on advocacy, they take centrist positions on issues and are able to transcend partisan politics and work on both sides of the political aisle. The approach has the advantage of building larger communities with diverse participants.

Among the organizations we studied, City Year has been the most deliberate about creating a culture of common ground.[6] It has consciously developed rites and rituals such as Physical Training, where corps members perform calisthenics each morning, in uniform and in a community's most public space. Rituals can help connect corps members, increase the visibility of the organization, and inspire others with a public demonstration of idealism.

From the outset, City Year has communicated its values through compelling stories, rituals, and symbols. The symbolism operates at a conscious and unconscious level. "Physical Training represents the myth that we are one humanity," explains cofounder Michael Brown, referencing the ideas of writer Joseph Campbell. "Myths are things that are truer than truth, public dreams we share when we are awake. Rituals are the way we access those public dreams. At City Year, we realized we needed myths *and* rituals."

The uniform that all staff and corps members wear is replete with symbolism, including everything from the colors (red for idealism and multicolored to represent diversity) to the idea of a military-style uniform to evoke national service. The City Year Web site talks at length about the symbolism of its logo—how the circle at the center represents "community and equality"; how the starburst symbolizes the release of human energy, idealism, and potential, with young people as a catalyst; how the triangles refer to Native American mythology and the goal of making decisions for the next seven generations; and how even the typeface references the Civilian Conservation Corps of the 1930s, a predecessor of City Year.

City Year has also documented its "founding stories," or myths that illustrate its core values—idealism, democracy, participation, optimism, and service. These stories are available in a published booklet and on the Web site, and include inspirational quotations from Robert Kennedy, Martin Luther King Jr., Mother Teresa, and Mahatma Gandhi. Its ubiquitous "Starfish Story," for example, recounts a tale of a little girl who found thousands of starfish washed up on a beach. She began throwing them back into the sea one at a time, despite the seeming futility of her act. Eventually, local villagers joined in, until all the starfish had been thrown back. The meaning of the story, as City Year interprets it, is that "idealistic acts, even highly symbolic ones, have the power to inspire others to act, and sometimes in numbers significant enough to make a major . . . impact on the problem."

Together, these myths, rituals, and stories communicate City Year's vision and values on multiple levels and inspire others to join the tribe. "It's all interconnected: the use of stories, the uniform, the concept of a diverse corps, the concept of service being a key element of democracy," says City Year board member Ilene Jacobs. "Somebody who doesn't have a passion for one element of the story might have a passion for another part. There are so many appealing hooks that draw people in and engage them."

CREATE MEANINGFUL EXPERIENCES

Successful nonprofits don't just express their values in a pitch—they give outsiders a chance to experience what they do. It's what the business world calls "experiential marketing." The approach goes much deeper than traditional communication techniques, and involves creating interactive, sensory consumer experiences with a product or service. In this case, however, the goal is not to convince people to make a purchase but to contribute to a cause. Great organizations engage outsiders through experiential and emotional events that allow them to take part in creating social change. They help people understand the organization, feel more connected to its values, and become active participants.

Some of the groups we studied, such as Habitat, have business models that make this experiential connection easy. "Habitat's recruitment of volunteers, its bonding with donors, and its personal connection can't be replaced," says David Williams, former chief operating officer of Habitat and now president of the Make-A-Wish Foundation. "In cancer research, you can't really give a volunteer a test tube and lab coat and say, 'Go to work.' People are enthralled with the opportunity to get their hands dirty. The interaction between the beneficiaries and volunteers is priceless; you work side-by-side and hear their struggle. It develops a momentum of its own with each new home."

The Exploratorium and Share Our Strength have experiential models as well. The Exploratorium helped pioneer the model of a museum as a place for experiential education. Visitors are participants in creating and making sense of their own learning experiences. Share Our Strength was founded on the premise that everyone can contribute and "share their strength" to fight hunger. By 2006 the nonprofit was holding approximately 150 events per year that were attended by more than seventy thousand people. It also invited a million people each year to participate in bake sales or find other ways to contribute their talents. "It's the simplicity of participation," says Share Our Strength board member Mike McCurry. "They have figured out how to mix philanthropy and pleasure." (Table 4.1 lists a number of "best practice" cultivation events.)

But not all nonprofits have easy experiential "hooks" like these three. The majority of the organizations we looked at have figured out how to *create* these experiences for supporters— either through experiential events, mission-related volunteer opportunities, or other chances to witness their work up close and in person. Although it wasn't part of their model, they actively sought opportunities to involve others in what they do.

City Year, for example, did not start out engaging the general public in its work. Its youth corps recruits people ages seventeen to twenty-five to spend a year serving their community at grassroots nonprofit agencies. But City Year aspired to involve more than its corps members—and it saw the value in reaching larger groups of people as donors, volunteers, voters, and evangelists.

Table 4.1. Top Cultivation Events.

Organization	Event
City Year	Serve-a-thons—one-day local volunteer events for thousands
	Visitor Days—anyone can visit and participate on given days
Environmental Defense Fund	White-water rafting trips for VIPs and top donors
Exploratorium	Overnight museum stays
Feeding America (formerly America's Second Harvest—The Nation's Food Bank Network)	National Hunger Awareness Week
Habitat for Humanity	Home Builder's Blitz and annual Jimmy Carter Work Project—high-profile housing builds
The Heritage Foundation	President's Club meetings—invitation-only gatherings for VIPs
Share Our Strength	Great American Bake Sale and Taste of the Nation—events organized by volunteers to raise funds for hunger
	Hinges of Hope—small VIP groups travel to impoverished regions
Teach For America	Teach For America Week—CEOs, politicians, celebrities, and others prepare a lesson plan and teach a public school class

Cofounders Alan Khazei and Michael Brown invented the Serve-a-thon, modeled after programs like walkathons in which individuals participate in an event and raise money for a cause. Similarly, the Serve-a-thon allows people to raise money for City Year while performing a day of community service. Between the time of their inception and 2007, Serve-a-thons engaged over ninety thousand people, who served more than 540,000 hours in their communities and raised $4.1 million for City Year. In the process, participants became champions for City Year, donating, volunteering, and even voting to support national service legislation.

"Experiential persuasion cuts through a lot of the static and overload of information," says Jim Balfanz, then chief operating officer and current president. "Experiential persuasion is one way City Year conveys idealism." City Year has an explicit "theory of engagement." The group has goals for the number of people it hopes to involve each year—it calls these evangelists its "witnesses and champions"—and hosts multiple events and service opportunities in addition to the Serve-a-thon. All these experiences combine to create deep relationships. "Once you touch, feel, witness, and experience what City Year is all about, it is hard to walk away from it and not be impressed," says Lisa Morrison-Butler, executive director of City Year's Chicago site.

Teach For America faced a quandary similar to that of City Year, and was equally creative in finding ways to convert outsiders to insiders and evangelists. The program was founded to recruit and engage young college graduates as teachers in America's high-need schools, and it has built an incredibly active alumni network. At the outset, however, there was no obvious way to engage outsiders in the nonprofit's teaching work—particularly as high-powered super-evangelists. Teach For America had to develop a new way to give individuals a taste of what it does.

So it invented Teach For America Week, an "annual nationwide event in which leaders from all professions spend an hour of their time teaching children from some of our nation's lowest-income communities."[7] Within a decade of the program's launch in 1997, hundreds of America's most successful leaders had participated, including the actor John Lithgow, Oprah Winfrey, former secretary of state James Baker, and former first lady Laura Bush. In addition to Teach For America Week, donors who give more than $5,000 are invited to local events, to observe in the classroom, or even to sponsor an individual teacher. As we'll see, hands-on experiences help Teach For America create powerful evangelists.

The Heritage Foundation is perhaps one of the least likely of the organizations we studied to actively involve individuals. After all, the stereotypical think tank is an ivory tower in which policy wonks produce lengthy reports that almost no one reads. Heritage turned this traditional model on its head. From the beginning, it built a grassroots constituency and a large base of individual donors who are actively involved in its work. Borrowing tactics from environmental organizations like the Sierra Club and other membership groups, Heritage launched direct-mail campaigns and held local events, resulting in over 275,000 members by 2006; by 2011 the organization boasted 750,000 members. "Going out to the grass roots was important to broaden our financial base," says Ed Feulner, founder of Heritage.

Heritage's approach goes beyond asking members to write a check. It holds a variety of regional and national events—including speaker events, conferences, and training sessions—that are open to members and the larger public. It also offers a tool kit for conservatives to take action in their local communities, as well as a variety of other ways for individuals to become more involved with the conservative cause.

We studied only a few groups that do not create experiences for large numbers of outsiders: the Center on Budget and Policy Priorities, Self-Help, and YouthBuild USA. They engage *targeted* groups critical to their success instead, but they are equally effective in creating meaningful relationships within these groups and in cultivating high-powered evangelists.

For example, the Center on Budget and Policy Priorities has exceptionally strong relationships with the media, which are critical as it seeks to influence national budget and policy debates. Founder Bob Greenstein and the Center's senior economists and policy experts conduct weekly conference calls to discuss the issues with the most respected reporters and editorial writers covering federal budget issues. This high-touch approach differs from most policy groups that issue generic press releases. Although budget analysis defies the notion of a participatory experience, the Center has pushed the envelope by reaching out to critical stakeholders. "We understand that reporters get nine thousand e-mails a day, and we work hard to break through," says Ellen Nissenbaum, now senior vice president for government affairs.

YouthBuild USA, too, is less focused on involving the general public, but is adept at cultivating critical supporters. Because it has focused on government and foundations for its funding, the nonprofit is only just now beginning to reach out to the larger public for donors and volunteers. Nevertheless, YouthBuild's success depends on creating experiential activities for congressional and state-level supporters, who are its true evangelists. Every year, founder Dorothy Stoneman brings hundreds of young people to Capitol Hill to meet face-to-face with members of Congress. She also invites key legislators to spend a day at a program site in order to witness it firsthand.

The experiential strategy has paid off. "A [number of] years ago, the House was debating the Housing and Urban Development appropriation for YouthBuild," recounts CFO B. J. Rudman. "Republicans voted to give money to YouthBuild, and some members asked why. 'All you have to do is visit a YouthBuild program to understand why we are [funding] it,' they replied."

CULTIVATE EVANGELISTS

Once people have had a positive experience with an organization and are convinced of its impact, they are much more likely to act as an ambassador on behalf of the cause. In all the groups we studied, we found this phenomenon time and again. When we interviewed board members, staff, program participants, alumni, and even volunteers, they all had their own story of conversion to tell. They ranged from people in entry-level positions to the most prestigious board members. Whether the nonprofits call these individuals evangelists, ambassadors, champions, or even guardian angels, all of them have figured out how to leverage powerful relationships for greater impact.

"When you commit yourself to making a difference in the world and share your passion and idealism with others, 'guardian angels' will emerge to help you," writes City Year cofounder Alan Khazei.[8] "There are many people just looking for opportunities to be a part of something larger than themselves, and to make a contribution to others. Often, at times when you least expect it and most need it, these guardian angels will appear to donate computers, volunteer their time, introduce you to someone who can support your work financially, or take you out to lunch to keep you going."

High-impact groups are particularly strategic about identifying, converting, and cultivating powerful individuals, or super-evangelists. They figure out who would be a good ally or ambassador—on the basis of that person's values or an interest in the nonprofit's cause—and deliberately recruit him or her as a board member or general supporter. In addition to former president Jimmy Carter, Habitat has converted countless other individual champions, including Bill Clinton, Al Gore, Newt Gingrich, Oprah Winfrey, and even rocker Jon Bon Jovi. All the other organizations we examined have at least one, and often more, of these super-evangelists as advisers or spokespeople.

They are not just celebrity faces associated with a cause. Most of them are deeply involved in the work of the institution and make it a high priority. "Jimmy Carter served three years on our board, and he never missed a meeting, never came late, and never left early," says Fuller, who founded Habitat. "He didn't take phone calls in meetings; he set a new standard." Timberland CEO Jeff Swartz served on the board of City Year for years, and has been a key player throughout the organization's growth. At the Exploratorium, Gordon Moore, cofounder of Intel, is an adviser who lends his time, counsel, and contacts. The examples go on and on. Table 4.2 shows a partial list.

TABLE 4.2. HIGH-PROFILE EVANGELISTS.

Organization	Evangelists
Center on Budget and Policy Priorities	Scholar William Julius Wilson, INDEPENDENT SECTOR CEO Diana Aviv
City Year	Bill Clinton, George H. W. Bush, Nelson Mandela, Timberland CEO Jeffrey Swartz
Environmental Defense Fund	Teresa Heinz Kerry, Joanne Woodward, venture capitalist John Doerr
Exploratorium	Intel cofounder Gordon Moore
Habitat for Humanity	Jimmy Carter, Jack Kemp, Jon Bon Jovi
The Heritage Foundation	Margaret Thatcher, Edwin Meese, Steve Forbes
National Council of La Raza	Henry Cisneros, PepsiCo Chair Steve Reinemund, actress Eva Longoria
Share Our Strength	Celebrity chefs Danny Meyer and Alice Waters
Teach For America	Gap founder Don Fisher, Laura Bush
YouthBuild USA	Senators John Kerry and Mike DeWine

These super-evangelists are often able to take an organization to the next level. By virtue of their political, social, or economic power, they can create organizational momentum. They attract attention, create legitimacy, and serve as powerful role models to others. Press and media attention follow, along with money, members, and volunteers. "[Jimmy Carter's] involvement quickened the pace," says Fuller. "As a former president of the United States, if he goes out on a construction site, the media shows up. More people learned of us faster." Evangelists such as Carter can also tap into their own social networks, opening doors for an organization in politics or making critical introductions to other influential leaders.

EDF has long gone after heavy hitters in politics and corporate America as part of its strategy to influence both government policy and business practice. Heiress and philanthropist Teresa Heinz Kerry served on its board until recently, and former eBay CEO Meg Whitman was an informal adviser. Whitman has attended the group's annual white-water rafting trip through the Grand Canyon (another best-practice VIP cultivation tool). Such powerful social networks allow EDF to broker a partnership with a large company or to call in favors when trying to pass critical legislation.

Perhaps the best demonstration of the ability to mobilize powerful evangelists on behalf of the environment occurred in the summer of 2006, when EDF turned to venture capitalist John Doerr for help in passing California's Global Warming Solutions Act (AB 32), the first statewide legislation of its kind and a model for federal legislation.[9] The group had a number of discussions with Doerr, a partner in the influential Silicon Valley firm Kleiner Perkins Caufield & Byers, and he eventually embraced the group's market-based approach to helping solve climate change.

But it wasn't until the proposed legislation stalled that EDF called on Doerr to use his influence. At the eleventh hour, Governor Arnold Schwarzenegger was undecided about whether he could adopt the recommendations of a state panel that supported emissions caps. In the midst of a reelection campaign, he wanted to be sure he'd have the support of the business community. One of his top policy advisers called a senior manager from EDF, who was able to fax a letter of support from Doerr, signed by other high-tech business leaders. Within hours, the governor announced his support of the legislation.

For Share Our Strength, cultivating super-evangelists has been part of its strategy from day one. Early on, founders Bill and Debbie Shore recognized the opportunity to involve celebrity chefs such as Alice Waters, Emeril Lagasse, and Thomas Keller in the fight against hunger. The chefs contributed their talents to fundraisers, but they also provided access to their social networks and patrons, who were often elite members of society. And they used their influence with other companies to help bolster Share Our Strength's sponsorship efforts. "One of the important things we did was to invest ownership of Share Our Strength in the chefs and restaurateurs," says Bill Shore. "Most of them say, 'That's my organization—I've been a member from the beginning.' So they are going out looking at deals for us."

The organization's American Express partnership, for example, came about because New York chef Danny Meyer started a local "charge against hunger" campaign at his restaurant. He then approached the group with the idea of expanding it nationally. Not only did Meyer bring Share Our Strength the American Express relationship, which netted millions of dollars for hunger relief, but he would personally host dinners for the organization that raised $200,000 each. He has been an important connector for the nonprofit.

Now Share Our Strength is looking to take these relationships to a more formal level through its National Culinary Council, made up of the connectors and opinion leaders in the restaurant industry who can bring their social networks to bear on hunger issues. "The Culinary Council will be small—only twenty to twenty-five people in the industry," says Debbie Shore, associate director. "They are wine consultants, food editors, chefs—people who have a distinctive national leverage point because of who they are and their personal networks. They are the innovators of cuisine, and the people who train the trainers as the heads of culinary schools. They have the ability to help us grow the organization."

Share Our Strength is also explicit about creating ongoing experiences for these core supporters and major donors as well as for the general public. Hinges of Hope is a new program that invites top supporters—celebrity chefs, corporate CEOs, leading journalists and authors—on tours to communities around the world where it works. These small groups visit a region with expert guides and board members, learning more about hunger issues and the impact of Share Our Strength's work in the field. "Hinges of Hope is a cultivation tool," says Chuck Scofield, chief development officer. "It's also about bearing witness to all poverty and hunger. We did a trip to Ethiopia with chefs and corporate leaders, and it really deepened their commitment to Africa."

BUILD A BELOVED COMMUNITY

Once groups have inspired people with their values, engaged them in emotional experiences, and turned them into evangelists, they are able to expand on these relationships to build entire communities—social networks—committed to the organization. In the next chapter, we will focus on how these nonprofits also create *organizational networks* of other nonprofits to expand their impact. This is where the definitions of "networks" and "communities" start to blur. But the distinction is academic. Great organizations leverage their organizational networks—whether regional sites, affiliates, or local allies—as a mechanism for reaching and engaging more individuals. In return they create a web of relationships and a larger community around the nonprofit and its cause.

These nonprofits then invest significant time and effort in sustaining these communities over time. Some are more adept than others at using technology: they have Web sites, send out e-mail updates, and actively use social media tools. However, technology is not a silver bullet. Although e-mail and social media can be important tools for staying connected, organizations also must provide opportunities for face-to-face connection. Individual members of the community need to remain connected at an emotional and experiential level in order to stay actively involved.[10]

In addition to providing ongoing opportunities to participate in their work, many great nonprofits use annual conferences or events as a way to convene their larger community and bring diverse stakeholders together. City Year has its "cyzygy" convention, Teach For America has its National Summit, Heritage has its Resource Bank Meeting, and the list goes on. More than just an inside gathering for staff or affiliates, conferences are often an opportunity for funders, volunteers, donors, site leaders, and other supporters to share knowledge and to network with each other. The entire tribe comes together, further reinforcing a feeling of community.

"A lot of what we do all year long shows up at the conference—it's our signature event," says Gerald Bornstein, chief operating officer of the National Council of La Raza, whose annual conference averages twenty thousand participants. "We bring in the affiliates, and we use it as a training opportunity, a networking opportunity, and a time to communicate our vision. We also give corporate America and politicians the chance to interact with our members. We communicate, we connect, and we celebrate and enjoy each other's company—it all comes together in the conference."

Another way successful nonprofits nurture their communities over time is through active alumni programs. Several of the organizations we studied foster the continuing involvement of their participants after they have graduated from the program, including Teach For America, whose corps members spend two years teaching in needy schools; City Year, whose participants spend a year performing community service; and YouthBuild USA, whose members spend a year developing their leadership and job skills building affordable housing.

Once people leave the program, they don't really leave the network. As you'll see in Chapter Five, on nurturing nonprofit networks, cultivating leadership for the larger field can be a strategy for social change in itself. Leaders go on to create and run other organizations working for a similar cause—or to be powerful evangelists in business and government on the organization's behalf. Alumni can form the core of a group's community, and they continue to give back to the organization—in time, money, or influence—long after their active participation has ended. They are the evangelists who, by virtue of their own deep experience with the nonprofit, continue to reach out and bring others in.

All three of these groups have exceptional alumni engagement programs and have figured out how alumni can become a key part of a larger community. A study by McKinsey and the Omidyar Network found several best practices among these three nonprofits and others that do this well: the groups recognize alumni as an integral part of the organization's programs; they treat alumni as equals and encourage them to self-organize; and they use technology and social media to increase the value of the community.[11]

Whether they are engaging past participants as active members of the community or creating experiences to convert outsiders to insiders, each organization has been able to develop a larger community that is self-sustaining. "For the social entrepreneur, the solution is to make the network itself the ends rather than means, to treat the network not as a tool for information or resources but as a community defined by a common set of values," says Joel Podolny, former dean of the Yale School of Management. "The community itself becomes the agent of change."[12]

Those involved become integrated into a larger community with shared values and beliefs, and are motivated to participate more deeply as donors, volunteers, and activists. As the organization grows, it attracts more attention, which brings in more resources—ultimately building a kind of perpetual motion machine. It's viral marketing, or self-organizing, at its best.

"The momentum builds on itself, and it becomes more about guiding it than pushing it," says Habitat's Stephen Seidel. "When I started working with the Twin Cities Habitat affiliate, few people had heard about us. We'd built one home and had a few under way. We grew to building twenty to thirty houses per year, and it kept growing. The more we grew, the more attention we attracted, and the more funding, more volunteers, the more corporations we were able to attract. It became this ubiquitous thing."

RIPPLES OF CHANGE

The strategy of giving people concrete experiences, creating evangelists, and sustaining these communities is not always the easiest path to follow. It takes much more time, energy, and initial investment than *not* involving others. And it's not always clear exactly how the strategy will pay off, or when. But these nonprofits do these things just the same, because they know that ultimately this approach can create a powerful lever for social change.

"Habitat has not chosen the easiest way to build houses," says Eric Duell, an international partner.[13] "The easiest way is like the construction companies do it, with paid skilled labor and lots of it. Habitat does not work this way because the ultimate goal is not the house, but [to transform] the people who participate in the building of that house, the families who will live in that house, and the society that they are part of."

The strategy often pays off handsomely. When they make a small initial investment in engaging individuals, groups can often catalyze much greater impact. They can tap individuals to create a diverse and sustainable donor base and reduce their own costs. They can mobilize supporters to vote on legislation or to boycott or support corporations. And they can leverage these individuals' power, influence, or social networks on behalf of a cause.

Ultimately these high-impact nonprofits seek to change society on a similarly wide scale, one person and one community at a time. City Year's vision is that one day, every young person will ask, "Where did you spend your city year?" Share Our Strength's mantra is that "it takes more than food to fight hunger," capturing its core belief that individuals make the critical difference.

Most of the nonprofits we studied have a way of expressing this process of building momentum. At City Year, they call the concept "ripples" to convey the ever-widening circle of social impact that flows from a single action to change groups, neighborhoods, communities, nations, and the world.

The ripples metaphor comes from a speech that Robert Kennedy made in 1966 at the University of Cape Town, South Africa: "It is from numberless diverse acts of courage . . . [and] belief that human history is shaped. Each time a person stands up for an ideal, or acts to improve the lot of others, or strikes out against injustice, he sends forth a tiny ripple of hope, and crossing each other from a million different centers of energy and daring, those ripples build a current that can sweep down the mightiest walls of oppression and resistance."[14]

CHAPTER FOUR HIGHLIGHTS

- **Turn outsiders into evangelists.** Most high-impact nonprofits create ways for many people to engage with their organization. And when they offer the *right* types of experiences, the best organizations convert their volunteers into passionate evangelists for the cause.
- **Build larger communities.** The best groups move beyond mere individual engagement to create larger communities of

supporters. Communities are treated as ends in themselves and can be mobilized for larger social change.

- **Follow the Rules of Engagement:**
  - *Communicate your mission, vision, and values.* Start by communicating your values, building a strong culture, and creating emotional "hooks" to engage and inspire others around your values.
  - *Create meaningful experiences.* Give volunteers meaningful experiences that align with the mission of your organization. Involve them in more than just volunteering or writing a check. Have them experience your work in person.
  - *Cultivate evangelists.* Convert your volunteers into evangelists who will spread the word among their social networks. Cultivate high-powered super-evangelists whose values and interests align with yours and who can help create organizational momentum.
  - *Build a beloved community.* Once you've built a larger community, cultivate it over time by providing ways for members to connect through conferences, communication tools, technology, and alumni programs.
- **Mobilize your communities as a powerful force for change.** If you follow these rules of engagement, you can create a powerful community of individual supporters that is ever expanding. You can then mobilize them for collective action, such as through coordinated media campaigns, lobbying, or large-scale advocacy.

CHAPTER FIVE

NURTURE NONPROFIT NETWORKS

The Exploratorium isn't anything like an old-fashioned science museum full of static, dusty exhibits. When we first visited for our research, the Exploratorium was housed in a cavernous warehouse in San Francisco's northernmost Marina District. Inside the eclectic space are interactive exhibits of gyrating titanium wheels, levitating beach balls, pulsing neon lights, and even a Tactile Dome that simulates how a blind person experiences the world. The Exploratorium has an atmosphere of calculated chaos. The place is teeming with children and their parents, and everyone is pulling ropes and pushing buttons with obvious delight.[1]

People who live outside Northern California may have never heard of the Exploratorium, even though it is one of the world's first hands-on science centers. The museum was receiving over five hundred thousand visitors a year by 2006, but it has not been particularly well marketed. Its facility is looking a bit worse for forty years of wear and tear. Senior staff members even admit that it is no paragon of nonprofit management. The culture has been one of radical creativity and constant innovation, not buttoned-down systems and processes. The organization has faced fundraising challenges, a difficult leadership transition after its founder died, and even a contentious unionization effort among its staff— hardly the stuff of management "best practices."

So you might wonder what the Exploratorium is doing in a book about some of America's greatest nonprofits. It doesn't even appear to meet the conventional definition of scale: it's located on one site in a single community. Yet despite these issues, the Exploratorium has had substantial impact on how we think about museums and how we teach science. Anyone who has ever taken his or her kids to a children's museum or visited any of the world's hundreds of interactive science and technology centers has indirectly experienced the power of the Exploratorium.

The museum is the brainchild of physicist Frank Oppenheimer, the late brother of J. Robert Oppenheimer, the father of the atomic bomb. Frank Oppenheimer designed the Exploratorium to debunk the notion that a museum could only be made up of dusty artifacts that hang on a wall or sit in a glass case. He envisioned a place where visitors could learn about science through mind-expanding experiences, a place where they could touch and interact with three-dimensional exhibits in an engaging and meaningful way.

From the day the Exploratorium opened in 1969, it has served as a model for interactive museums around the world, many of which were established in the 1970s and 1980s.[2] In fact, Oppenheimer was eager to help them beg, borrow, and steal his ideas. "The Exploratorium served as a touchstone in the field of science centers," says Robert Semper, director of the Exploratorium's Center for Teaching and Learning. "It was a place that people came to that provided resources to help them start interactive museums of their own. It was in the DNA of the founder to create a support structure for other people doing this work."

Although the Exploratorium was not the only leader of this larger movement—the U.C. Berkeley Lawrence Hall of Science and the Ontario Science Center in Toronto[3] were other influential organizations—it was the most active in spreading its innovations. Early on, the Exploratorium developed multiple programs to help other institutions replicate its model. The museum raised federal funds (through a program called the Fund for the Improvement of Postsecondary Education) to develop new science centers on university campuses and in local communities. Within three years, the nonprofit had helped launch twenty-one interactive museums in the United States alone, including the Children's Museum of Manhattan and the Discovery Place in Charlotte, North Carolina.

The Exploratorium has always seen itself as a museum without walls. Rather than simply shore up resources for its own organization, the Exploratorium actively helped other non-profits copy its model. "We have a philosophy of sharing to the point of giving it away," says Debra Menaker, chief financial officer.

What would possess an inventor to give away his secrets? Exploratorium's approach is akin to Coca-Cola's posting its secret recipe on the Internet for anyone to copy and then paying to train PepsiCo in how to make better soda. In the business sector, such "open-source" strategies are rare. Unlike the operating system Linux, which allows anyone to copy, modify, and improve its popular software, most businesses develop new ideas and then aggressively guard their company secrets. But the Exploratorium realized that by giving away its model and building a global network of interactive science centers, it could reach more people and have greater impact.

An open-source network strategy is not without its challenges, however. Even though the Exploratorium has shared resources and expertise with many of the science centers in existence today, for most of its history it asked for nothing in return. The museum does not cobrand with its informal affiliates. "It works against us sometimes in terms of branding," says Pat Murphy, a science writer who directs the Exploratorium's publications programs. "People say, 'We've got an Exploratorium here in Cleveland.'" Nor does it seek to control the quality of museums in its larger network. At a minimum, it charges a fee for loaned exhibits through a program introduced by Oppenheimer's successor, Goéry Delacôte, but for years the museum made no money from its imitators. (The museum is now run by Dennis Bartels, who became CEO in 2006.)

Even though it may not always get credit for this role, the Exploratorium is recognized among its peers for what counts the most: catalyzing a worldwide hands-on science education movement. It has achieved such remarkable impact precisely *because* it shared valuable resources—funding, knowledge, exhibits, and talent—with members of its informal network.

Delacôte, like other leaders at the Exploratorium, understands the value of the network strategy: "The future is not in large organizations; the future is in the network, and servicing other organizations."

ADOPTING A NETWORK MIND-SET

When we set out to write this book, we expected to learn about how great nonprofit organizations are led, managed, and grown. But as we wrote in the Introduction, we found something quite different. Building an organization is only part of the story. *These high-impact nonprofits work with and through other organizations—and they have much more impact than if they acted alone.*

As we explored this attribute in depth, we were struck by the enormous amounts of time and energy these groups spend sharing funding, expertise, leadership, power, and credit with like-minded allies. They build networks of other nonprofits in their field—with either formal or informal affiliations—and they work in coalitions to achieve collective goals. At times they make significant short-term organizational sacrifices to move the larger cause forward—they put their long-term vision and desire for impact above their own self-interest. And they do all this while managing and growing their own organizations.

What they *don't* do is focus exclusively on building their own empires or hoarding resources. Instead, they increase their impact by giving knowledge and resources away. "The focus of National Council of La Raza is on improving life opportunities for Latinos and fighting discrimination," says Emily Gantz McCay, former executive vice president. "You can't do that by building the organization. You have to do it by building the field."

When we first observed this phenomenon, we weren't sure what to call it. "Collaboration" is an overused buzzword. It can imply simply being nice instead of being strategic. And jargon such as "building capacity," "training and technical assistance," or "coalition building" didn't quite capture it either—these are all tactics, but to what end? The organizations we found do all those things, and then some. Some leaders in the nonprofits we studied talk about this phenomenon as "building a movement," others call it "building a field," and yet others refer to "building a network." They used these terms to speak about both organizational structure and the way in which groups operate.

Ultimately, we decided that these terms were all different ways of describing the same thing. The real difference between these nonprofits and many others lies in the way they work with and through other organizations to achieve greater good. Just as they mobilize communities of individual supporters to achieve social change, they also leverage their nonprofit networks to increase their impact. For simplicity, we call this approach a "network mind-set."

Although the word *network* emphasizes a structure or a formal affiliation, in fact these groups actively build the capacity of their like-minded allies, regardless of whether they share formal ties or a brand name. Some groups, such as Feeding America (formerly America's Second Harvest—The Nation's Food Bank Network) and Habitat for Humanity, have formal affiliates with whom they share their brand. Other groups, such as the Exploratorium and Heritage, have only a single site, but they have broad informal networks that they have used to spread their model or achieve more impact. And some of these nonprofits—City Year and Teach For America, for example—have corporate structures, with regional sites or offices that report into headquarters, but they still work in coalitions with other nonprofits in their fields. (See Table 5.1.) Regardless of their organizational structure, these nonprofits all exhibit a collaborative mind-set and a set of behaviors that increase the ability of the whole to achieve more than any individual part.

TABLE 5.1. NETWORKS CAN HAVE FORMAL OR INFORMAL AFFILIATIONS.

Informal Nonprofit Networks	*Formal Affiliated Networks*
Center on Budget and Policy Priorities	Feeding America *(more than 200 member food banks)*
City Year	Habitat for Humanity *(2,100 global affiliates)*
Environmental Defense Fund	
Exploratorium	National Council of La Raza *(300 local affiliates)*
The Heritage Foundation	YouthBuild USA *(226 affiliates)*
Self-Help	
Share Our Strength	
Teach For America	

At its most basic, a network is a group of related things that work together to achieve a larger goal. Think of the network of computers that forms the Internet, or the network of streets, roads, and highways that makes up our transportation grid. Collectively, these things are bigger and more powerful than their individual components. Similarly, a network strategy allows these nonprofits to reach more people and to have far more social impact than they could through their own organization. Through their networks they have improved access to resources, and they have greater depth in more communities. In short, they do more with less—it's the ultimate leveraged strategy.

Most nonprofits have an "organization orientation," which keeps them focused more on building their own enterprise at the expense of others. These nonprofits seek to scale their impact by growing their own institutions—producing more, adding more programs, and building out the organization to meet demand. Although this approach can lead to an incremental increase in impact, it does not provide the fastest or most direct route to greater social change. Table 5.2 compares an organization-centered approach to a network orientation.

TABLE 5.2. DEFINING THE NETWORK MIND-SET.

	Organization Orientation	Network Orientation
Mind-set	Competition	Collaboration
Strategy	Grow the organization	Grow the network or field for impact
Typical behaviors	Compete for scarce resources	Grow funding pie for all
	Protect knowledge	Share knowledge
	Develop competitive advantage	Develop skills of competitors
	Hoard talented leadership	Cultivate and disperse leadership
	Act alone	Act collectively
	Seize credit and power	Share credit and power
Structure	Centralized	Decentralized

We were initially surprised to find that these nonprofits collaborate rather than compete. After all, competition is natural in any human endeavor, whether the players are operating in the public, private, or social sectors. Indeed, not every nonprofit sees the pie as ever expanding; many view other organizations as competitors for funding, recognition, or top talent. Even though management experts suggest that cooperation rather than competition can be a better strategy in the long run, it is not always in an organization's immediate self-interest to collaborate.

But high-impact nonprofits see beyond their immediate short-term interest and recognize that they can achieve far more if they collaborate rather than compete. Although the network mind-set at first glance might appear generous, even altruistic, it is actually better described as a function of enlightened self-interest. *These groups work with and through their nonprofit networks in order to have greater impact themselves.*

By acting collectively, these organizations also have more power and influence over government and business. Because they represent many voices, they can exert greater influence on public policy or corporate behavior, as we demonstrated in Chapters Two and Three. Further, because they have more members in their networks and therefore a larger platform for distributing their ideas, programs, or services, they have more opportunities to engage and influence individuals and the public at large. They can also scale their impact more quickly, more efficiently, and with less direct expense than they could if they were simply to grow their own organizations site by site.

How to Nurture a Nonprofit Network

Each of the twelve nonprofits in this book taps into the power of networks in different ways. But they generally share four tactics:

1. **Grow the pie.** High-impact nonprofits often fund other organizations in their network or field, regardless of formal affiliation. Sometimes they lead collaborative efforts to gain resources for the network; sometimes they individually raise funding that they redistribute; and sometimes they help other

organizations improve their own ability to fundraise. They are more focused on growing the pie for the larger cause than they are on grabbing their own slice. They want to increase resources for their cause because it increases their overall impact.

2. **Share knowledge.** These nonprofits actively share their knowledge and expertise with other organizations through research, publications, and replication manuals, and build the skills of their allies through training programs, conferences, and workshops. By increasing the efficiency and effectiveness of members of their networks, they are able to have more influence as a collective.

3. **Develop leadership.** The majority of these organizations develop leadership for the larger network, field, or movement, nurturing talented employees and developing the next generation of leadership. They magnify their impact indirectly, increasing both the personnel capacity of other organizations and their own social connections within the network.

4. **Work in coalitions.** Once these groups have built formal or informal networks, they often go beyond their inner circle to form larger coalitions and mobilize their network for collective aims. They work in coalition with others, playing both lead and secondary roles, and they share the credit for their successes.

Although not every organization we studied pursues all four tactics simultaneously, most of them pursue a majority. And although some of these nonprofits built their network by creating formal affiliations with other nonprofits, the majority of groups did not. Regardless of their particular organizational structures, all high-impact nonprofits exhibit a network mind-set. They work with and through other nonprofits to achieve greater social change.

GROW THE PIE

One of the biggest advantages of working in a network is that it allows groups to increase the funding pie for everyone. A number of these organizations raise funds from individuals, foundations, or the government and then regrant the money to other organizations in their field. Sometimes they grant funding without having any formal affiliation, freely giving money away without getting anything in return other than greater impact, as the Exploratorium did. In other cases, the central nonprofit requires some brand affiliation, or adherence to standards, in exchange for financial support. In yet other cases, the organization indirectly helps like-minded allies by sharing valuable donor lists, assisting with proposal writing, or building fundraising skills.

YouthBuild USA shares wealth, knowledge, leadership, *and* power with a broader network of affiliates. Activist Dorothy Stoneman founded the group in East Harlem to "mobilize teenagers to become a positive force for change" by redeveloping dilapidated housing in their neighborhoods. But Stoneman's vision was always larger than the initial project: "My goal was to build a movement that could change the conditions of poverty and discrimination in which children are growing up across America," she says. "I didn't set out to create a program to be taken to scale; I set out to create a *movement* of young people taking charge of their lives and changing their communities."[4]

She remembers one consultant's misguided advice to focus on building her own organization and to see other nonprofits as competition. "Think of this as a business," the consultant said. "The product is what you give to young people. The market is the young people who need your help. Your competitors are other nonprofit organizations in the community who also offer opportunities to young people. You are competing with them for a limited pool of resources to fund your program."

Stoneman's reply was, "No, we're not going to think of it that way. The other nonprofits are our *partners*. Our job is to collaborate with them to increase the pool of resources so we can collectively meet the needs of all the young people. Competition is counterproductive under these circumstances."[5]

Stoneman always saw collective action as her primary strategy. When there was demand in New York to copy her group's model, she organized a network called the Coalition for $10 Million to seek funding from city government for additional programs. When that effort succeeded and demand for the YouthBuild model continued to grow, she went on to organize a national coalition of 250 community-based nonprofits to lobby for federal funding to spread the model and the movement. "The federal government has a lot of money—it's the best way to scale out quickly," she says. (See Chapter Eight for details on YouthBuild's funding strategy.)

When the YouthBuild Coalition obtained its first $40 million from the Department of Housing and Urban Development (HUD) in 2003 to replicate the program nationally, Stoneman refused to channel the funding through her own organization. If YouthBuild USA had acted as the intermediary, Stoneman feared its programs would have been capped in size at around $25 million, because of federal funding guidelines. Although this amount of money would have been a big coup for the organization, it would have limited the potential size of the larger network.

Stoneman sacrificed her organization's own interest for the greater good. "We decided we didn't need to control the money," she says. "We had trust in community-based organizations, and we had a desire to get it out into the field." Through its federal funding, the YouthBuild network grew from a few sites in New York City to a national alliance of 226 organizations with combined annual revenues of $180 million as of 2006. Together they reached sixty thousand young people in a decade and channeled nearly $650 million in federal funding to nonprofit sponsors of YouthBuild in low-income communities.

The upside of this strategy was that YouthBuild USA could scale up more quickly than if it had grown site by site. But there was also a drawback. By not acting as the intermediary, YouthBuild relinquished control of funding decisions to HUD, while contracting back to the agency as a technical assistance provider. And by not channeling the much larger $118 million in government funding, YouthBuild USA's own budget has remained much smaller, at $17 million in 2006—most of which supported the network through training and technical assistance.

Stoneman doesn't regret the choice. Although she may at first glance seem unduly generous, she does not naively pursue network building over more self-centered approaches. She knows she has had more impact by relinquishing some control and empowering the network. "It was a strategic decision," she says. "We could have set it up where the money went to the national organization, but then we would have been nothing more than a demonstration project. The jury is still out on that decision. It's a trade-off between control versus impact."

SHARE KNOWLEDGE

In addition to sharing financial resources, all these organizations share knowledge and actively build the skills of other nonprofits in order to increase their effectiveness. They don't just hoard information—they give it away to help the so-called competition succeed.

A few of them, such as Exploratorium and YouthBuild USA, actively give away their model as a replication strategy; others help like-minded allies be more successful by providing training or technical assistance. Many do both. Most share knowledge passively through publications and printed or online materials that document best practices. And many of them also actively convene their affiliates or local sites through conferences and provide training sessions, workshops, or even hands-on consulting.

The Center on Budget and Policy Priorities shares information and expertise with state and local groups, and in the process has dramatically expanded its impact.[6] Instead of growing its own organization, it works with established nonprofits to build their capacity to do budget analysis and advocacy work. In the business world, this unheard-of strategy would be akin to Starbucks partnering with the neighborhood coffee shop to enter a local market—without taking any profit for itself.

Unlike YouthBuild, the Center never aspired to build a national movement. Bob Greenstein launched the Center in 1981 with support from the Field Foundation in response to enormous budget cuts in social programs during the first Reagan administration. Its mission was to analyze the impact of federal budget decisions on the nation's poor and to advocate for programs that benefited the least well off. At the outset, Greenstein's exclusive focus was on federal policy analysis and national advocacy. He had little interest in building a larger network. "We never had a huge plan for expansion," he says.

In its early years, the Center enjoyed a growing reputation among political insiders. "[Its] numbers, which are trusted across the ideological spectrum, often speak for themselves," stated the *Washington Monthly* in 1988, when it ranked the Center one of the five best public interest groups in Washington.[7] Despite this success, the Center's impact was increasingly limited because of its focus on *federal* budget analysis and low-income policy issues. More and more, decisions about funding and implementation of government programs were being made not in Washington but at the state level.

With the prodding and financial support of several national foundations, the Center launched the State Fiscal Analysis Initiative in 1993 to take its model to the state level. Rather than open regional offices and compete with existing nonprofits, the Center decided to help existing organizations build their own capacity to conduct budget analysis. To achieve this, the Center provides information and training to state nonprofits on issues ranging from budget analysis to the implementation of low-income programs.

The initiative started with a few modest grants to fund twelve state-based groups, and had grown into a network supporting nearly thirty groups with more than $7.5 million in foundation funding as of 2006. "It allows us to be a lot bigger than we would be comfortable with on our own," says Iris Lav, a former deputy director. "We wouldn't want to have offices in thirty far-flung states and be responsible for their output."

The result has been significant and measurable impact. For example, the Center's state-based network helped protect *$24 billion* in state-level funding for state programs by 2005, including those serving low-income Americans. In 2001 and 2002, Congress had passed a series of changes to the tax code related to estates and businesses that significantly reduced the revenue available for social programs that states administer. The Center worked with state-based groups to help them understand how these tax changes would have decreased *state* tax revenues as well; it helped target legislators and the media with an advocacy campaign protesting the changes contained in the legislation. In the end, thirty-four state legislatures refused to conform their tax codes to one or both of these federal changes, which over four years saved

$24 billion in state funding for services that benefit the poor and other populations.

By sharing information and building up state organizations' ability to conduct budget analysis, the Center expanded its impact faster, more efficiently, and with fewer resources than if it had pursued a top-down expansion. It was able to tap into the individual networks of state and local organizations, which already had community contacts and knowledge of the state legislators who would be most receptive to their calls.

The Center's strategy comes back to the *network mind-set*. The organization saw that enabling other groups to succeed at policy analysis helped it achieve its own goals much more efficiently and effectively. "We're in this to have impact," says Lav.

DEVELOP LEADERSHIP

One of the most important—and least tangible—ways these nonprofits build the strength of their nonprofit networks is by developing and sharing their most valuable asset: people. They don't hoard talent; instead, they share it with the field. Granted, *talent* and *leadership* are somewhat nebulous buzzwords that mean many things to many people. Further, a people-based strategy takes much longer to pay off, and its impact is far more difficult to measure than that of more concrete approaches.

But developing talent and leadership can be a powerful tool for building a network, movement, or field, as Teach For America has learned.[8] The group's mission is "to build the movement to eliminate educational inequity by enlisting our nation's most promising future leaders in the effort." But few outsiders understand its longer-term strategy for change. By slowly and steadily building a vanguard for education reform, Teach For America is having an impact that is far greater than what it can achieve in any single classroom or school district, despite its critics.

The organization boasted twelve thousand alumni by 2007, and although most were still in their twenties and thirties, these former corps members have been increasingly assuming powerful leadership positions. Alumni now run some of the nation's most acclaimed schools. They bring fresh experience to school boards and elected office. And they channel the resources of the corporations where they now work toward education and social reform. Overall, Teach For America estimates that more than 60 percent of its alumni are still working full-time in education, and of those who have left education, almost half are working directly on other issues that have an impact on low-income communities.[9]

Scratch the surface of any new education institution today, and you're likely to find Teach For America alumni leading reform. Program alumni Mike Feinberg and Dave Levin cofounded KIPP (Knowledge Is Power Program), a nationwide network of charter schools, many led by their fellow alumni. Another former corps member, Michelle Rhee, founded the New Teacher Project and later went on to serve as chancellor of the Washington D.C. Public Schools and has become a national advocate for ending teacher tenure. Former staff member Kim Smith started New Schools Venture Fund, which by 2006 had attracted more than $50 million in philanthropy to fund innovative education models. Another former staff member runs the Eli Broad Foundation, which invests millions of dollars each year to train and develop school administrators. At the same time, Teach For America alumni have infiltrated the corridors of power in other sectors: they serve as policy advisers to senators, representatives, and governors; they have made partner in prestigious law and consulting firms; and others are executives at major corporations.

Teach For America's leadership development work has helped seed a larger movement of disparate organizations connected by loose ties and strong values. This network of leaders has helped access government and private resources for education reform, put more pressure on government and large institutions to change policies, and shaped strong and capable leaders in schools throughout the country. Although the impact is indirect and hard to measure, it is no less powerful or important.

Like Teach For America, a majority of these twelve nonprofits formally dedicate time and effort to developing the next generation of leaders (see Table 5.3)—many of whom go on to work for other organizations in the larger field. Some of the groups, particularly the youth organizations, pursue the strategy as an integral part of their social change model. Others make a priority of recruiting, training, and cultivating new young leaders in large numbers.

TABLE 5.3.   DEVELOPING YOUNG LEADERS.

Organization	Formal Youth Leadership Programs
City Year	Youth corps and alumni program; Young Heroes
Exploratorium	Young Explainers; teacher training programs
Habitat for Humanity	Campus chapters; Collegiate Challenge
The Heritage Foundation	Young Leaders Program
National Council of La Raza	Young Latino Leaders Program
Teach For America	Teaching corps and alumni program
YouthBuild USA	YouthBuild corps and alumni program

City Year and YouthBuild USA were founded to train and develop the next generation of leaders. Both organizations spend considerable resources to instill lifelong leadership skills and foster a commitment to becoming actively engaged citizens. YouthBuild's alumni base of fifty thousand and City Year's eight thousand former corps members (as of 2006) had formed a powerful force for change as they entered the working world and continued to advocate on behalf of low-income communities. One City Year study showed that its graduates were far more likely than their peers to vote, volunteer, and take civic leadership roles in their communities, regardless of race, education, or income level.[10]

Although some of these organizations do not have explicit leadership development programs, they nevertheless see such development as a key component of their talent management strategies. They may recruit, hire, train, and develop a senior leader within their organization, only to have that person leave for another nonprofit. Indeed, because groups often reach a limit to their own growth, often the only way to move up is to move out. But when these nonprofits lose a leader to another organization, they are simply gaining an ally in the field.

"NCLR has been a fantastic grooming ground for young Latinos and Latinas," says Tom Espinoza, CEO and president of the Raza Development Fund. "They have worked with us and then gone on to do a variety of work in many areas. The infrastructure of people who have left us has paid dividends to the entire community."

Such strong social networks help build the backbone of the organizational networks that successful nonprofits use as a force for good.

WORK IN COALITIONS

In the same way that they share funding, expertise, and talent with other organizations, these high-impact nonprofits are also willing to share power and credit while mobilizing the network for greater impact. They learn to increase their influence over larger systems by working in coalitions and alliances.

These high-impact nonprofits leverage their own formal or informal affiliates, and organize larger coalitions, for a number of ends: to raise public awareness of an issue through coordinated PR campaigns, to change public behavior, to influence policy decisions at the federal or state level, or to access resources. As discussed in Chapter Two, collective action is a powerful strategy for increasing effectiveness in advocacy. By acting together, these nonprofits have much more power than they would alone. For high-impact groups, this sometimes means leading a coalition, but it can also mean following another organization's lead and working behind the scenes.

City Year played both roles in advancing the national service movement.[11] At times it led a larger coalition, and other times it played a supporting role. Alan Khazei and Michael Brown launched City Year in 1988 to engage diverse youth in a year of community service. From the outset, the two founders deliberately positioned City Year as a demonstration project for federally funded national community service. They knew that achieving such an ambitious goal would require much more leverage over the federal government than they could achieve alone.

City Year was a latecomer to the larger national service movement, which had been building for two decades to pressure the federal government to fund community service programs. By the mid-1980s, intermediaries like the National Association of Service and Conservation Corps (NASCC) and Youth Service

America were working to unite many different players—including conservation corps, inner-city groups, and school-based service-learning programs—into a grand coalition to pressure Congress to pass national service legislation.[12] Even though it was the new kid on the block, City Year played a critical supporting role in this larger movement.

By engaging inner-city and suburban youth alike, City Year helped create broad political support among the public. The nonprofit also aggressively courted bipartisan political leadership and persuaded them of the importance of the national service cause. City Year was named a demonstration project under the first Bush administration's Commission for National and Community Service, and after Bill Clinton was elected president, he held it up as a model for what became AmeriCorps. City Year lobbied on Capitol Hill for the legislation, and used relationships with corporate leaders such as Timberland CEO Jeffrey Swartz to influence the national debate.

Although City Year obviously benefited as an organization from federal funding, it never put its own interests above the collective, and it didn't try to dominate the movement—or take all of the credit. "They were really good about showing the diversity of the field, about putting all sorts of groups forward," recalls Shirley Sagawa, a former Hill staffer who was instrumental in drafting the first national service legislation. "If it made more sense to put the head of NASCC up in a speaking role, they did it. If it was better to put [business educator] Ira Jackson up there to speak to the business sector, Michael Brown would do it without hesitation."[13]

A decade later, City Year took a more active leadership role in the field when AmeriCorps was threatened with serious budget cuts in 2003. Khazei and Brown organized a coalition of national service leaders, which included two other organizations featured here: Teach For America and YouthBuild USA, among many others.[14] The Save AmeriCorps campaign resulted in thousands of signed petitions to Congress, full-page advertisements in major newspapers donated by Starbucks and other corporations, and countless stories in the local press. The television program *West Wing* even wrote an AmeriCorps-related budget fight into one of its scripts. By mobilizing thousands of players and leveraging the power of collective action, City Year was able to help save AmeriCorps. "We were stronger together than we were apart," says AnnMaura Connolly, senior vice president.

Although City Year suffered budget cutbacks in the short term—its corps member funding was slashed almost in half—in the long run, its big-picture goal was preserved. The coalition won $100 million in restored federal funding the following year. "It goes back to the larger vision: seeking to expand the power of citizen service," says Alison Franklin, then communications director. "The cuts were a threat to both the [City Year] corps itself and to the concept of citizen service."

Mobilizing a network and sharing power and credit are not without their drawbacks. During 2003, then CEO Alan Khazei worked overtime and shifted his focus to leading the national coalition, and staff members involved with the effort experienced a radical increase in workload. Meanwhile, the organization's expansion activities were put on hold, and its very existence was threatened by funding cuts. Was it worth the sacrifice? Many of City Year's supporters didn't agree with the nonprofit's choices. They worried that the organization's relentless pursuit of national service advocacy was eclipsing its focus on internal organizational needs. "People don't always 'get it,'" says City Year's Connolly. "But it's the role we have chosen."

These high-impact nonprofits all realize that sometimes achieving larger impact means forgoing personal gain. And sometimes it means sharing credit and power to be a greater force for good. As Emily Gantz McCay, former executive vice president at National Council of La Raza, sums it up: "We deeply believe at NCLR that you work in coalition with other groups— you share the credit, and you share the work." Senior vice president Charles Kamasaki echoes her philosophy: "At the end of the day, it's not about getting our name in the paper but about getting that change."

WHEN TO GO YOUR OWN WAY

Although network building and collaboration emerged as a pattern across many of the nonprofits we studied, not all the organizations pursued this strategy at every juncture or to the same degree. An organization's approach depends on its own goals and orientation and on the larger environment in which it operates. In some cases, the groups were not so much building a field as trying to disrupt or transform a field. Or they were operating in environments already well populated with entrenched players. This was particularly true for Environmental Defense Fund (EDF) in the environmental field and Teach For America in the field of education.

EDF discovered that in its quest to "find the ways that work," it sometimes needed to part ways with other environmental groups. It was among the first to embrace corporate partnerships, when other green groups accused it of selling out. (See Chapter Three for more details.) And it sees coalition building for advocacy purposes as just another tool in its kit, not its modus operandi: "We work in coalitions when they are effective, but we also don't hesitate to go our own way and drop out of a coalition if justified," says Annie Petsonk, international counsel.

Teach For America is also viewed as a maverick in the larger, well-established education field. It works in partnership with organizations that its alumni have created, and collaborates with other national service programs, as in the Save AmeriCorps campaign. But Teach For America's collaboration stops there. Many established institutions in the education field do not view Teach For America as a team player. In fact, the organization has sought to shake up the education establishment, including powerful teachers unions.

One possible reason for this approach is that when EDF and Teach For America began to grow, they operated in large fields that were already crowded with other players, and they introduced solutions that ran counter to the prevailing wisdom of the time. EDF moved toward corporate partnerships, which were initially anathema to most environmentalists. Teach For America's solution to the problem of educational inequality was to radically transform the way teachers are recruited, trained, and placed, which directly challenged the establishment's position.

Sometimes one field perceives a nonprofit as not being collaborative, when in fact that organization collaborates in a different area. For instance, most affordable-housing groups have historically viewed Habitat for Humanity as isolationist in the housing field. Although some Habitat affiliates have worked closely in coalition with other housing or economic development groups at the local level, many have not. But much of Habitat's focus has been on building a network among the faith-based community and churches, which it has done successfully. In this way, Habitat defined its field as religious groups, and built a network through those channels, not in the housing field.

PULLING IT ALL TOGETHER

The Heritage Foundation demonstrates how all these tactics—sharing funding, knowledge, leadership, and credit—can come together to make a network more powerful and to seed a much larger movement. Heritage exemplifies the network mind-set and strategy in action.

When Heritage was founded in the early 1970s, most think tanks were quiet backwaters of research that did nothing to actively promote their agendas.[15] Heritage changed all that. It was the first think tank to proactively market conservative policy to the public, Congress, and the White House. In the process, it helped catalyze a much larger conservative movement.

Heritage is credited with helping Ronald Reagan sweep into office in 1980 and influencing his policies once he was in the White House. It helped propel Republicans to their Contract with America takeover of Congress in 1994, and later spurred the transformation of many states from "blue" to "red" as conservative issues came to dominate the national debate. More recently, the Tea Party has embraced many of The Heritage Foundation's fundamental ideas about the role of government.

The Heritage Foundation achieved this influence through an informal network and a strategy of shoring up its conservative allies at the grassroots level. In 1977, Heritage formed the Resource Bank, which began as a handful of policy analysts and has since grown to include more than twenty-five hundred experts and nonprofits. Heritage network members can attend an annual spring conference where they debate the latest policy issues and share strategies for advancing conservative policy agendas. They also can attend Heritage-sponsored workshops on analyzing legislative proposals and receive help with marketing and fund-raising. Heritage provides all its assistance free of charge, to virtually any conservative proponent who seeks it.

When Resource Bank member John Andrews founded the conservative Independence Institute of Denver, for instance, he combed through Heritage's database to identify local donors. "Who else would tell you the major donors in your state and provide a printout of their names?" asks Andrews incredulously.[16] Rather than see the regional group as a competitor for local funding, Heritage saw it as an ally fighting for the larger conservative agenda.

Heritage also helped its conservative allies get their message out. It built two state-of-the-art radio studios at its headquarters two blocks from the U.S. Capitol for conservative leaders and opinion makers. "Our studios are available at no charge to our allies in the battle," says Rebecca Hagelin, vice president of communications and marketing. And Heritage provides training on everything from communication skills to organizing and policy advocacy. "I was astounded to learn that I had a budget to train other conservatives, whether from Capitol Hill or a grassroots person from Iowa," says Hagelin. "Heritage seeks to strengthen the movement, not just itself."

The Heritage Foundation has helped nurture the next generation of conservative leadership as well, ensuring the sustainability of the movement. Through a prestigious paid internship program, which includes housing in Washington, Heritage grooms college students for future positions in the marketplace and with other conservative groups. "We see young interns as the root," says Stuart Butler, vice president of domestic and economic policy studies. "They could potentially staff other organizations, or come back to us."

What sets The Heritage Foundation apart from other conservative organizations, and most think tanks in general, is its remarkable dedication to building, cultivating, and coordinating a network of allies. This network in turn serves as an important hub for the larger conservative movement. Heritage does not see other conservative groups as competition. Instead, it helps them raise funds, build their skills, and develop leadership to increase their impact.

Although generous, Heritage's collaborative approach is hardly altruistic. It is, in fact, a strategy for realizing its own goals. "[Leaders] Ed Feulner and Phil Truluck have always had a vision for building the field," says Becky Norton Dunlop, Heritage vice president of external affairs. "We're not in competition with other organizations. We're one piece of the conservative movement, and whatever we can do to help others represent the conservative view, we will. Our view is that the conservative pie is large and growing."

NETWORKS ARE THE FUTURE

Networks and open-source platforms are popular these days in the high-tech industry. Social networking sites, such as Facebook and LinkedIn, have transformed the way we think about community at the individual level. And open-source technology platforms such as Linux—along with such user-driven Web sites as Wikipedia—have also tilted the playing field toward collaboration over competition.

There's a paradigm shift under way in the private sector. In *The Starfish and the Spider: The Unstoppable Power of Leaderless Organizations,* the authors examine the impact of this emerging network structure.[17] Their point is that if you decapitate a spider, it will die. But with headless starfish, if you cut off an arm, the old starfish will simply regenerate a new arm, and the other arm will grow into a new starfish. Spider organizations have rigid hierarchies, top-down leadership, and centralized decision making (think militaries, traditional corporations, and bureaucratic governments). Starfish, in contrast, are highly decentralized, relying on peer-to-peer relationships, widely distributed leadership, and collaborative communities united by shared values. They are exemplified by such groups as Burning Man, Alcoholics Anonymous, and the Apache Nation.

The advantage of these decentralized networks is that they require little initial investment, scale quickly, are highly adaptable, and are hard to destroy. They are also disrupters. The starfish organization can present a serious challenge to traditional spider businesses, as the peer-to-peer file-sharing network Kazaa did when it undermined the mainstream music industry by allowing free music downloading and became the target of copyright lawsuits in return.

The starfish model is a perfect metaphor for nonprofits, which are more decentralized, are united around communities with shared values, and practice more distributed leadership. They are the ultimate peer-to-peer networkers, working through others to transform government, business, or public behavior. In fact, the authors look at the social sector role that networks have played in the antislavery movement and in the spread of innovations like Alcoholics Anonymous.

Although there's a link between social networks and social movements, we are only now beginning to understand the important role that networks play in achieving social change. It's popular to pay lip service to collaboration, but few groups actually do collaborate or understand how and why doing so can be in their strategic self-interest. Following a network strategy is not without its challenges. At times it requires organizations to make sacrifices and choose pathways that they otherwise would not pursue. And it requires taking a longer-term, bigger-picture view to see beyond immediate self-interest or ego to what will ultimately create more benefit for the whole.

But a network strategy is a more highly leveraged approach to achieving social change. The traditional way to scale an organization's impact is to build and fund new locations one by one. Expansion takes longer, requires more capital, and attains power slowly. But by scaling a *network,* nonprofits distribute the costs, scale more quickly, and have more immediate power through collective action. Networks wield additional public influence over large institutions; they create more ways to engage individuals at the local level; and they offer a larger distribution platform for services or ideas.

The lesson here is that organizations seeking to scale their social impact should look to a network of allies, not just to the departments within their organization's four walls, as the engine of change. This network mind-set will help make short-term strategic choices clearer. Because in the end, even though they may be invisible to outsiders, nonprofit networks are among the most powerful forces that an organization can channel for the greater good.

CHAPTER FIVE HIGHLIGHTS

- **High-impact nonprofits adopt a network mind-set.** Great nonprofits collaborate rather than compete with their social sector peers. They don't see other groups as competition for scarce resources. Instead, they understand that only by working collaboratively with like-minded allies can they have more impact.
- **To build the larger field, share resources and empower others.** Successful organizations help other organizations succeed by sharing hard-to-attain resources—money, special knowledge, training, and a growing pool of talent. They engage in most or all of these practices:
  - *Grow the pie.* They help expand the funding pie for all, or redistribute resources to the network or field.
  - *Share knowledge.* They share information openly and provide training to other nonprofits to increase these groups' capacity.
  - *Develop leadership.* They invest in building leadership for the larger field and share their talent with like-minded allies.
  - *Work in coalitions.* Whether or not they have a network structure, these nonprofits work in formal and informal alliances to advance the larger cause.
- **Give credit where credit is due.** The best groups look for ways to share credit and shine the spotlight on other organizations. They join coalitions and decide when to lead and when to play a secondary role—and put equal effort into both. Often the most influential player in a coalition is the one that operates from behind the scenes.

CHAPTER SIX

MASTER THE ART OF ADAPTATION

When Share Our Strength founder Bill Shore and his sister, Debbie, decided to start a nonprofit in 1984 to fight hunger, they began with an approach that was at once simple and counterintuitive. Instead of mailing out letters seeking support from the usual cadre of antihunger activists, they reached out to an entirely new group of people who care about food—gourmet chefs and restaurateurs. The Shores believed that these professionals would have an affinity for hunger issues and could be inspired to donate to the cause.[1]

One of the first people to respond was Alice Waters, the Berkeley, California, chef and owner of Chez Panisse, who is renowned for her passion for locally grown food. Waters sent Share Our Strength a $1,000 contribution. "She can do more than write checks," thought Bill Shore. So the Shores asked Waters to help them reach out to other opinion leaders in the restaurant industry. Soon chefs from all over the country were donating to the cause, and Share Our Strength had raised $20,000 for hunger relief.

By 1986, the brother-sister duo was working on Senator Gary Hart's presidential campaign in Denver, and running Share Our Strength on the side. While there, they convinced local chefs to host a food-and-wine benefit for their fledgling nonprofit. The chefs volunteered to provide a sampling of gourmet dishes to guests, whose entrance fees were donated to Share Our Strength. The group, in turn, gave away the proceeds to programs fighting hunger.

The event raised a modest $10,000, but more than the money raised, it taught the Shores something valuable: whereas only a few of the chefs had answered Share Our Strength's direct mail request for a $100 donation, they each volunteered to contribute about $800 worth of materials and labor to the event. Their time, in-kind donations, and status were worth far more than cash to the nonprofit.

Share Our Strength changed its tactics, moving away from its previous direct-mail strategy. In 1988, it launched a national series of events called Taste of the Nation, modeled on the Denver prototype. Within two years, the events had expanded to eighteen cities and had raised about a quarter-million dollars. By 2007, Taste of the Nation was held in more than sixty communities and had raised more than $40 million to fight hunger.

This success led Share Our Strength to experiment with other events that leveraged people's strengths to raise money for hunger relief. It launched A Tasteful Pursuit, an elite gathering sponsored by Lexus that features seven-course dinners with celebrity chefs, as well as events such as the Great American Bake Sale, which has engaged one million volunteers in their communities. These humble bake sales raised over $3 million in two years to help end childhood hunger. Share Our Strength also built its most lucrative initiative to date, the American Express Charge Against Hunger campaign, which alone raised $21 million over four years.

Not every new venture was an unmitigated success, however. One flop was the short-lived Taste of the Game, an extension of the dinner concept into the field of sports. The idea was compelling: big-name coaches and athletes would donate their time to teach kids football; parents would buy tickets to the event to raise funds. But on the big opening day, things went awry. It rained— a big deal, given that only outdoor activities were planned. And football coaches just didn't demonstrate the same passion for hunger as chefs. So when the pilot project ended, the organization abandoned the effort.

Dine Across America was another washout. The idea was to ask the thousands of chain restaurants like Applebee's and Chevy's to donate a portion of their profits to charity. "We decided it was not successful, because we wanted it to reach a million dollars in revenue immediately, and it only reached $250,000 in the first go-round," says Ashley Graham, director of leadership. Share Our Strength staff members were unsure whether the program fell short because the idea was unsound or because they failed to allocate sufficient resources to improving the program over a longer period of time.

In order to learn from these failed experiments and improve its "research and development" process, Share Our Strength turned to its McKinsey-trained managing director, Pat Nicklin. Nicklin applied her experience as a business entrepreneur to create internal systems that help staff evaluate new ideas and conduct more rigorous reviews of existing programs. Under the system, staff members now write business plans for new program ideas, which the senior management team periodically reviews.

"Staff seem to appreciate the added layer of process, as the historical lurching after one idea or another didn't pay off in the end," says Nicklin (who has since left Share Our Strength). "Taste of the Game cost hours of every team member's time." Echoes longtime staffer Graham: "Pre-Pat, we always had an entrepreneurial approach to our business. We were great at setting BHAGs [Big Hairy Audacious Goals], but we weren't always great at identifying the way to get there."

Today, Share Our Strength's creativity flourishes—along with its ability to execute on its best ideas. Rather than stifling new ideas and imposing pointless bureaucracy, the new system allows the organization to focus scarce resources where it can have the most impact. It doesn't have time and energy to waste on new programs that are unlikely to succeed. As staff members learned, a bit of discipline can serve as an effective counterbalance to unbridled innovation.

Share Our Strength is a role model for innovation. Sure, it has come up with some creative, even brilliant, ideas. But it can also *execute* on these ideas, expand them when they bear fruit, and shut them down when they fail. Along the way, the group has created systems for evaluating new and existing programs that have increased its efficiency without dampening its entrepreneurial spirit. In short, Share Our Strength has mastered the art of adaptation.

THE CYCLE OF ADAPTATION

Like Share Our Strength, each of the twelve organizations in this book is highly adaptive—able to perceive changes in the environment and develop new approaches in response. We believe this is a critical component that allows them to continually increase their impact. When they perceive a gap between their vision and their results, they aren't afraid to modify their approach to be a greater force for good.

Adaptive capacity is one term used to describe this phenomenon—and high-impact nonprofits have it in abundance. "It is one thing to deliver a program . . . [and another] to know where and how to change programs and strategies so that the organization is delivering on its mission," write the authors of *High Performance Nonprofit Organizations.* "For an organization to be more than the sum of its programs, it needs the ability to ask, listen, reflect, and *adapt.*"[2] Christine Letts and her coauthors argue that a nonprofit's ability to develop adaptive capacity is essential to increasing its effectiveness and therefore its impact.

Yet these qualities are surprisingly hard to come by in the social sector. On the one hand, many established, larger organizations become mired in bureaucracy or stuck in old ways of approaching social change that no longer work. They fail to recognize that the world is changing around them, and they are unable to modify their programs and tactics on the basis of signals received from the external environment or from key stakeholders.

On the other hand, thousands of start-ups pride themselves on being entrepreneurial and innovative, generating countless new ideas—and often reinventing the wheel. They are bursting with creative energy, but they lack the management capacity, systems, and resources to bring these ideas to full fruition. And when new programs fail, these organizations are unable to learn from their mistakes. As the authors of *Ten Rules for Strategic Innovators* point out, it's much harder to execute on ideas than come up with them in the first place: "The limits to innovation have less to do with creativity, and more to do with management systems."[3]

But the nonprofits we studied have discovered how to walk the fine line between creative innovation and structured execution. They exhibit the ability to listen, innovate, learn, and modify their approach—they have mastered what we call the "cycle of adaptation," as illustrated in Figure 6.1.[4]

We believe that mastering the cycle of adaptation is critical to success. Precisely because they exist at the intersection between markets and governments—which are constantly changing—successful

FIGURE 6.1.   THE CYCLE OF ADAPTATION.

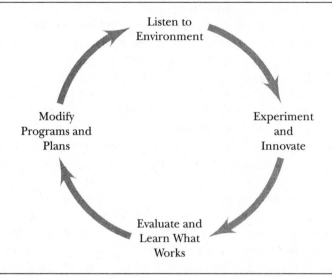

Listen to
Environment

Experiment
and
Innovate

Evaluate and
Learn What
Works

Modify
Programs and
Plans

Note: This figure draws on concepts from such established frameworks as the Japanese Plan-Do-Check-Act (PDCA) model and Kolb's Learning Cycle.

nonprofits must continuously adapt in order to remain relevant. For example, as public policies change or as political parties come and go, an advocacy approach must change in response. Or as social needs are met through changes in the economy or markets, a group must identify new opportunities to help their constituents.

Given how important adaptive capacity is, we wanted to understand specifically what drives change in the first place—and *how* groups develop, evaluate, and modify new program opportunities in light of their overall strategies and goals.

WHAT DRIVES INNOVATION?

Sometimes the impetus for change comes from an external source, as an organization's environment shifts and the group responds. Other times, change is the result of internal dynamics: an organization evaluates its programs and decides to alter its course because it sees a gap between its goals and its actual results.

We observed that "staying close to the customer," to borrow a business phrase, is the most common impetus for adaptation. Groups listen closely to their constituencies and stakeholders, including clients, donors, volunteers, and partners in all sectors of society. They are able to track changes in customer needs, and they perceive new opportunities for solving social problems as they solicit feedback. Share Our Strength launched the Taste of the Nation event series because it realized that chefs were more interested in donating their time and talent than writing checks. The group listened to chefs' interests and needs, and was then able to capitalize on an opportunity to engage them more effectively.

Frequently, external forces disrupt a nonprofit and compel it to redesign its programs. For example, Feeding America (formerly America's Second Harvest—The Nation's Food Bank Network) historically created food banks where slightly damaged but edible packaged food could be stored and redistributed.[5] But the food industry has changed significantly over the last decade, moving away from canned goods into ready-to-prepare meals and fresh produce. Increasingly, many grocery stores devote more square footage to fresh produce and deli sections. Rising societal concerns about diet and nutrition among the privileged have trickled down to affect the types of food available to the hungry. Feeding America saw these changes and responded to them, altering its supply chain to accommodate fresh produce, developing prepared meal programs, and integrating new procurement models to adapt to changing trends in the food industry.

"Basically, we're chasing trends of the food industry," says former CEO Bob Forney (who is now deceased). "Now we have to have not just pallets for canned and packaged goods, but a new food transport system with refrigerators. We have to move [produce] quickly or it will perish." Making this change wasn't easy, or cheap. Feeding America had to develop a new online distribution system that uses the latest technology to allocate fresh produce quickly and efficiently to local food banks. And it invested in refrigerated trucks and warehouses to store goods in transit.

Had Feeding America not been able to listen and respond to these changes, the organization could still be distributing dented cans, fulfilling an important need. But it wouldn't have been creating the degree of social change that it does today, feeding many more people in much healthier ways. "It's dynamic, not static," says Al Brislain, former vice president. "You have to adapt to the environment around you. You can't impose your reality on your environment."

One reason the nonprofits we studied are so adept at responding to external cues is that they must work outside the boundaries of their individual organizations to achieve greater impact. In Chapter Two, we demonstrated how both providing direct services and advocating for policy change lead to greater impact. This dual business model enhances an organization's ability to innovate, with on-the-ground programs informing advocacy, and vice versa. Likewise, in Chapter Five we saw how working with local affiliates and through less formal networks also keeps a group's ears to the ground. The organization's networks inform it about what is working, what isn't, and what more can be done. And in Chapter Three, we saw how savvy nonprofits successfully partner with businesses and stay attuned to changes in markets.

But an external event doesn't always trigger change. Many times, adaptation arises from within the organization itself. Share Our Strength launched an advocacy campaign after a great deal of introspection on the eve of its twentieth anniversary. It just wasn't satisfied with the progress it was making toward its goal of alleviating hunger in America. "I'd asked people to go away and come back with what they thought was the *most compelling*, the *boldest* assertion of impact we could make over the next twenty years," says Bill Shore. "We needed to find something that people could get their arms around."

Staff members generated a host of ideas, one of which was the ambitious notion of ending childhood hunger in America. That fall in New York City, Share Our Strength held its Conference of Leaders, a private event for senior advisers that includes top chefs, restaurant owners, and chief executives from its corporate partners. Although the original purpose of the event was to focus on operations, conference attendees provided useful input on the nonprofit's strategic direction.

"We started to talk about the End Childhood Hunger in America strategy, and everyone got very excited," says Shore. Instead of rejecting the idea of advocacy, as some staff members had feared, the group's corporate partners actually *championed* the move into the political arena. Shore recalls their response: "You're telling us there's a goal line and you know where it is, and you can get across it? We want to be part of it."

Share Our Strength dramatically shifted its priorities as a result, starting with an effort to define how a single city like Washington, D.C., could eradicate childhood hunger. "We did it to make sure that we could actually *end* hunger (as opposed to just alleviate it), and we wanted to hold ourselves accountable for something more achievable than ending all hunger, worldwide," says managing director Nicklin. "As a result, we've had to fundamentally change who we are as an organization. We're changing the way we work with our grantees—we're now consultants, collaborators, and strategists, as well as grantmakers. And we're changing the way we raise money, by partnering with foundations in addition to continuing our cause-marketing and events."

A process of introspection can lead an organization not only to introduce new programs but also to eliminate old ones. We'll see later in this chapter that the organizations that are most aggressive about evaluation shed old programs nearly as often as they create new ones, freeing up resources to pursue fresh opportunities and improve high-potential offerings.

DIFFERENT CULTURES SUPPORT ADAPTATION

Once we better understood what prompted these twelve organizations to change, we looked more closely at how they developed the specific capacities needed to adapt. As we explored the ways they hatched new ideas and then evaluated and modified their programs, we observed that the groups had a range of styles. We mapped these approaches along a continuum ranging from loose to structured, as shown in Figure 6.2.

Some of these organizations are more organic in their approach—innovation just seems to happen. They value experimentation and hands-on learning, and are more likely to have a creative culture and idiosyncratic evaluation rather than rigorous systems. We decided to call these nonprofits "the Free Spirits." At the other end of the spectrum, some groups have developed

FIGURE 6.2. DIFFERENT CULTURES SUPPORT ADAPTATION.

The Free Spirits		The MBAs
• Center on Budget and Policy Priorities	• Environmental Defense Fund	• Feeding America
• Exploratorium	• National Council of La Raza	• City Year
• Habitat for Humanity	• Share Our Strength	• The Heritage Foundation
• Self-Help	• YouthBuild USA	• Teach For America

rigorous processes to guide their adaptation. When we visited them, they felt like well-oiled machines. They are run more like businesses, with clear strategic planning processes, strict policies guiding new program development, and rigorous evaluation. We typecast these organizations "the MBAs."

Finally, a few organizations fall somewhere in between—they have a combination of openness, innovation, and structured evaluation. Typically, new nonprofits start out on the Free Spirit end of the spectrum, and evolve toward a greater amount of structure. That's the natural life cycle of most organizations, whether they are for-profit or nonprofit. Over time, and through sometimes painful experiences, entrepreneurial groups develop more formal ways to innovate.

THE FREE SPIRITS

A number of these organizations take a freewheeling approach to adaptation. They emphasize experimentation and action, they're impatient with any process that smacks of bureaucracy, and they pride themselves on being "doers" not "planners." Their cultures can only be described as creative and innovative, as opposed to systematic or structured.

Self-Help is the ultimate Free Spirit. Staff members unanimously describe the organization as innovative and hands-on.[6] "We lend, innovate, do more lending, then go advocate to large

institutions to change," says Randy Chambers, who was chief financial officer and is now president of Self-Help Credit Union. For
Self-Help, it's important to be active in the financial market, using
a single lending deal as a stepping-stone to the next breakthrough
innovation.

In Chapter Two we told the story of a Self-Help client, the
school bus driver, who was in danger of losing his home. This
single encounter led the nonprofit to discover that tens of thousands of others were victims of similar lending abuse. Within three
years, Self-Help had launched a new affiliate organization, the
Center for Responsible Lending, which has since helped groups
in twenty-two states pass anti–predatory lending laws and, most
recently, significantly influenced legislation at the federal level
through the Dodd-Frank Act. (For updated details on how it did
this, see Chapters Ten and Eleven.) Because it was responsive to
its clients, Self-Help was able to quickly identify a problem and
implement a solution. "We're small enough and nimble enough to
turn on a dime," explains CEO Martin Eakes. "We don't dillydally
or have a nice process where we all sit around in a room with a
whiteboard on the wall. We would rather put our toes in the water
as a test than study to death a proposed plan of action."

This bias toward action is due, in part, to the field in which
Self-Help operates. Lending to disadvantaged populations was a
new industry at the time Eakes founded the organization, so there
wasn't a lot of historical precedent. "In this field, there is not a
lot of market research or third-party data about our [clients],"
says Bob Schall, president of Self-Help Ventures Fund. "The information is hidden, or it doesn't exist. So you cannot do a lot of
advance planning. You have to be in the market first to gain information about the market and to test what works."

Even Self-Help's system for evaluating new program ideas
can best be described as loose. Toni Lipscomb, former president
of Self-Help Credit Union, explains the process: she evokes the
image of a bull's-eye to illustrate how new program ideas config-
ure around a central point. The center of the bull's-eye represents
the organization's core mission—closing the wealth gap between
poor and minority borrowers and the rich. Ideas with the potential to hit this central target are supported, with less emphasis on
their profitability. "The operating assumption is that the farther

an idea is from the mission target, the more the product or program must contribute to Self-Help's financial sustainability," notes Lipscomb.

One program to emerge from this process was a new initiative to extend credit to child-care centers serving low-income populations. Historically, Self-Help had focused its lending in areas that enabled low-income people to build assets, such as through owning their own home or business. Child-care centers did not help individuals build personal wealth per se. But Self-Help soon discovered that local business and home owners were better able to maintain their assets when their children received stable, quality care. So child-care center lending moved closer to the center of the Self-Help bull's-eye.

Such an approach to idea vetting is a fairly simplistic system that works for a group such as Self-Help, which manages against a double bottom line. (That is, it measures its success both in terms of financial returns and social impact.) The group has access to real financial metrics that quickly indicate the financial success or failure of new lending programs: borrowers either repay their loans or they don't. Self-Help can get by with trying things out, listening to market feedback, and keeping what works.

For other organizations, such as the Exploratorium, measuring impact is inherently more difficult.[7] The museum aspires to help people learn about science and to influence how science is taught in public schools, but there is a real artistic element as well. The impact of the organization has as much to do with inspiration, awe, and the creative process as it does with hard facts. These intangibles are even more challenging to evaluate, so it's not surprising that the Exploratorium takes a loose approach to adaptation. Scientists and artists are constantly experimenting with new exhibits to present physical phenomenon in ways that will teach and inspire visitors. The culture is one of constant change and creative destruction.

When you walked into the Exploratorium's original warehouse space in San Francisco, the first thing you'd see through a glass wall was a machine shop where artists and engineers in welding glasses assembled new exhibits. Sparks would fly as they banged metal against anvil, the clanging was almost audible through the window. The creative process was exposed for all to see, setting the tone for the rest of the museum. At the

Exploratorium, visitors are invited to interact and experiment with all the exhibits and to rediscover the joy of learning. Across the street in the organization's headquarters, the atmosphere was similarly unstructured. Housed in an old army barracks, the offices were a rabbit warren of cubicles. Bright posters, Escheresque art, and photographs of scientific phenomena hung on the walls. Desks were piled high with paper, gadgets, and news clippings. The culture was (and still is) decidedly creative and nonconformist.

The Exploratorium's organizational structure, which is modeled on a university, supports this culture of innovation. It has avoided imposing too many managerial layers, or too much discipline, for fear of squelching creativity. "We have a flat non-hierarchical structure that is conducive to creativity," says Robert Semper, director of the Center for Learning and Teaching. "A group can organize around an idea rather than around a structure. Ideas can originate from anywhere. Anyone can put their hand in and try something out to make it work." Staff members are given free time to tinker with pet projects.

One drawback to having so much creative freedom is a corresponding reduction in rigor. By its own admission, the Exploratorium has sometimes sacrificed managerial efficiency on the altar of inspiration. And it recognizes the inherently difficult nature of evaluating creativity and learning. "It's very difficult to measure our impact," says Pat Murphy, director of publications and editorial. "We've added a research component and we work with evaluators, but it's never going to be easy." The Exploratorium measures what it can, but it doesn't let numbers stand in the way of having impact on a more intangible level.

CEO Dennis Bartels, appointed in 2006 as we were concluding our initial research, emphasizes that alternative approaches are critical to the organization's creative culture and to its ability to remain innovative. "The Exploratorium is a place of strange juxtapositions: What happens when you put art and science together? When you make the invisible visible? What happens when you ask impossible questions?" Without artists to help scientists translate complex phenomena into exhibits, it is hard to imagine that the Exploratorium would have achieved such extraordinary impact with visitors, or in the science field at large.

THE MBAS

Another cluster of successful organizations falls on the opposite end of the adaptation spectrum. Organizations such as Teach For America, The Heritage Foundation, and Feeding America are meticulous about evaluating and measuring their programs, and are sticklers for strategic planning. They are certainly innovative, but they seem to learn as much from evaluating and planning as they do from *doing*. Their approach is more akin to companies in the pharmaceutical industry, with elaborate R&D pipelines and staged processes.

Teach For America's headquarters is a picture of stark modernity and hushed professionalism.[8] The converted warehouse space in Manhattan's Garment District is minimalist: ceilings are lined with exposed pipes, floors are unpainted concrete, and conference tables are cold steel. Staff members pass by briskly with a serious air. Meetings are held to talk about recruiting quotas and to optimize strategies on campuses across the country. Like an elite military force, the Teach For America team is talented, dedicated, and disciplined. The organization is all business.

Teach For America's management team tracks data as if their lives depended on it. They focus like a laser beam on evaluation. Although its approach may have been looser in the early years, today the organization obsessively collects data about the performance of its teachers in the classroom. Teach For America takes evaluation so seriously that it recently hired a psychologist to deconstruct the personal attributes of the corps members whose students made the greatest academic gains. He identified the key factors that distinguished great teachers from the merely good—the most noticeable of which was having a "strong internal locus of control."

Teachers who exhibit this attribute, said the psychologist, distinguish between what they can and can't control and then work to change every factor they can. For instance, if one teacher's student is falling behind in math—not because of aptitude, but because he lives in a crowded house—the teacher will try to get the student into a more suitable environment for doing homework.

Such insights caused a dramatic shift in Teach For America's recruitment strategy. It moved away from targeting education majors or the stereotypical "Peace Corps do-gooder" on campus, and instead placed students with proven leadership ability at the top of its list. The nonprofit now proactively competes for the attention of recognized campus leaders, such as the sports team captains, newspaper editors, choir directors, and student government officers—individuals who might not have considered teaching until the group pursued them and persuaded them to enlist.

Teach For America also invests considerable resources in surveying its corps members throughout their two years of service to evaluate their experiences. It then adjusts admissions, training, and support programs to ensure that the teaching corps improves every year. "No other teacher training program or school district takes this approach of gathering such extensive data and using it to drive constant annual revisions in the program model and delivery," claims Teach For America in a grant proposal. "This approach has allowed us to consistently improve student outcomes over the past years even as our corps has grown."[9]

Teach For America complements its internal assessments with independent external evaluation of its programs. The organization participated in a 2004 Mathematica Policy Research study that compared the academic gains of students who had Teach For America teachers with those who had other teachers. The study found that despite working in the highest-need classrooms in the country, corps members "produced higher test scores than the other teachers in their schools; not just other novice teachers or uncertified teachers, but also veterans and certified teachers," according to internal documents.

Unlike Teach For America or the many other nonprofits that evolve toward increased structure over time, The Heritage Foundation started out that way from the beginning. It is meticulous about measuring performance, and rigorously plans throughout the year.[10] The staff attribute this culture to the CEO. "Ed Feulner was a graduate of Wharton, and he brought a very focused, businesslike view of the way it would be run," says Kim Holmes, vice president of foreign policy. The approach has permeated the organization.

Feulner's MBA training—and his impact on the institution's culture—shows in its outward appearance as well. The Heritage Foundation offices are more blue-chip corporation than grassroots nonprofit. The floors are marble; the walls are paneled oak. Conference rooms are lined with custom-built shelves, stacked with books on conservative policy, politics, and business management. A large collection of publications and DVDs from management educator and motivational speaker Brian Tracy, who serves on the Heritage board, was displayed in the room where we interviewed Heritage staff.

True to form, Heritage's senior leadership team functions in a crisp, corporate manner. They are sticklers for evaluation and planning. "Our constant attempt is to figure out how effective we actually are," says Stuart Butler, who at the time was vice president of domestic policy. "We just had a meeting about our Web site: Is it having the impact that it should? Is the information correct? Is it doing what we want? In a nutshell, we don't engage in a level of self-delusion that assumes that if we just produce something, everyone will read it."

Heritage devotes substantial resources to strategic planning. Strategy meetings are held monthly, quarterly, and annually, and the top leadership—from Feulner on down—all attend. Monthly half-day senior management meetings are reserved for the evaluation of new opportunities, and short-term troubleshooting. "If anyone has an idea or a project they want to present, that is a good place to start," says Holmes. "If there is a problem brewing, it surfaces." An annual senior management retreat is used to address the organization's long-term strategic plans and to track progress against the bigger picture. "We focus on how we are going to do things differently," explains Butler.

The result of this strategic planning process has been that Heritage can make better decisions about what to do and also what *not* to do. A good example of a program it let go is *Policy Review*, the nation's first journal of conservative policy analysis and a publication that helped establish Heritage's credibility in its start-up years. Later, once Heritage had grown in influence, management made the difficult decision to spin off the magazine to Stanford University's Hoover Institution, which was better suited to publishing an academic journal.

"It was a wrenching case," recalls Stuart Butler. *Policy Review* was one of Heritage's hallmark products, and leaders were attached to the publication. But the organization's rigorous strategic planning process led it to determine that the journal had become a financial drain and that management time could be better directed elsewhere.

MASTERING THE CYCLE OF ADAPTATION

Whether an organization is a Free Spirit, an MBA, or somewhere in between, each of the groups discussed in this book is able to successfully execute on all four steps of the cycle of adaptation. It's also true that some perform better at certain stages than others do. MBAs are great at evaluation and *process* innovation, whereas Free Spirits are better at experimentation and *product* innovation. (See Figure 6.3.)

But wherever they end up on the spectrum, and whatever their unique style, all twelve nonprofits exhibit a baseline level of adaptive capacity. Specifically, they must be able to effectively listen to the environment, experiment and innovate (either for product or process improvement), evaluate and learn what works, and, finally, modify their approaches on the basis of new information.

FIGURE 6.3.   HIGH-IMPACT NONPROFITS CAN EXCEL AT DIFFERENT PHASES OF THE CYCLE OF ADAPTATION.

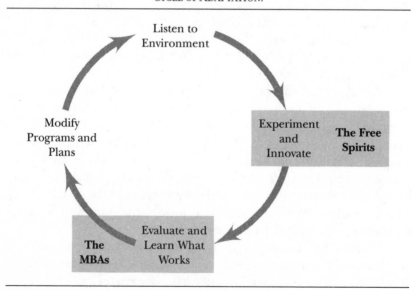

LISTEN TO THE ENVIRONMENT

Adaptation begins with listening for external cues in the environment and looking internally for opportunities to increase impact. These skills are enhanced in organizations that focus on working with and through other sectors of society to achieve greater change. For instance, maintaining a large network of formal affiliates and informal nonprofit allies helps a group stay in touch with the grass roots, as does working through local sites or regional offices. Working with business helps it stay attuned to changes in the market.

One of the reasons the National Council of La Raza (NCLR) has continuously adapted is that it maintains a wide network of affiliated organizations, and works closely with other nonprofits in coalitions. These partners provide critical feedback from the grass roots, help generate and test new ideas in local communities, and provide a channel for implementing new programs that the national office develops. Similarly, NCLR engages in both advocacy and service, using one program area to inform another. The result is an organization that has been able to evolve and increase its impact over time.

"We have been able to grow by staying attuned to the times and the necessities of the community," explains Gerald Borenstein, chief financial officer. "This used to be an active civil rights organization; that was important at the time, and still is. But we have realized that it's also about education and having access to society's benefits. It's about creating wealth and opportunities for the community. NCLR has evolved into an organization that tries to meet the needs of the community today."

EXPERIMENT AND INNOVATE

As organizations perceive new opportunities, they must design new programs and then bring them to market. Sometimes they create entirely new breakthrough programs, akin to product innovation in the for-profit world; other times, they focus on making internal processes more efficient and doing a better job of delivering their programs, which is known as process innovation.

The organizations in this book master both product and process innovation in a variety of ways. Sometimes they develop new products and services spontaneously as they operate in the marketplace, such as when Self-Help developed and tested new lending tools. Others develop new program ideas through a more structured R&D process, such as the one at Share Our Strength, in which staff write business plans. And some focus more on continuously improving what they already do, such as Teach For America, which constantly refines its recruiting process to make it ever more efficient and effective. Regardless of which type of innovation a group focuses on, there are a number of attributes that enable innovation.

One important means of encouraging innovation is to deliberately recruit staff with diverse professional experiences. Both Environmental Defense Fund (EDF) and the Exploratorium hire brilliant staff from eclectic backgrounds and put them together to come up with unusual solutions. EDF employs scientists, economists, and lawyers to develop its innovative market-based solutions to environmental problems. The Exploratorium brings artists and scientists together to invent new ways of presenting complex physical phenomena that appeal to children and adults alike. Other groups we studied have similarly diverse staff members, representing multiple perspectives on an issue.

Another key to fostering innovation is to encourage cross-team collaboration and break down barriers between organizational departments. At The Heritage Foundation, departments are organized around issue areas, such as health care and trade policy. Many nonprofits are structured in this way, but one of the drawbacks is that it can lead to the silo effect, a competitive dynamic in which individual departments jockey to obtain scarce organizational resources.

To mitigate against this tendency, Heritage staff members are required to participate in formal cross-team meetings and collaborations designed to share information and foster creativity. And Heritage staff elect to go one step further: "We developed ad hoc [cross-department] groups within Heritage that are sort of like entrepreneurial teams in charge of moving forward," says Stuart Butler. "These small groups understand all of the inner workings of the organization." The teams can understand problems from multiple perspectives and see how new solutions fit within the larger strategic context.

Evaluate and Learn What Works

Equally important to innovation is the process of learning what works and what doesn't. Government or foundation funders require all nonprofits to conduct program evaluation, at a minimum through updates on their progress and results. However, some groups take evaluation far beyond the formal requirements and use it as an opportunity for organizational learning and continuous improvement. One organization that has been particularly thoughtful about evaluation is YouthBuild USA. "There's a real emphasis on outcomes and data collection here," says Suzanne Fitzgerald, president of the affiliates network. "I came from a business environment, and was amazed at what YouthBuild was doing."

When she first joined the organization ten years ago, data weren't utilized effectively at the program level. But now YouthBuild has an IT system to track information "with attention to real outcomes, not feel-good stories," she says. Local YouthBuild affiliates report monthly to national headquarters about how participants are doing on a number of dimensions: GED or high school diploma acquisition, attendance, program graduation, job placement, continuing education, and post-program wages. If something isn't working well, YouthBuild USA can respond quickly—and track opportunities for long-term improvement across the network.

Another strategy for improving programs is to study and copy comparable organizations' best practices. The technique is known as *benchmarking* in the business world, and many of the organizations we studied use it to understand what is possible and to gather new ideas about how to improve. Sometimes they benchmark against external companies in the private sector, sometimes against other nonprofits, and often within their own affiliate network.

When City Year wanted to improve its financial systems, it approached Cisco Systems for help. Nancy Routh, vice president of development, knew that the technology company closed its accounting books every day, as opposed to the monthly norm, giving the firm real-time financial knowledge. Meanwhile, City Year closed its books on a quarterly schedule. "Why can't we close our books every day like them?" asked Routh. City Year leaders worked with Cisco executives to improve its IT and financial systems, enabling it to close its books daily. "We have this notion of learning from the best, no matter what sector," Routh says. "When we wanted to learn technology, we went to Cisco."

Teach For America also reached out to the corporate sector early on, in this case to benchmark its recruiting process. It studied the techniques of top-notch consulting and banking firms such as McKinsey and Goldman Sachs, copying such strategies as one-on-one networking and individualized follow-up. The irony is that Teach For America now out-recruits those firms on many college campuses.[11]

At critical times in their evolution, many organizations have also engaged external consultants who can help them learn and magnify their impact. Early on, City Year used a team from Bain & Company to help it develop a national expansion plan. Teach For America used a pro bono consulting team from the Monitor Institute, a benefit of its relationship with funder New Profit Inc., to develop a major fundraising campaign. EDF hired an independent nonprofit consultant in New York City to drive its five-year strategic plan in 1997. And when we visited NCLR, it had just engaged The Bridgespan Group (a nonprofit spin-off of Bain) to develop a strategy for rethinking its relationships with members of the affiliate network.

MODIFY PROGRAMS

After programs are developed, implemented, and evaluated, high-impact organizations use their accumulated knowledge of what works to inform future activities. Whether launching a new program or adapting an existing one, many of these organizations are exceptionally good at capturing, codifying, and then sharing knowledge to modify their programs and improve performance. They use their larger networks—whether they comprise formal affiliates, regional offices, or informal allies—to benchmark best practices and identify what's working at the local level.

City Year even adopted a moniker for its approach: SAIL (standardize, align, integrate, learn). Before it began using SAIL, each local site invented its own fundraising events and held them at different times; now the organization is more coordinated in its approach. The SAIL process was tested out on City Year's new Starry Starry Night dinners, an innovative event developed by a local site, which turned out to be an excellent fundraiser. City Year decided to take the events national, working with the local office to determine best practices, document the process, and then share it with other sites in order to modify their fundraising programs. Now all of City Year's sites hold Starry Starry Night dinners during the same time of year, allowing for national press coverage and greater fundraising results.

YouthBuild USA is also proficient at sharing best practices across its network of affiliates to modify its work. It publishes handbooks for local sites, conducts numerous training sessions, and involves site leaders in several layers of councils that guide and set policy for the organization. "Identifying high-performing sites, what practices they follow, and giving that information back to the rest of the sites" has been a major priority for YouthBuild, says Fitzgerald.

Finally, every one of the organizations we studied makes annual gatherings for all staff and for local sites and affiliates a top priority. These conferences are often multiday events during which local sites, or affiliates, present new models or best practices, and national training is conducted. The organization as a whole can focus on strategy. These gatherings are an opportunity for the groups to constantly modify their plans in light of new lessons learned, or changes in the larger environment.

EDF places such a premium on its annual all-staff gathering that the CEO insisted on holding the event during its most challenging fundraising year, following the 9/11 terrorist attacks. The choice was significant, given that EDF employs nearly three hundred staff members spread across offices in nine cities nationwide, with some working abroad. "At the beginning, I didn't fully appreciate this retreat," says Jane Preyer, now director of the southeast office of EDF. "There can be heated issues that come up—and it costs a lot. But it's a unifying thing. It helps us know what is going on in the larger organization. We highlight successes, lessons learned, models, and examples."

WHAT *NOT* TO DO

Each of these stories sheds light on how groups mastered the four stages of the cycle of adaptation. We believe that this ability to master the art of adaptation is a key factor that differentiates these groups from less successful organizations.

Many nonprofits fail to find this delicate balance. They are either so freewheeling that their cultures are more chaotic than creative, or they are so structured that they become hidebound and paralyzed. But high-impact nonprofits are able to work with this tension. And they have learned one of the most important lessons of adaptation and of strategy: it's as much about what *not* to do as it is about which ideas to pursue. For every new program they add, they often cut something else that is having less impact.

A mistake that highly creative, chaotic organizations often make is trying to sustain too many programs at once and not prioritizing among them. Running myriad programs consumes precious resources: they suck in talent, burn grant dollars, and command management time and attention. Being spread too thin can quickly impede a group's ability to achieve greater impact. One nonprofit we know lists three dozen "priority programs." Organizations like these trip over themselves and their programs; they could increase their effectiveness if they learned to focus on a few projects with the greatest potential for real impact.

Containing chaos is not easy. Sometimes organizations are forced to let go of pet projects, because they would otherwise implode. In her book *One Day, All Children . . . ,* Teach For America founder Wendy Kopp writes about struggling to launch a national youth teaching corps while also incubating new programs such as TEACH!, which trains existing teachers in public schools, and the Learning Project, a New York City regional charter school group.[12]

Kopp eventually spun off these programs as separate nonprofits so that Teach For America could focus on its core offering: the teaching corps. The decision wasn't easy, however. It meant that Kopp had to let go of devoted staff, including veteran corps members who helped create the organization. It also meant that Teach For America could not ensure the spin-offs' survival: TEACH! thrives today, but the Learning Project eventually closed its doors. But after cutting these projects loose, the organization was able to focus its resources on improving its main program—and saved itself from demise.

This winnowing process is essential to continuous adaptation. After all, adaptation is not just about innovation or creating new programs—it is also about learning and change, and discarding what isn't working to make room for new ideas that have the potential for greater impact. Every group discussed in this book has some mechanism for assessing new ideas in light of its overall strategic direction, and for deciding what *not* to do, as it makes room for new possibilities and programs.

The processes these organizations use to decide on their organizational priorities vary dramatically—some are more structured, some more organic. But they all ask themselves similar questions in deciding what to keep and what to let go. They are able to self-reflect and ask, *What are we good at? Where can we have the most impact? Is anyone else already doing this?*

Nearly thirty years into its history, EDF engaged in its first formal strategic planning process. After a year of assessment and planning, the nonprofit decided to narrow its priorities and focus on four critical areas: oceans, climate/air, health, and ecosystems. EDF used several simple questions to determine whether programs fit with its larger strategy: Is the issue critical to the environment? Do we have the competency to do it well? Are other groups already working on it? EDF then divested from programs—such as population—that didn't fit the four new areas, that didn't use a core competency, or that were being addressed effectively by other groups. It focused instead on areas where it could have the most impact.

At the other end of the spectrum within the social sector are those nonprofits that gravitate too much in the direction of structure. They become bureaucratic, adhere too closely to their plans, and remain inflexible in the face of shifting circumstances. Either they are unable to respond to change or they lack the creativity to generate and launch new ideas. Often these are older, well-established organizations that have grown ossified over time, with a loyal funding base that propels their current programs and creates a "lock-in" effect. Although they may continue to provide vital services, they miss opportunities to increase their impact.

But the nonprofits we studied have managed to increase their effectiveness without becoming overly bureaucratic. Share

Our Strength, for example, could have rested on its laurels after launching the successful Taste of the Nation event, continuing to deliver an innovative program that has raised millions for hunger relief. Instead, it forged ahead with new opportunities, developing cause-marketing partnerships such as the American Express Charge Against Hunger. Share Our Strength parlayed these cause-marketing experiences into a new business, launching Community Wealth Ventures as a for-profit subsidiary designed to help other groups develop earned-income capabilities. (See Chapter Three.)

The decision to build the new enterprises didn't come without risk. Allocating resources toward new ideas caused Share Our Strength to miss the opportunity to build Taste of the Nation into an even larger success. "The downside is that if we had wanted to grow Taste of the Nation to $10 million annually, we could have," reflects Ashley Graham, director of leadership. "I think, to both our benefit and our detriment, we are extremely agile and adaptable."

The challenge for every nonprofit is to find the sweet spot between exploring new opportunities and shoring up the best existing programs. This means balancing discipline and freedom, and honing the ability not only to innovate but also to evaluate, learn, and modify plans based on new data. As we've illustrated in this chapter, maintaining that tension is extraordinarily challenging. But high-impact nonprofits have learned to strike that balance and find ways to sustain innovation over time. They are true masters of the art of adaptation.

CHAPTER SIX HIGHLIGHTS

- **Great nonprofits constantly adapt and modify their tactics.** Because successful organizations leverage the power of other sectors—government, business, other nonprofits, and the general public—they must be unusually receptive to outside signals, agile enough to change course, and flexible enough to respond to new opportunities.
- **Find the balance between stifling bureaucracy and unbridled creativity.** Less successful nonprofits may excel at generating new ideas, but they can't fully execute on them because they lack structure. Other organizations become mired in

bureaucracy and are unable to change. But high-impact nonprofits strike the balance between structure and innovation.

- **Master each step of the cycle of adaptation:**
  - *Listen.* Stay tuned to external cues from the environment and to ideas generated within the organization, and perceive opportunities for change.
  - *Experiment and innovate.* Develop new ideas for programs (product innovation) and constantly improve your existing programs and how you deliver them (process innovation).
  - *Evaluate and learn.* Rigorously assess what works and what doesn't work; share information across your network.
  - *Modify.* Alter future plans based on the results of evaluation. This can include changing the overall direction of the organization or sharing knowledge across existing sites to improve all programs.
- **Different styles support adaptation.** Some organizations take a more free-spirited approach to adaptation, emphasizing hands-on experimentation. Others approach innovation more systematically, with rigorously constructed plans and systems; they learn as much from evaluating and planning as from doing. A few groups fall somewhere in between.
- **Successful nonprofits focus on what *not* to do.** As these organizations change, they cut programs as often as they add new ones. This can mean making tough choices, but by winnowing out the old, they make room for the new to emerge.

CHAPTER SEVEN

SHARE LEADERSHIP

Edwin Feulner is not a shy and retiring person. The president of The Heritage Foundation reminds you of a burly football coach as he vigorously shakes your hand. The oversize desk in his office is cluttered with political tchotchkes and awards for speaking, policy leadership, and work with several presidential administrations.[1]

Feulner loves to regale visitors with stories of political brinkmanship, and recounts going head-to-head with an arch nemesis: "I was in a debate with Ralph Nader, who accused us of being a 'Coors foundation,'" he recalls. (Joseph Coors provided a seed grant in 1973.) "And I said, 'We actually receive only 1 percent of our funds from them, and we have over *two hundred thousand supporters,* while you won't tell us how many you have.' Point, set, match." Feulner likes a good fight—and even more, he loves to win.

Over the years, Feulner has helped turn Heritage into "the most influential public-policy think tank in Washington, D.C."[2] It wasn't always smooth sailing, however. During its first few years, the nonprofit went through several early directors before members of the board approached Feulner to become president in 1977. He was staff director of the House Republican Study Committee, so he knew the ins and outs of politics. But unlike many policy wonks, who are often more comfortable behind the scenes, Feulner had the makings of a great, and charismatic, leader.

By now, you might think that the point of this story is that nonprofits need a larger-than-life figure at the helm. But you'd be missing the most important aspect of Feulner's strength as a leader: *his ability to share power with others.*

When you ask people outside the Beltway to name the president of The Heritage Foundation, many scratch their heads. Policy experts we spoke to rarely mentioned Feulner's name in the same breath as Heritage. Unlike Focus on the Family, which is closely identified with its founder, Dr. James Dobson, or Ralph Reed, the former director of the Christian Coalition who is a brand unto himself, The Heritage Foundation is not overly associated with any individual. And that's just the way Feulner wants it. "The objective has always been to build an institution that will outlive me," he says. "It has been deliberate. I don't claim to be unduly modest or humble, but it is more important that the institution has made its mark."

Feulner's secret? He has a unique combination of charismatic yet egoless leadership. He gives power away, rather than hoards it.

Perhaps the most telling example of his leadership style occurred when Feulner was first offered the job. He immediately called up his friend Phil Truluck, who was working on the Hill, and said: "I'll take the job, but you have to come with me." Truluck accepted, becoming Feulner's second-in-command. For more than thirty-five years now, the two men have built a powerful organization. By 2006, Heritage had grown to a budget of $40 million, employed two hundred staff, and deployed a network of two thousand informal grassroots affiliates and policy leaders, as well as 275,000 members who volunteered on behalf of the ideas Heritage was championing. (Heritage has since doubled in size and tripled its membership, as we explore in Chapter Ten.)

Heritage's remarkable success owes a lot to the shared leadership of Feulner and Truluck. They possess highly complementary skills: Feulner is an extrovert who exudes energy and vision, whereas Truluck is more internally oriented. From the outset, Feulner positioned Heritage as part of a larger movement, and focused on marketing conservative ideas to Congress and the public. Truluck focused more on managing and growing the organization, building up Heritage's signature policy research program. "They have a great partnership: Ed's a visionary, Phil is very practical, and they are both very savvy," says Kim Holmes, vice president. Beyond their shared leadership, by 2006 Feulner and Truluck had built an institution of leaders, starting with a powerful executive team of eight vice presidents, many of whom had been with the nonprofit twenty years or more. Truluck recalls when they first adopted this organizational structure: "It was around 1981, and we had grown. . . . All of a sudden I had sixty-five people reporting to me, and Ed [Feulner] had five. No one had designated me 'Number Two,' but I was. So we did a simple organizational chart: Ed was at the top, I was underneath, and we created a tier of VPs under me. That has enabled us to continue to grow."

We spent a great deal of time studying Heritage's success, and came to see that this structure, with its broadly distributed leadership, provided the critical capacity Heritage needed to sustain its growth and impact. Not only did Heritage have two long-tenured leaders at the helm, but it had built bench strength throughout the organization in the form of a large and empowered executive team. In addition, Heritage was governed by a highly engaged board, with many members who have served for decades.

By having so many leaders, Heritage has been able to cultivate critical relationships, influence federal policy, develop a large individual donor base, and run high-powered marketing campaigns to promote its message. This triumvirate of leadership—the shared executive leadership, a broad tier of senior managers, and a strong and supportive board—has created an unstoppable organization.

The Power of Collective Leadership

This model of shared leadership is not what we expected to find. After all, in business—and in much leadership literature—the individual heroic leader is often exalted. Many books on leadership focus on the traits and behaviors of leaders, or the relationship between leaders and followers. In just the past decade, theories of "collective leadership" have begun to gain traction, but for the most part, leadership is still thought of as an individual act. Great leaders are praised for their individual competencies, attributes, or distinguished personalities. In other words, attention has focused more on leaders than on leadership.

Within the social sector, older models of individual, heroic leadership endure. The social entrepreneurship movement is fascinated with the role of the lone entrepreneur; less attention is paid to collective leadership and entrepreneurship as a collaborative act.[3] Fellowship programs such as Ashoka and Echoing Green emphasize and reward the individual over the organization. Many nonprofit leadership programs and awards still focus on the executive director, rather than on an entire team. And too many nonprofits are known for their charismatic, visionary founders who have a hard time sharing leadership and who use their organizations to promote their grandiose visions rather than build institutions that will outlast them.

We're not discounting the role of the individual as a leader—indeed, the twelve organizations featured in this book would not have achieved such high levels of impact without the exceptionally gifted entrepreneurs who led them in their growth. These nonprofits have all had highly strategic, extremely intelligent leaders who have stayed with their organizations for long periods of time, whether the leader was the founder or joined the organization later in its history. (See Table 7.1, which highlights the tenure of these leaders.)

But strong leadership doesn't only exist at the very top of high-impact nonprofits; rather, it extends throughout the organization. CEOs of high-impact nonprofits share a commitment that goes beyond their own egos, and they use their leadership to empower others. Every one of the twelve groups we studied now has an empowered executive team and a strong second-in-command. And like Heritage, they almost all have large, enduring, and engaged boards. They have distributed leadership throughout their organization, and often throughout their larger network of allies and affiliates as well.

Although we can't prove a simple cause-and-effect link between collective leadership and organizational performance, we have come to believe that sharing leadership has in fact enabled these nonprofits to have more impact. Because they focus so much on influencing players outside their organizational boundaries, they need to manage hundreds of relationships and access many networks. Further, working across sector boundaries to advocate for policy change, partner with business, build a network, or

TABLE 7.1. LONG-TENURED LEADERS (AS OF 2006).

	Number of CEOs	Tenure (in Years), Name of Founder or Growth Leader ♀
The Heritage Foundation	♀ ♀	33 (Feulner)
National Council of La Raza	♀ ♀ ♀ ♀	31 (Yzaguirre)
Habitat for Humanity	♀ ♀	29 (Fuller)
Self-Help	♀	26 (Eakes)
Center on Budget and Policy Priorities	♀	25 (Greenstein)
Share Our Strength	♀	23 (Shore)
Environmental Defense Fund	♀ ♀ ♀ ♀	21 (Krupp)
City Year	♀	19 (Khazei and Brown)
Teach For America	♀	17 (Kopp)
YouthBuild USA	♀	17 (Stoneman)
Exploratorium	♀ ♀ ♀ ♀	16 (Oppenheimer, Delacôte)
Feeding America (formerly America's Second Harvest—The Nation's Food Bank Network)	♀ ♀ ♀ ♀ ♀ ♀ ♀	4.5 (average for all seven)

engage thousands of individuals takes many different skills—not all of which can be found in one person. And the problems these groups are trying to solve are complex, requiring large-scale systemic solutions involving many stakeholders.

Recent research suggests that a collaborative model is more effective in such a complex environment. "Complex social problems, like improving the public schools, are fundamentally different from technical problems, and the effective exercise of leadership depends on understanding this distinction," write Ron Heifetz, John Kania, and Mark Kramer in their 2004 *Stanford Social Innovation Review* article, "Leading Boldly."[4] "Adaptive problems are entirely different . . . many different stakeholders are involved, each with their own perspective[, and] no single entity has the authority to impose it on the others. The stakeholders themselves must create and put the solution into effect."

Our research strongly supports the notion that leading a nonprofit is quite different from leading a business—and therefore requires a more collaborative type of leadership. The CEO of a business has formal authority, and can use a more executive style of leadership to compel people to act. By contrast, leaders in the social sector lead through influence, not authority, and must convince others to act by force of their convictions alone.

This doesn't mean that the role of the executive director isn't important—on the contrary, the top leader sets the tone for the whole organization. "The point of the collaborative leadership paradigm is not that leaders are unnecessary," writes leadership scholar Greg Markus.[5] "Rather . . . organizations are more likely to thrive within complex, continuously changing environments when leadership comes from many places within the organization, drawing upon the complementary assets of group members and not confusing leadership with formal authority."

Although the executive director of a high-impact nonprofit might have vision, he or she can't single-handedly build an organization while catalyzing a larger movement and changing entire systems. No single director could possibly have as much impact by hoarding power, relationships, or information, or by making himself or herself the decision-making bottleneck. In fact, only by giving power away and empowering others do these groups develop networks and movements large enough to catalyze widespread social change.

ONE STYLE DOESN'T FIT ALL

Thousands of articles and books have been written about leadership, many of which focus on the individual attributes of a leader. Business management author Jim Collins, in his book *Good to Great*, described the "Level 5" leader as an individual who paradoxically embraces both personal humility and professional will. These leaders possess strong professional resolve and focus more on building their organizations than on feeding their egos. "Level 5 leaders channel their ego needs away from themselves and into the larger goal of building a great company," writes Collins. "[T]heir ambition is first and foremost for the institution, not themselves."[6]

In this respect, our findings are similar to those of Collins—great nonprofit leaders, like the best business leaders, are successful because they put their organization's interests ahead of their own egos. In fact, we believe that the CEOs of the twelve great nonprofits we studied take the Level 5 leadership concept one step further. They not only put the interests of their *organizations* ahead of their personal egos, they often put their *overall cause* ahead of their *organization's* interests (a theme we explored in Chapter Five).

Where our findings about successful nonprofit leaders differ from Collins's description of great corporate CEOs is in the realm of personality styles. Collins observed that Level 5 leaders are most often described as "quiet, humble, modest, reserved, shy."[7] However, the *Forces for Good* leaders couldn't all be described as humble, shy, or particularly mild mannered. No one would say that Millard Fuller of Habitat for Humanity International, Ed Feulner of The Heritage Foundation, Dorothy Stoneman of YouthBuild USA, or Alan Khazei of City Year are quiet, or that they operate behind the scenes. Although these leaders can check their egos at the door, that does not mean they lack personality. On the contrary, many of the leaders we studied are highly dynamic, extroverted, outwardly inspirational individuals.

We actually found that the leaders of high-impact nonprofits are quite different from one another in their individual leadership styles. The myth of a single type of leader who can succeed is just that—a myth. Many kinds of leaders can be successful at running high-impact social sector organizations.

For example, Wendy Kopp was initially so introverted that she would avoid interactions with Teach For America corps members, because she didn't know what to say to them.[8] She was much more interested in staying up all night developing fundraising plans than in chitchatting over coffee.

Yet despite her shyness, Kopp was still able to persuade countless others to support her cause—from donors who wrote big checks to college graduates who turned down lucrative job offers to teach in inner-city schools. Because Kopp was so passionate about fixing American education, she turned her personal conviction into inspiration—and used this to overcome her initial weaknesses as a leader.

Today Kopp is described as an incredibly focused and disciplined leader who inspires her staff to achieve greater results. She leads by example, setting a tone for the whole organization. "Wendy is the magic bullet at Teach For America," says Kevin Huffman, then a vice president of the organization. "People outside the organization tend to label her as a visionary, but that damns with faint praise. She is astonishingly efficient and effective at both the people and project level. She gets things done at a very high level, and sets a higher bar for the office. It's different from any place I've ever worked."

And those who have heard Bill Shore of Share Our Strength speak so eloquently in public would be surprised to learn that he has had to work at addressing large crowds. Like Kopp, Shore is an introvert. By his own account, he spends a third of his time thinking deeply, riding his bike, and reading books on diverse topics such as science and religion. Shore uses this solitary time to dream up new ideas, remain inspired, and write. In addition to building an organization that had raised more than $200 million for hunger relief by 2006, Shore has authored three books that explore people's motivations to give back through nonprofit work. He has also transcended his own introversion to become a highly effective and inspirational speaker.

Unlike Kopp, Shore is less interested in managerial details and more externally focused. He is described as an inspirational leader who spends much of his time building relationships and persuading others to act—whether by writing a check, hosting a dinner, or entering into a multimillion-dollar cause-marketing partnership. "Bill is just an amazing asset because he can speak about the cause and write so well," says sister and cofounder Debbie. Adds Chuck Scofield, vice president and former development director: "He is a connector of ideas and people. He's an innovative and creative thinker. He is inspirational—he's the reason I'm still here."

On the other end of the extroversion spectrum are leaders such as Alan Khazei of City Year, Dorothy Stoneman of YouthBuild

USA, Fred Krupp of Environmental Defense Fund (EDF), and Ed Feulner of Heritage. Khazei is like a nonstop politician—but rather than campaigning for elected office, he is stumping for national service. (Khazei departed City Year in 2006 and later ran for the Senate seat left vacant by the late Ted Kennedy.) Krupp is widely credited with helping to professionalize EDF, but he's equally effective lobbying politicians, corporate CEOs, or billionaires to support solutions to global warming.

Dorothy Stoneman, by contrast, has been described as "an organizer straight out of the 1960s." She is also brilliant at politics and lobbying, but comes across as more of a grassroots activist than as a polished insider. But anyone who has met her—Republican or Democrat—quickly realizes that she is a force to be reckoned with. Her staff describe her as "relentless, dogged, and determined," a reputation confirmed by YouthBuild USA's success at obtaining large federal appropriations for YouthBuild programs, regardless of which party is in power.

Self-Help founder Martin Eakes is also cut from the 1960s activist mold. His staff describe him as passionate and humble, and "a Level 5 leader, a servant leader," quoting Jim Collins. He doesn't look the part of a powerful financial mover and shaker, but he's a man who was controlling $1 billion in assets and wielding significant influence with such industry titans as Sandy Weill, former Citigroup CEO and chairman at the time we were conducting our research. Eakes has also been accused of micromanagement, as he gets involved at all levels of the organization—from lobbying legislatures to reprogramming computers.

Twelve high-impact nonprofits—and more than twelve inspirational leaders, with radically different personalities. Yet the more we looked, the more we realized that they all had one critical quality in common: *they shared power and leadership in their quest to be a greater force for good.*

Despite their individual differences, these leaders have all demonstrated a willingness to distribute leadership among others both inside and outside their organizations. Although they may not have started out this way, they all now recognize that they cannot increase their impact by hoarding power. The only way to get to the top in the social sector is to give power away.

Two at the Top: The Second-in-Command

Although several of these nonprofits might appear to have been started by a lone social entrepreneur, a number of them had shared executive leadership from the outset. City Year was cofounded by friends Alan Khazei and Michael Brown, just as Share Our Strength was cofounded by brother and sister Bill and Debbie Shore. Heritage had Feulner and Truluck from very early on. And YouthBuild USA, though strongly identified with founder and president Stoneman, was actually cofounded along with her husband, John Bell, who currently spearheads leadership development within the network. The National Council of La Raza (NCLR) was founded by a collective group of Hispanic leaders, but early on appointed Raul Yzaguirre as director. (His title later shifted to president and CEO.) He in turn built a larger leadership team, and was later succeeded by Janet Murguía.

A few of the organizations we studied, such as Teach For America, Feeding America, and the Center on Budget and Policy Priorities, were started by a single individual, but fairly quickly grew into a shared leadership model. Others, such as Self-Help, Habitat for Humanity, and the Exploratorium, were started by one charismatic social entrepreneur and took much longer to evolve into collective leadership. Their founders had a harder time letting go.

But regardless of the timing, the primary leader eventually realized the need to appoint a strong second-in-command to help run the organization. All these organizations now have the equivalent of a chief operating officer (COO) working closely with the executive director. It really is two at the top—whether this second-in-command is called a COO, an executive vice president, or senior vice president, the role is similar. This second leader is more often an internal manager, focused on operational issues, while the executive director is more often the external leader, concerned with vision, strategy, issue leadership, relationship building, or fundraising. The split echoes the distinction between leadership and management drawn by authors Warren Bennis and Burt Nanus: "Managers are people who do things right, and leaders are people who do the right thing."[9]

The timing for appointing a second-in-command—and the precipitating factors—varied from organization to organization. For some nonprofits, such as YouthBuild USA, the board prompted the founder to let go and appoint a COO. As one board member recalls, "When I first joined the board, I had concern that the organization was purely directed by Dorothy [Stoneman]. She was doing everything without an executive management team. With board encouragement, she set out to find a COO." Tim Cross was promoted to COO, and Stoneman shifted to focus on being the public face of the organization as Cross managed internal operations. (Cross now runs YouthBuild's international expansion.)

In several of the cases we studied, it took a crisis moment for the primary leader to let go. These moments occurred when the founder-director either contemplated leaving or in fact left the nonprofit for a brief time, allowing a second leader to assume more power and responsibility. Often this break with routine also allowed the founder to release some control and begin to share power and leadership more broadly.

After ten years as cofounder and CEO of City Year, Alan Khazei left on a one-year sabbatical to get married and travel around the world. During this time, other City Year leaders, including cofounder Michael Brown, took on more responsibility. Khazei eventually left the organization in 2006, but only after he and Brown ensured that there was a strong leadership team at the top. They named Brown as CEO, internally promoting COO Jim Balfanz and recruiting Colonel Robert Gordon, a military leader from West Point who shares Khazei's relationship skills, as the senior vice president for civic leadership.

In some cases, it was the original second-in-command, or cofounder, who needed to be moved aside as the organization grew. Share Our Strength was cofounded by executive director Bill Shore and his sister, associate director Debbie Shore. Their longtime friend Kathy Townsend managed internal operations. After twelve years of this arrangement, it became apparent that the organization had grown beyond the skills of the founding team. It needed real operational expertise. Bill Shore recruited Pat Nicklin—a former McKinsey consultant who had run several businesses—as managing director.

"We were really late in doing it," says Bill Shore. "The managers of the organization were the people who had been there the longest, not those with management skills. It was hard, but Pat was really graceful, and my sister was really graceful at moving over." Debbie Shore concedes that it wasn't easy for her to let go. "I was on the border of not being able to evolve," she says. "You have to learn that it's not about you, or your way—it's about the organization. You really have to keep evolving as a leader, but most founders don't do this well." Debbie Shore still plays a senior leadership role in the nonprofit.

Self-Help went through a similar transition more recently—one also precipitated by the growth of the organization. As founder Martin Eakes recalls, "We reached a point where we had twenty senior people reporting to me. Nobody can adequately do feedback or intervention with twenty people! We had an organizational consultant come in who made a joke that 'Half the people report to Martin, and the other half think they do.' Up to a certain size that worked, but then I became the bottleneck."

Eakes put in place a new structure by 2006 that elevated four senior staff members to the senior management level. At the same time, he appointed Eric Stein as COO. "Eric has the authority," says Randy Chambers, now president of Self-Help Credit Union. "If Martin [the CEO] is out of the office, all the staff knows that we can count on Eric to cover for Martin."

LETTING EXECUTIVES LEAD

In addition to having a strong second-in-command, these nonprofits have something else that sets them apart: a remarkably strong senior executive team. It's not just "two in a box," but a whole team at the top. Often this shared leadership extends beyond the headquarters of the organization to include the executive directors of local sites, in the cases where the group has formal affiliates.

"At a typical nonprofit, the person at the head is almost the whole organization, but that's not really true here," says Charles Clark, YouthBuild USA's vice president of asset development. "YouthBuild is not successful just because of Dorothy [Stoneman].

She enables the two hundred executive directors of local sites out there who are really doing the work. She has been more of a founder and enabler."

It is of interest that most of the nonprofits we studied have a handful of senior leaders who have been with the organization an extraordinarily long time. These executives are not only loyal but also empowered to speak and act on behalf of the group. They have both authority and accountability for their divisions, and make decisions such as hiring and firing without executive director approval. On the basis of our knowledge of the sector and our experience with many other nonprofits, we believe that these strong, empowered, and enduring executive teams differentiate high-impact nonprofits from their less successful counterparts.

Many leaders are never able to evolve and truly share power at the top. Although they may have executives in title, they are unable to let go, or to retain their senior staff. "I know an organization with a strong reputation, but it's built on the charisma of a single individual," says Emily Gantz McKay, former executive vice president of NCLR. "I do know they've had a real problem keeping senior staff. When you see an organization whose success is all based on the individual, and it is not able to maintain strong [managers], you worry about it."

By contrast, NCLR is an excellent example of a high-impact nonprofit with an empowered and enduring executive team.[10] Initially launched by a collective of Hispanic leaders in Phoenix as the Southwest Council of La Raza, the organization went national in 1972 and moved its headquarters to Washington, D.C. NCLR grew significantly after Raul Yzaguirre was named director in 1974 and worked to strengthen the nonprofit's mission, key programs, and organization. (Former Clinton staffer Janet Murguía took over as its first woman president and CEO in 2005, when Raul Yzaguirre retired after more than thirty years at the helm.)

Yzaguirre is thoughtful and soft spoken. His former staff describe him as "old-world" and patrician without being paternalistic—he has a quiet power. Born in the 1930s, he grew up with activist parents in the American Southwest, and began doing community organizing at age fifteen. An early formative experience came later when he worked for the War on Poverty under Sergeant Shriver. When originally appointed as director of NCLR at the age of thirty, Yzaguirre had the insight to hire strong leaders who would complement his own strengths and weaknesses. "One of my most important talents is being creative," says Yzaguirre. "I have ten ideas, and eight of them are worthless; but the two that are good are what makes the organization. And I surround myself with people who are not shy about telling me which are which."

By 1978, Yzaguirre had too many direct reports, and the organization moved to a structure with several vice presidents. He came to rely on Emily Gantz McKay as his second-in-command, and she was named executive vice president in 1983. Although Gantz McKay left NCLR in 1994, she spent more than twenty years with the nonprofit in various roles.

As the organization grew, it recruited a number of younger leaders who have subsequently evolved into senior roles. For example, Charles Kamasaki, a local activist from NCLR's Texas office, joined the national office in 1982 and has been with the organization ever since, currently serving as senior vice president. Among the other NCLR senior staff with exceptionally long tenure as of 2006 were Cecilia Muñoz, former vice president of the Office of Research, Advocacy, and Legislation (ORAL) (eighteen years); Sonia Pérez, vice president of affiliate member services (sixteen years); and Lisa Navarrete, vice president of public information (eighteen years). Several others who had equally long tenure had only recently left or retired.[11]

"One of the ways Raul [Yzaguirre] and NCLR were effective was [in creating] the vice president tier—it was very critical," says Marco Davis, former NCLR leadership director. "There was a core of vice presidents who really knew what they were doing, and had a great relationship with each other. So Raul could let them go— they were able to excel and make day-to-day decisions." This structure also freed up Yzaguirre to focus on developing new program ideas, building external relationships, fundraising, and executing high-level strategy.

The most critical point to emphasize is that these are not vice presidents in title only—they play a substantial leadership role both inside and outside the organization. "We empowered and trained our staff to become spokespersons for our organization," says Yzaguirre. One good signal that Yzaguirre truly shared power came when Muñoz was awarded a MacArthur Fellowship "genius grant" in 2000, an honor usually reserved for executive directors. She has had a major impact as a leader on immigration policy in her own right. (Muñoz left NCLR in 2009 when she was appointed by President Obama as U.S. director of intergovernmental affairs.)

The Exploratorium presents a slightly different case in shared leadership—and illustrates the dangers of not developing a strong executive team as an organization grows.[12] In fact, it took the founder's death and the hiring of a new executive director before the Exploratorium evolved to a more collective leadership model.

Founded by the visionary and charismatic Frank Oppenheimer in the late 1960s, the museum operated informally under his leadership. Oppenheimer was less interested in building an organization than in catalyzing a movement to change science education, so he didn't spend much time on things like management, budgets, or systems. The nonprofit was thrown into chaos when he died in 1985. There was no formal management structure, second-in-command, or empowered leadership team—and no succession plan.

"After his death, [the Exploratorium] almost didn't survive," says Christina Orth, chief of staff. "But people were committed to his vision and legacy. People didn't want to let this die." The organization operated under several interim directors while a search was conducted. The first executive director brought in from the outside was rejected by the staff after only two years as not being a good cultural fit. Ultimately, five years passed before the board hired Goéry Delacôte, a director at the National Center for Science Research in France.

"I took over when it was almost ready to die and took it to the grown-up phase," says Delacôte, who introduced professional management practices to the organization. (In 2006, Delacôte decided to move back to Europe after nearly fifteen years running the nonprofit; he was replaced by a former Exploratorium executive, Dennis Bartels, who had most recently been running another science education nonprofit. Bartels continues to run the Exploratorium today.)

Part of Delacôte's strategy, in addition to building management systems, was to develop a strong executive team. "Goéry [Delacôte] wasn't a publicity hound; the spotlight wasn't on him," says board member Ann Bowers. "In contrast to other nonprofits,

Goéry was building a team. Their ideas were listened to, they were respected, and they were definitely part of the decision-making process. In other organizations, the sun shines on the director—but I don't think you build an organization that way."

GREAT LEADERS LAST

In studying these successful executive directors and their top teams, we were struck by the fact that many of them have extraordinarily long tenure. Although about half of the groups we studied had been through at least one executive transition (some had withstood several), half were still founder led at the time we concluded our research in 2006. Almost all of them, however, have had one executive director at the helm for decades. In the cases in which the founder left early, it was an early successor we call the "growth leader" who took on a founder-like role and who stayed with the nonprofit a long time.

This finding was surprising because the data show that most nonprofit executives last an average of only four years on the job. A CompassPoint study titled *Daring to Lead* looked at executive turnover in the social sector and found that just 25 percent of nonprofit executives expect to stay in their jobs for more than five years.[13] In the business sector, most CEOs last around five to seven years. Leaders like Jack Welch at GE—who was in the CEO role for twenty years—are much more rare.

But among the groups we studied, the leaders had stayed, on average, twenty years as of 2006. (See Figure 7.1.) Further, many of them have a few senior executives who have also been with the organization for a long period of time, as in the case of NCLR.

Why have these high-impact leaders stayed so long? After all, it's not for the money. By nonprofit standards, these executives are well compensated, but they could all earn more in the private sector. (We explore compensation in Chapter Eight.) And it's not as though these jobs are easy—on the contrary, leading in complex, changing environments without a lot of formal power is challenging, to say the least. From our interviews with nonprofit CEOs, we came to see that they stayed because they are so passionate about their cause—their role is not just a job, but a *calling*.

Figure 7.1.   CEO Tenure Much Longer Than Average.

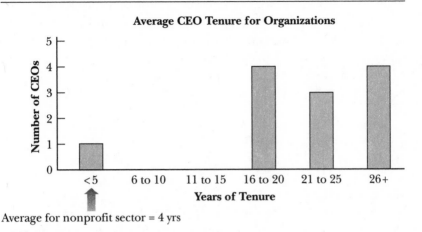

Average CEO Tenure for Organizations

Average for nonprofit sector = 4 yrs

Note: Figure illustrates CEO or growth leader tenure as of 2006.

"The novelty doesn't wear off," says Fred Krupp, president of EDF. "If what you really want to do with your life is have an impact on things that matter, then what I am doing is so satisfying." These leaders all share a relentless focus on results and a desire to have real impact—which often takes decades, not years.

Further, we believe that the very success of these executive directors has enabled them to stay longer—success breeds success. As these organizations achieve real impact, their leaders accumulate more reasons for staying, both financial and emotional. *Daring to Lead* noted that larger organizations have leaders with longer tenure, speculating that "presumably the nature of working at a larger organization—higher pay, more staff support, and perhaps prestige and community influence—make sticking it out longer seem more desirable."[14] Nonprofit boards are less likely to force a transition if both the leader, and the organization, are successful.

Although some might argue that such long tenure is unhealthy (and with a megalomaniac director, it would be), we believe that continuity among these executives and senior managers contributes to success. For one thing, executive directors and senior managers spend much of their time cultivating relationships—if a leader leaves, some of these are lost. Similarly, most nonprofit work relies on tacit knowledge embodied in the staff; when top leaders leave, the organization loses accumulated wisdom and skills. And because the issues that nonprofits are trying to solve are so complex, constant leadership turnover causes the organization to focus more internally, rather than on external results. Leadership continuity keeps them headed down their path to success.

FOUNDER'S SYNDROME AND SUCCESSION PLANNING

Not surprisingly, many less successful nonprofits do not share the longevity, depth, or breadth of leadership of these high-impact organizations. Within the sector as a whole, turnover is rampant, burnout rates are high, and many organizations struggle just to stay afloat. We know many cases of nonprofits led by charismatic but egocentric individuals who are unable to let go and truly share leadership—a phenomenon known as founder's syndrome. These groups run the risk of imploding, as the Exploratorium almost did, when their founder either leaves or dies. Succession planning is an important, but often neglected, issue within the field.

As Phil Truluck of The Heritage Foundation observes of his peers, "Quite frankly, a lot of these conservative groups were started by strong individuals who were never willing to release control of the organization," he says. "It will be a real problem over the next ten years as they retire. A lot of them have never delegated things down."

Habitat for Humanity is the only nonprofit we studied that is only now moving toward a model of greater shared leadership—after a difficult founder transition.[15] Habitat was started by the classic visionary entrepreneur, Millard Fuller, who was uninterested in organizational management and did not develop a broad and empowered executive team—though he did have a small group of critical people on whom he relied.

Habitat was cofounded in the late 1970s by Fuller and his wife, Linda, as a Christian housing mission. Fuller was tireless in his efforts to promote Habitat, and the organization's success can be attributed in large part to his entrepreneurial and inspirational leadership. "You can't discount the necessity of the charismatic, visionary founder," says Denny Bender, former senior vice president of communications. "Habitat flourished because of Millard's insatiable drive to rid the world of substandard housing. It's an engine that's essential to rapid growth; it attracts the support and resources necessary to grow. A good idea is not enough—it takes someone to lead the parade."

Despite his ability to inspire others, however, Fuller was much more interested in building a movement than an organization— and he expected others to be as tireless and self-sacrificing as he was. "The key ingredient of a movement is abandon—you sell out to the movement," says Fuller. "Martin Luther King sold out to the cause and gave his life for it. You don't hold back: You get up at 5 AM and go until midnight. That's what it takes: passion, commitment, dedication. You don't build a movement being concerned about pension plans and salaries."

Not surprisingly, Fuller didn't pay much attention to things such as staff capacity, salaries, or other management systems— all of which started to cause problems as the organization grew. Ultimately, senior staff and the Habitat board worried that the movement would collapse without a strong organization to sustain it. "The board said, 'We don't want to be called a movement—you can't plan a movement, and we want Habitat to be something you can plan and move forward,'" recalls Clive Rainey, former director of community relations. "Movements don't last; organizations do."

Eventually, the Habitat movement was in danger of eclipsing the organization's ability to effectively manage its network and sustain its impact. Despite sensational external impact and a fabulous reputation, Habitat was chaotic internally. Staff morale was low, and the organization was stretched too thin and was dependent on many volunteers who didn't necessarily have the skills to manage a multimillion-dollar global nonprofit. Although the board wanted to build internal capacity, Fuller was less interested. He and the board disagreed on his authority and succession planning. The struggles became public knowledge when a former employee accused Fuller of sexual harassment. Eventually Fuller was fired by the board.

The transition that followed was difficult for some staff members, but Habitat came through it successfully. Fuller went on to launch another housing organization, and the board conducted a national search for a replacement, while an interim leader filled in. (Fuller died in 2008, shortly after the first edition of this book was published.)

The nonprofit ended up hiring a CEO with impeccable credentials: Jonathan Reckford, a self-described born-again Christian, a former executive with Best Buy and Disney, an executive pastor of a large Presbyterian church, and an MBA from Stanford. Reckford combined passion for the housing cause, a personal commitment to the faith-based community, and the managerial experience needed to run a billion-dollar global organization.

As the Habitat case illustrates, founder's syndrome is a significant issue in the nonprofit sector—and one that can imperil an organization if not handled well. Of the twelve organizations we studied, seven are still led by founders (or the primary growth leaders), and are only now beginning to discuss succession planning. The other organizations we studied have all undergone at least one leadership transition, if not several. One organization—Feeding America—has had a new executive director nearly every five years, in part because it is a "bottom-up" nonprofit whose headquarters report to its many local food-bank members.

In fact, during the course of our research, five of the twelve organizations we studied underwent a leadership transition at the top. In addition to Habitat, NCLR, the Exploratorium, and City Year, in 2006 Feeding America brought on former Delta Airlines senior executive Vicki Escarra as their seventh (and current) CEO.

Interestingly, none of these nonprofits appointed a CEO successor from within, despite having strong executive teams. By contrast, most successful for-profit businesses promote new CEOs from within their own company.[16] The fact that these high-impact organizations have all recruited a new executive director from outside is somewhat surprising, given their bench strength. We attribute this to the fact that high-impact nonprofits often need a charismatic, externally oriented leader to speak on behalf of the organization and appeal to outside constituents, whereas the COO and executive teams often perform a more managerial function.

Many of the other organizations we studied had just begun to address the issue of founder transition. YouthBuild USA had only recently developed a senior management team and expanded organizational leadership beyond founder and president Dorothy Stoneman. Although it didn't yet have a formal succession plan in place, its leadership was much stronger than even five years before. "If I were hit by a truck, YouthBuild would survive," says Stoneman. "We now have a COO, four senior vice presidents, and five vice presidents—and another level of senior program managers with five to ten years' experience."

Share Our Strength is another organization strongly identified with its founder, Bill Shore. It has not yet addressed the issue of succession planning, although there is a strong executive team in place. "Bill Shore is inseparable from Share Our Strength—he is a huge asset," says Mike McCurry, board member and former Clinton presidential adviser. "But I think there is some recognition that we will have to be able to project stability and continuity beyond the founder. An organization has to transcend the founder if it is to be successful."

The Invisible, Invincible Board

No discussion of nonprofit leadership would be complete without addressing the fundamental role of the board in leading an organization. Many experts we interviewed, however, almost uniformly failed to mention this role. It didn't come up as a critical success factor among senior managers, outside stakeholders, or even board members themselves. This was somewhat surprising, given the amount of attention paid to building strong boards within the social sector.

However, most of the *executive directors* we interviewed maintained that their relationship with the board was critical. It is "true but not new": if the board isn't effective, it can sink an organization, but if things are going well, the board rarely gets credit. Perhaps that's the hallmark of a truly great nonprofit board—it plays a significant role leading the organization, but it does so from behind the scenes.

Some fascinating trends emerged once we started teasing out the various threads of our research. The high-impact boards we studied are fairly large in size, and they have a handful of long-tenured members. The executive directors share power with their boards—neither one is really on top or has ultimate control of the organization. The boards are highly engaged; they work well with the executive leadership and have evolved as the organization has grown, although their governance models and roles vary depending on the context in which they operate.

The size of these boards, particularly in comparison with corporate boards, was eye opening, ranging from twenty to forty people as of 2006. (See Table 7.2.) Perhaps this is because high-impact nonprofits must engage so many stakeholders, both internal and external, to have impact. They need broad boards that represent a range of skills, backgrounds, and social networks. "It has to be a mix: you have to have people with money and people representing the community," says the Exploratorium's Delacôte. "A board has to be a mirror of the society in which it is functioning."

Like the continuity of leadership among the executive directors and senior staff we studied, there is also a great deal of continuity of leadership on the boards of high-impact organizations. Many of these groups have board members who have been around for years—although they balance this continuity with some turnover to allow for new energy and ideas. "We have six

TABLE 7.2. LARGER THAN AVERAGE BOARDS (AS OF 2006).

	Number of Board Members
Environmental Defense Fund	42
Exploratorium	28
National Council of La Raza	26
Teach For America	26
Habitat for Humanity	25
Feeding America	21
City Year	21
The Heritage Foundation	20
Share Our Strength	20
Center on Budget and Policy Priorities	16
YouthBuild USA	15

board members who have been here for more than twenty-five years," says Virginia Carollo Rubin, development director of the Exploratorium who also served as interim director during several executive transitions. "They are really dedicated. There's something about this place that feeds them—the activity, the mission, the vitality of the place. People aren't here for a personal agenda or for the distinction."

The executive directors and top teams have all found a way to actively share leadership with the board to further their mission. In most cases, the organization is equally led by the executive director and the board—each has a critical but different role to play. This was an interesting finding given that many boards tend to micromanage or play an incredibly hands-on role, often doing much of the work, particularly in start-up or early growth phases. But in these high-impact nonprofits, the board balances its power with that of the executive director and senior staff, or works in partnership with them, rather than dominating. We believe that this balance reflects both a shared leadership model internally and that these groups are in a more mature stage in the life cycle of organizational growth.

In some cases, an organization started out being led and dominated by a founding board, but then transitioned to stronger executive director leadership and shared power. For example, NCLR had a controlling but unaccountable board when Raul Yzaguirre first took over in 1974. (The nonprofit was founded by a collective group that then appointed Yzaguirre director.) He didn't have either the authority or accountability he needed as executive director, so he confronted the board with a request for change—and threatened to walk away if they wouldn't give him more power to make critical operating decisions without board approval. In other words, he lobbied for shared leadership, rather than a hierarchical model with the board on top.

"We had a strong board chair with a political agenda, and we were defined by his relationships and affiliations," recounts Yzaguirre. "It was just a runaway board. It was unaccountable, and it made the staff unaccountable." To its credit, the board gave up some of its power in order to prevent Yzaguirre from quitting. From that time on, he and the board were able to operate effectively together in a true balance of power.

198 Forces for Good

These boards have a high level of engagement; more critical, they have a positive relationship with the executive director. Research shows that many nonprofit executives do not have constructive relationships with their boards, a factor often cited as a reason for high turnover. "Executives who are unhappy with their boards are more than twice as likely to be planning near-term departures as those who have positive perceptions of their boards," according to *Daring to Lead*.[17] The study found that only one in three nonprofit executives strongly agreed that their "boards challenge them in ways that make them more effective" or viewed their boards as "an engaged leadership body."

Our research seems to echo this general perception. Although we don't have deep data on the board-executive relationship, our observation is that these executives have a strong and supportive relationship with their boards. "Most of my colleagues were always saying, 'I hate my board,'" says Delacôte of other science museum directors. "But I was always saying the opposite. The work relationship was superb."

The role that the board plays varies from organization to organization. Most play a fundraising role (with the exception of YouthBuild USA and Self-Help), and board members help the nonprofit access resources either directly or indirectly, through social networks. "Fred pays a lot of attention to building a very engaged board," says Marcia Aronoff, senior vice president for programs at EDF. "A lot of cultivation [of donors] comes from the board making introductions to their networks. It's a huge part of our resource strategy." As we saw in Chapter Four, board members are often the group's most powerful evangelists, helping make introductions or broker critical relationships in government and business.

Further, most of these executives say their board is quite involved in helping set high-level strategy and in advising the top executives on critical issues. For this reason, they are often deliberately diverse, rounding out the skills or backgrounds of the senior team, with a mix that often includes people with legal, marketing, or finance expertise, or experience and networks in government or business. (This may be another reason for their large size.)

Many boards have also gone through transitions as the organizations themselves have evolved. For example, the Share Our Strength board "started out as friends and family—a founder's board, really," says Bill Shore. "We didn't pick people for their name, or ability to give resources. We picked them for their ability to think strategically. Then we outgrew that board, and looked for communications experience, corporate experience, and so on. It's a very different board today but still pretty engaged."

One thing is certain, however: strong leadership requires that an organization maintain a delicate balance of power among the executive director, the executive team, and the board. As F. Van Kasper, chairman emeritus and board member of the Exploratorium, says, "You have people [on the board] who have bought into a mission statement that is strong, and they are very committed. So it can create a very dedicated staff and board environment. I think that consistency of the two working together has really provided for the success of the organization."

LEADERSHIP MATTERS

At a time when the social sector is growing in size and importance, the need for skilled leadership has never been greater. And as our findings illustrate, leadership is needed not just at the executive director level but also among senior managers, board members, and site staff. Despite the importance of shared leadership, however, it's not always easy to find the top talent that nonprofits need.

All the organizations in our research cited lack of talent as the second most significant barrier to growing their organization and expanding their impact, just after lack of funding. And studies show that the social sector is facing an impending leadership crisis. Just as demand is growing, supply is falling, due to the number of baby boomers retiring, a high rate of burnout among nonprofit executives, and the failure of most organizations to develop human resources within their organizations. Although these nonprofits have done a good job cultivating leadership within their organizations—including paying top talent, as we'll see in the next chapter—that doesn't mean it has been easy for them. They go out of their way and invest time, money, and significant energy in sharing leadership throughout their organizations.

As Tom Tierney, founder of the nonprofit consulting firm Bridgespan, wrote in an important report on the topic, more nonprofits should follow this example: "It takes long, hard work to build an excellent leadership team. Many successful business CEOs spend well over half their time on people-related issues. In contrast, executive directors of nonprofits tend to devote the lion's share of their time to fundraising."[18]

Leadership matters a great deal to nonprofits, in part because they are primarily service organizations whose assets are intangible; their programs and services are only as good as the people they hire and retain. All the more reason that the social sector needs to wake up to new models of leadership. A report from the Center for Creative Leadership says, "To expand leadership capacity, organizations must not only develop individuals, but also develop the leadership capacity of collectives (for example, work groups, teams, and communities). They must develop the connections between individuals, between collectives within the organization, and between the organization and key constituents and stakeholders in its environment."[19] Of course, all of this is easier said than done, but our nonprofits provide some examples of how to get started.

By cultivating internal leadership and building bench strength, high-impact nonprofits have shored up their capacity to support growth. By building strong and engaged boards and developing a supportive partnership between the board and the executive director, they ensure longer tenure. Ultimately, these nonprofits have learned that true power, both professionally and organizationally, comes not from concentrating authority and responsibility at the top but from spreading it as widely as possible. It comes from a culture of leadership that permeates the organization, one that freely gives power away.

CHAPTER SEVEN HIGHLIGHTS

- **Great nonprofit leaders share power.** Wise CEOs recognize that they must share power if they are to unleash and magnify the potential of their organizations. They learn to let go to have greater impact.
- **Let many leadership styles bloom.** There is no one type of leader who is most successful at creating a high-impact

organization. Instead, many different styles can succeed (charismatic, humble, strategic, detail oriented) if leaders are willing to put their cause, and their organization, above their own egos.

- **To relinquish control, hire a COO.** Many CEOs either start with or eventually hire a second-in-command. Regardless of his or her title, this person usually focuses more on internal management, so that the director can focus more on external leadership.

- **Empower your executive team.** The best nonprofit leaders build their bench strength by creating strong executive teams and giving these top managers real authority and accountability for the organization's success. This approach helps retain top talent over time.

- **Great leaders last.** Many of the executives at these nonprofits have been with their organizations much longer than the sector average, or even the typical CEO. Longevity and leadership continuity help these nonprofits succeed.

- **Develop a succession plan.** Great leaders also know when it's time to go. Create a transition plan with the board that prepares for that day. Get ready for the change by cultivating leadership within the organization and preparing to hire a new director from the outside.

- **Build a big and strategic board.** Although the trend these days is toward smaller boards, the nonprofits discussed in this book all have relatively large and diverse boards. But quality matters, too. Board members should be highly committed and should bring a diverse range of skills, perspectives, and social networks to help the organization and its cause.

- **Balance power.** Many leaders try to minimize their interactions with their board, or they perpetually fight with them, whereas great nonprofits have a positive relationship with the board. They share leadership to advance the larger cause.

CHAPTER EIGHT

SUSTAINING IMPACT

Teach For America was only a few years old when its founder and president, Wendy Kopp, found herself facing a mutinous staff. The entire organization had convened in August 1992 in Los Angeles for its second summer training institute, an annual program designed to train new teachers before sending them out into classrooms. But after more than two chaotic years in start-up mode, staff members were fed up with the long hours and low pay, the absence of organizational systems, and the unclear decision-making authority. Staff members told Kopp they would jump ship if things didn't change. The episode became known as the "coup de Kopp."[1]

To make matters worse, the mutiny dovetailed with a major funding crisis: Kopp needed to raise $700,000 within four weeks to avoid shutting the doors. It was the perfect storm. At that moment, Teach For America was on the brink—not of breakthrough impact, but of implosion.

Kopp had launched the ambitious group in 1989, based on an idea she developed in her senior thesis at Princeton University. Teach For America would be a national teaching corps, placing young college graduates in America's neediest schools, while working simultaneously to reform the larger educational system. From the outset, Kopp's vision was grand. She disregarded early advice to start with a single pilot site and scale up slowly, insisting that her idea would require an immediate national presence and a corps of five hundred teachers.

"Almost everyone advised me to start smaller," she recounts in her book, *One Day, All Children.* . . . "I should recruit fifty people for one site, learn from that experience, and then expand from there. But this perspective was counter to my very conception of what Teach For America would be. This was not going to be a little nonprofit organization or a model teacher-training program. This was going to be a movement."

Kopp nearly killed herself to launch this movement. She worked twenty-hour days for the first year, at times only sleeping "every other night," she says. Passionate and persistent, she obtained donated office space in New York, scrounged up borrowed furniture, and sent out thousands of fundraising letters. She also recruited a small staff of young education advocates to join her crusade. They traveled around the country, recruiting the first class of corps members from college campuses, without yet knowing where the teachers would be placed, how they would be paid, or what support they might need. They were making it up as they went along.

Like most start-ups, the organization was in constant crisis mode those first few years. Meetings regularly ran until three in the morning; few management systems were in place; everyone was paid the same meager $25,000 salary; and the entire staff reported to Kopp. To make matters worse, most of the recent college grads Kopp hired had never held a real job before, let alone operated a national nonprofit. The organization ran on idealism, caffeine, and the largesse of foundations and individual donors who dared to take a risk on her dream.

Although she was able to persuade her staff to stay after the "coup," Kopp realized she was in over her head. So when she received a lucrative job offer to join Edison Schools, an education start-up run by entrepreneur Chris Whittle, she was sorely tempted to abandon Teach For America in exchange for less overwhelming responsibility. Ultimately, Kopp declined his offer, but not before a concerned Whittle loaned her a top executive, vice chairman Nick Glover, to help her sort out her financial and organizational crisis.

Glover convened a three-day retreat at the Waldorf-Astoria Hotel in New York with Kopp and a handful of her most trusted staff members. He told the group to put more time, energy, and resources into fundraising and to balance out its large program staff with more development employees. (At the time, Kopp and one other colleague were the only ones raising funds, while sixty staff members worked on the program side.) He also advised Kopp to put together a senior management team and to delegate more responsibility. Glover convinced her to let go of the egalitarian pay structure, and he helped implement some basic management and decision-making systems to help things run more smoothly.

"It worked," writes Kopp. "Within weeks Teach For America felt like a different place. [The] organizational difficulties had taken their toll. . . . But we had refined our approach to selecting and training corps members. We had beefed up our systems for providing them with ongoing support. We had raised the funding we needed to cover our costs. And Nick Glover had restored my sense of possibility. With the lessons he taught us, I figured we could accomplish anything."

Teach For America wasn't out of the woods just yet. Following the coup were what Kopp now calls the "dark years," a lean time in which many of the group's initial grants expired. The nonprofit was also stretched thin, with too few staff members running too many programs and a lack of the organizational resources needed to sustain rapid growth.

But that first crisis marked a real turning point. It was the moment when Teach For America, at the brink of failure, realized that it needed to build an *organization* to sustain its *movement*. Over the next few years, Kopp and her senior team cut less critical programs, reduced costs to meet their actual budget (rather than continuously raising more money to support too many programs), created a long-term fundraising plan, developed management systems, and invested in organizational capacity and people. With this stable foundation, Teach For America finally began to take off.

Today, the organization is widely considered to be one of the great success stories of recent times. By 2006, Teach For America had grown to encompass a staff of 650, a budget of $70 million, strong leadership, and an increasingly recognized brand. (By 2011, its budget approached an astonishing $240 million.) The organization—and its influential alumni—have become a force to be reckoned with in the education field. But had a few things gone differently back in the early 1990s, we might not be writing about it in this book. Indeed, the group might have been yet another nonprofit to fall into the chasm between high expectations and insufficient organizational capacity.

CROSSING THE CHASM

Like Teach For America, many of the organizations we've written about have faced difficult times. Although they are truly great in terms of what they have achieved, their impact hasn't come easily—even though it may look that way in hindsight or from a distance. For the majority, success has been a bumpy road rather than a smooth path. Several of the organizations we studied faced near-death experiences, when they almost imploded or ran out of money, or when their operations couldn't keep up with their ambitious goals.

For the National Council of La Raza (NCLR), the moment of reckoning came early in its history, not long after Raul Yzaguirre had stepped in as director in the late 1970s. (His title later shifted to president and CEO.) At the time, NCLR received more than half of its funding from government grants, which were slashed after Ronald Reagan was elected president in 1980. The nonprofit's budget went from $5 million to less than $2 million almost overnight, and NCLR was forced to lay off 70 percent of its staff. It wasn't clear that the group would survive, until Yzaguirre formed a corporate council and aggressively pursued alternative sources of funding.

Many of the other organizations in our sample have faced their own crises of funding or capacity, times when it looked as though they might not pull through or when their organization was stretched too thin. And the social sector is littered with has-beens and also-rans—nonprofits that have a good idea but never achieve significant impact, or those that are unable to sustain impact because they haven't been able to secure the basics. "The gap between the capacity of nonprofits and the size of the problems they are attempting to address often looks more like a chasm,"[2] writes William Foster, who at the time was a director at The Bridgespan Group, a nonprofit consulting firm.

Despite the desire among many groups to get to a certain scale—or even just to maintain steady state—it is incredibly difficult to do so. All nonprofits face barriers to finding ongoing funding and to investing in their own infrastructure and organizations.

For one thing, most nonprofits don't have a revenue stream to cover their costs, as successful for-profit companies do. They can't depend on profit margins—they exist to correct market imperfections and to provide for those people who can't always pay. Instead, they must ask third parties (foundations, government, individuals) to donate more money each year to deliver on their mission. "Most companies eventually become self-funding," says Eileen Jacobs, a City Year board member and former business executive. "But nonprofits don't have that luxury. Most nonprofits do not have huge endowment funds; they have to sell their story year after year. Having to raise money to live day-by-day is tough."

Businesses also have access to sophisticated capital markets to raise additional money as they expand. Corporations can issue stocks or bonds to invest in their organizations as they grow, and they can tap into an impressive array of financial institutions designed to meet their needs at each stage of development, including "angel" investors, venture capitalists, investment bankers, and various lending firms. But the social sector's capital markets are not as developed, a topic that scholars and practitioners have recently begun to study and discuss.[3]

There is also a *disincentive* for nonprofits to invest in the critical organizational elements—people, infrastructure, and systems—that make success sustainable. In the private sector, investors recognize the importance of not just investing in a product but also supporting the company behind that product. As Christine Letts, William Ryan, and Allen Grossman argued in their influential 1997 *Harvard Business Review* article, "Virtuous Capital," nonprofit investors have a great deal to learn from their for-profit counterparts.[4] The social sector has inherited an erroneous belief that every penny should go directly to programs rather than overhead, as if programs could deliver themselves.

As a result of these dynamics, most nonprofits have a more difficult time reaching the minimum scale that they need to achieve their goals, let alone maintaining the same size or even building a broader platform for future impact. Our point is not that these organizations need to be *huge* to have big impact. On the contrary: the Center on Budget and Policy Priorities has achieved significant impact with its $13 million budget, as has Habitat with its $1 billion global budget as of 2006. (See Figure 8.1.) These two groups have very different missions and goals, which lead to very different business models and funding strategies, as we'll see later.

FIGURE 8.1.   TOTAL REVENUES (2005).

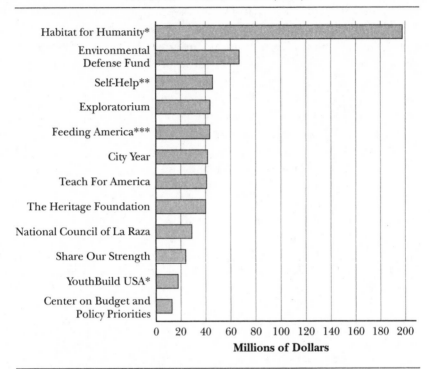

Notes: *Headquarters only—does not include affiliate budgets.
     **Net revenue spread.
     ***Does not include value of in-kind donations.

But once a nonprofit gets to the size it deems effective to support its strategy, it can have difficulty *sustaining* its organization and its impact.

Herein lies the challenge: most social entrepreneurs want to scale up or at least sustain their current levels of impact, but they face a powerful countervailing force. All the leaders discussed in our book grappled with how to get more bang for their buck, how to maximize their results without increasing their costs, and how to raise enough capital to build their organizations. Great nonprofits know that they must continually close the gap between their outward-looking vision—their constant desire for greater impact—and their need to invest in themselves.

Three Critical Elements to Sustain Impact

In the previous chapters, we've illustrated how these twelve great nonprofits leverage forces outside their organizational boundaries in order to achieve more impact. In addition to focusing externally, however, they also need to be able to deliver on their promises. Although we recognize that not all the groups are perfectly managed, neither can they afford to neglect the basics, such as keeping good people, raising money, and building the right infrastructure. At the same time that they work externally to *increase* their impact by applying the six practices, they must also invest internally to *sustain* their impact. It's not "either-or"; it's "both-and."

Reaching for ambitious goals and building organizational capacity can be mutually reinforcing: by working with and through other sectors, nonprofits can also find the financial resources necessary to sustain themselves. External partners—government, business, individuals—often provide money, in-kind donations, credibility, volunteer labor, and other critical resources. As we've seen in the preceding chapters, successful groups can influence government as both a *means* to funding and as an *end* in itself—to achieve policy change. Similarly, they can work with businesses to obtain resources for their cause and to influence business practices. They can engage individuals and work through nonprofit networks to raise funds; they can also mobilize these networks to achieve grassroots or cultural change.

High-impact nonprofits recognize that there are three critical elements needed in order to maintain and deepen their impact over time: *people, capital,* and *infrastructure.* These are the "necessary but not sufficient" ingredients that enable them to build "good enough" organizations. In our view, none of these elements really constitute a practice, but they are nonetheless essential to these organizations' ability to sustain their impact.

1. *People:* **develop a people strategy and invest heavily in top performers.** Every one of these organizations cited their staff as a critical success factor. Although all nonprofits rely heavily on employees, we discovered that great nonprofits

have developed particular capacities for hiring, developing, and retaining top talent that can serve as examples for other organizations.

2. *Capital:* **find the *right* sources of funding.** None of these groups could keep going without having one or more sustainable funding mechanisms—the critical input that fuels their outputs or impact. Their sources of support may vary, but successful groups integrate fundraising with their strategy, and they find ways to diversify these sources over time to reduce their financial risks.

3. *Infrastructure:* **invest in overhead, despite the pressure to look lean.** All the groups have reached a point in their growth at which they needed to invest heavily in information technology, buildings, or management systems and build their own organizational capacity. They've found creative ways to raise capital for these needs.

PEOPLE: INVEST IN TOP TALENT

In Chapter Seven, we saw how great nonprofits retain their senior leaders over time, first and foremost because they empower their top team. When asked what keeps them at their jobs, many top managers cite a passion for the mission, the ability to make a difference, and the other committed people with whom they work. The same goes for midlevel and junior staff. Most often, people initially gravitate toward nonprofit work for purpose and passion.

But intrinsic motivation is not always enough to retain people, particularly over long periods of time. Successful nonprofits have learned that they need a *people strategy* to keep the best and brightest talent on their teams. Surprisingly, only about half of the organizations we examined have a formal human resources director or department. However, all of them have learned to do a few things right with respect to their senior staff, and these policies tend to trickle down to midlevel managers and entry-level positions as well.

Focus First on What, Then Who

Many of the nonprofits we studied said that it's important to "get the right people on the bus," and a few even quoted Jim

Collins's book *Good to Great*, which included a chapter on that topic.[5] Collins claims that successful businesses need to focus on "first who, then what." That is, if they first get the right people on board, they can then figure out where and how to steer the bus, in terms of their strategy and tactics.

But in the nonprofit world, it's actually "first what, then who." All the organizations we studied are guided first and foremost by their *mission,* and this purpose is the primary reason a person will take the job. These groups look for new hires with a passion for their mission, and a strong cultural fit. In other words, they already know where the bus is headed; they're looking for good people who are going in the same direction. Although the strategy or tactics may change over time, their overall cause is unlikely to change.

"For us it's mission first," says Martin Eakes, founder of Self-Help. "You can't work at Self-Help longer than a week and not have someone raise the question, 'Is this in line with our mission?' This is not a place where people come for a paycheck. If this is not a calling, and you're not primarily motivated by the mission, get off the bus and leave us a seat."

Some of the nonprofits go so far as to say that a person's fit with the organization's mission matters even more than basic skills. "The skills matter, but they matter less than the passion, because you can learn the skills," says Cecilia Muñoz formerly of National Council of La Raza. "The focus and commitment you can't learn—that's what makes good advocates."

Pay to Play

Although nonprofit leaders don't take their jobs *because* of the money, in order for them to stay (particularly those raising families or those without a second income or independent wealth), it is important to establish a base salary that at least makes the financial equation palatable. It is one thing to take a low-paying job just out of college to follow your bliss, and another thing entirely to support a family or face retirement on a $40,000 salary, particularly in major urban areas. Unlike the stereotypical nonprofit, these organizations don't burn out their talent with entry-level wages. *It's both mission and then money that matter, in that order.* Indeed, a recent study confirmed that nonprofit executives who are very dissatisfied with their compensation are twice as likely to leave within a year as executives who are satisfied.[6]

We discovered that successful groups are willing to compensate generously to attract and retain top talent. They "pay to play." Ten out of the twelve organizations discussed in this book aim to compensate at the higher end of the nonprofit pay scale, relative to other organizations of the same size and in similar fields and regions. (See Figure 8.2.) They didn't all start out that way—most paid the paltry salaries that characterize any start-up—but over time, they have moved to the top tier.

FIGURE 8.2.   WELL-PAID EXECUTIVES (2005).

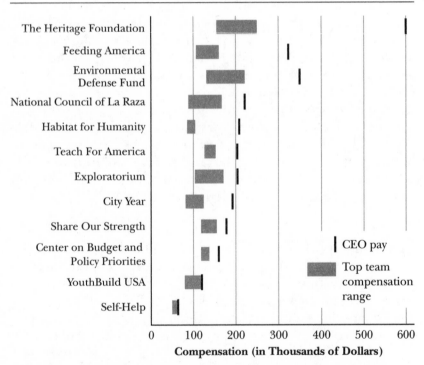

Note: This figure includes data from 2005 or the most recently available year before 2005. Data were provided by the organization or were taken from the organization's 990 form published by GuideStar, and include salary and bonuses where applicable, but not benefits.

These nonprofits also offer competitive benefits, which enables them to keep their best performers. They don't constantly rely on young people who are willing to work for lower wages but who don't have the experience or expertise necessary to generate substantial impact.

Environmental Defense Fund (EDF) came to this conclusion about fifteen years into its growth. "In the early 1980s, the board didn't have a pension or benefits plan," recalls Michael Bean, a senior attorney who had been with the organization twenty-four years at the time. "They had to ask, 'Do we want to keep the good people we've hired, or . . . have a staff constantly in their twenties with new ideas?'" The board voted for the former, and increased compensation and benefits to keep senior people, many of whom joined the organization in the 1970s.

Although senior-level salaries are still lower than in the private sector, compensation at these organizations is competitive among their peers. Some are even able to entice talented leaders from business, who take pay cuts to work on issues they care about. Offering respectable salaries makes a difference. For example, vice presidents at many of the groups discussed in this book earned $130,000 or more per year in 2005. In addition, many of the organizations provide high-quality health care and retirement benefits.

Only two organizations in our sample did not compensate at the top of the nonprofit pay scale at the time we studied them. Under newly appointed CEO Jonathan Reckford, Habitat for Humanity began moving from paying 20 percent lower than other Christian nonprofits to compensating at the median level. But for years founder Millard Fuller relied heavily on unpaid staff, who worked full-time in return for "Pig-checks," or certificates that could be redeemed at the local Piggly Wiggly grocery store. These volunteers didn't necessarily have the skills required for their jobs as the organization grew.

Self-Help has a similarly ideological view, based on a philosophy that the spread between the highest- and lowest-paid positions should be small and that external markets should not determine the value of an employee. Under founder Martin Eakes's formula, top salaries at Self-Help in 2005 were capped at around $63,000 (much lower than the other organizations we examined). However, the nonprofit has raised entry-level salaries, so that the lowest-paid staff members make relatively more than their peers at other nonprofits. In this sense, Self-Help also takes compensation off the table. It doesn't even attempt to compete in the talent marketplace—it has made an ethical, not an economic, choice about compensation. You join Self-Help for the mission, not the money. (Whether this compensation approach is sustainable remains to be seen; several staff members questioned it in our interviews with them.)

In addition to paying well, some of the groups have moved to performance-based pay. The Heritage Foundation was an early pioneer of the approach. "We [were] one of the first think tanks to set up a goal system in the 1980s," says Philip Truluck, executive vice president. "Other groups come out and ask how they can be as great as we are. Well, goals are set and goals are measured. We are still one of the few [nonprofits] that set up a bonus system."

Create Nonmanagement Career Paths

People often come to work in the social sector because they are passionate about an issue such as education or the environment, and they have skills or deep knowledge in the area. But in many nonprofits, the only way to move up is to take on more management and administrative responsibilities. The move often takes leaders away from their core competencies, such as advocacy, research, writing, or running programs.

Although all the organizations we examined have promoted internal people into management, many have also created nonmanagement career paths for star senior staff: economists, scientists, policy researchers, analysts, or other experts. "There was a view that moving up into management meant success. But we tried to create career paths that weren't automatically management. If you are a great researcher, then you can stay here. I wish I had pinpointed that beforehand," says Truluck of The Heritage Foundation.

In many ways, these groups are structured more like a university—with a division between administration (management) and faculty (subject experts)—than like a typical business. In fact, a number of them, particularly those that have a strong research, analysis, and advocacy component, have PhDs on staff, including the Center on Budget and Policy Priorities, the Exploratorium,

EDF, and The Heritage Foundation. Their ability to keep subject experts, along with talented managers, means that they have high retention rates in the senior ranks. We believe that this is a fundamental factor for sustaining impact at extraordinarily high levels.

"The other day I calculated that around thirty people are here today who started during [founder Frank Oppenheimer's] time," says Robert Semper, director of the Center for Learning and Teaching at the Exploratorium. "In my case, it's because I've been able to get involved and have had enough learning opportunities that have allowed me to maintain my engagement."

Let Go of Underperformers

"You never wish you'd waited longer to fire an employee who wasn't working out," says Bill Shore, founder of Share Our Strength. He and the other CEOs we met have had plenty of hiring successes, but they've also made some blunders along the way. It is hard for any manager to let go of a committed individual who has a passion for the cause but who is underperforming or isn't a good fit.

Because nonprofits are mission based and tend to be more "touchy-feely" than businesses, they can often fall into the trap of hanging on too long to people who aren't working out. Organizational effectiveness suffers: efficiency remains lower than it could be, and talented staff members can become demoralized when they see underperformers being indulged. More important, with limited resources and ambitious goals, these groups need strong staff to achieve the level of impact to which they aspire. Anything else just won't cut it. Although not every organization we studied has learned this, many have mastered the art of firing.

"You perform or you're out," says Kevin Huffman, then vice president for strategy at Teach For America. "People who don't hit their fundraising goals here don't last long in their roles. If a regional director is not performing, or they are not a good fit, they are counseled out. . . . Every person at Teach For America has defined goals and a sense of accountability."

Fred Krupp at EDF echoes the tough-love approach. "We have a philosophical commitment to firing people," he says. "When I see program managers or departments that are not letting people go, that is when I know to meet with the managers. We have

280 people, and we imagine that we are changing the world. If we do not have the very best people we can find, if we view ourselves as coddling, then we're done."

All these organizations have achieved a virtuous cycle of talent management, and it can be hard to tease out cause and effect. Are these nonprofits successful because they've figured out how to develop leaders and keep top talent over time? Or do people stay mainly because the organizations are so successful and have reached a certain size and stability? Studies show a correlation between the size of an organization and its ability to retain talent. Ultimately, it's probably a bit of both. People like working for a successful organization that is having real impact. They feel they are making a difference, they are surrounded by interesting and motivated colleagues, they are likely to be paid well and find new challenges as the organization grows, and hence they are more likely to stay. Because good people stick around, the organization continues to do well. It's a self-reinforcing cycle.

CAPITAL: FIND THE *RIGHT* SOURCES OF FUNDING

There is no magic formula for raising the money needed to fuel your work—every organization has had to blaze its own trail. Initially we found stark differences in capital structures and a diversity of funding sources among these nonprofits. But as we looked closer, we realized that there were a few interesting insights that can be helpful to any group seeking to raise funds to sustain its impact.

We observed that high-impact nonprofits don't treat fundraising as a stand-alone function of management; it is highly integrated with their programs, their mission, and their strategy. In some cases, fundraising is actually part of their "theory of change." The best organizations have a financial strategy that is aligned with their larger vision for creating social impact. These nonprofits choose to pursue funding from the government, the private sector, or individuals not just because they are good sources of revenue but because they can help solve the problems these nonprofits are trying to address.

As we saw in Chapter Five, Dorothy Stoneman lobbied the federal government to create a national YouthBuild program, in part because she knew that's where she could find a large infusion of cash to expand quickly. But Stoneman also pursued federal appropriations because, as a former civil rights activist, she had a deeply held belief that government *should* help low-income youth. Working with government was part of her larger strategy for delivering impact. "We believe the federal government has a responsibility to address these issues and offer a solution," she says. "It was my political conviction that we had a responsibility to work with the government."

Likewise, when The Heritage Foundation set out to "win the war of ideas," it realized that the traditional think-tank approach was insufficient for promoting policy ideas to the general public. As we saw in Chapters Four and Five, Heritage built a conservative *movement*, working with a network of other nonprofits and engaging 275,000 donor-members by 2006 in the process. (By 2011 it had reached 750,000 members.) Its theory of change supported, and was supported by, its fundraising strategy.

Michael Brown and Alan Khazei of City Year pursued corporate support—along with federal AmeriCorps funding—from the outset, as we saw in Chapters Two and Three. They were part of a new generation of social entrepreneurs who believed it was critical to involve the business community in their vision for national service. The first pilot program was funded with $250,000 from five corporations, and today the group generates a large percentage of revenues from a wide range of corporate sponsors, in addition to receiving significant funding from government and foundations.

Like City Year, many high-impact nonprofits realized that they needed to diversify their revenue base if they wanted to sustain their impact. Indeed, as might be expected of organizations of this age (fifteen to forty years) and size (over $10 million), the majority had diversified their funding sources to varying degrees by 2006 to decrease their risk. (See Figure 8.3.) But simultaneously, many have continued to pursue a dominant source of support, with more than 50 percent of their revenues coming from one of the following places: government, individuals, corporations,

Figure 8.3. Sources of Revenue (2005).

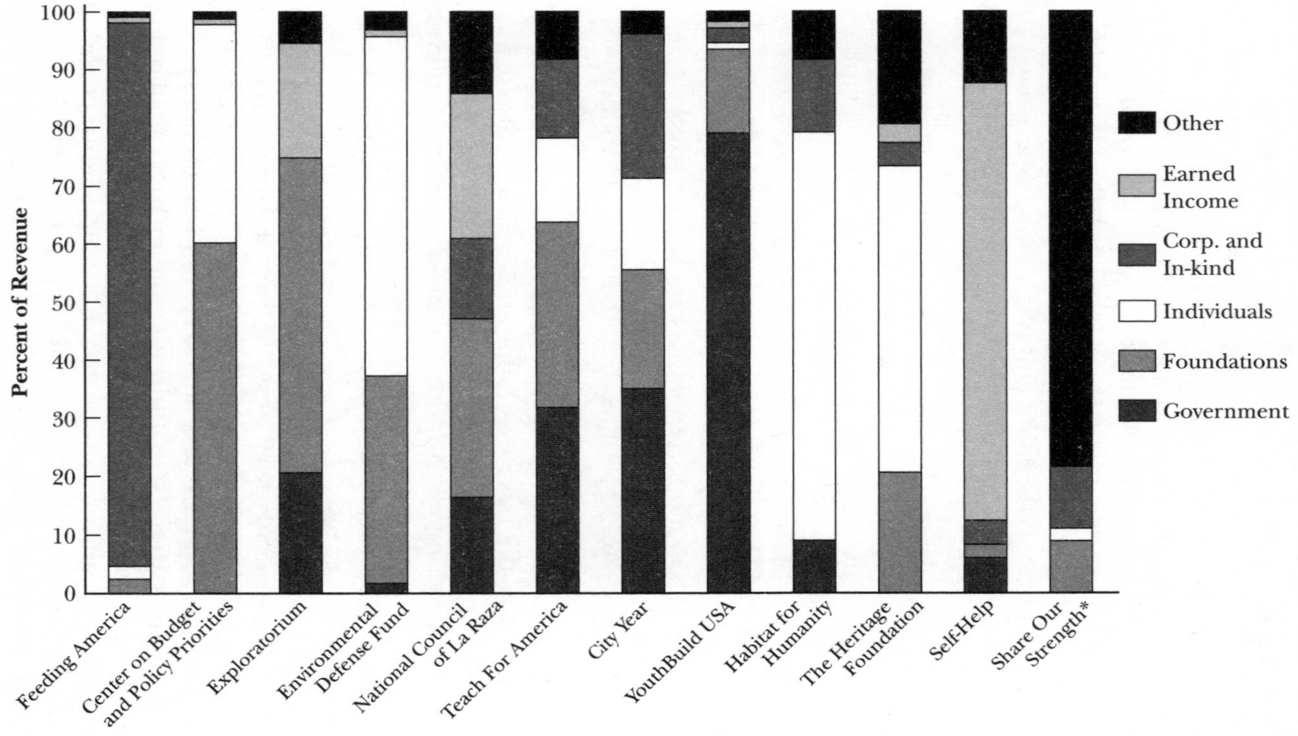

*Note: Other includes revenue from events that is passed directly to Share Our Strength grantees.

218

earned income, or foundations.[7] We explore each of these sources in the next sections.

Government: Mobilizing Public Funds for Social Impact

Almost half the organizations we examined lobby the government—at the federal, state, and local levels—for appropriations and contracts. They pursue policy change because they believe that their programs are important enough to receive broad public support. In this way, changing public policy can be both a means of obtaining funding and an end in itself. (It is important to note that some nonprofits engage in policy advocacy but do not accept government funding because to do so would represent a conflict of interest.)

For organizations that have pursued government funding, many experienced rapid growth once they received the money. Government funding probably gives the quickest bang for the buck, as it requires less of an initial investment to obtain than other sources. Government grants or contracts also are often substantially larger than any other single funding source. "That's where the big money is," says YouthBuild USA's Tim Cross. "You're never going to find an annual outlay of $65 million from any single corporation or foundation. To even begin to meet the need, the feds have to be in the picture."

For YouthBuild USA, pursuing significant government funding was essential. Not only did it provide a lot of money and fulfill Stoneman's belief in the role of taxpayers, but government also provided the distribution muscle that YouthBuild needed to spread its model quickly throughout the country.

Relying heavily on government funding also has its risks, however. YouthBuild USA learned this lesson in the mid-1990s, when a change in administration and subsequent budget cuts briefly reversed its steep growth curve. In just a few years, YouthBuild had gone from a small local program in one city to a national network of 226 local programs with combined annual revenues of $180 million, fueled by federal grants of $40 million to $65 million per year. But when Congress changed hands in 1996, major cuts forced the program to scale back. By 2006, YouthBuild USA still depended on federal contracts for 70 percent of its budget, but the organization has since been working hard to diversify its funding base *within* federal sources, as well as through individual and corporate support.

YouthBuild USA made other trade-offs in pursuing federal funding: it relinquished a great deal of control over its network to the federal agency, HUD. As we discussed in Chapter Five, the organization decided not to control the total appropriation and "own" its affiliate programs—sacrificing some control over the members in its network. Instead, it chose to scale out the YouthBuild model more quickly and to allow other nonprofits to apply for federal grants.

Achieving widespread impact as rapidly as possible was a fundamental part of YouthBuild USA's social change strategy, and government funds were the primary mechanism for scaling its impact. For YouthBuild, the trade-off was worthwhile.

Individual Donors: Capitalizing on Citizen Support

A number of the nonprofits we examined have built large individual donor bases and rely primarily on those sources to sustain their organizations and impact. Groups that receive substantial funding from individual donors include Share Our Strength (from fundraising events), Feeding America (from individual donors), EDF and The Heritage Foundation (from membership bases), and Habitat for Humanity (from direct marketing and events). For these organizations, engaging volunteers, members, and individual donors in their mission has been critical to their strategies for increased impact. Not surprisingly, a number of these groups also excel at engaging individuals in experiential activities and at inspiring evangelists.

The most dramatic—and counterintuitive—example of an organization effectively raising big money from individual citizens is The Heritage Foundation, with its 275,000 donor-members as of 2006 (and more than 750,000 today). Its broad, diverse individual funding base has resulted in large part from Heritage's ability to build a highly influential conservative movement and to engage individuals in its cause, as we illustrated in Chapter Four. Moreover, its funding base has allowed Heritage to turn down money that comes with strings attached and has given the organization enormous strategic freedom. CEO Ed Feulner recounts a story about the time when a high-profile corporate leader disagreed with Heritage's view on trade: "He asked if we would change our position." Feulner says he pulled out the man's check and ripped it up.

Individual engagement is also a significant part of Habitat for Humanity's theory of change. As we noted in Chapter Four, Habitat did not choose the most efficient or cost-effective way to build houses for the poor. But its vision was always much larger than just building homes; it wanted to mobilize volunteers to work alongside the recipients of the home, and in the process, build an antipoverty housing *movement.*

Since its inception, Habitat has engaged more than a million volunteers in its movement, and as a result, the organization also has one of the strongest brands in the world. This in turn bolsters its ability to raise significant dollars from the individuals who volunteer and from ever-widening circles of their friends and colleagues.

Although building a large, renewable individual donor base certainly has its rewards, doing so requires a significant investment of resources. Most of the nonprofits that rely on individual donations have larger development staffs, with larger budgets, than those organizations that rely on government or foundation support. For example, as of 2006 EDF had forty development staff members responsible for collectively managing thousands of relationships.

Corporations: Applying Private Dollars to Social Change

Corporations have been a source of both funding and in-kind support for a number of the organizations discussed in this book. As we saw in Chapter Three, many of the high-impact nonprofits we studied find ways to work with business. Although only one of them is predominantly reliant on corporate funding (Feeding America [formerly America's Second Harvest—The Nation's Food Bank Network], which received nearly $500 million in donations of food and related products from corporate partners when we were concluding our original research), many use corporate funding to supplement their income.

For instance, City Year creates engaged partnerships with companies, as we saw in Chapter Three. "Our goal was never to just get a check," says Michael Brown. "From the beginning, we asked sponsors to get involved, come out and do service, and begin seeing service as a vehicle to bring people together." These corporate relationships not only provide City Year with much-needed funding, but also create mutual benefits for the companies and the nonprofit, spread City Year's message of national service to an important audience, and hold it accountable to a wide constituency. Corporate dollars are the *right* dollars for supporting City Year's theory of change.

NCLR is another nonprofit we studied that moved away from reliance on government funding after significant cuts were made in the early 1980s. Instead, the group began to cultivate a large number of corporate supporters. "I think traditionally, a lot of nonprofits relied on federal funding," says CEO Janet Murguía. "Raul learned some hard lessons about diversifying. He understood that a little earlier than others and put it into practice—looking at foundations and also the business community, and growing those relationships."

Earned Income: Driving a Double Bottom Line

Self-Help appeared to be perhaps the most financially sustainable of all the organizations we studied, because it generates a large portion of its revenues through earned income. But as we discussed in Chapter Three, it is the exception, not the rule. Earned income is such a powerful source of revenues for Self-Help because its business model for economic development is completely aligned with its mission and social impact goals. It is truly a double-bottom-line business.

Self-Help generates earned income from capital instruments, such as mortgage-backed securities and low-interest loans, which involve the core products it offers customers. These revenues gave the organization incredible freedom and financial stability as the housing market grew. As mentioned in Chapter Three, the metaphor that Self-Help staff members often use is "two wheels of the bicycle": the front wheel is the mission of the organization, and the back wheel is the financial engine that propels its growth. "Our bicycle [is] a consistent financial base that allows us to innovate and take risks," says Bob Schall, president of Self-Help Ventures Fund. "We're not held hostage by funders to do certain things or not do certain things."

None of the other organizations we studied had attained the same level of financial independence as Self-Help had by 2006. Their strategies for achieving social impact are less aligned with a profitable business model. Still, some were making real efforts to increase their sources of earned income, in ways that were clearly in sync with their mission and strategy for impact. For example, the Exploratorium received 15 percent of its revenues from admission fees, which was actually a smaller percentage than many museums. But it had also developed other income through the sale of publications and the rental of exhibits, both of which extend its social impact as well.

Foundations: A Mainstay for Many Nonprofits

Some organizations' missions lend themselves to relying more heavily on foundations, particularly those with strategies that preclude them from accepting funding from the government or the private sector for conflict-of-interest reasons, such as EDF, Heritage, and the Center on Budget and Policy Priorities. Foundation support can be useful for a variety of purposes, including research, launching new ideas, and evaluation of existing programs. And although the groups we studied received concentrated funding from other sources, they all have received additional support from foundations.

Of the nonprofits we studied, the Center on Budget and Policy Priorities has been the most reliant on foundation support, with 90 percent or more of its funding coming from major foundation grants throughout most of its history. Since 2000, it had received grants totaling $34.4 million from nearly thirty foundations by 2006; its largest foundation funder provided 13 percent of the total grants awarded. Because the Center lobbies the government on budget issues, it would be a conflict of interest to take taxpayer dollars. And historically the group has not diversified into individual support, although it is just beginning to do so. By 2006, the Center received 35 percent of its funds from smaller donors.

Although these days it is popular to critique "traditional" philanthropists for making short-term, relatively small grants, notably a number of the nonprofits we studied have long-term relationships with foundation funders, who have stuck with them over *decades*. The Ford Foundation and the Surdna Foundation, in particular, have played a critical role in funding many of these groups over time. If your organization has a clear strategy, a strong track record of success, and a mission compatible with the goals of the foundation, at least a few institutional funders seem willing to invest for the long haul. "We do have these long-standing relationships with our funders, and they have seen a return on their investment," says Kathryn Greenberg, the Center's director of development.

INFRASTRUCTURE: INVEST IN OVERHEAD

Finding great people and raising ongoing funding are two significant challenges facing all nonprofits, but there is a third challenge as well. Within the social sector, organizations are discouraged from investing in the very things they need in order to build their own capacity and sustain their impact: systems and infrastructure.

Unfortunately, individual donors often do not want to pay for organizational overhead, preferring that their dollars go directly to programs. In the business world, it is widely recognized that having a superior company enables success. It takes money to make money. But in the social sector, the idea still remains difficult for donors to grasp. "This is the real challenge for many nonprofits—how do you get the funding to match the work that you need done, knowing that you need some flexibility?" says Janet Murguía, CEO of NCLR. "It's very difficult to get unrestricted dollars."

At some point in their evolution, almost all the groups we studied needed to raise substantial capital, above and beyond their annual operating costs, to invest in the development of their organizations. And they've been both persistent and creative about funding necessary things like buildings, computers, and additional staff to manage their rapidly expanding programs. In fact, many ran "growth campaigns" to invest in the critical systems and teams they needed to keep up with program growth. They often structured campaigns as one-time events rather than folding them into annual operating costs, which helped keep their overhead ratio low as well as generate momentum and excitement among funders.

Teach For America and City Year both conducted growth campaigns not unlike the more familiar capital campaign that nonprofits hold when raising funds to purchase a building. Both organizations had reached a point at which they could no longer sustain their growth with the systems and infrastructure they had. They needed to invest in the basics to shore up day-to-day operations and close the chasm between their ambitious goals and their ability to deliver.

City Year's campaign raised $30 million for organizational capacity from 1999 to 2004, with the goals of "maximizing impact, growing to scale, building sustainable resources, and increasing leverage." City Year was incredibly strategic about linking these critical capacities with its ability to both sustain the current level of impact and have greater impact in the future.

It worked with a formerly anonymous funder, Atlantic Philanthropies, to provide the lead grant of $10 million, and raised a total of $30 million over five years. The funding was invested in twelve critical areas of "enterprise-wide business processes, management systems, and organizational capacities," which included things like recruiting software, systems to engage and mobilize the alumni network, a public policy "Action Tank," information technology, staff development, and strategic planning.[8]

"It was [cofounder] Michael Brown's idea for a capital campaign to build the capacities we needed to grow," says board member Ilene Jacobs. "We had not seen this approach before, but it made a huge amount of sense. With every new site, it felt like we were reinventing the wheel. We realized we needed to have the systems—finance, training, and development tools—to run the organization much better. There has been a high return on that investment. Now we are well positioned to grow and run the organization much better."

Teach For America's goal was to double its budget from $20 million to $40 million in the five years ending in 2005, and was seeking to double it again by 2010. (Instead, Teach For America actually *quintupled* in size, which we explore further in Chapter Ten.) To achieve this, the group deliberately identified individual and foundation donors for the campaign and approached them for growth funds separate from ongoing needs. With a campaign mentality and a rigorously constructed plan in place, Teach For America met its revenue goals, despite the fact that the years following the 9/11 terrorist attacks were one of the most challenging fundraising periods in recent American history for many nonprofits. (To learn how it fared during the Great Recession, please see Chapter Ten.)

The organization also used some of this funding to build a robust operating reserve, so that it had enough cash on hand to cover six months of operating costs. The strategy allowed it to resist dipping into growth funds to support annual expenses when setbacks occurred. When Congress threatened to cut AmeriCorps in 2003, Teach For America's teacher education awards were cut. Still, the organization covered the cost of the awards with funds from its operating reserve, while keeping its programs running.

A key to the success of both Teach For America and City Year was the deliberateness and discipline with which they approached growth campaigns. Their leaders realized that they needed to step out of the day-to-day fundraising grind and focus on the bigger picture in order to build a sustainable organization. They couldn't keep living from grant to grant, without being more strategic about how their funding and their organization supported their long-term aspirations. This took conviction and leadership at all levels of the organization. "Michael brought the board along with him," explains Jacobs.

At Feeding America, the challenge was to raise funds for the major technology upgrades needed to support its complex food transportation systems. Initially, large funders were reluctant to invest in such mundane things. "ConAgra was the first big donor to the technology campaign—and they initially didn't want to fund it," says David Prendergast, senior vice president for technology and planning. "They wanted to fund the Kids Cafe program. But our development department said, 'We can't do these things unless we improve our infrastructure.' So they made an initial, multimillion-dollar, multiyear grant."

Prendergast says the nonprofit had to be strategic and persistent about its fundraising plan. "We were successful in putting together a technology plan," he says. "We then went out and got significant funding of $12 million over a five-year period to do the things we needed to do." Although it does cost money to maintain technology, the ongoing costs are much less than the initial investment and can be manageably folded into the operating budget.

Other nonprofits conducted more traditional capital campaigns, for a building or for an endowment used to increase their financial sustainability. NCLR raised $35 million in the last few years of Raul Yzaguirre's tenure, using the funds to buy a building, invest heavily in infrastructure, and set aside a financial cushion to subsidize ongoing operations. "There is no question that we will be able to raise much more money once we put these systems in place," says CEO Janet Murguía, underscoring the adage that it takes money to make (or raise) money. "It's going to be a lot easier—our plans will allow us to demonstrate how we can be credible and effective."

Of course, because of their investment in infrastructure, these organizations don't always meet traditional measures of nonprofit success—despite some groups' efforts to structure campaigns as separate from annual operating budgets. The most common measure used to evaluate nonprofit performance is the ubiquitous overhead ratio, which shows how much money a group spends on its programs (or services) versus how much it spends to maintain its own operations (administration, fundraising, and so on). Not all of the nonprofits we studied score well on these conventional measures, as Table 8.1 illustrates.[9]

The problem with using these metrics is that they fall into the trap of measuring financial inputs or ratios as a proxy for success, rather than measuring *impact,* or the amount of change accomplished with that investment.[10] Worse yet, they assume that nonprofits can implement programs without any infrastructure or support. They may encourage donors to support groups that spend too little on people, IT systems, or management, which can lead to weak organizations at best, or accounting trickery at worst.

TABLE 8.1. CONVENTIONAL RATINGS DON'T ACCOUNT FOR IMPACT.

Organization	GuideStar Rating (2005 or 2006)
Feeding America	★★★
Center on Budget and Policy Priorities	★★★★
City Year	★★★★
Environmental Defense Fund	★★★
Exploratorium	★★
Habitat for Humanity	★
The Heritage Foundation	★★★
National Council of La Raza	★★
Share Our Strength	★★
Teach For America	★★★
YouthBuild USA	★★

Note: Self-Help is not rated.

The nonprofits we identified, however, don't spend too much time worrying about these metrics. They spend what they need to sustain their impact.

A PLATFORM FOR FUTURE IMPACT

As these groups have learned, it's not enough only to focus externally—they must also build strong organizations. For some, particularly those that are still growing rapidly, it is like playing a never-ending game up of catch-up. As they grow and expand, they must build their organizational capacity to fill in the gap between their expectations and their effectiveness. Other nonprofits we studied have already reached their own "steady state" and are content to remain about the same size as they are today. Figure 8.4 gives an overview of the growth trajectory of these nonprofits through 2005.

As Figure 8.4 illustrates, these nonprofits have taken many different paths to growth. A few scaled up their operations relatively quickly. Teach For America and City Year were both founded around 1990, and within fifteen years were raising annual revenues on par with more mature organizations such as EDF and The Heritage Foundation. Others grew at a moderate pace and then shot up in a moment of breakthrough impact, such as when Self-Help received a $50 million Ford Foundation grant and combined it with investment capital from Fannie Mae.

And although some organizations had begun to intentionally level off their growth at the time of our research, several were in the midst of major expansion campaigns: Teach For America and EDF were set to double their budgets over the next few years. EDF was undertaking a growth campaign to reach a budget of $100 million in the five years following 2005. "We're at a real tipping point," says David Yarnold, former executive vice president. "We're poised at this place where our success going forward will be all about our ability to execute. It's not about having enough money—we have a network of allies and donors, and just need to figure out how to activate them. It's all about execution. We're building the airplane while flying it."

Teach For America was almost midway through its five-year growth campaign to double in size as the first edition of this book

FIGURE 8.4. REVENUE GROWTH PATHS (2005).

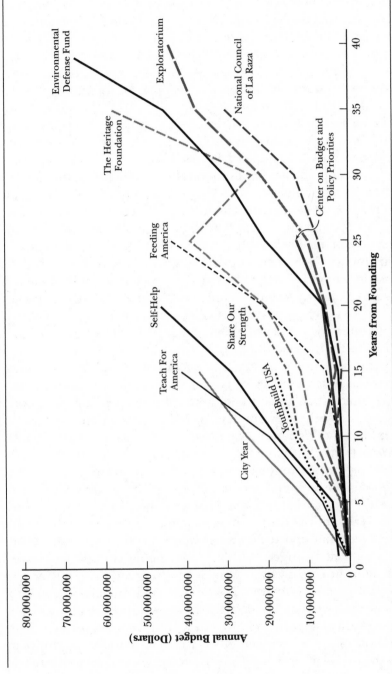

Note: Historical data for Habitat for Humanity International are not available. Feeding America's revenue does not include value of in-kind donations.

went to press. The goal was to take the budget from $50 million to $100 million, and the campaign more than succeeded; by 2010, Teach For America had grown to $240 million. "Scale is critical to our success," says founder Wendy Kopp. "We have to play such a numbers game. We have to have a critical mass of corps members within communities to make them feel part of something larger, and influence the consciousness of the country." The group has worked with the Monitor Institute, a consulting group, to identify the critical capacities needed to expand the organization and increase its impact exponentially.

On the flip side are organizations like Heritage and the Center on Budget and Policy Priorities, which, at the time of our initial research, were not interested in growing much more. Because they focus mainly on advocacy, and work through informal networks at the state and local levels, they don't actually need to grow to have more impact. "I'm very skeptical of growth," says Stuart Butler, vice president of Heritage. "I think there's a danger of inefficiency with size. I already spend a significant amount of time navigating Heritage—I think that is a cost. We've tried to keep it to around two hundred staff for a while." Still, by 2010, both Heritage and the Center on Budget had doubled in size.

For others, the challenge isn't necessarily to raise more money to grow, as much as it is to focus on shoring up the organization. For Habitat, which already had twenty-one hundred affiliates globally as of 2006, the new emphasis is not on growth but on sustainability and on deepening the quality and impact of participants in the network. With a new CEO in place, Habitat is finally building the organization needed to support its global movement.

Share Our Strength is similarly focused on building its internal capacity. "We're really good at raising money for others, not ourselves," says Pat Nicklin, former managing director. "We've been good at coming up with corporate partnerships and events that raise money for hunger. But we're not as good at raising working capital for the organization. We keep putting our oxygen mask on other people, not ourselves. It's ironic—everyone else is trying to diversify into what we are doing, and we're going the other way."

Regardless of which choice these nonprofits make, it's clear that most of them have demonstrated that they can sustain their current levels of impact, if not increase them over time. They recognize that they have to attract talented people, empower them, and compensate them adequately; that they have to invest money to raise money; and that they must build sufficient organizational systems to remain effective. And they do all these things despite powerful countervailing forces.

Although the challenges to building nonprofit capacity are real, they are not insurmountable. These groups have already proved themselves to the world, and they hold more power over their futures than most people realize. "It becomes a self-fulfilling prophecy, whether you operate with fear or you operate from the place of, 'This is our plan, and we are going to execute against it,'" says Kopp of Teach For America. "You really can control your own destiny."

CHAPTER NINE

PUTTING IT INTO PRACTICE

What makes great nonprofits great?

That was the question that prompted us to undertake this ambitious project in 2003. When we first started down this path, we weren't sure what we would find, and we remained open to the unexpected. We were not disappointed. As some of our initial assumptions proved incorrect, we discovered a new way to understand how great nonprofits have great impact.

Being an extraordinary nonprofit isn't about building an organization and scaling it up. It's not about perfect management or outstanding marketing or having a large budget. Rather, it's about finding ways to leverage other sectors to create extraordinary impact. Great nonprofits are catalysts; they transform the system around them to achieve greater good.

In the previous chapters, we unveiled the six practices that high-impact organizations use to create larger systemic change. They work with government, business, individuals, and other nonprofits to achieve more than they could alone. They constantly adapt to their environment to stay relevant. They share leadership and power within and beyond their organizations, empowering others to become forces for good.

Sure, you might think; this all makes sense, in theory.

In reality, if you're like the vast majority of nonprofit leaders, you are consumed with the complexity of running your organization. You may be in a massive fundraising crunch, racing to meet your budget projections before the end of the fiscal year. You could be dealing with major personnel issues—contentious salary negotiations, vacant senior positions, or underperforming field staff. Simultaneously, you're probably worried about program evaluation and how best to serve your true customers—those who benefit from your services. Meanwhile, you've got to keep your board continuously focused on the most strategic, long-term priorities. It can be overwhelming just staying afloat, let alone having more impact.

So stop. Before you phone that foundation officer and ask her to prerelease next year's grant to close this year's gap; before you post yet another job announcement; before you command an emergency meeting of your board; before you overhaul your signature program; before you fix the Web site, just stop. Stop and think.

What are you trying to achieve? What is the real change you want to see in the world—and how does what you're doing today lead to more impact tomorrow? Are you focused on the most important activities, or are you letting constant crises drive your agenda? We know—we've both been there. It's all too easy to let the urgent become the enemy of the important, and the perfect the enemy of the good.

Consider what you've read in this book. If you give it serious thought, we believe that you will start to see things differently and approach your work in new ways. When you put this book down, the one thing we hope you'll remember is that you can't achieve greater social change by spending most of your time focused *only* on your own organization. Even the most efficiently managed nonprofits, the groups that are "run like a business," will fail to reach their full potential if they only shore up their internal capacity to deliver programs. You can't neglect your organization, but neither should you let it eclipse your larger purpose: to have impact.

Too often in this sector, we let the tail wag the dog. We've become so focused on process that at times we've forgotten to focus on results. We get caught up in measuring the wrong things, because the things that really matter are often more difficult to measure. We all know that nonprofits must focus much of their time, energy, and financial resources on sustaining themselves. But that alone isn't enough.

As we learned from these great nonprofits, to achieve greater social change you must also focus on those things that are external to your own organization. The answer to our question, *What makes great nonprofits great?* is this: greatness is about working with and through others, as counterintuitive as that might seem. It's about leveraging every sector of society to become a force for good.

THE VIRTUOUS CYCLE

Throughout the previous chapters, we've shown how high-impact organizations bridge boundaries, and work with others to achieve greater levels of change than they could accomplish alone. Initially, some of them started out using only one or two of the six practices we identified, adding more over time as their organizations grew in size and experience. And as we learned, the more practices they used, the more influence they had. Each element reinforced the others in a virtuous cycle, as the nonprofit gained credibility and power.

At this point, an example might help bring this message into clearer focus. As we noted in Chapter One, the six practices can interact in a way that creates tremendous forward momentum for an organization. Self-Help is the perfect example of how this happens.

From the outset, Self-Help's mission has been to create wealth for minority and poor families.[1] For the first few years, founder Martin Eakes helped low-income clients start small businesses by providing loans and technical assistance. But Self-Help's clients were often in precarious financial situations. As soon as a crisis hit, their companies fell apart. So Self-Help shifted its focus to helping them acquire an even more basic economic asset: a home. It has subsequently expanded into other programs, each one focused on the economic empowerment of America's low-income and working poor.

We saw in previous chapters how Self-Help leverages each of society's major sectors to achieve high impact. In Chapter Two, we illustrated how Self-Help's relentless advocacy efforts helped pass legislation in more than twenty-two states by 2006 to curtail predatory lending, the abusive practice that effectively strips assets away from the poor. And although these policy wins were not sufficient to prevent the U.S. housing market crash and ensuing recession, vulnerable borrowers in those states where stronger regulations existed did not suffer as badly as those in other states. In Chapter Three, we described how Self-Help created the nation's largest secondary mortgage market for low-income borrowers, partnering with such companies as Wachovia and Fannie Mae to create more than $4 billion in home loans. As mainstream companies have taken up Self-Help's social innovations, the group has pioneered models in other areas.

Self-Help didn't create a brand-new mortgage market and help pass legislation across the country by building its own organization. It did it by working through others and leveraging the power of both business and government. Self-Help could have remained focused on growth through an expansion of its credit union services. But Eakes recognized that his organization's financial power and distribution muscle would always be minuscule compared to the might of the commercial lending industry, and his group's political power would always be less than the government's. He knew Self-Help had to convince banks to adopt his innovation, and it had to persuade the government to regulate predatory lending.

To do this, Self-Help had to build a network of nonprofit allies in North Carolina and in the twenty-two states where it has helped pass legislation through its work with other local community development financial institutions (CDFIs). Although the group doesn't actively engage huge numbers of individuals as volunteers or donors, mainly because it doesn't need the money, it has created a number of evangelists for its cause within the highest levels of corporate America and government. CEOs of national banks have gotten behind Eakes's crusade. And leading political figures take his calls, even though most of the public has never heard of him or his organization.

Self-Help is successful on these fronts because of several other important practices as well. For one, it has mastered the art of continuous innovation and adaptation. Its mission—to create wealth for poor families—has stayed the same, but its tactics, its programs, and even its strategy have changed. It started out making business loans, then morphed into making home loans for low-income borrowers, and over time ramped up national policy advocacy and added a host of other programs, including real estate development.

As Self-Help has grown, Eakes has also distributed leadership throughout the organization and its three affiliated organizations: the Center for Responsible Lending, Self-Help Ventures Fund, and Self-Help Credit Union. Eakes recently appointed a COO and has a growing cadre of senior executives on whom he can rely. And like all great nonprofits, Self-Help has built a solid organizational foundation on which to sustain and expand its impact. It recruits and retains top personnel, despite offering lower-than-market salaries, and invests in systems and infrastructure to support its business model. And because it works in financial and real estate markets, Self-Help has found ways to generate enough earned income to cover its operating costs and to continue to expand its programs. Its back wheel of the bicycle—earned income—continues to power its front wheel: the mission.

Self-Help shows how all the practices can come together. Because the group marshals vast networks of nonprofit allies in North Carolina and beyond, and works well in coalitions with other CDFIs, it has more power to influence government and public policy. It has built a network for advocacy at the state and local levels as well, with new offices opened in Oakland, California, and Washington, D.C., and its policy experts have been catapulted onto the national scene in the wake of the 2008 recession and the need for massive federal housing regulation reforms.

Because Self-Help has proven that low-income people are creditworthy and can generate a profit for banks, the organization has been able to influence companies such as Wachovia, Citigroup, and other commercial lenders to adopt its innovative programs and reach historically underserved populations. And because Eakes has cultivated these powerful allies in corporate America, he can use their influence to help convince government to regulate the predatory lenders that operate at the fringes of the banking industry.

Each element of Self-Help's strategy helps reinforce the others. Working with high-level political leaders can create credibility with business, and vice versa. And having a network of extended relationships gives the nonprofit more leverage at the bargaining table. Self-Help has built a significant base of power and uses it to influence other institutions.

When we examined how these powerful practices interact with one another, we began to see how high-impact nonprofits operate within the larger, dynamic *ecosystem* of societal institutions. As Self-Help found, no single organization holds the key to unleashing billions of dollars in credit to poor borrowers. Rather, it lies in the collective hands of America's largest financial institutions, its state and federal policymakers, and its networks of nonprofits and individual activists. Together they interact in a larger system, and a group such as Self-Help can help connect and align these various forces to magnify the greater good. *The solutions to society's most pressing problems lie in the collective, not in any single institution.*

THE SIX PRACTICES IN ACTION

Our findings have significant implications for how we understand, run, fund, and support nonprofits. If we now know this is what it takes to have more impact, then we need to understand how to cultivate these qualities in the social sector. How do we build the critical capacities needed to help organizations think outside their own four walls and become catalysts for change? How do we provide incentives that reward these behaviors, rather than provide disincentives to those nonprofits that invest in their abilities to sustain impact? *How does society channel its resources to the most effective agents of change—those groups with real impact?*

First, the social sector needs new ways of understanding and cultivating leadership if it is to succeed. If nonprofits are to maximize their impact as these twelve groups have, top executives will need to bridge boundaries and understand how to influence without authority. They will need to see the larger system and their role in it—not just their own interests. (When we talk about nonprofit leadership, we mean not just the executive director but also the executive team, the site or affiliate directors, and the board.)

These leaders need to be influential enough to convince the CEOs of global corporations to change their ways and to make the business case, as well as the moral case, for doing so. They also need to be capable of persuading a congressperson to pass legislation based on the larger collective interests they represent. They need to be savvy enough to create *meaningful* opportunities for individual volunteers to engage with the organization. And they need to rally the support of their like-minded peers, organizing and working in coalitions and networks while sharing credit and resources with others.

Above all else, nonprofit leaders must learn how to share power and how to empower others—if they aren't already doing so. They can't rely on authority or formal position to persuade. Instead, they must use the power of purpose and solutions to convince others to follow their lead. They are neither CEOs who can command and control, nor are they elected officials who can move the levers of political power. They themselves must be forces for good.

Our work has implications for other sectors of society as well, including donors, business executives, government leaders, and the general public. *Leaders in these areas should look for opportunities to support organizations that have the greatest impact.* To identify them, we need new ways of measuring success. Indeed, because high-impact organizations are catalysts or intermediaries working to transform larger systems, it becomes much harder to assign credit for success. And the benchmarks for larger systemic change are often much harder to quantify.

How do you begin to change the way *you* approach or support social impact? The following sections outline what you can do to apply the practices presented in this book, whether you are a nonprofit leader, a donor or funder, a corporate executive, an elected official or policymaker, a volunteer, or a concerned citizen. (Our Additional Resources section may help as well.)

NONPROFIT LEADERS

If you run one of the 1.5 million nonprofits in the United States today, you have a unique opportunity to increase your impact: adopting the practices outlined in this book can help you achieve even greater levels of social change. The following checklists can assist you in putting these practices to good use. However, they are only a starting point. Before you begin implementing anything, it makes sense first to do your research, tap the wisdom of experts, and develop a plan.

Practice 1: Advocate and Serve

Policy advocacy alone is a powerful force for good, because it leverages the enormous resources of government. When you combine advocacy with programs on the ground, you gain even more traction against the problems you are trying to solve. The two together are more powerful than either is alone. But most nonprofits fall into the trap of "either-or": they either provide direct services *or* conduct research and pursue policy advocacy. High-impact nonprofits realize that this is a false dichotomy, and they refuse to choose.

If you are an advocacy organization, think about ways you might add grassroots programs or services to increase your impact, as The Heritage Foundation and the Center on Budget and Policy Priorities did. And if you're a direct service provider, look for ways to engage in policy reform—whether at the local, state, or federal level—as all the organizations in our study did. The checklist in Exhibit 9.1 outlines some tips to keep in mind as you develop advocacy efforts.

Practice 2: Make Markets Work

High-impact nonprofits don't see business as the enemy; they see it as a potential force for good. They don't avoid markets; they harness market forces. They do this in three ways: they change business practices, either by decreasing businesses' negative impacts or increasing their positive effects; they partner with business to leverage corporate power and resources, through cause-marketing or traditional sponsorships and philanthropic grants; and some even run their own businesses to generate earned income. Depending on which path an organization decides to pursue, the checklist in Exhibit 9.2 can provide some initial guidance.

Practice 3: Inspire Evangelists

Great organizations find ways to turn volunteers and donors into evangelists for their cause. They express their core values, create meaningful experiences to engage outsiders, cultivate evangelists, and sustain and connect their expanding communities of supporters. The ideas in Exhibit 9.3 can help you put these strategies into practice.

EXHIBIT 9.1. ADVOCATE *AND* SERVE.

What to Do	How to Start
☐ Start at the top.	The top leadership in your organization, including the board, must initiate and support efforts to move into advocacy.
☐ Know the law.	Consult with lawyers and lobbying experts to make sure you fully understand advocacy regulations and implications.
☐ Develop a plan.	Talk to other nonprofits who have done this; do your research. (See Additional Resources.)
☐ Hire policy experts.	Insiders with access and know-how can accelerate your advocacy efforts enormously.
☐ Find flexible funding.	Some funders shy away from politics, so find alternative sources of support for your advocacy efforts.
☐ Practice bipartisanship.	Most nonprofit issues appeal to the broad middle, not political extremes; work with politicians on both sides of the aisle.
☐ Preserve your integrity.	Never sacrifice your core principles or fudge the data to make your case; once you lose credibility, you lose influence.
☐ Leverage your network and individual supporters.	Working in alliances and cultivating communities of individual supporters can lend much power to advocacy.

EXHIBIT 9.2. MAKE MARKETS WORK.

What to Do	How to Start
☐ To change the world, change business.	Recognize that the private sector holds tremendous power that can be harnessed for the greater good.
☐ Decide which path(s) to take.	Depending on your issue and your business model, one or more of the three paths described in Chapter Three may make more sense.
☐ Do your homework.	There are many resources on partnering with business or starting a business that can be of help. (See Additional Resources.)
☐ Hire people with business backgrounds.	To work with business effectively, include people on your staff who understand the corporate world.
☐ Find the right partner.	If you decide to partner with business, make sure you do your due diligence and find a good fit.
☐ Understand and manage your risks.	Each path you may take will entail risks that you can anticipate and mitigate.

EXHIBIT 9.3. INSPIRE EVANGELISTS.

What to Do	How to Start
☐ Be strategic about engagement.	Be deliberate about how you cultivate communities of supporters; invest time, energy, and resources in it.
☐ Start with core values.	Express your core values to attract others who are interested in your cause; make your story inspiring and engaging.
☐ Create meaningful and emotional experiences.	Even if you don't have obvious opportunities to do so, think of ways to concretely engage outsiders.
☐ Inspire and cultivate evangelists.	Convert outsiders to insiders, and cultivate super-evangelists who can help you increase your influence.
☐ Nurture and connect the community.	Treat your larger community of supporters as an end in itself, not just as a means to an end.
☐ Mobilize the community for change.	As your community expands, you can leverage it to effect broader social change.

Practice 4: Nurture Nonprofit Networks

In addition to engaging individuals in larger communities of supporters, you also need to work with other nonprofits to have more power and impact. Either develop your own network of affiliates or build coalitions and alliances. Don't view other groups as competitors for scarce resources, but rather as allies working for the same cause. Invest time, energy, and resources into building the capacity of others to become forces for good. In the end, you'll all win. Try some of the ideas in Exhibit 9.4.

Practice 5: Master the Art of Adaptation

To work effectively outside your organization, you must be responsive to your environment and able to adapt. This requires building the capacity to be continuously innovative: listen to external cues, experiment with responses, evaluate the new programs and modify as necessary, and continue to repeat the cycle. Groups that become mired in bureaucracy and that resist change—or that generate a host of new ideas but have no structure to their creativity— are doomed to be less effective. High-impact nonprofits find the balance through the strategies outlined in Exhibit 9.5.

Practice 6: Share Leadership

If you are the CEO of a nonprofit with a growing staff, you can begin to increase your impact by delegating real responsibility to your senior management team, second-in-command, board, and local site leaders. There will come a point when you cannot make all the decisions for the organization—at that point, you can let go of power and empower others around you. Exhibit 9.6 is a checklist of some preliminary steps that can help you begin this journey.

Sustaining Impact

Finally, we urge you to focus your nonprofit on the basic elements that support these six practices and help you sustain impact. Although you can't let the organization become your entire focus, neither can you completely neglect it. You must constantly work to bridge the gap between your external orientation and goals and your organization's capacity to deliver results. You need great people, sustainable funding, and basic systems and infrastructure. The checklist in Exhibit 9.7 can serve as an initial guide.

EXHIBIT 9.4. NURTURE NONPROFIT NETWORKS.

What to Do	How to Start
☐ Collaborate, don't compete.	Start with a mind-set that puts impact above self-interest; high-impact nonprofits don't see peers as competition.
☐ Develop a network strategy.	Whether or not you have formal affiliates, you can find ways to build networks, movements, and the larger field.
☐ Grow the pie.	Look for ways to increase resources for the field; share resources within your network.
☐ Share knowledge.	Use your expertise to help strengthen other nonprofits' ability to advance the cause.
☐ Develop leadership.	Cultivate leaders not only for your own organization but also for your network of allies.
☐ Work in coalitions.	Lead and work in coalitions; learn how to share power and credit with other groups.
☐ Know when to go your own way.	Know when collective action is the answer, and when you need to disrupt a particular field.

EXHIBIT 9.5. MASTER ADAPTATION.

What to Do	How to Start
☐ Balance creativity and structure.	Find the balance so that you become neither trapped by bureaucracy nor overwhelmed by too many new ideas.
☐ Listen to your environment.	Pay attention to external cues from your clients and stakeholders; use your network or programs to "listen."
☐ Experiment and innovate.	Try new ways of doing things: innovate around promising practices, programs, or processes.
☐ Evaluate and learn.	Test how the innovation is doing; evaluate results and learn; decide what needs to change.
☐ Modify programs.	Modify your programs or processes as a result of what you've learned; share this knowledge within your network.
☐ Repeat the cycle.	Continue to listen, innovate, learn, and modify as necessary.
☐ Focus on results, not tactics.	Stay focused on closing the gap between your performance or tactics and what you are trying to achieve.

EXHIBIT 9.6. SHARE LEADERSHIP.

What to Do	How to Start
☐ Learn to let go.	It's up to you to share your power; distributing leadership unleashes more potential for the entire organization.
☐ Appoint a second-in-command.	Focus on external leadership tasks and hire a strong COO to handle internal operations.
☐ Build your executive team.	Hire and keep top talent; share power and authority with your top team.
☐ Nurture leaders in your network.	Cultivate leadership in your network; top leaders can advance from within or join your allies in the field.
☐ Develop a strong and engaged board.	Effective nonprofit CEOs have a positive balance of power with their boards and engage them in what matters most.
☐ Embrace shared leadership.	Model a new form of distributed leadership that is less hierarchical or dependent on formal positional authority.

EXHIBIT 9.7. INVEST TO SUSTAIN IMPACT.

What to Do	How to Start
☐ Find the right balance for your organization.	Decide on what your organization needs to sustain its impact, and invest heavily.
☐ Focus on what, then who.	Hire based on cultural fit and mission and then give people the latitude and development they need to succeed.
☐ Pay to play.	Pay top talent relatively well, ideally at or near the top of your field.
☐ Find sources of ongoing funding to diversify risk.	Find the right mix of funding and manage your risks.
☐ Fuse fundraising with your theory of change.	Integrate your fundraising strategy with your overall vision for change; government, business, and the public are potential sources of funding as well as a means of leveraging social impact.
☐ Resist pressure to look lean.	Don't let funders or the media dictate how you choose to spend money on things like overhead.

Foundation Leaders, Philanthropists, and Donors

If you are a philanthropist, we believe that our findings have implications for the way you fund and support nonprofits. Whatever kind of donor you are—whether you are an occasional check writer or a professional philanthropist—you can use the six practices to evaluate which organizations to fund and how to support them in the best ways possible.

We believe that financial resources in this sector should be channeled to the highest-impact organizations or to those that have the potential to get there. If the first wave of philanthropy in the United States was "basic charity" (give a man a fish), and the second wave was "enlightened charity" (teach a man to fish), then we believe the next phase can be "systemic social change" (revolutionize the entire fishing industry, to paraphrase Bill Drayton).[2] Funders have a real opportunity to leverage their investments.

Whatever your level of giving, consider which groups are most deserving of your hard-earned resources. The stock market is a good analogy. Investors don't put their money into just any company; they look for the businesses that will provide the highest return on their investment. Donors, too, can look for organizations that can give the highest potential return in terms of results.

As a starting point, foundations can consider investing in organizations that work with and through others to generate greater impact. Rather than withdrawing their funding as soon as government, corporations, or individual donors step in—as some do— foundations can see these as signs of greater leverage for their valuable grants. They should "double down" on the best organizations. Of course, this means learning how to recognize the value of leverage, which is much harder to quantify than things like "cost per volunteer."

City Year offers one example. The organization's budget was $42 million in 2005. If you judged City Year's impact only according to the corps members it employs in its sixteen sites each year, you might conclude that its program costs seem high. But using cost per volunteer is the wrong metric to evaluate success, because it doesn't take into consideration other ways in which City Year has impact.

If you believe, as we do, that the federal AmeriCorps program wouldn't be where it is today without City Year's relentless advocacy, you must also factor in the hundreds of millions of federal dollars leveraged for other community organizations, and the hundreds of thousands of AmeriCorps volunteers who have given back to their country. And City Year has worked with, and transformed, hundreds of corporate sponsors, helping them connect to their communities. It has helped build not only the national service field but also the social entrepreneurship field. City Year develops so much more than its individual corps members—it has helped change the system around it.

Of course, it is harder to quantify the impact City Year has had through its advocacy efforts or its work with business. And information like this is not always published on an organization's Web site, let alone on ratings Web sites—you have to ask for it. We need new ways of measuring success in the social sector—and we need new systems and intermediaries to tackle this challenge.

In the meantime, if you want to evaluate whether an organization is capable of providing the highest return on your philanthropic dollars, you could use the six practices outlined in this book to screen for nonprofits that are having substantial impact. And you could start by investing in the twelve organizations profiled here. But they're just a handful of the many nonprofits that are achieving great impact and that deserve support.

BUSINESS, GOVERNMENT, AND CITIZEN LEADERS

Corporate leaders who want to become more socially and environmentally responsible can look for nonprofit partners that are uniquely positioned to help them achieve their goals. Of course, there will always be extreme activists protesting the evils of capitalism, but there are also pragmatic groups such as Feeding America (formerly America's Second Harvest—The Nation's Food Bank Network), Environmental Defense Fund, or Share Our Strength that want to work *with* companies. They can help your company change its practices, in ways that allow you to do well while also doing good. The six practices can help you evaluate whether or not an organization is geared to leverage the resources you can provide.

Government leaders can also use these practices to select non-profit partners. As government continues to outsource many programs, it should also consider nonprofits an excellent source of policy innovation and proven solutions. As we showed in Chapter Two, high-impact organizations combine programs on the ground with policy research and advocacy, and are able to test and implement ideas. This approach can help ensure that a policy solution actually works.

If you are a private citizen, whether you volunteer regularly, serve on a nonprofit board, or simply write a check to your favorite group, you too can apply our findings. You can begin by using these six practices, and our framework, to evaluate whether the organization you are working with has high impact. In addition, you might want to assess the nonprofit according to the ideas we presented in Chapter Four. We found that high-impact organizations are particularly adept at creating meaningful experiences for their supporters. These nonprofits build and nurture larger communities and empower people like you to become active participants in social change.

BECOMING A FORCE FOR GOOD

The nature of philanthropy today is changing, as donors seek more evidence of impact from their donations. Businesses are changing too, as corporations become more socially and environmentally responsible—and are increasingly under pressure from major investors to do so. Government policy is also being transformed, as more decisions are made at the state and local levels and as legislatures outsource more programs to nonprofits. All these forces are converging to create a unique opportunity for social change.

So it's not surprising that high-impact nonprofits are changing as well. Rather than just providing services or basic charity, they are doing much more. In the process, they are redefining what it means to be an effective nonprofit. The leaders of today's civil sector offer promising practices for others to emulate. Indeed, there is a notable difference between high-impact nonprofits and

EXHIBIT 9.8. THE NEW NONPROFIT PARADIGM.

High-Impact Nonprofits Do This	*. . . Not This*
☐ Work externally with all sectors of society	Focus exclusively on their own organization
☐ Use leverage to change entire systems	Use only organizational growth to scale impact
☐ Do whatever it takes—short of compromising their core values	Would rather "be right" than "win"
☐ Advocate for policy change and run programs	Only provide direct services; avoid politics
☐ Harness market forces and work with business	Avoid working with business or capitalism
☐ Engage outsiders in meaningful experiences; build long-term relationships	Treat volunteers as free labor or donors as check writers; focus on transactions
☐ Nurture networks of nonprofits; build the field	See fellow nonprofits as competitors
☐ Constantly adapt and balance creativity with structure	Become mired in bureaucracy or get overwhelmed with too many ideas
☐ Empower others to lead and take action	Maintain a command-and-control hierarchy and allow the CEO to be the hero
☐ Invest in the basics: people, fundraising, and systems	Neglect building basic infrastructure through insufficient spending on overhead
☐ Focus on impact and measure progress against results or larger systemic change	Focus on process; measure inputs, not outputs

those that are not living up to their full potential. Exhibit 9.8 summarizes what we see as the new and old paradigms.

Nonprofits operate at the intersection of society's major sectors. The best of these organizations take advantage of their unique role and their unprecedented opportunity to create greater impact. To win at the social change game, it's not about being the biggest or the fastest or even the best-managed nonprofit. The most powerful, influential, and strategic organizations *transform others* to become forces for good.

PART THREE

NEW LESSONS FOR NEW TIMES

CHAPTER TEN

THRIVING IN TUMULTUOUS TIMES

The global financial crisis and Great Recession have dramatically influenced the state of the world and the stability of the nonprofit sector, as we noted in the new Introduction. So as we prepared to research and write this updated edition of *Forces for Good*, we wanted to know how the twelve high-impact nonprofits we originally featured had fared during these tumultuous times. After all, the management genre is rife with books highlighting the best practices of particular companies at a moment in time, only to see a few of those firms fail mere years later. Such is the dynamic nature of commercial markets—reflecting Schumpeter's cycle of creative destruction.

So we were curious: Had the original twelve high-impact non-profits we featured retrenched during the recession? Had some of them gone under or become a shadow of their former selves? Or, in fact, had they weathered the storm? And, if so, what might they teach *all* nonprofits about how to survive in difficult times? We interviewed their senior leadership teams in summer 2011 to get an update and see what we might continue to learn. (For a list of interviewees, please see Appendix F.)

EVER GREATER IMPACT

We were happy to discover that these twelve nonprofits have continued to positively change the lives of millions in the short term, while also initiating systemwide changes to ensure impact for

253

years to come. Far from shrinking during the downturn, they've actually seized the economic crisis as an opportunity to continue increasing their impact. In fact, the majority of these nonprofits have *significantly grown* during the last five years, during the worst economic conditions in seventy years. One group grew nearly seven times its size (Teach For America, from $41 million to $277 million in annual revenues); four essentially *doubled* in size (the Center on Budget and Policy Priorities, City Year, Habitat for Humanity, and The Heritage Foundation); and a number of the other organizations grew their annual revenues at healthy rates between 2005 to 2010, despite a few bumps along the way. (See Table 10.1 for a list of the five-year compound annual growth rates [CAGRs] for the twelve nonprofits.)

These organizations have not just survived the Great Recession, they've *thrived.*

TABLE 10.1. REVENUE GROWTH 2005–2010.

	2005 ($M)	2010 ($M)	Five-Year CAGR (%)
Center on Budget and Policy Priorities	13	27	16
City Year	42	79*	13
Environmental Defense Fund	69	101	8
Exploratorium	44	56	5
Feeding America	543	720	6
Habitat for Humanity	1,000(1B)	1,600(1.6B)	10
The Heritage Foundation	40	81	15
National Council of La Raza	29	47	10
Self-Help	75	107	7
Share Our Strength	24	37	9
Teach For America	41	277	47
YouthBuild USA	18	26	8

*Note: City Year budget data is for FY2011.

Take Feeding America, known as America's Second Harvest when the first edition was published. Since the 2008 recession, this antihunger group has engineered creative ways to feed the millions more needy adults and children who have lined up at food bank doors—nearly doubling the amount of food that it distributes annually. "The kind of people who are in the food bank lines today are different," says Feeding America's CFO Janet Gibbs. "It's not just the chronically unemployed or homeless; it's also regular middle-class people whose houses went upside down, or the breadwinners lost their jobs." Likewise, Share Our Strength has managed to reduce childhood hunger in several states over the past few years by expanding access to free breakfast and lunch programs during the downturn.

On the housing front—one of the hardest-hit industries—Self-Help finally succeeded in its quest to pass federal legislation to stop abusive predatory lending and protect vulnerable borrowers from losing their homes and businesses, as we explain in more detail later in this chapter. Meanwhile, Habitat for Humanity has continued to build homes with low-income families worldwide, while also ramping up its advocacy for fair housing for all, both here and abroad.

In the education field, despite plummeting U.S. public school performance, City Year has helped turn around graduation rates in some high-risk schools by shifting its strategy to focus more on educational outcomes than on various kinds of community service. Simultaneously, Teach For America corps members have continued to achieve student gains in their classrooms, while the program's alumni have begun changing entire school systems through their leadership and public advocacy.

These are just a few examples. Each of the twelve organizations has continued to demonstrate remarkable impact since we concluded our original research in early 2006. And the fact that many of these organizations have managed not just to survive but to *accelerate* their growth through an economic downtown is equally impressive.

This is especially affirming considering that the subjects of similar corporate studies have not fared so well. *In Search of Excellence*, the seminal 1982 management book by McKinsey consultants Tom Peters and Bob Waterman, was subject to a tough postpublication critique. According to the *Business Week* article "Oops! Who's Excellent Now?" within two years of publication, one-third of the forty-three "excellent" companies that Peters and Waterman had profiled faced financial difficulties.[1]

For the twelve organizations featured in *Forces for Good*, five years later there are not yet any "oops" stories.

THE PARADOX OF COUNTER-CYCLICALITY

But can we attribute the success of these organizations during the Great Recession to the six practices? One could argue that these nonprofits' success over the past few years is due to the *paradox of counter-cyclicality*: it is well established that when the economy dips and unemployment, poverty, homelessness, and hunger rise, donors turn to help those most in need. So even in the Great Recession, when foundation endowments and investor portfolios dropped 30 percent or more, overall giving *increased* to nonprofits providing direct services to the most vulnerable. "We heard from our donors, 'Maybe this year our gift to the museum or our alma mater can wait,'" says Feeding America's Gibbs.

Feeding America was perhaps the most dramatic example of a nonprofit that grew *because* of the global financial crisis, rather than in spite of it. Today the organization moves 3.3 billion pounds of food to feed millions of hungry people in America, and it has grown annual revenues 76 percent since 2005, with a 6 percent CAGR over the period. The demand for donated food has never been greater, as more individuals and families visited food banks and tapped into federal and state assistance programs during the recession.

Yet the paradox of counter-cyclicality has had no effect on many of the twelve organizations we studied: several are far from the front lines in providing direct services to those hit by the recession. One would expect that as attention and resources shifted to those serving the most vulnerable, nonprofits focused on other areas would bear the brunt. This may have been true for many nonprofits. But consider this: The Heritage Foundation, Environmental Defense Fund (EDF), and the Exploratorium do not provide direct services to the poor—yet they all managed to grow and extend their impact during the downturn.

The only organization to suffer a real setback was Self-Help, which, as a major lender of home and business loans to low-income borrowers, was at the center of the housing crash. Although its own clients were less likely to default than other subprime borrowers—because they had been carefully selected, had affordable fixed mortgages, and were offered foreclosure prevention—many found their home values decreasing, and a number became unemployed. At the same time, Self-Help had major Wall Street lending partners calling back capital, forcing the organization to repay significant loans on a day's notice. Self-Help's conservative financial policy of building its net worth and keeping reserves allowed it to weather the storm. (Self-Help currently has $1.5 billion in assets and $327 million in net worth.)

Luckily the crisis did not prevent Self-Help from achieving extraordinary impact. After the mortgage market contracted and loan purchases from banks dried up, Self-Help shifted its emphasis to foreclosure prevention and expanded its local work with at-risk credit unions in working-class communities, to ensure that they could continue serving their members.

In addition, Self-Help ramped up its advocacy efforts. The goal? Along with the Center for Responsible Lending, one of its affiliates, Self-Help saw an historic opportunity to help correct faulty federal lending policies that enabled the subprime debacle in the first place. Self-Help founder Martin Eakes and his team were among the chief architects of the Dodd-Frank Wall Street Reform and Consumer Protection Act, which passed into law in 2010—perhaps the most significant financial regulatory reform effort since the Great Depression. It instituted national protections for vulnerable borrowers for which the organization had intensely fought for years, but was previously able to win only at the state level.

All in all, we can conclude that performance of almost all of our twelve nonprofits has been quite remarkable either in spite of, or because of, the effects of the Great Recession. In part, we believe this is due to the virtuous cycle they have created—or what Jim Collins might call the "flywheel." Because these non-profits have had substantial, and substantiated, impact on issues they care about, they represent sound investments at a time when donors are more carefully scrutinizing their giving. As we discovered in our initial research, success begets success, and this seems particularly true when times are tough. These nonprofits have also been willing to continue to adapt and change in response to the times.

EMBRACING CHANGE

Like Self-Help, each of the twelve organizations adapted quickly to the changing economy and continued to scale its impact in significant ways, often by leveraging the six practices. The news was heartening. It affirmed that these were truly extraordinary organizations and assured us that the "six practices of high-impact nonprofits" were reliable guides for maximizing impact no matter what the external context. As we interviewed leaders from each of these high-impact nonprofits, we discovered several patterns that appeared to be common across the portfolio in terms of how they responded to their changing environment.

First, as mentioned earlier, the majority of the nonprofits managed to grow their revenues significantly, and all twelve continued to scale out their impact. They did so in some cases by expanding existing programs and services or by launching innovative new initiatives, but all continued to leverage the six practices—working with and through government, business, nonprofit networks, and individual community members to advance their causes. (In the next chapter, we'll explore in more detail *how* they applied these practices during a downturn.)

Internally, the organizations underwent profound changes as well: half successfully weathered a CEO transition since 2005—including Habitat for Humanity's tumultuous replacement of its charismatic founder Millard Fuller and installation of CEO Jonathan Reckford. A number of them continued to evolve their boards and senior leadership teams. And several, including National Council of La Raza (NCLR), restructured their affiliate relationships to provide greater accountability and effective use of their networks. One organization, Habitat, moved its headquarters from Americus to Atlanta, Georgia; another, the Exploratorium, began construction on a new San Francisco waterfront venue, which will be completed in 2013.

Many of the twelve organizations also made significant strategic changes during the past five years: City Year shifted from providing multipurpose national service opportunities for its corps members to focusing on education reform. As the Exploratorium prepares to move into a new building, it is also expanding its programs to reach diverse audiences, including more adults and Latinos. Feeding America underwent a major rebranding from its former name, America's Second Harvest; and Environmental Defense Fund added back to its name "Fund" after a brief stint as Environmental Defense. The Center on Budget and Policy Priorities beefed up its external marketing and communication efforts and its use of social media, which historically had not been as strong as its policy research.

By 2005, each of the organizations had already survived three or four recessions since their founding (all were established between 1965 and 1993), and each had gone on to achieve more impact. However, this financial crisis was far more severe than any economic downturn the organizations had ever before experienced. So we wanted to know: just *how* were our twelve nonprofits able to grow through the deepest recession since the Great Depression?

LESSONS FOR CHALLENGING TIMES

From our interviews with CEOs and other senior leaders of these nonprofits, and from studying how they responded to their changing environment, we learned several critical lessons about how to thrive in tumultuous times:

LESSON 1: ACCELERATE INTO A DOWNTURN

We found it notable that almost every leader we interviewed had just launched or was partway through a major growth campaign when the recession hit in 2008. Yet instead of causing setbacks, the onset of the recession was a force propelling them forward. Rather than putting their foot on the fundraising brake, as so many nonprofits did, most of them actually accelerated into the downturn and increased their development efforts.

In 2006, Habitat for Humanity had set an ambitious goal of growing from $1 billion to $4 billion in five years across its global network of affiliates; although it had fallen short as of 2011, it still managed to *grow* its annual global revenues to $1.6 billion, and it's on track to hit $4 billion in the next few years.[2] Jonathan Reckford, Habitat's CEO, noted in an interview that the nonprofit figured out how to turn the economic crisis into an opportunity to promote its cause and raise more money to solve underlying problems.

City Year's transformative growth during this period was equally dramatic: two years prior to the recession, CEO Michael Brown had led an intensive strategic planning exercise. His cofounder, Alan Khazei, had departed City Year in 2005 to start ServiceNation, and later ran for the late Ted Kennedy's Massachusetts Senate seat before losing in the primary election. At the time, City Year had grown to more than $40 million, with sites in twenty-one cities, and had successfully advocated for the federal AmeriCorps national service program for years. But Brown felt that City Year could achieve more targeted, measurable impact. "We needed to show that national service wasn't just nice, but necessary," says Brown.

So City Year engineered a whole new strategy. It shifted its entire focus from deploying corps members to a range of community organizations, where they performed multiple kinds of service, to dedicating itself instead to serving students in the most struggling schools—the "dropout" factories identified in national studies. Growing from $42 million in 2005 to nearly $80 million in 2011, and introducing a robust new state-based funding stream, City Year has now repositioned itself as a high-impact contributor to improving educational outcomes in America's toughest schools. If the original City Year model could be likened to a Swiss Army knife, with something for everyone, its new education-intensive strategy is more like a surgical knife. As Brown says, "Leaning into our strategy allowed us to grow through the recession."

Feeding America was another nonprofit that was serendipitously well prepared for the downturn. At the time the recession took hold, the nonprofit was in the midst of a major rebranding campaign, led by Vicki Escarra, who was appointed CEO in 2006.

Bringing deep marketing experience from her career as a senior executive at Delta Airlines, Escarra recognized that if the organization wanted to elevate awareness of hunger in America, it had to renew its brand. The name America's Second Harvest—The Nation's Food Bank Network wasn't well understood by the public, so after much market research and careful consideration, the group decided to change the name to Feeding America—despite grumblings from some member food bank leaders who had weathered several previous switches. (Over the years, the organization's name had incrementally morphed from Second Harvest to America's Second Harvest to America's Second Harvest—The Nation's Food Bank Network.)

The timing of the new name was eerily prescient. Just as news of the recession was breaking, Feeding America was rolling out its new logo and awareness campaigns, which helped capture the attention of donors in a different way. The organization realized a 27.5 percent increase in fundraising from FY2008 to FY2009 as their brand recognition jumped 30 percent nationwide. Just as millions of donors were looking for opportunities to meet immediate needs, Feeding America rose up as a visible, high-impact vehicle. It also opened up fresh corporate partnership and media opportunities, such as a $17 million partnership with American Idol and a significant deal currently on the table with Dr. Phil. These high-profile gifts would not have been possible had the group stuck with any of its prior names. "The biggest gift I will give this organization as a leader is the name change," says Escarra.

Lesson 2: Stay Close to Your Donors

The moment Ed Feulner, CEO of The Heritage Foundation, recognized the potential financial repercussions of the recession, he tasked his development staff with an unusual request: he instructed them to call every single one of Heritage's major donors. "Don't ask for money or for confirmation of their support," he advised. "Instead, ask: 'How are you doing? How will the downturn affect you?'" From those conversations, Heritage deduced that major gifts would be down about 10 percent in the upcoming year. Although the organization had just ratified a five-year strategic plan and approved an annual budget, Feulner announced a hiring freeze and a cap on all salary increases.

Then Heritage took another bold step: it ramped up fundraising and intensified its direct marketing campaign. "We went full force," explains Feulner. "Those who do well in recessions come out strong. We didn't want to show weakness. So we went full bore on direct marketing. Other nonprofits were so spooked by early 2009 that they withdrew from fundraising and direct marketing." The result? Heritage's first-quarter revenues in 2009 were the best the organization had seen in years. Between 2005 and 2010, the organization doubled in size to $81 million and nearly tripled its dues-paying membership base from 250,000 to more than 700,000 members. Its ambitious goal is one million members by 2013.

Of course, the outpouring of support could also be attributed to another factor—namely, the election of Democrat president Barack Obama, which fired up conservative activists. But Heritage's cunning development approach should not be discounted: the major donors they contacted in 2008 conveyed sincere appreciation for Heritage's outreach. Feulner explains that they said, "You're the only one that's called to ask us that. We're cutting all contributions back 10 percent." The information was invaluable because Heritage could adjust its budget accordingly in the short term, until it could obtain bearing on the longer-term financial situation.

The Exploratorium is another organization that leveraged the economic crisis to advance its own fundraising efforts by cultivating new donors. Executive director Dennis Bartels assumed leadership as we were completing our earlier research in 2006. When the recession hit in 2008, the organization had just announced a $300 million capital campaign to relocate from its founding site in the Palace of Fine Arts to a prime waterfront property at the doorstep of downtown San Francisco, which would dramatically increase its visibility and accessibility. So at a time when most arts organizations were suffering financially, the Exploratorium doubled down on development and has thus far raised most of the capital required to finance its move.

"Private individuals who deeply believe in us are at the core of this campaign," says Bartels. The Exploratorium has long appealed to high-tech leaders in Silicon Valley, given its focus on science and engineering. Gordon Moore, the cofounder of Intel; Ann Bowers, wife of the late Robert Noyce (also cofounder of Intel); and Bill Bowes, the founder of Amgen, have all served on the nonprofit's board. But in light of the capital campaign, the group redoubled its efforts to attract younger digerati donors—including twenty- and thirty-something leaders of the social media revolution, such as Reid Hoffman, founder of LinkedIn, and Jack Dorsey, founder of Twitter, among others.

"We've had eight gifts of eight figures or more," says Bartels of the high-touch capital campaign. "But really the building is a Trojan horse for all the other great stuff we want to do inside of it and in the community." In addition to cultivating individuals who can make substantial gifts for the Exploratorium's expansion, the group has also forged partnerships with some interesting and alternative social networks: the DIY/maker movement and the Burning Man Project. Although individuals in these groups may not all be billionaires, the affiliations are certainly elevating the Exploratorium's profile and brand.

LESSON 3: PLAY BOTH OFFENSE AND DEFENSE

Not every one of the twelve organizations grew between 2008 and 2009; some stayed relatively flat, and a few took temporary hits. For instance, NCLR laid off a few staff, instituted an executive pay freeze, and implemented other cost-cutting measures until fund-raising stabilized.

Share Our Strength CEO Bill Shore cut back early in the recession in response to the sentiments of his board. "I used to be the guy who said, 'You have to be willing to take risks; don't be so hung up on this one increase,'" explains Shore. "But when you are financially unstable, literally every $200,000 decision can preoccupy the board for hours. If financial stability is a football, when you have it, you call your own plays. When you don't have it, you're in a defensive crouch."

But by 2010, both NCLR and Share Our Strength had regained velocity. NCLR's CAGR was 10 percent; Share Our Strength had grown to $37 million in revenue and more than doubled its staff as it intensified its state-based campaign to end childhood hunger using a networked approach.

Self-Help had the most dramatic story of switching from offense to defense—literally in one day. Randy Chambers (CFO at the time and now president of the Self-Help Credit Union) recalls how the scene unfolded the day after Lehman Brothers filed for Chapter 11 bankruptcy protection on September 15, 2008. "It was the day the world stood still," he recalls.

At nine the following morning, Self-Help received an e-mail from a major Wall Street bank requesting that the nonprofit pay back $35 million in overnight loans by the end of the day. "We had been borrowing from this bank every day for three years, and they'd renewed every day up until that moment," Chambers said. "Three major Wall Street banks were suddenly gone, and now the fourth was calling us to get paid. We had six different creditors who lent us between $10 million to $100 million, which we rolled over every day for three years. And now they either didn't exist or were requesting immediate repayment."

Self-Help staff set up a war room to deal with the crisis. "Where are we going to get $35 million by the end of the day?" Chambers asked. They puzzled out how they would borrow the funds from one of their other lenders so that they could pay the Wall Street bank without having to default. "It was a very harrowing experience," he says. Once the nonprofit secured the reserves, they quickly began strategizing how to further diversify Self-Help's business model so that it would never be dependent on a single loan partner again.

LESSON 4: FIND OPPORTUNITY IN CRISIS

Fred Krupp, the twenty-seven-year leader of EDF, made the point succinctly in our interview, when talking about the 2010 oil spill disaster in the Gulf of Mexico: "Don't let a good crisis go to waste." It's advice that many of the twelve nonprofits have taken to heart in the past five years, in response to the economy and other natural disasters.

The Gulf Coast oil spill clearly had severe impacts on the ecosystem and local economy, but immediate action taken by EDF and other environmental groups resulted in the "biggest ecosystem restoration effort ever in the history of the planet." As Krupp puts it, "We had been working in Louisiana for years on restoring wetlands. The attention given to the Gulf by the spill has created an opportunity to work with others. Congress introduced a bill that would dedicate billions of dollars of BP's penalty to restore wetlands in the Gulf."

The other nonprofits also faced crises that they leveraged to turn a bad situation into something with more positive outcomes. Habitat for Humanity was instrumental in responding to Hurricanes Katrina and Rita in New Orleans and the U.S. Gulf Coast (2005) and to the Indian Ocean tsunami (2004). Although these both took place during our initial research, it was only in hindsight that they proved to be pivotal moments in the nonprofit's evolution—bringing together the board, donors, staff, and volunteers in the response and altering the organization's strategy.

"Of course we all pray that there will be no disasters," says CEO Reckford, who took the helm just before these crises hit. "But when they do occur, you have to be willing to adjust your efforts and thinking to meet the need. Both Katrina and Rita and the Indian Ocean tsunami were rallying points to kill cultural sacred cows about how we scale. If you think about Habitat, it was designed to do a little bit in a whole lot of places. With both events, we went much deeper in a smaller place and time. We built twenty-five thousand homes in response to the tsunami and two thousand in the Gulf region post-Katrina. It forced us to think about doing some things differently."

This experience led Habitat to expand its strategy from focusing primarily on building single homes to embracing many more diverse ways of ending poverty housing around the world.

In the wake of Hurricane Katrina, Teach For America increased its commitment to New Orleans, a community in which it had been working since 1990. Rather than just scaling up or out, the organization has learned—like many local or smaller nonprofits—how to scale more deeply in one place. In this case, Katrina literally destroyed much of the existing infrastructure, creating a blank slate on which to build from scratch. As the community rebuilt the city and the school system, Teach For America responded to the increased need for educators, providing a critical infusion of human capital to the city's highest-need schools.

"It was a huge crisis for New Orleans, yet it became a critical moment for the community to transform their education system," says founder Wendy Kopp. Teach For America now has more than 350 corps members teaching in the New Orleans area and over 450 alums working throughout the region. In addition, 20 percent of local principals are alumni, and many other charter schools in the area are part of Teach For America's extended informal network—fueling efforts to transform an entire school district. "We think New Orleans has the potential to be a system-level proof point, and we are excited to be working alongside many others as part of that effort."

BENDING HISTORY

Reflecting on the turmoil of the past few years, we were reminded of a phrase popularized by the Reverend Martin Luther King Jr. during the civil rights era: "The arc of the moral universe is long, but it bends toward justice." Since the onset of the Great Recession in 2008, it has seemed to many nonprofits that the arc of justice has bent in the wrong direction. While millions in the United States continue to suffer from unemployment, poverty, hunger, and homelessness—not to mention those suffering abroad—it makes for a heavy counterweight against society's espoused ideals of equality, opportunity, and prosperity for all.

Yet, as we have documented in this chapter, the twelve organizations we studied have continued to push with all their might against the weighty forces of collapsed markets, faltering governments, and a spiraling global economy. They have continued to feed millions, house hundreds of thousands, improve the toughest schools, and secure health care for the most vulnerable despite it all. That many of them grew their annual budgets through the Great Recession is remarkable.

Even more noteworthy is that the growth did not necessarily correlate with traditional avenues of organization development, such as opening new sites or expanding programs. Instead, the twelve groups scaled their impact by continuing to tap into greater forces outside their four walls—working through government, business, other nonprofits, and individuals—to propel greater results. We continue to be awed and humbled by the work of these organizations and by their impressive results. Indeed, they are trying to bend the arc of history back toward justice. And over and over again, we saw the twelve organizations leveraging the six practices of high-impact nonprofits to do this—a theme we explore further in the next chapter.

CHAPTER ELEVEN

DEEPENING THE SIX PRACTICES

When we set out to revisit the original twelve high-impact non-profits five years after our initial research, we were curious about what we might find, as Greg Dees alluded to in his Foreword. We suspected that some of these nonprofits might have cut back on certain practices given the austere times, or that a few might be struggling. But as noted in the previous chapter, every one of the organizations has not only survived the recent downturn but actually thrived. Sure, some of these groups needed to take temporary defensive positions and shore up their internal organization, but none of them maintained that internal gaze for long. They continued to go on the offense and to find new ways to increase their external impact, even as the world changed around them.

Rather than cutting back on the six practices, several organizations have, if anything, significantly increased their use of a practice to increase their impact. For us this validated that we had uncovered reliable pathways for scaling impact, ones that hold true despite radically different circumstances from those under which we'd conducted our initial research. In fact, we've come to believe that an important reason these nonprofits have thrived is that they've continued to harness many or all of the six practices for their cause.

In this chapter, we look at how all six practices have been refined and deepened by the twelve organizations in the past five years. We share how many of these groups leaned heavily on one or more of these practices during the downturn to increase their impact, whether or not they were growing their budget or organization. As with the first edition, we hope these stories will inspire you and give you some new concrete examples that you might emulate.

ACCELERATING ADVOCACY

As we explored in Chapter Two, that these organizations combined service *and* advocacy was one of the counterintuitive findings that emerged from our original research, considering that most nonprofits have traditionally done one or the other, but not both. It's a practice that we believe has sustained the twelve high-impact nonprofits through good times and bad. If anything, several of the organizations actually accelerated their advocacy during the downturn; doing so provided a hedge against potential cutbacks in services, and leverage for greater impact at a time when government programs were threatened. Not only did these groups continue to advocate, but many of them expanded to include local, state, and federal advocacy as part of their strategy. A few of the nonprofits that had only just started advocating five years ago have actually made a strategic shift to lean much more on this lever.

Habitat for Humanity provides perhaps the most compelling example of an organization that dramatically strengthened its advocacy in the past few years, while continuing to directly serve communities. Recognizing that the nonprofit would never be able to build enough houses to serve everyone in need, Habitat adopted a new strategic plan in 2006. "The headline of the plan," explains CEO Jonathan Reckford, "was that Habitat would be a *partner and catalyst* for worldwide action." The move was designed not just to focus on building homes but also to facilitate broader impact by advocating for decent housing for all. "It was a shift in focus from houses built to families served," Reckford told us. "We can serve people through housing, but we also want to serve them through advocacy."

The organization established a staff advocacy team at its Georgia-based headquarters while growing a virtual campaign among its volunteers—one that soon included ninety thousand advocates in the United States alone. Overseas Habitat volunteers and staff became leading advocates for systemic reforms that would enable more families and individuals to secure decent affordable housing. The global effort focused on securing home ownership and property rights, particularly among women in countries where they had been denied these rights. For instance, as Habitat volunteers built homes in Southeast Asia during the past five years, they titled each property in the woman's name. Habitat also joined in coalitions with other nonprofits to adopt the same approach, thus seeding widespread change and empowering women who historically had not had land rights to be legally safe and secure where they lived.

As it more actively embraced advocacy, Habitat did not abandon its commitment to direct service, but actually expanded it in other ways. Under Reckford's leadership, the organization finally let go of its long-held practice of only building new individual homes, in order to embrace a broader portfolio of housing solutions. The nonprofit began buying up empty and foreclosed homes, rehabbing and renovating salvageable existing homes, and conducting weatherization and repairs. This enabled Habitat to dramatically expand its programs in certain parts of the United States that it had historically overlooked, such as densely populated urban areas where land was at a premium and building new single-family homes too costly.

The antihunger organization Share Our Strength provides another story of increased advocacy at both the state and national levels leading to greater impact. Interestingly, this organization was founded by Bill Shore, a social entrepreneur who'd once worked for Senator Gary Hart—yet policy advocacy was noticeably absent from the nonprofit for its first two decades. Eventually, like all of the other organizations in our book, Share Our Strength realized that it could not achieve as much impact if it didn't move into advocacy.

By 2006, Share Our Strength had put a firm stake in the ground with respect to its strategy: "End childhood hunger by 2015." This was, as Jim Collins would say, a Big Hairy Audacious Goal (BHAG)—one that could not be achieved simply by expanding its programs. Around the same time, Share Our Strength leaders made a disturbing discovery: there were twenty million children in America eligible for a free breakfast and lunch, but only nine million were receiving the aid, and almost none were getting meals in the summer. Ironically, all of the funding was already available through existing federal antipoverty programs— it just wasn't being used.

"It was one of Washington's best-kept secrets," says Shore. "These kids are completely voiceless. They have no lobbyist. They make no PAC contributions. Yet there is a billion in federal funding just sitting there; it has already been approved, and they are simply not getting it. Nothing is a stronger testament to their lack of voice."

Shore's next move was to go directly to state governors to help them access this funding. "We realized that there was this real lack of attention to the issue. Governors had access to state and local funding for these programs, but none of the antihunger organizations had been to see them." In partnership with established local organizations, Share Our Strength reached out to governors and identified three states—Maryland, Colorado, and Arkansas—to pilot a program to increase access to aid. By 2011, Maryland and Colorado had seen increased participation of low-income children in these free meal programs, and a subsequent reduction of childhood hunger.

Self-Help is an example of a nonprofit that actually used advocacy to sustain its impact at a time when it was forced to scale back its services—in other words, advocacy was the perfect hedge. Self-Help was hard hit by the housing market collapse and recession; its home loan program slowed markedly as mortgage lending ground to a halt. But because Self-Help pursued a dual strategy of serving and advocating, it continued to increase impact through its advocacy, while moving into new program directions by working with struggling credit unions in local communities.

Self Help's Center for Responsible Lending had already built a reputation for passing effective state laws curtailing predatory lending, but it couldn't get federal legislation passed because of the powerful mortgage industry lobby. When the economy collapsed, federal lawmakers were finally convinced to overcome opposition and tune into what Self-Help had been preaching for a decade—resulting in passage of the Dodd-Frank Wall Street Reform and Consumer Protection Act in 2010. Had Self-Help not been actively advocating while also serving clients directly, its impact would have declined precipitously.

It's also important to note that not every advocacy effort was a success: Environmental Defense Fund (EDF) has been a leading proponent of climate change legislation for decades—expending millions of dollars, thousands of hours of staff time, immeasurable political capital, and myriad other resources to support cap-and-trade legislation to curb U.S. carbon emissions. Unfortunately for EDF, the bill passed in the U.S. House but stalled in the Senate. The organization has now taken the fight to the global and local levels, focusing on other countries and on cities and states to pass similar legislation. For other nonprofits, one group's victory was another's defeat. Even as the liberal Center on Budget and Policy Priorities celebrated the passage of Obama's health care plan, the more conservative Heritage Foundation chalked it up as a loss for its free-market ideology.

In sum, these twelve nonprofits won some policy battles and lost some—as is the nature of politics. But the point is that each put more effort into the advocacy game at the local, state, federal, and even global levels. And by doing so, many of them continued to increase their impact irrespective of what was happening to their programs and services.

Making Markets Work for Good

In our original research for Chapter Three, we found three ways that great nonprofits harness the power of markets and the private sector: they change business or industry-wide practices, partner with companies, and, in a few cases, even run a business themselves to generate earned income. When we went back to these twelve nonprofits, we again found that many of them continued to expand their efforts in this area. Despite the volatile nature of economic markets and cutbacks in some industries, a number of these nonprofits actually leaned into or ramped up their corporate partnerships and market-based approaches during the downturn.

Feeding America (formerly America's Second Harvest—The Nation's Food Bank Network) provides an excellent example of using all three of the aforementioned levers for greater impact. The onset of the Great Recession and increasing unemployment meant that millions more people in America needed emergency food assistance. As noted in the Chapter Ten, the nonprofit responded by expanding the amount of food it distributes by 65 percent, from 2 billion to 3.3 billion pounds annually, to feed nearly forty million people. But the group didn't do this by opening up 65 percent more food banks or pantries. Instead, Feeding America tapped into the power of the private sector and honed its practice of "making markets work" to source new supplies and push more food through its established distribution channels.

Under the leadership of new CEO Vicki Escarra, Feeding America expanded beyond its traditional corporate partners—food giants such as ConAgra, Kraft, and others—and developed new relationships with major retailers. Escarra and her team discovered that just as high-growth companies such as Walmart, Target, and Kroger were expanding their grocery aisles, these industry leaders were also throwing away millions of pounds of edible food. This included meat, cheese, eggs, and other items that were within their sell-by date, but were just not selling for various reasons. Feeding America was able to add 660 million pounds of new food to its supply chain by salvaging this "shrink" and redistributing it to the poor.

Meanwhile, Feeding America also went straight to the original source: the farmers who were growing the food. The nonprofit learned that millions of pounds of potentially edible produce—fresh tomatoes, potatoes, corn, and other crops—never made it off the farms. If the price wasn't good or the market was volatile, growers plowed under perfect crops rather than lose money bringing them to market. So in 2009, Feeding America established its new Produce Program, forming partnerships with farmers and promising them that Feeding America "would get that food out of the field, package, and ship it," says CFO Janet Gibbs. This new initiative added an additional annual 462 million pounds of food for hungry people—all by taking advantage of market dynamics and decreasing waste in the system.

Other high-impact nonprofits continued to strengthen and build out their partnerships with businesses, in some cases helping change business behavior. EDF, which we covered extensively in Chapter Three, has expanded its corporate partnerships even further, with the explicit purpose of helping businesses become more sustainable. Most notably, EDF has deepened its relationship with Walmart, helping the global corporation "make an organization-wide commitment to greenhouse gas reduction from its own stores and its supply chain," says Fred Krupp. The nonprofit has also established a partnership with numerous corporations to recruit and place ninety-six summer MBA interns, who focus on identifying ways to increase energy efficiency. And through the online Innovation Exchange, it has begun to crowdsource and share ideas across companies about ways to make business practices green.

EDF has also gone on to establish new ways of creating trading markets for environmental benefit. Even though cap-and-trade legislation failed to pass in the U.S. Senate, the organization has taken the fight to Europe, where similar carbon trading markets are in effect, and to India and China, the newest frontiers in the fight to tackle global climate change. "We came away from that fight realizing we're stuck in Washington, D.C., but we're not stuck outside Washington," says Krupp. "We're taking the fight to China, Brazil, to U.S. cities and corporations where we can demonstrate that we can reduce emissions, make the transition to clean energy, *and* create jobs."

One of EDF's latest, and most successful, forays into market-based approaches has been its establishment of successful catch-share programs to help stabilize fish populations. (Fishermen are given an ownership share in the stock of fish, and therefore have economic incentives to "leave fish in the bank," as it were.) "The biggest thing that has happened for us in the last five years is our fisheries work. If you'd told me then the results we'd be getting, I'd have laughed it off," says Krupp. "Now, primarily because of EDF's work to get the federal government to agree to this program, 75 percent of the fish caught in U.S. waters are in catch-share systems. This makes a huge difference—these fish populations are going to recover. In the Gulf of Mexico alone, the red snapper catch is up 40 percent in the last three years."

Last, a number of the twelve nonprofits have continued to forge corporate partnerships to leverage the resources of business for their cause, in the form of philanthropic donations, cause-marketing partnerships, in-kind donations, volunteer time, and so on. Several nonprofits that had been less strong on this practice have enhanced their efforts to partner with the private sector in the past few years—despite the fact that it has been a challenging time for business as well.

Notably, the Exploratorium has increased efforts to attract corporate sponsorships for its new waterfront location, just in time for the 2013 America's Cup sailing race, to be held in San Francisco Bay. It has also formed partnerships with local tech titans Google, Lucas Studios, and Pixar to explore furthering what's known as the DIY ("Do It Yourself")/maker movement. In addition, the Exploratorium has grown its business development unit to license and produce tinkering kits and other branded elements that may lead to large consultancy contracts for others promoting movements like DIY.

INSPIRING MORE EVANGELISTS

In Chapter Four, we described how high-impact nonprofits build and nurture social networks, or large communities of evangelists who champion their cause. They do this by sharing their values and their stories, and by giving their volunteers and donors real visceral experiences with their mission, which in turn inspire these people to go out and recruit others. Eventually this creates large ripple or "network effects," whereby these groups empower and engage others in their work. It is truly a virtuous cycle.

When we revisited the twelve nonprofits, we found that they have continued to advance this practice—if anything, they have now turbocharged it with social media, which was only just emerging when we conducted our first research. (Our first edition excluded many Internet-based high-impact groups, such as Kiva and MoveOn.org, because we limited our sample to nonprofits founded before 1995. In addition, social media was not yet ubiquitous when we concluded that research in 2005.) Perhaps this is the practice that has been advanced the most by external forces—after all, online channels and social networks now give all nonprofits cheaper, more effective ways to reach out and communicate to many more people, thus inspiring more evangelists for their cause.

Take The Heritage Foundation, which is well on its way to enlisting a million members. As of 2011, it already counted 750,000 on its official roster—up 300 percent from when we left off in 2005. If any organization is bent on inspiring a movement of evangelists, it is Heritage. (And in case you aren't a member, this think tank acts more like a conservative Sierra Club than it does a Brookings Institute.) Counter to most think tanks, which continue to operate as ivory towers churning out reports, Heritage—with some help from the Tea Party—has built a national movement of individuals who are impassioned evangelists for the conservative cause.

Heritage has done this primarily through direct marketing (both online and offline), doubling investment at the height of the recession and receiving more contributions than ever. But it has also targeted high-net-worth individuals who want to take up Heritage's cause. "We've continued to inspire evangelists among recent retirees," says CEO Edwin Feulner. "There was a former corporate CEO from Iowa who said he'd give us $100K a year, but he also wanted to volunteer half-time. He was briefed on the policy side and by our development staff, and he's now out there working on our behalf. This is the kind of talent we couldn't possibly pay."

Teach For America also continued to expand its impact by engaging its alumni in the broader effort to ensure that kids growing up in poverty get an excellent education. By 2011, its long-term theory of change was finally crystallizing as TFA alumni were experienced enough to assume positions of real power and influence. Michelle Rhee, a noted Teach For America alumna, was appointed chancellor of D.C. Public Schools, taking on teachers unions by championing a plan that would enable teachers to opt into performance-based pay while opting out of tenure. Though Rhee was ultimately ousted by the next mayor, her tenure resulted in a new union contract that saw the D.C. Public Schools become one of the fastest-improving K–12 systems in the nation. Other noteworthy alums include KIPP charter school cofounders Mike Feinberg and Dave Levin, and senior leaders at many major education reform foundations and nonprofits.

Other examples of inspiring evangelists abound. Habitat for Humanity has been busy turning hammers into votes; as discussed in the section on advocacy, Habitat enlisted more than ninety thousand of its volunteers as advocates for housing reform. National Council of La Raza (NCLR) has also been building up its network of Latino advocates through local outreach so that it can bring the power of individual, grassroots advocacy to its policy campaigns. And the Exploratorium has used its capital campaign as a catalyst to engage even more people. "The work on the capital campaign is getting more individuals inspired," associate executive director Robert Semper says. "The physical experience of being in the museum makes you a strong evangelist for museums and for science education. But because of the campaign, more people who didn't know our story are now coming in."

The Exploratorium, along with the other high-impact nonprofits, is accelerating this approach of inspiring and engaging others through its use of social media. Although the twelve nonprofits vary in terms of their level of sophistication using these new tools, several of the earliest adopters have figured out how to strategically integrate online and offline engagement opportunities and leverage the power of social networks to inspire more evangelists and grow their communities.

"We've been trying to change with the Web world," says Semper. "Five years ago we were developing experiences online like the ones in the museum—there were lots of pages and content. Now we're trying to create material that's bite-sized and that's useful on mobile. We just redid our Web site about a year ago, and we're making it adaptable to new forms of social media. We're also trying to marry cyberspace and physical space, so you can experience the Internet in the building itself, and you can extend your visit outside the building."

Integrating online and offline networks to create seamless transitions between the two is perhaps the next great frontier of engagement. Other nonprofits would do well to learn from and copy early adopters such as the Exploratorium.

NURTURING THE NETWORKED NONPROFIT

In Chapter Five, we illustrated how the twelve high-impact nonprofits worked with other nonprofit organizations to build networks, collaborating rather than competing. In some cases, they do this through formal or informal "affiliates," which are part of the organization's overall distributed, or federated, structure. In other cases, these nonprofits form alliances, coalitions, or partnerships with nonaffiliated nonprofits that share a similar cause, if not the same exact mission or brand.

This time around, we were interested in understanding more deeply how these twelve groups continued to leverage their nonprofit networks. For those with affiliates, how did they think about maximizing this decentralized structure for greater learning and impact? For those without affiliates, had their approach to collaboration and field building changed given the economic downturn? What we found was that rather than increasing competition in a fight over ever-scarcer resources, these high-impact nonprofits realized that they could actually be more effective and efficient and have more impact if they teamed up and invested deeply in building and strengthening their networks rather than going it alone. In some cases they continued to "grow the pie" for their field; in other cases, they figured out how to share resources and collaborate in order to literally do more with less.

Of all the high-impact nonprofits we studied, NCLR has focused most intensely on nurturing its network of more than three hundred nonprofit affiliates. (NCLR affiliates are independent 501(c)(3) organizations that may identify as NCLR affiliates by name, but are not required to.) So even though NCLR was one of the few nonprofits we studied to face a financial setback in 2008–09, it was still able to expand its impact by strengthening its network.

Starting in 2008, NCLR set out to recategorize the way it worked with affiliates so that they could ultimately become more efficient and realize greater economies of scale. "NCLR and our affiliates had gotten away from why we were connected. We were trying to be 'everything' to all of our affiliates," says NCLR CEO Janet Murguía.

The first step was to segment the affiliates strategically into three categories and to define more clearly what the relationship with NCLR would entail. For General Affiliates, there are minimal expectations on either side; the ties were kept loose. Program Affiliates largely receive some funding directly or indirectly through NCLR, but are required to execute certain programs according to specified standards; there is a medium level of commitment and control. Advocacy Affiliates form a special category, and NCLR figured out how it could better support them in state and local advocacy work and team up on national campaigns. NCLR also examined strategies to better engage the next generation of emerging affiliates with targeted resources and training, so that they can grow into more stable and high-impact local organizations.

NCLR was betting that if it could form stronger partnerships with local affiliates and bolster their capacity, these would lead to stronger communities, stronger cities, and ultimately greater impact on Latino causes. "It all ties back to NCLR's overall strategy and mission," explains Murguía. Early results are promising: one of the indicators that NCLR tracks is affiliate engagement, which has increased across the board. For example, participation in NCLR's 2011 Advocacy Day in California had more than 325 participants—up from mere dozens in earlier years.

Similarly, Habitat for Humanity undertook a review of its global affiliate structure just after CEO Jonathan Reckford took the helm. Reckford led the organization through a painful but productive process of scrutinizing its nearly three thousand affiliates across 120 countries, and made the decision to consolidate some, scale back operations, and pull out of a few countries altogether. Some staff who were acolytes of founder Millard Fuller and his vision of global expansion initially resisted the change—it ran counter to their movement-building culture. But Reckford, a Stanford MBA with decades of private sector experience, questioned why Habitat couldn't focus on deepening its impact in the places it already operated by consolidating some affiliates and forcing greater accountability among the ranks. More isn't always better—sometimes it's just more.

A key part of City Year's strategy also has hinged on a networked approach, though in this case it has not been about a distributed structure. (Although the nonprofit operates in multiple locations, it is a tightly controlled, single organization.) Rather, City Year has formed strategic partnerships and alliances with other nonprofits in adjacent fields. Its Diplomas Now program, launched in partnership with the nonprofit

Communities in Schools, is an education reform initiative that blends whole-school reform with social services. The program uses elements of a proven approach developed at Johns Hopkins University, which structures a school in smaller units so that teams of teachers oversee manageable numbers of students. The program also provides professional development and peer coaching for teachers, customized academic help for students, and added instruction in math and literacy—which is where City Year comes in.

Through the partnership, City Year sends teams of corps members to Diplomas Now schools to run after-school programs and team up with teachers to help the students with attendance, behavior, or academic difficulties. Meanwhile, Communities in Schools provides social workers to counsel the most seriously troubled students. The partnership leverages the relative strengths of both organizations and leads to better outcomes for students than either nonprofit could achieve alone.

Share Our Strength's recent advocacy campaign, End Childhood Hunger, also relies heavily on building coalitions and working *with and through* other nonprofit partners. Rather than expanding to new sites, Share Our Strength instead focused on identifying existing partners at the state level to join as allies in the fight to end childhood hunger; Share Our Strength then shared funding with them and helped build their capacity to advocate for local changes. In Colorado, for instance, Share Our Strength partnered with Hunger Free Colorado and Governor John Hickenlooper to launch the No Kid Hungry Colorado campaign. The campaign has been credited with increased participation among children eligible for food assistance programs, such as summer meals, school breakfast, after-school snack, and SNAP (Supplemental Nutrition Assistance Program). Similar local networks and alliances exist in Maryland.

Tim Cross, the former COO of YouthBuild USA who is now leading YouthBuild's international expansion, summed up this networked approach well: "Our model won't work unless partnerships are forged and managed so that they are mutually beneficial," he says. "It's important to have transparent discussions about how collaboration can benefit the respective institutions, and to talk about brand and how credit is shared. And you have to have commitment to outcomes. Ultimately it's about getting the model right and then ceding local control. I don't know any other way to do this kind of work."

These are all excellent examples of highly leveraged approaches that tap into the power of decentralized nonprofit networks. Instead of functioning as highly centralized or hierarchical organizations, expanding out programs and services from the top down, these nonprofits reach out to their affiliates and to other partners to advance their causes from the bottom up as well. It's an excellent example of how great nonprofits don't focus on building their own empires—instead they find value in building the larger field.

CONTINUOUSLY ADAPTING

Clearly, as illustrated in the previous chapter and in the examples we've described in this one, the ability to respond nimbly to the shifting economic, political, and social trends over the past five years is a hallmark of the twelve organizations we have examined. It is what has enabled them not only to survive but to thrive in extraordinarily difficult times. We've touched on numerous examples of their ability to read cues in their external environment, innovate, and respond accordingly—but there are a few that truly stand out.

The Exploratorium, for example, has long been radically innovative, as we underscored in Chapter Six. Although not terribly buttoned-down in its management style, it is a great example of harnessing the power of creativity and of constantly evolving its strategy to respond to changing times. This capability is not an afterthought or coincidence, but rather an intrinsic element of the Exploratorium's culture that its leadership deliberately cultivates. "You have to actively foster adaptive capacity," Semper says. "It's about being strategically opportunistic. You don't want to have zero strategy and be completely free-form, but you also don't want to be too rigid and locked in. There are always multiple ways to get to where you want to go." In other words, adaptive capacity has to do with using judgment about when and how to respond, with which tool or approach.

Several of the twelve nonprofits have made some fairly radical shifts in the past five years. Take the Center on Budget and Policy Priorities, which was previously focused on its inside-the-beltway strategy of federal budget analysis and influence on the Hill. Today the Center has built on this core strength, but dramatically expanded how it communicates with larger audiences.

"The Center of today is not in the same category as it was five years ago—we're really at a different, higher level," says founder Bob Greenstein. "Then we were known for the caliber of our analysis and the strategic use of it, and our work had impact through policymakers and the mainstream media. But in the past five years, our communications capability has been transformed. We're now using Twitter, social media, and blogs, and have transformed how we reach people. From an organizational perspective, it's much more decentralized—you have to be in order to deal with a twenty-four-hour news cycle and with social media."

The Center's conservative counterpart, The Heritage Foundation, has also made some important shifts to increase its adaptive capacity. In addition to changing its strategy and ramping up its membership and fundraising, Heritage has also carved out a particular part of the organization dedicated to focusing on policy innovation. One of the nonprofit's senior policy leaders was put in charge of a new Center for Policy Innovation, which Feulner describes as a "Steve Jobs kind of unit, designed to come up with our equivalent of the iPod." The team in this center is tasked with "going out and thinking big thoughts outside our normal structure, and then coming back with big solutions."

Other examples of innovation and deliberate adaptation among these twelve nonprofits abound, and have been covered more thoroughly elsewhere in this or the previous chapter:

- City Year's transformation from a general-purpose service organization to a youth corps trained and focused to intervene in the nation's toughest schools
- EDF's successful launch of its market-based catch-share programs to help stabilize U.S. fish populations
- Feeding America's move to partner with farmers and effectively create a market for underpriced crops that would

otherwise be plowed under; its decision to completely
overhaul its brand
- Habitat's decision to consolidate and strengthen its affiliate
  structure, while simultaneously shifting its strategy to embrace
  multiple approaches to creating more affordable housing for
  all, including greater advocacy
- NCLR's strategic reorganization of the way it works with
  affiliates to become more efficient and realize greater
  economies of scale
- Self-Help's ability to find $35 million in one day to pay off its
  overnight loan and avoid defaulting; its ability to ramp up
  advocacy at a time when its direct lending was stalled by the
  economic crisis
- YouthBuild's expansion into sixteen countries, taking its
  model for educating and employing low-income youth to
  populations with great need

None of this is to say that innovating is easy—in fact, these
nonprofits acknowledge the difficulty of orchestrating major
changes. The difference between them and less successful nonprofits is that they make the changes anyway. They are not content
to stand still, but constantly keep adapting in pursuit of greater
impact. As Randy Chambers recalls, "Self-Help doesn't take for-
ever to turn around, but it's also not a speedboat that turns 360
degrees in five seconds. It took us a little while after the crash to
figure out how to grow our ability to do loss mitigation. Our goal
when the meltdown started in 2008 was, How quickly can we turn
this battleship? We've been pretty successful, but it did take some
experimenting with what the best intervention was."

SHARING LEADERSHIP IN
TUMULTUOUS TIMES

The last of the six practices is certainly not the least important. In
fact, sharing leadership helps knit the other practices together—
with strong and distributed leadership, these organizations
can continue to adapt, engage others, influence entire sectors,
change systems, and sustain their own organizations. In networked

organizations, strong relationships and trusted leadership are the social "glue" that binds everything together. If leadership were to become too concentrated in just a few individuals, these nonprofits would cease to have the same impact. They must literally share their vision and work with others to magnify their results.

When we explored the concept of shared leadership in Chapter Seven, we looked at several different layers: how high-impact executives manage to last so long and yet not become the bottleneck in their organizations; how they build strong and distributed leadership teams; how they cultivate, engage, and share leadership with their boards; and even how they develop leadership in their external networks and larger fields. We've taken to characterizing these as three legs of a stool (or four, if you count external network leadership, as we explore in Chapters Five and Twelve). Each leg is needed to maintain balance and impact.

All these multiple ways of sharing leadership continued to resonate in our second round of research. The senior leadership teams for these nonprofits still include an impassioned and exceptionally talented CEO (not always the founder), paired with a strong second-in-command (COO or equivalent), surrounded by highly skilled senior teams and large, dedicated boards of directors.

One trend that was particularly striking—and that perhaps was correlated with the age of many of these groups (around thirty to forty years)—was that fully *half* of the twelve nonprofits sustained a CEO transition during the last five to six years. Some of these changes were already under way when we were completing our first research, but it was too early to determine if they had been successful. Others have undergone these transitions more recently.

Now, circling back, we're able to report that these groups have successfully navigated the turbulent waters of executive transition—and many have come out even stronger. We believe that this is precisely because their leadership wasn't overly concentrated in the founder or CEO; rather, these organizations had strong teams and boards that could lead through and beyond the transition. Table 11.1 lists the organizations that since 2005 have either installed a new CEO or announced a forthcoming transition.

TABLE 11.1. MULTIPLE LEADERSHIP TRANSITIONS.

Organization	New CEO or Founder	New CEO Tenure
City Year	Cofounder Michael Brown became CEO when cofounder Alan Khazei departed after 25+ years in office.	2005 to present
Exploratorium	Dennis Bartels replaced outgoing CEO Goéry Delacôte and turned over much of the leadership team.	2006 to present
Feeding America	Vicki Escarra replaced outgoing CEO Bob Forney.	2006 to present
Habitat for Humanity	Jonathan Reckford replaced founder Millard Fuller and also appointed new members to the senior team.	2005 to present
The Heritage Foundation	Ed Feulner, president of 30+ years, will step down in 2013.	TBD
National Council of La Raza	Janet Murguía replaced Raul Yazaguirre.	2005 to present

Paradoxically, these executive transitions often enabled the organizations to share leadership in new ways by distributing authority even more fully. City Year cofounder and CEO Michael Brown explains that when outgoing CEO Alan Khazei departed from the organization after twenty-five years of coleadership, it was no longer two at the top. But that didn't whittle it down to just one. "It opened up space to expand the leadership potential of the entire senior team," says Brown. "I needed the expertise of the other team members, and with Alan gone, instead of relying just on me, we allowed others to step up to the plate."

The Center on Budget and Policy Priorities has also made a concerted effort to build out its leadership team; even though founder Bob Greenstein is still involved, he is less and less central to the group's work, by design. "We have strengthened the bench of our senior management," he says. "This has been very important, as we've been getting bigger; now the division structure is much stronger. The division directors have roles in managing people and policy and product in their areas." The Center has also made similar changes to its board, bringing on new board members and new blood. "We've really followed a lot of the best practices for nonprofits and board changes."

In fact, as many of these nonprofits have been on rapid growth trajectories, they have had to expand their talent base and invest in their human assets in order to support and sustain their rapid growth. Teach For America is the most dramatic in its expansion, and it has invested heavily in shoring up its scale with concerted efforts to recruit, hire, retain, and develop extraordinarily talented leaders.

"We were really overdue in realizing what structures and investments we needed to make internally," says Wendy Kopp. "We recruited a new senior team in 2006; we needed a whole new level of leadership if we were going to get where we were trying to go. That team came in, and midway into the first year we concluded that the growth goals were doable, but that the staffing plan was insufficient. We've made a huge commitment to leadership development in our own organization and put enormous resources into every piece of that puzzle—into recruiting and selecting staff and into our development and talent pipeline. We now have more than one hundred people working in human assets."

In addition, Kopp made a move to share her own leadership at the top. She appointed Matthew Kramer president, while retaining the CEO title. "That was critical," Kopp says. "It was becoming clear that the external and internal demands were just too much for one person. Matt has made a real difference by fostering entrepreneurship at every level of the organization. We've developed our own leadership competency model and internal systems . . . which enabled us to find the right leaders and develop them internally."

Self-Help has made a similar effort to expand its leadership base both within its organization and among its local affiliates. "We're much stronger than we were five years ago," says Chambers. "We've built a strong group of senior managers." The challenge for Self-Help now, as it has merged with or acquired many local credit unions and rolled them up to be part of its larger network, is "How do we absorb the staff that's in retail day to day? That's a challenge. Also, how do we develop our human capital further down in the organization, and make sure that folks several levels down from the CEO are getting opportunities for growth?"

A VIRTUOUS CYCLE

As the examples we've described in this chapter demonstrate, the six practices of high-impact nonprofits are not static. Adaptive nonprofits continue to refine them, strengthen them, and embed them more deeply into the fabric of their organizations. The more they increase their use of the practices, the more impact they have—leading to greater influence and greater impact, in a reinforcing loop. As we've seen, in the past few years many of the twelve nonprofits strengthened their commitment to advocacy; others found novel ways to make markets work; some forged new networks or embraced social media to inspire more evangelists; and they all continued to invest in developing shared leadership. It goes without saying that they all exemplified the capacity to adapt and innovate, a capacity critical to navigating turbulent times.

Yet we recognize that as successful as the organizations have been during these past few years, and as much as they continue to scale out their impact, they still have far to go. They are each in relentless pursuit of a Big Hairy Audacious Goal, whether it is to end childhood hunger in America, create equal access to a quality education, or build affordable housing for all. As they continue to strive for these ideals, they leverage every tool available, band together with other nonprofits, forge partnerships with the public and private sectors, and inspire individuals to join their cause. They are never satisfied; their vision of the future and their ability to shape it are always expanding outward. They clearly have not let the Great Recession stand in their way. By deepening their commitment to the six practices, these organizations have become even stronger forces for good.

CHAPTER TWELVE

FORCES FOR *LOCAL* GOOD

When *Forces for Good* was first published, it gave us the opportunity to engage with nonprofit and philanthropic leaders across the country as the two of us traveled widely, speaking, advising, and facilitating workshops. The question we heard most often from our audiences was, *Can the six practices be executed by local and regional groups with smaller budgets—or are they applicable only to large organizations operating at national or global scales?*

Good question. Unlike the twelve organizations we initially studied—all of which were selected based on having "scaled up" to national or global impact—the vast majority of nonprofits in the United States are relatively small, locally focused, and resource constrained. Understandably, they don't want to risk spending time and effort on practices that might not be applicable to their context, particularly in a challenging economy.

At the same time, the question misses an important point. None of the twelve organizations we profiled in the first edition sprang into existence fully grown, with budgets in the millions. To take just two examples, Teach For America was launched by a college student on a miniscule budget in a borrowed office, and Habitat for Humanity was founded *after* Millard Fuller had already given away his fortune. Rather, these groups reached the size and scale they are today *because* they used the six practices to grow and achieve impressive levels of impact.

And yet we know that the vast majority of nonprofits don't have national—let alone global—ambitions. What drives most local and smaller organizations is not growth per se, but the desire to achieve deep impact *in their own communities*. Although we had a strong intuition that nonprofits of any size could benefit from the six practices to have deep rather than broad impact, we hadn't yet studied any smaller local nonprofits to find proof—until we undertook this updated edition.

In this chapter, we provide emerging evidence, based on new research, that the six practices can be used by smaller and local nonprofits to increase the impact in their own communities. Take one of our favorite examples—the Little Theatre on the Square in Sullivan, Illinois—a small but mighty nonprofit that uses all of the six practices to punch above its weight.

THE SIX PRACTICES AT THE LOCAL LEVEL

At the apex of a 2009 performance of *Annie* at the Little Theatre on the Square, strong winds howled, rain fell, and the lights went out. Undaunted, Little Orphan Annie pushed through her bring-down-the-house finale, even as a tornado threatened to touch down nearby.

Located in the heart of America's corn belt, in Sullivan, Illinois, the Little Theatre is the only professional performance space between Chicago and St. Louis, Missouri. Sullivan, with a population of forty-four hundred, is a typical rural town, yet the quality of the Little Theatre's productions isn't that different from those at more renowned regional theatres, such as Chicago's Steppenwolf. It's the interesting mash-up of the bucolic setting and big-city drama that surprises: the nonprofit has become a cultural beacon in a community more known for its corn than its cabaret.

This small but mighty nonprofit has sustained its impact for more than half a century: it has survived tornadoes, episodic private and government support, and even a brief bankruptcy in the 1980s. Yet today the Little Theatre provides world-class artistic programming on a relatively modest budget of $1.5 million. It boasts a 418-seat venue, hosts more than fifty thousand patrons a year, and provides traveling dance and drama classes to more than sixty thousand students in area schools. Rather than scaling up nationally, the Little Theatre has focused instead on having deep impact in a specific region. In this sense, it represents the perfect case of how a local nonprofit (one decidedly smaller than the original twelve) can employ the six practices to strengthen its own community. Here's how it does it.

First, Little Theatre has *advocated* to local government for financial support, despite having a history of mixed relations with city officials. (The Theatre is liberal leaning in a mostly conservative town.) When the city council initially refused to provide public funding for the theatre, its enterprising executive director, John Stephens, proposed a creative solution: the city could charge a 5 percent tax on ticket sales and share the proceeds with Little Theatre after taking a small commission. Today this tax generates $50,000 a year for the nonprofit.

The Little Theatre also *makes local markets work* by thinking like a business. To better utilize the theatre's floor space, Stephens opened the Second Act Gallery, which displays work by local artists and generates a 30 percent commission on sales. It also launched educational programs in which employees teach drama to local children and adults, serving 350 paying students a year. And through a touring program, added in 2004, Little Theatre actors have visited 180 schools, performing for over a quarter-million students and generating more than $2,000 per week in additional revenue. In addition, the theatre has been an early adopter of new technologies—for example, promoting online ticket purchases and automated monthly credit card donations.

Like many local nonprofits, the Little Theatre is particularly adept at *inspiring evangelists*. It offers personalized engagement opportunities for patrons, such as a Friends program that includes invitations to private receptions, question-and-answer sessions with actors, opening- and closing-night parties, and backstage tours. Select Friends are invited to attend an annual trip to New York City and receive free backstage tours to Broadway shows, among other perks. These high-touch cultivation efforts have paid off: "When our donors got back from the first trip, they'd already paid $2,000 each. But everyone made an unexpected second donation much bigger than the first," says Stephens.

The theatre also taps into the power of *nurturing nonprofit networks*. It introduced an affiliate advertising model, in which participating local nonprofits drive their members, donors, and volunteers to the theatre and receive a percentage of ticket sales. More recently, it launched the Coalition of Theatre Organizations, a regional network of school-based community theatres across the Midwest. Individual members can purchase a card that provides discounts on tickets to any theatre in the network.

To effectively leverage the power of each of the local sectors we've mentioned, the Little Theater has also *mastered the art of adaptation*. It pays close attention to external cues so that it can respond quickly to changes and seek out new opportunities. The nonprofit evaluates its programs and approaches, and knows everything from how far and how frequently audience members travel to attend performances, to how they buy tickets—whether by phone, in person, or online. Then it uses these data to adapt its approach.

Finally, the Little Theatre presents a creative example of how a local nonprofit *shares leadership*—in this case, by extending leadership beyond its four walls to include nonprofit networks and loyal patrons in advancing its cause.

Although the Little Theatre's performance is remarkable given its limited budget, it does not stand alone—over the past five years working in the sector, we've gathered increasing anecdotal evidence that the six practices can be applied by a wide variety of local nonprofits to have greater impact. So when we set out to do new research for this updated edition, we particularly wanted to find further examples of how local and smaller nonprofits can use this approach.

Over the summer of 2011, we conducted new research on thirteen smaller nonprofits—with budgets ranging from $800,000 to just under $5 million, from varying locales, and representing different issues. (See Exhibit 12.1 for a list of the ten that appear in this chapter.) In this chapter, we have distilled our lessons learned about how the six practices play out in a local context. Some of the nonprofits highlighted here came to our attention because the executive director attended one of our presentations, or we knew of them through our own networks. Others were referred to us by funders and experts with deep knowledge of local social sector organizations. (For an overview of our selection and research process, see Appendix F.)

Regardless of how the nonprofits in this chapter surfaced, we included them because each seemed to be applying some or all of the six practices with success. Unlike our original research, we didn't go out and choose a sample of smaller nonprofits in order to inductively derive what makes them tick. This time we already had our framework; we wanted to deductively test our hypothesis that the six practices could be applied locally to increase an organization's impact. We hope that by studying these high-impact smaller nonprofits and sharing their stories, we might inspire other leaders to learn from them—and perhaps even adopt similar approaches.

PRACTICE 1: ADVOCATE *AND* SERVE

Will never had a chance. His father was a drug dealer and his mother an addict, so it wasn't surprising that Will, the oldest of six children, was homeless and dealing drugs by age fifteen. One day he got into a terrible fight, resulting in the death of another man. Although he claimed self-defense, Will was charged with murder, and ended up facing life in prison.[1]

Will's case was brought to the Georgia Justice Project (GJP), an Atlanta-based nonprofit founded in 1986 with a holistic mission: to provide the indigent criminally accused with quality legal representation and access to social and employment services. GJP took Will's case, fought hard at his trial—and lost. But GJP stayed with Will for the long haul, visiting him in prison and communicating with his family. The group won a motion for a new trial and got Will's life sentence reduced. After ten years in prison, Will is now on parole, working every day at a job GJP helped him obtain. With the assistance of this small nonprofit, Will has turned his life around.

Although it is remarkable, Will's success story is not unusual for GJP. But the nonprofit is fighting against the odds: the U.S. criminal justice system deals primarily with low-income people, many of whom commit nonviolent offenses and receive legal representation by overworked public defenders. The result? Conviction rates are over 80 percent, with almost every defendant being sentenced to prison. Upon release, most parolees receive a

EXHIBIT 12.1. PROFILES OF SMALL AND LOCAL NONPROFITS.

Organization Name	Service Region	Issue Area(s)	Budget	What It Does
A Home Within	27 U.S. cities	Foster care, mental health	$0.80 M	A Home Within seeks to heal the trauma of chronic loss experienced by foster children and to improve the foster care system by building positive lasting relationships and continuous connections through direct services, professional training, public awareness, and advocacy.
Federation of Appalachian Housing Enterprises (FAHE)	Kentucky, Tennessee, Virginia, West Virginia	Housing, community development	$5.00 M	FAHE is a clearinghouse for financial services, including conventional as well as unconventional products, in the Appalachian counties of Kentucky, Tennessee, Virginia, and West Virginia. FAHE also establishes the infrastructure necessary to implement scalable housing solutions.
Georgia Justice Project (GJP)	Georgia	Criminal justice	$0.80 M	GJP's work is divided into two categories: (1) criminal defense representation combined with long-term social services and employment support; and (2) Coming Home, comprising a legal counseling program and a policy initiative that work together to remove the barriers (collateral consequences) to employment and housing created by a criminal history.
Little Theatre on the Square	Illinois	Arts	$1.50 M	Founded in 1924, the Little Theatre on the Square is a theatre in Sullivan. Centered in an agrarian community, it is the only professional theater between Chicago and St. Louis. It's outreach program has reached 26,000 students since 2004.
Live Local Alberta	Alberta, Canada	Community development	$1.00 M	Based in Edmonton, Live Local helps citizens, independent businesses, and communities ensure ongoing opportunities for independent entrepreneurs, prevent the displacement of locally owned businesses, and promote citizen engagement. The nonprofit supports the growth and development of community-based business by providing services to members and encouraging local purchasing.

Meet Each Need with Dignity (MEND)	California	Social services	$2.40 M	MEND serves as many as 32,000 individuals per month while remarkably keeping operating costs at 5 percent, and is the largest, most efficient, and most comprehensive poverty relief organization in the San Fernando Valley.
The Mission Continues	Individual fellowships across the United States	Veterans, community service	$4.50 M	The Mission Continues challenges post-9/11 wounded and disabled veterans to serve once again in their communities through its fellowship program. A typical fellowship covers twenty-eight weeks, during which the Fellow serves at a local charitable organization for 20 hours per week. It also promotes programs through which veterans perform community service alongside civilians.
Partnership to End Poverty	Oregon	Economic and workforce development	$0.65 M	Partnership to End Poverty is a convener of resources for innovative solutions to poverty in Central Oregon. The organization has two programs that best typify how it leverages the power of its networks: faith-based networks and Project Connect.
RYASAP	Connecticut	Juvenile justice	$3.20 M	RYASAP is an urban and suburban youth and community development coalition serving the Greater Bridgeport region, with local and statewide programs in juvenile justice advocacy, young adult leadership, and asset-based youth community development training and consultation. RYASAP's mission is to create healthy communities free of the harm caused by substance abuse, crime, and violence.
Safe Kids Canada	Toronto, Canada	Children's health and safety	$1.50 M	Safe Kids Canada began in 1992 to address the leading cause of death and a significant cause of hospitalization to children and youth (1 to 14 years): preventable accidents. Over almost 20 years, the organization has grown into a credible source of evidence-based practices for professionals and of key messages for parents and media, and is an active advocate for changes to policy and legislation.

$25 check and a bus ticket home. It should come as no surprise, then, that two-thirds of poor inmates released from prison return within three years. The current system isn't merely ineffective—it's fundamentally broken.

The experience of GJP staff working directly with clients afforded them greater visibility into the systemic barriers that prevent their clients from avoiding prison and improving their life prospects. GJP staff learned that any court-involved person— whether proven guilty or not—could be denied housing and employment for life. "We're talking about severe impediments to climbing out of poverty," explains executive director Doug Ammar, who began to recognize that GJP could help more people if it added advocacy to its portfolio. So in 2004, GJP launched the Coming Home program, using staff attorneys and volunteer lawyers from area firms to correct clients' criminal histories and advocate for sentence modifications. In 2010 alone, the program directly assisted more than six hundred clients.

GJP embraced other forms of advocacy as well—for example, teaching classes, such as Civil Consequences of Criminal Convictions at Mercer University Law School, and hosting forums on these issues around the state. In 2009, GJP and Mercer Law published their joint research on barriers facing ex-offenders in a book titled *Collateral Consequences of Arrests and Convictions*. The book raised awareness and helped prompt Georgia legislators to redraft the "expungement" statute (a law that makes it difficult to erase criminal histories). The result was Georgia State House Bill 663. If passed in 2012—which looks likely—the law would restrict public access to records of any criminal charges that did not result in a conviction, thereby potentially improving the lives of thousands.

Operating on an annual budget of just over $800,000, this small but mighty nonprofit is achieving remarkable outcomes. Between 2009 and 2011, fewer than 10 percent of GJP's clients have been sentenced to confinement (versus an 80 percent national average for similar populations), and 59 percent of its cases have resulted in nonconvictions. GJP has helped break the cycle of poverty and crime for many of its previously incarcerated clients. Its recidivism rate is only 17 percent—a remarkable result when compared to the national average of 70 percent. Now, by adding advocacy, GJP has dramatically deepened its impact across Georgia. As Ammar says, "We knew that with one stroke of the pen, we could influence thousands more lives."

OVERCOMING THE BARRIERS TO ADVOCACY

Like the majority of local nonprofits, GJP started out providing direct services to low-income clients. As its experience grew, so did GJP's understanding of the systemic barriers preventing its clients from receiving fairer treatment in the courts and ultimately escaping poverty. Within two decades, the organization moved into advocacy, but the move was not seamless.

GJP's experience is not unique. It mirrors that of many smaller nonprofit organizations in the United States—including those we profile here and others we've encountered in our travels. From our research and through our direct experiences, we've come to recognize a few basic barriers that local and smaller nonprofits face in their efforts to embrace both service and advocacy. In fact, this practice is arguably the most difficult for local nonprofits to pursue—but also one with the greatest leverage. Here we describe these barriers, along with creative ways that GJP was able to overcome them.

1. **Lack of funding**. For GJP, one big hurdle was convincing funders to support its advocacy work. Its first grant actually came from the Washington, D.C.–based organization Equal Justice Works, followed by a grant from the Georgia-based Sapelo Foundation. GJP used these early funds to make advocacy the responsibility of one staff person, who also conducts direct service and educational activities. Tapping into national networks for start-up advocacy funding is a creative way to overcome the initial financial hurdle. It also allows the organization to lay the groundwork for subsequent outreach to local donors and offer them the comfort that they aren't the first money in.
2. **Limited staff time**. GJP's use of this funding to support part of one person's time, rather than underwriting a new full-time position, was also a practical way to overcome constraints around the use of staff time for advocacy. GJP also uses its

staff attorneys in policy advocacy; and in 2011, GJP retained an adviser to help the organization navigate the halls of the Georgia statehouse. By sharing advocacy work across the organization, GJP was able to dramatically maximize impact while spending only 8 percent of its overall budget in 2010 on policy work.

3. **Resistance to the "L word"—lobbying.** Local nonprofits face another very real constraint to advocacy—overcoming both their own aversion to it and fears among funders. "I should admit," says Ammar, "I was one of the early points of resistance to advocacy work." But he explains that he soon began to see that policy and advocacy work would enable GJP to reach many more people. Convincing funders was another challenge; one of GJP's main advocacy donors requested anonymity, which is reflective of a larger trend in philanthropy. Just as many nonprofits shy away from advocacy, many foundations also eschew it.[2] GJP has learned to be very deliberate about its language. "We prefer the label 'policy advocacy,'" says Ammar, "and we do not use the term 'lobbyist.'" Other local organizations refer to their policy advocacy work as "civic engagement" or "community organizing." Whatever the moniker, nonprofit leaders clearly have found that euphemisms make their policy advocacy more palatable to their supporters—but no less effective.

OTHER APPROACHES TO ADVOCACY

GJP represents one example of a local nonprofit successfully overcoming some of the typical barriers to advocacy. As we noted in Chapter Two, policy lobbying is just one form of advocacy—and one of the hardest for nonprofits to embrace. But there are many other pathways to raising awareness for a cause and pursuing systemic change, as Figure 12.1 illustrates. Several of the local nonprofits we studied focused more on grassroots advocacy or leveraging networks for advocacy, in addition to focusing on direct policy lobbying.

RYASAP (Regional Youth Adult Social Action Partnership), a $3.2 million organization based in Bridgeport, Connecticut, approached advocacy by creating a local alliance to change the

FIGURE 12.1.   ADVOCACY HAS MANY DIMENSIONS.

Source: L. R. Crutchfield, J. V. Kania, and M. R. Kramer, *Do More Than Give: The Six Practices of Donors Who Change the World* (San Francisco: Jossey-Bass, 2010), p. 46.

state's juvenile justice policies. The nonprofit had long aspired to improve the lives of young people in Connecticut, which has one of the nation's highest rates of adult incarceration of juveniles. RYASAP started out providing mostly counseling services to court-involved youth, but by 2001, executive director Bob Francis had joined forces with a broad coalition of local nonprofit service providers, child advocates, judges, law enforcement officers, case workers, and other representatives from the juvenile justice system to collectively address the treatment of youth. With a seed grant from a local private funder, the Tow Foundation, the groups formed the Connecticut Alliance for Juvenile Justice to coordinate their actions and collectively lobby for policy change.

Instead of dedicating the time of an internal staff person to lead the lobbying effort—as GJP did—RYASAP took a different approach: it offered to house the Alliance, which in turn hired a lobbyist. That way, the broader coalition of nonprofits collectively shared the resource; no single local nonprofit had to pay—or account for—a full-time advocate. The Alliance was ultimately instrumental in achieving significant legislative reforms, including replacing the local juvenile court and detention center, moving youth care out of centralized state facilities and into local residential communities, and raising the age of jurisdiction (the age at which a young person could be tried and sentenced as an adult) from sixteen to eighteen. As a result, recidivism and juvenile incarcerations have decreased, and low-income youth in Connecticut's system are now receiving much fairer treatment.

Another group we studied, Safe Kids Canada, has fundamentally changed public behaviors nationwide by practicing grassroots advocacy, building national networks, and pursuing policy change—on a modest national annual budget of $1.5 million. The nonprofit was started in 1992 when Dr. David Wesson, a surgeon at Toronto's Hospital for Sick Children, realized that many of the injuries to young children he was seeing were caused by accidents that were preventable.

Today the nonprofit works with more than two thousand Canadian organizations to conduct research, raise awareness, and facilitate interactions among practitioners, policymakers, and the public. Its partners deliver health promotion and prevention programs to meet the unique needs of their respective communities. And through its Web site and Safe Tip Line, Safe Kids responds directly to more than twenty-five hundred calls and e-mails each year from parents, caregivers, and health professionals looking for safety information. In 2010, the Safe Kids Web site had 900,000 views and 200,000 downloads of its policy papers—it's a great example of how a nonprofit leverages both new and traditional media to advocate for its cause.

Because of its grassroots approach and national network, Safe Kids had the credibility to influence federal legislation on baby walkers, bike helmets, booster seats, and pool fencing. Now the organization employees a full-time public policy specialist, whose job is to monitor child-injury issues in the federal, provincial, and territorial legislatures. Largely due to the organization's efforts, Canada has experienced a 37 percent decline in childhood injuries, hospitalizations, and deaths since 1993. Not bad for a national nonprofit with a relatively small budget.

Just as we observed in the twelve larger national nonprofits, high-impact local organizations don't just focus on *either* providing direct services *or* advocating for change. They find creative ways to effectively do both—whether by combining them in-house, joining up with peer organizations to form coalitions, or reaching out to the grassroots to drum up support for their campaigns.

PRACTICE 2: MAKE MARKETS WORK

In the rural Appalachian community of Rowan County, Kentucky, a local resident named Robert was living in a worn-down trailer with holes in the floor, loose wires hanging from the walls, and no insulation. Determined to buy a home, Robert spent three years repairing his credit before applying for a bank loan—only to be turned down because the salary he earned working with developmentally disabled adults was too low, despite his perfect credit score.

The banker told him to call the Federation of Appalachian Housing Enterprises (FAHE). Within a week, Robert was attending the group's homeownership classes and was connected to FAHE's unconventional mortgage products. FAHE approved Robert for a $44,000 first mortgage at 3 percent interest and a $30,000 deferred second mortgage. Two months later, he had moved into his own home. "Compared to where I used to live, now I feel like I'm in a castle," Robert says.

FAHE is based in Berea, Kentucky, and also serves residents in the Appalachian regions of Virginia, West Virginia, and Tennessee. According to Jim King, CEO and president, the local economy has "half of the good numbers, and double the bad." The median income is half the national average. "Our educational attainment is low; our substance abuse is high; unemployment is high. It's a geography that's rural and tough to work in. Capital doesn't flow well here," says King.

Despite these impediments, FAHE has managed to create a self-sustaining market for thousands of aspiring home owners. The regional network provides a variety of services, including financing and support for the purchase of existing homes by low- and moderate-income families, the construction of affordable housing, and comprehensive community development. In 2011, FAHE— which has an operating budget of $5 million—deployed around $45 million in capital to reach six thousand families in Central Appalachia through a network of fifty member organizations in 140 counties. The group collectively touched three times the number of families it had five years earlier and deployed five times as much capital.

FAHE was founded in 1980 by two dozen community development financial institutions (CDFIs) that came together to collaborate and achieve some economies of scale. After more than a decade, they realized they were failing to adequately serve the five million people in need of better housing in Appalachia. "Around 2005, you saw lots of organizations providing similar services," King says. "We reached capacity at about two thousand families a year we were helping. At that rate, we'd have to go a long way to achieving any real impact. We needed to make a change and do something different."

So in 2006, King challenged FAHE's members to grow in a decade from serving two thousand families per year to serving eight thousand in a year. Meeting this goal started with an overhaul of FAHE's core business, servicing loans. King says that his staff had historically treated low-income borrowers differently, hesitating to collect on loans. "Why can't we collect from them like anyone else?" King asked them. "It gets in the way of scaling our approach."

Another key step to growing the local Appalachian mortgage market was to reorganize the FAHE network into "compacts" to aggregate its financial capital and business acumen in order to better serve demand. Newly centralized loan servicing and mortgage origination allowed for more targeted resources, producing better results and saving money, which was then passed back to members. FAHE also worked with local capital markets to provide profitable investment opportunities by increasing the community's supply of affordable rental housing subsidized by the federal Low Income Housing Tax Credit (LIHTC).

"Making markets work is not just about financial markets," King says. "It's looking at the market of available agencies as well, and aligning them for maximum impact. One can't happen without the other."

MAKING *LOCAL* MARKETS WORK

Like the twelve high-impact national nonprofits, FAHE tapped into the power of private markets to fuel its mission of creating economic opportunity for disadvantaged borrowers. As discussed in Chapter Three, high-impact nonprofits leverage the power of the private sector to advance their causes in three ways. They change business or industry practices, partner with business, or run a business to generate earned income. With our new research, we've gained additional insight into how these three approaches play out locally, and FAHE serves as a prime example.

First, FAHE changed local business practices by creating a regional nonprofit network and growing it to scale, and by focusing on populations overlooked by traditional private-sector companies. Second, it worked with and through existing businesses to make the market function better, partnering with private banks and local CDFIs to create low-income housing with LIHTC subsidies. Finally, FAHE has a self-sustaining business model that generates revenue for the organization. (FAHE generates 75 percent of its $5 million budget from earned income—two-thirds from interest from its portfolio and investments, and another third from fees for services.)

Now you might say that FAHE has been able to make local markets work because it operates more like a traditional lending business, one that happens to serve low-income customers. And you'd be right. Unlike FAHE, the vast majority of nonprofits aren't trying to adapt traditional business models to low-income communities. So that's why we looked for examples of other nonprofits that found creative ways to make local markets work for their cause.

Partner with Business

For many local nonprofits, their efforts have less to do with trying to change business behavior than with leveraging the assets of the private sector to increase their reach or self-sufficiency. In our interviews with local leaders, we learned that they recognized the risks associated with partnering with business—tensions over controversial programs, fear of "selling out," mission-creep—but this did not dissuade them from forming mutually beneficial relationships. In fact, nonprofit-private partnerships were common to all our local groups.

Of all the groups we interviewed, we found the Partnership to End Poverty, which focuses on ending poverty in rural Oregon, to be one of the most remarkable in its approach to corporate partnerships. In 2008, CEO Scott Cooper had a vision of a twelve-thousand-square-foot educational facility in remote Prineville, where technology would be used to offer college and workforce development classes. But building a distance-learning facility like this one was far beyond the scope of local resources.

Enter Bend Broadband, a corporation that had previously supported Partnership projects with cash and in-kind donations. "When a federal grant came out to expand broadband access in the region, we both decided independently to pursue it," Cooper says. "We didn't know of each other's intentions, but when we found out we were chasing the same dollars, it was simple to suggest that our construction of a distance-learning facility ought to be wired by the local company. So we supported the company's application as a benefit to low-income people."

Ultimately, both organizations received federal grants. The Prineville facility opened in September 2011, and already has two hundred students seeking an associate degree, thanks to state-of-the-art broadband connectivity. In this case, the Partnership's success lay in not viewing the other organization's application as competitive and instead seeking a way to move both projects forward and benefit the region twice over. Applying this win-win mind-set, the Partnership formed a true alliance with a company that created value for both parties—and, most important, created opportunity for a higher level of combined impact than either organization could achieve alone.

We also observed examples of more classic business-nonprofit partnerships, in which a local company provides financial and in-kind support directly to a community nonprofit.

Meet Each Need with Dignity (MEND), for example, is a holis-tic social service organization based in Southern California, which adopts a very pragmatic approach to its many corporate part-nerships. "We understand that in this economy, we need to work with businesses on their terms," says CEO Marianne Haver Hill. "Sometimes they want good press. Sometimes they want to show their employees that they care about the community. As long as it benefits our people and it's not all for show, we will work with them."

RUN A BUSINESS

As we mentioned in the new Introduction, these years of eco-nomic uncertainty have forced nonprofits to adjust to dimin-ished philanthropic and public resources, often while also facing increased demand for their services. So it's not surprising that many of the high-impact local nonprofits we've encountered have cultivated diverse revenue streams, including earned income. Although it's not a useful approach for every nonprofit, running a small business, if successful, can be an important stepping-stone toward greater self-sufficiency and economic stability. In some cases, these groups actually catalyze new markets and are able to earn income at the same time.

Live Local Alberta illustrates the ability of innovative nonprof-its to both make a market and make a living. Founded by Jessie Radies, the nonprofit coordinates and networks other groups and individuals helping Canadians in Edmonton to eat, dine, and shop locally. It all started in 2007 when Radies, a former PepsiCo execu-tive, discovered how challenging it was to source local, sustain-able foods for an independent restaurant she had started with her husband, a chef. So she began to network with local growers and other independent restaurants to try to make their food economy more efficient and more effective. "I recognized that every other independent restaurant was in same boat, and we were all compet-ing with each other and taking market share," says Radies. "If we worked collaboratively instead, we could actually grow the market for independent restaurants."

Ultimately, using a networked approach, Live Local helped build a vibrant sustainable food market while also contributing to the regional economy. Today the nonprofit aggregates and offers over eight hundred food products from more than seventy Alberta food producers and growers on its Web site, where the products can then be purchased by individual consumers and restaurants. Live Local runs the supply chain infrastructure as well, from warehousing to delivery. According to Radies, now $45 of every $100 stays in the community when consumers buy from a local food producer, as opposed to around $13 when buying from a national or global chain. All told, Live Local has already generated $500,000 for local food producers in Alberta.

Even better, the nonprofit has built an enviable business model, which allows it to thrive without relying heavily on charitable contributions. It generates 75 percent of its annual $1 million in revenue through many different earned income streams. Live Local charges membership dues to its network, takes a small percentage of revenue from food passing through its online and distribution platform, sells gift certificates to local restaurants, and runs a loyalty program. "We operate a lot of our programs like a business—there has to be a revenue stream *and* a benefit to the community," says Radies. "We're always looking for the win-win-win. We're for local business, local food, and local nonprofits. We want our local economy to be vibrant and sustainable and prosperous."

Practice 3: Inspire Evangelists

All he remembers is a flash. In April 2004, National Guardsman Anthony Smith was in Iraq when he took a direct hit from a rocket-propelled grenade. His hip was destroyed, and he lost his right kidney, his right arm below the elbow, and his vision in his right eye. Smith's injuries were so severe that he was initially placed in a body bag, until a nurse noticed that he was still breathing. Two months later, he woke from a coma. Despite all this, Smith says that what hurt the most was not finishing his tour of duty: "If people want to have a purpose, it comes from helping your fellow man."

When he returned home, Smith was given a fellowship with The Mission Continues, an organization that creates service opportunities for injured veterans returning from the Middle East. The nonprofit was founded by veteran Eric Greitens, who had his own brush with death in 2007, when he was a Navy SEAL on tour in Fallujah. His team was hit by a suicide truck bomb, delivering a severe head wound to the Marine standing next to him, but leaving Greitens without serious injury.

Back in the United States, Greitens went to visit his injured friend—and discovered an opportunity. "I was part of a long line of guys coming to say thank you for your service," Greitens says. "What these men really needed to hear was that *we still need you.*" At the time, several organizations had sprung up to support returning vets, "but 90 percent were sending gift baskets . . . and the other 10 percent were advocating on Capitol Hill," says Greitens. He believed that veterans needed something more than charity or public benefits. "What didn't exist was something to challenge veterans to get back into meaningful service to their communities."

Greitens combined his combat pay with several friends' disability checks to fund the first fellowship. The Mission Continues has subsequently awarded 180 fellowships, with 500 more slated for 2012, enabling vets such as Anthony Smith to continue to serve their country. Today Smith uses martial arts to teach moral character to young students. "As young people see and hear about my struggles, I hope they'll be encouraged to pursue their own dreams," he says.

Greitens soon realized that he was able to reach only a limited number of veterans, although the fellowships have had an impact on individuals such as Smith. His aspirations were larger: he wanted to challenge veterans of all eras, and civilians of all ages, to serve their country by giving back. "The total population of the United States that has served [in the military] is less than 1 percent," he says. "We knew we had to get lots of people shoulder to shoulder with injured veterans in a shared environment." So The Mission Continues began setting up service projects where civilians and veterans could volunteer together to refurbish schools, clean memorials, or run blood drives. "Anything," says Greitens, "to get citizens to see these vets as something more than charity."

The group's widespread evangelism for service has quickly become a powerful force. Within three years, sixteen thousand civilians had participated in one-day events with fifty-eight hundred vets. And donations to the nonprofit climbed from $227,000 in 2008 to $6.25 million in 2011. Donor-advised fund Goldman Sachs Gives and the Draper Richards Kaplan Foundation invested early, and soon Target and Home Depot joined as sponsors. Now the organization operates on a $4.5 million annual budget. "The 'challenge versus charity' aspect of our work is something people really respond to," Greitens says. "That's a unique and powerful point of view, and it's the theme our evangelists get behind."

If Greitens had continued to pursue his original idea of only awarding fellowships to veterans, by now he might have reached several hundred men and women returning from duty. But by tapping into the power of individuals, and building a burgeoning movement of veterans and civilians, The Mission Continues has inspired tens of thousands of people to give back. And although this nonprofit is no longer local—it is quickly becoming a national force—it is a great example of an organization that started small and has used the power of the six practices to scale up.

If you judged The Mission Continues only by its fellowships, you might be underwhelmed. But if you look at the greater movement the organization has created and the social networks it has built, you see a much larger picture. The practice of inspiring evangelists lends itself uniquely to local and smaller nonprofits. It's different from the first two practices we've addressed in this chapter because the barriers to implementing it aren't so high. For instance, unlike policy advocacy, engaging individual volunteers as ambassadors for your cause doesn't require a lot of funding, and it's not controversial with donors. If anything, it has become even easier and less costly with new social media tools.

The inherent challenge to inspiring evangelists instead lies in creating *meaningful* experiences that lead to sticky relationships. It's not rocket science, but effectively inspiring evangelists requires focused attention and the willingness to invest some time and money in activities that may have minimal short-term benefit but can be valuable long-term investments. This means investing in face-to-face and experiential activities—not just online social networking platforms. Although these new technology tools are powerful, they function best as complements to real-world activities rather than as substitutes.

SHARE YOUR STORIES

The road to inspiring local evangelists and building strong social networks begins with capturing the attention of individual supporters and enticing them to spend their time and attention on your cause. This process starts with persuasive storytelling—about the organization's mission, values, and impact—that establishes a strong *emotional* bond with individuals you seek to reach.

Take an example provided by the Partnership to End Poverty, profiled earlier in this chapter. Two years ago, CEO Cooper had grown weary of his tried-and-true PowerPoint presentation—long on data and short on feeling—and decided to do something different when asked to speak at a local lunch. He titled his talk "What You Don't Know About Me," and called on two prominent community members to help deliver his message.

First, Cooper asked the audience to list some stereotypes of people living in poverty. "Dirty," one audience member volunteered. "Mentally ill." "Unmotivated." "Uneducated." "Minority." Then he asked a well-known local city manager to step up to the podium. This man talked about how he was raised as a migrant worker, traversing the western United States with his seven brothers and sisters, attending twenty-two schools, and at one point being placed in special education because he was so behind in school. Yet today he was a well-known civic leader.

A city councilmember spoke next. She shared how she'd been a successful bank vice president in Denver, but lost her job. When she gave birth to a baby that was lactose intolerant, she couldn't afford the special food it needed. She says she would lie on the floor and wish she could die. "Do you know what it's like when you can't feed your own child?" she asked a stunned audience. She says she was saved by kind neighbors who quietly slipped coupons under her door.

"No one knew those stories—and there wasn't a dry eye in the house," Cooper says. "People come out of the woodwork when they're in a safe place to tell stories about their brushes with poverty. There are more people who have those stories than you'd think." These powerful and personal stories, shared by well-known community leaders, captured the attention of the audience in a way that no PowerPoint presentation or annual report ever could. Of course, the approach required taking an emotional risk and a leap of faith on the part of the speakers, but clearly it paid off.

Engaging your evangelists to speak passionately in public is only one avenue for sharing your organization's story. Local and smaller nonprofits can also leverage mainstream or social media, or publish articles and books, to get their message out. "Having your story out there is one of the greatest growth accelerators," says The Mission Continues' Greitens, who is the author of the *New York Times* best seller *The Heart and the Fist*. "It doesn't have to be a book, obviously. But having some sort of content that precedes you is invaluable. It creates evangelists quickly because your message is stated on your terms. It's a way of extending the shared experience."

USE SOCIAL NETWORKS TO BUILD BELOVED COMMUNITIES

Once a local nonprofit has captured people's attention with a compelling articulation of its mission and story, it then needs to create meaningful experiences for supporters that cement their commitment to the cause. As we learned in our initial research, it's not enough merely to talk about the organization—you need to get people involved. And the more social the activity, the stickier it becomes.

For the Partnership to End Poverty, that vehicle is Project Connect, a volunteer-driven social service delivery system. "We have eight hundred people volunteering at our events," Cooper says. "They are on the ground, getting hands-on experience about what it means to live in poverty. We then provide them with a kit so they can frame a conversation, go run a program, or talk about the subject." Cooper calls the Partnership's evangelists his "boots on the ground," relying on them to provide knowledge of what's happening in the field and to inspire other local evangelists.

Another group to successfully nurture its social networks is A Home Within. Founded in San Francisco in 1994, this nonprofit group provides free long-term mental health support to current and former foster youth. Founder Dr. Toni Heineman recognized the critical need among foster children for long-term, stable relationships, and she sensed a willingness among many private therapists to help out. So she started a network of therapists who each provide free care to one foster child for as long as needed. In exchange, the now hundreds of therapists have exclusive access to a national network of colleagues.

"What people don't realize is that being a therapist can be an incredibly isolating profession," said Heineman. "What young therapists are hungry for is a continuation of that community and network they had in school. We were responding to a need in the therapist community as much as we were responding to a need for therapy in the foster care community." A Home Within inspired its evangelists in the therapy profession by creating meaningful experiences for its volunteers and helping nurture and grow this community over time.

In fact, the final step to deepening relationships with your evangelists is to build a "beloved community"—a strong social network—around your volunteers, connecting them more deeply to each other and to the organization and its cause. This takes time and resources, but many local nonprofits are committed to bringing together their supporters at annual events—whether retreats, dinners, galas, conferences, serve-a-thons, outdoor runs, or other social functions. The trick is to develop an event that uniquely fits the work of the nonprofit and creates meaningful ways for volunteers to connect with each other and with the cause. Other groups are learning how to use online tools and social media to keep their volunteers and supporters connected between events.

PRACTICE 4: NURTURE NONPROFIT NETWORKS

Just as the Partnership to End Poverty uses the power of evangelists as "boots on the ground," it also nurtures more formal nonprofit networks in order to extend its reach across a central Oregon service area of seven thousand square miles, half of which is rugged terrain. With a small staff and a budget of $650,000, the organization knows that this is the most leveraged approach to achieving social change for twenty thousand area residents living in poverty.

The nonprofit began building out a network in 2009, when Cooper came across data that he found stunning: nearly half of all referrals to the Partnership's services came from faith-based groups, and the vast majority—85 percent—were initially directed to the wrong agency. "There was a chronic inefficiency in our system," Cooper says. "The denominations didn't work together or talk to each other. They didn't have reason to." So Cooper convened a series of meetings among local faith-based agencies to lay the groundwork for a more formal network. His goal: enable each organization to improve outcomes for low-income clients through better coordination among all the agencies. Cooper envisioned a whole that was greater than the sum of its parts.

Cooper structured the network into five teams and introduced regular monthly meetings. The meetings provided a forum for these myriad groups to begin collaborating. They quickly identified redundancies in their services and learned how their referrals to social service groups could be expedited. As the network grew and trust was developed among members, they also learned they could consult with each other on challenges or on issues in which some groups were stronger than others. Today, fifteen to twenty people attend on behalf of each church—hailing from far-reaching areas such as La Pine, Prineville, Redmond, Madras, and Bend. (Although the majority of members represent churches, several also come from other social service nonprofits.)

The Partnership's strategy of nurturing a local network has paid off: already its members have raised $10,000 for cash-strapped schools around Prineville by encouraging congregants to hold yard sales on behalf of a community fund, while another group in Madras created a common, coordinated intake system for all clients seeking help from faith-based institutions. "Now we have clothing banks, food banks, and community gardens all working together," Cooper says. "It's amazing how they have responded."

The Partnership is a relatively small nonprofit, but Cooper's vision for its potential to end poverty is big. "A nonprofit like ours is too small to have the answers to everything," he says. "To have a broader impact, we bring people together who have the answers, and whose combined knowledge and resources work better together than apart."

Better Together

Over and over, as we encountered local high-impact nonprofits, we observed how they intuitively understood the potential for working through nonprofit networks rather than going it alone. For every one of the groups we studied, investment in networks is not only a strategic choice—it is often *a means of survival.* This may be particularly true in a depressed economic period, when resources are fewer and needs are greater, but the practice works equally well in good times. As we pointed out in Chapter Five, building networks can at first seem altruistic, but ultimately it's also about enlightened self-interest. Like their larger counterparts, these smaller nonprofits nurture their networks in addition to building healthy organizations, emphasize collaboration and coordination over disconnected competition, and prefer to grow their impact rather than their empire.

As we studied how local nonprofits apply this practice, we also gained new insights into how the practice of nurturing nonprofit networks is closely interwoven with inspiring evangelists. There's actually a lot of overlap and synergy between the two practices. Attracting and cultivating relationships with individuals is not only an effective means of spreading the word about an organization's mission but also a first step to creating one-on-one bonds with people who work in peer nonprofits. These social ties can form an important building block in the process of creating more formal organizational networks.

The Challenges of Networks

Building networks can provide real benefits to nonprofits—such as learning, sharing resources and ideas, engaging others, capturing economies of scale, coordinating action, and increasing impact. But that's not to say it's always easy. Much of the external environment, including how grants are made and how impact is assessed, continues to reinforce organization-centric behavior, rather than collaboration. There are a number of challenges for nonprofits that pursue this path, including some we explored in Chapter Five: letting go of some control over your brand, demonstrating impact, and getting credit for work.

Like their larger counterparts, smaller nonprofits also risk losing control of their brand. The flip side of relying on networks is that each member of the network still has its own identity—and individual needs can sometimes be in tension with collective needs. This is particularly challenging for nonprofits that are part of loosely affiliated networks. Executive director Sheila Rice of NeighborWorks Montana explains, "In the public's mind, if they don't see our logo, they might not know they're utilizing a service that's part of our network. We have twenty-four partners, all of which have their own identities." She also talked about a related challenge: the dilution of the identity of the collective network. "Each organization in the network has its own culture, and as new people come in, the understanding of who we are and what we do is bound to dissipate with time unless we continually reinforce our value."

Another challenge to the networked nonprofit is that it can be more difficult to demonstrate impact to funders or to take credit for action. Because they are small and often underresourced, local groups spend an inordinate amount of time working through networks, but they risk not receiving "credit" from funders. It's both harder to measure collective action and harder to assign causality. "It is a little hard to get the credit we perhaps deserve when it comes to articulating our impact," says Cooper of the Partnership to End Poverty. "But that's the deal you make. You need the network to have impact. If we worked alone, we'd have a far worse problem."

As Cooper's words illustrate, just as large organizations struggle with these challenges of working through networks, so do smaller nonprofits—but they often pursue this path anyway, because its benefits outweigh its costs.

Practice 5: Master the Art of Adaptation

These stories illustrate how high-impact local nonprofits apply the first four of the six practices in *Forces for Good* by looking outside and working through each sector—government, business, other nonprofits, and individuals—to advance their causes. And to successfully carry out these *external* practices, high-impact local nonprofits exhibit two key *internal* traits: they are extraordinarily *adaptive,* and they *share leadership.* These two attributes actually describe how well the nonprofit mediates its internal-external boundaries: Is it able to take information in? Is it able to share power and extend influence out?

The ability to perceive changes in the external environment and adapt with innovative solutions is a core, elemental trait of any high-impact nonprofit—large or small. It's not necessarily hard to do, but it does require being open to input and being intentional about the practice of organizational learning and reflection. As we wrote in Chapter Six, most nonprofits begin adaptation with listening for external cues in the environment and looking for opportunities to increase impact. Then they continue through the cycle of adaptation, which includes three additional components: experimentation and innovation, evaluation and learning, and modification of programs and plans. (See Figure 6.1, "The Cycle of Adaptation.")

Let's look again at the Little Theatre on the Square, described at the outset of this chapter. This Midwestern arts group has been highly attuned to signals it receives from the outside: public support for arts funding is on the decline; private funding is increasingly competitive; and traditional theatre audiences are aging out, as younger generations spend their leisure time on new media. If the Little Theatre doesn't continue to respond and to adapt its programs and plans accordingly, the show literally will not go on. Here's how the Little Theatre uses the cycle of adaptation to stay relevant:

- **Listen to the environment.** At the end of each show, John Stephens, the executive director, collects feedback from the audience. He also lets members help with the process of choosing shows for the following season. The Little Theatre also started the Coalition of Theatre Organizations, to help smaller regional and school theatre programs in the Midwest share information and learn from each other; this helps the theatre stay in touch with the grassroots.

- **Experiment and innovate**. "It's obviously a creative environment with lots of ideas, especially around promotion," Stephens says. The Little Theatre has a robust social media presence because experimentation is relatively inexpensive, enabling microadaptations to giving campaigns. It also experiments with other kinds of programs, such as opening the art gallery, or new artistic productions.
- **Evaluate and learn what works**. One value of social media is that it can be tracked and quantified. Stephens knows where his audience comes from, what time they buy tickets, and which e-mail blasts are opened. "We measure everything," he says. This measurement extends beyond the online world to collection of feedback from multiple sources, on multiple programs.
- **Modify programs**. "What you don't do is just as important as what you do," Stephens says, citing examples of programs the Little Theatre has eliminated or changed. "We can't do everything. Ideas are all around us. It all comes back to what will have the greatest impact and can be managed practically."

Like the Little Theatre, all the local nonprofits we studied are highly skilled at adapting. The Partnership to End Poverty recognized it couldn't effectively serve the population of vast Central Oregon alone, so it launched a regional network of faith-based and social service nonprofits to create greater impact. The Mission Continues started with a few soldiers turning their combat pay into fellowships, but altered its course to build a national movement of civilians and veterans serving their country. GJP moved into advocacy when it realized that it could dramatically change more lives by changing the law. And FAHE challenged its network to dramatically increase its production in order to reach more underserved families in the region.

PRACTICE 6: SHARE LEADERSHIP

As we stepped back and thought about how these local nonprofits adapted to their changing environments, we saw a pattern similar to one we found in our initial research: their strong adaptability was closely linked with their ability to *share leadership*. For smaller and local nonprofits, the practice of sharing leadership often extends beyond their four walls as they entice nonprofit peers, donors, volunteer evangelists, and stakeholders to take on the work of the organization.

Originally, we defined the practice of shared leadership primarily as an *internal* organizational trait—the capacity of the CEOs of the twelve large national nonprofits to share responsibility and authority with their senior management teams, their boards of directors, and other key stakeholders. But as we studied these cases of smaller and local nonprofits—so many of which are cash constrained, understaffed, and overworked—we saw more clearly how the shared leadership practice extends to organizations and individuals *outside* the organization's four walls. Sharing leadership is a nuanced practice that requires nonprofit executives to empower others and learn to *let go,* because inherent to the practice is relinquishment of control. In this sense, it merges with practice 4, nurturing nonprofit networks, and practice 3, inspiring evangelists.

Consider MEND. This local nonprofit was launched in a San Fernando Valley, California, garage in 1971 by a small group of Catholics and Protestants to help the neediest residents of their community. Today MEND offers a holistic suite of programs that range from providing hot meals and showers for the homeless; affordable medical, dental, and vision care; adult job training and literacy programs; after-school student tutoring; and even a regional adopt-a-family Christmas program. As if that weren't enough, MEND isn't just a pantry but a food bank as well, supporting thirty smaller charities in the San Fernando Valley region.

In all, MEND serves as many as thirty-two thousand individuals per month, and in certain departments, the numbers continue to grow. Since the recession hit in 2008, applications to some MEND programs have increased 400 percent, yet the organization has never had to wait-list an individual for food, clothing, or educational services. MEND has met increased demand by expanding its volunteer force 24 percent and its total number of donated hours by 39 percent—the equivalent of more than twenty full-time employees.

How does an organization with just twenty-four paid staff administer this vast offering of services without maxing out on its own capacity to give? The answer is to *share leadership*—in this case, extending leadership out to its networks of individual evangelists and other local nonprofits.

CEO Marianne Haver Hill has been with MEND since 1987, but her leadership is not of the command-and-control variety that characterizes too many organizations. Instead, MEND delegates real leadership responsibilities down the line, with one big difference: its workers are almost all volunteers. A total of thirty-two hundred MEND volunteers donate 12,970 hours to the organization per month, accounting for 99 percent of the organization's total labor. MEND now pushes 95 percent of its overall budget, cultivated almost entirely from private sources, directly to clients.

MEND's volunteers don't just provide services; they also participate heavily in organizational leadership and in setting strategy. MEND prefers to have a new program be run by volunteers until it merits a dedicated staff member. Volunteers also write grant proposals, mount public relations campaigns, lead orientations with other community organizations, and manage shifts in the food bank and medical clinic. A recent research project by the Taproot Foundation on the use of volunteers identified MEND as its "gold standard."[3]

"When I talk about sharing leadership with our volunteers, people say to me, 'Volunteers can't do that,'" Haver Hill says. "But I think that when volunteers are educated about the mission, and a performance standard is set, their leadership provides a tremendous advantage. They're not just leaders—they are authentic evangelists as well. A number of people have come to us as donors or volunteers because they heard a presentation by one of our volunteer leaders and responded to that person's enthusiasm. If it's a risk to allow volunteers to work in an official capacity, well, that risk has been rewarded tenfold by what comes back to us."

MEND demonstrates several other key best practices we discussed with respect to sharing leadership *within* its organization as well:

- **Two at the top**. Taking a cue from the original *Forces for Good* research, MEND recently adopted a CEO-COO model, installing Jenny Gutierrez to oversee all programs and facilities, while Haver Hill focuses on public relations, fundraising, and development. This job split has enabled both women to have more impact and to feel less overwhelmed.
- **Great leaders last but let go**. Haver Hill's twenty-five-year tenure is proof positive that MEND cultivates long-term leadership—but it's not a victim of founder's syndrome either. The couple who started MEND, Ed and Carolyn Rose, remain on the board and continue to volunteer, but have long since relinquished any officer responsibilities. They realized they couldn't be the bottleneck to the organization's growth, and graciously let others lead.
- **Build a big and strategic board**. MEND has sixteen board members currently, with plans to scale up by eight to ten members soon. Members of the board—ranging from the vice chancellor of the Los Angeles Community Colleges to a retired law partner who now drives a MEND food rescue truck—are highly committed and possess a diverse range of skills.

In sum, high-impact nonprofits like MEND embody the practice of shared leadership both inside and outside their organizations. They artfully combine adaptive capacity with the instinctive ability to share leadership with those around them, not just because they are benevolent, but because doing so is also the most direct route to deepening their impact. Call it enlightened self-interest, but it's what makes these good nonprofits *great*.

GREATER GOOD

Beyond their common use of many of the six practices, these small but mighty nonprofits share a key trait with the larger high-impact nonprofits we profiled: their obsession with impact. Almost to a one, they focus on effecting local systemic change, be it through economic, social, cultural, or political means. But rather than making these sweeping changes with massive resources, they punch far above their weight. They tackle big issues by leveraging local advocacy, networks, evangelists, and markets to have more impact. In fact, these groups are particularly adept at leveraging both social and organizational networks, along with adapting to changes in their environments and sharing leadership.

Whether your nonprofit is large or small, the six practices can expand your organization's range of action. We've shared in this chapter a variety of examples that demonstrate how local and smaller nonprofits have done it, and we hope these stories will inspire you to strengthen your own application of the six practices. To help you get started, we include in the next chapter a simple diagnostic tool designed to assist you in assessing how well your organization is applying the concepts in this book, and to highlight opportunities for enhanced impact.

As we wrote in the first edition, "The answer to our question, *What makes great nonprofits great?* is this: greatness is about working with and through others. . . . It's about leveraging every sector of society to become a force for good." In addition, we can now say unequivocally that the answer to the question that began this chapter—*Can the six practices be executed by local and regional groups with smaller budgets?*—is a resounding yes!

CHAPTER THIRTEEN

FORCES FOR GOOD
DIAGNOSTIC TOOL

As the authors of *Forces for Good,* we are frequently invited to conduct evaluations and provide strategic advice, as well as give presentations and facilitate workshops and board retreats, for nonprofits, foundations, and corporations of various sizes and types. In preparing for some of these engagements, we developed this simple diagnostic tool as a means for leaders to quickly assess their organizations according to the six practices of high-impact nonprofits discussed in our book. For instance, executive directors of nonprofits have distributed versions of this survey to staff and board members in order to gauge their perceptions of organizational performance vis-à-vis the concepts in *Forces for Good.* Sometimes the survey was distributed by one of us, and responses were collected and collated anonymously; other times the organization's leader directly distributed the survey.

We invite you to use or adapt this tool in order to solicit staff and key stakeholder input for your own organization. A scoring key is included at the outset; the lower your score, the greater the perception that your organization has mastered that particular practice (or subset of activities within a practice). Conversely, the higher your score, the greater the perception that the organization could strengthen its efforts in that area of practice.

For more information about the six practices of high-impact nonprofits as well as upcoming presentations by the authors of *Forces for Good,* please visit www.forcesforgood.net.

SCORING KEY

1 = Strongly agree   2 = Agree   3 = Disagree

Practice 1: Advocate *and* Serve

1. My organization advocates for policy reform, in addition to providing direct services.

    1   2   3

2. My organization effectively combines service and advocacy, drawing on direct service programs to inform advocacy agendas, and vice versa.

    1   2   3

Practice 2: Make Markets Work

1. My organization changes the way local, national, or global businesses fundamentally operate.

    1   2   3

2. My organization builds effective, win-win alliances with companies.

    1   2   3

3. My organization is funded in part by revenue generated from sales of products or services.

    1   2   3

Practice 3: Inspire Evangelists

1. My organization creates meaningful, emotional experiences for volunteers.

    1   2   3

2. My organization deliberately cultivates high-profile evangelists.

    1   2   3

Practice 4: Nurture Nonprofit Networks

1. My organization embraces a network mind-set, working collaboratively with other groups to advance the larger cause.

    1   2   3

2. My organization shares knowledge, cultivates fieldwide leadership, and develops collective resources within our network or field.

    1   2   3

Practice 5: Master the Art of Adaptation

1. My organization evaluates what works using practical tools designed to track *outcomes,* not just *outputs.*

    1   2   3

2. My organization can effectively launch new programs and also terminate programs that don't produce sufficient results.

    1   2   3

Practice 6: Share Leadership

1. The executive director of my organization effectively shares power and decision making with the senior team and board of directors.

    1   2   3

2. My organization deliberately develops emerging leaders within the organization and also within our larger network.

    1   2   3

PART FOUR

APPENDIXES AND RESOURCES

RESEARCH METHODOLOGY
FOR THE FIRST EDITION

We decided to write this book because we wanted to know how great nonprofits have achieved high levels of impact—how they scaled their social impact—in a relatively short period of time. We hoped to uncover useful lessons to share with organizations that aspired to similar results. In our research, we followed an inductive case-based methodology, also known in academia as "grounded theory."[1] This appendix includes more extensive detail about our methodology, building on the overview in Chapter One.

Our research followed four phases. In the first phase, we defined "high impact" in the context of the social sector, and established basic boundaries for our work. In the second phase, we devised a multistage process to select a diverse sample of nonprofit organizations that met our criteria and that would be useful in generating new insights. We conducted case-study research on the selected organizations in the third phase, then developed case summaries. In the fourth phase, we analyzed multiple sources of data and identified cross-case patterns that we believed could help explain these nonprofits' impact. We tested emerging patterns and hypotheses with advisers and practitioners, and went back to the data and organizations in an iterative approach. Finally, from these analyses, we constructed the general theory that is presented in this book.

PHASE 1: DEFINING "HIGH IMPACT," ESTABLISHING RESEARCH PARAMETERS

Our first major challenge was to define success in a sector that has no universal means of measuring it. As we noted in Chapter One, unlike the for-profit sector, where total returns to shareholders and other financial metrics are commonly used to judge business performance, the nonprofit sector has no accepted universal measure of success. Rather, outcomes vary according to the organization's mission, model, and issue area. They are inherently more difficult to quantify.

The quantitative data available about nonprofits focus mostly on budget information, filed on 990 returns to the IRS. When we first began this research, we initially examined revenue growth rates for a variety of nonprofits, looking for patterns in the data, and thinking we might use that as one selection criterion. Research advisers Bill Meehan and Brian Trelstad of McKinsey & Company helped develop and guide this initial analysis. However, we determined that relying on financial information was a misleading way of assessing organizational impact. Budget data are useful for gauging things like revenue growth, spending on administration versus programs, and overall financial health. However, *budgets are not useful for measuring impact or effectiveness.* Unlike in the business sector, money in nonprofits is only an input, not an output or a measure of value created. Other researchers have discussed this challenge of measurement and metrics in great detail.[2]

We knew that in order to create a workable definition of success, we would need to somehow gauge an organization's *impact.* Because we could not use any of the currently available numerical measures of performance, we had to devise our own method. We also needed to set parameters that would make our research meaningful and useful to practitioners, so we created the following definitions and boundaries during the first phase of our research. We used these to screen and select organizations for further study.

- **Scale of impact.** Because we were interested in the question of scaling social impact, we limited our focus to organizations that had achieved impact at the *national or international level* (or both). This immediately excluded countless nonprofits achieving significant impact at the local level.

- **Geographical location.** We limited our study to organizations that were founded *in the United States,* because comparing groups across different social, political, and economic contexts would introduce apples-to-oranges comparisons. And from a practical perspective, we didn't have the resources to conduct global research. (However, a number of the U.S.-based nonprofits we studied have expanded their operations abroad.)
- **Time frame.** We wanted to examine organizations that had scaled their social impact *in a relatively short period of time* and that had *sustained that impact for at least ten years.* We focused on organizations founded after 1965 but before 1994. We believed that it would be most useful to study nonprofits that had succeeded under similar social, political, and economic conditions.
- **Type of nonprofit.** We also limited our study to public-serving charitable organizations with 501(c)(3) status. As our research progressed, we also decided to eliminate religious organizations and member-serving organizations, such as fraternities and other social clubs. Last, we selected only groups that must raise the majority of their funding year-to-year. This meant eliminating grantmaking foundations and organizations that were sustained by the wealth of a single funding source. These organizations do not face the same capital constraints as most nonprofits.
- **Conflict of interest.** Because coauthor Leslie Crutchfield was employed part-time by Ashoka during this research, we eliminated it from consideration.

With these broad parameters in mind, we created a two-pronged definition of impact. The first part involved a measure of concrete outputs, such as the number of people served, products produced, or direct influence on policy. We asked, *Did the organization achieve substantial and sustained results at the national or international level?* We looked at a variety of data to confirm these results. The second part of our definition was more abstract and qualitative. We wanted to study organizations that had achieved the most *significant* impact on a system or provided a model that other groups had adopted. Next we confronted an even bigger challenge: selecting a sample of organizations that met our definition of success.

PHASE 2: SELECTING A SAMPLE OF HIGH-IMPACT NONPROFITS

We followed a number of detailed steps in this phase to select a representational sample of nonprofits that also met our research criteria.

NATIONAL NONPROFIT CEO PEER SURVEY

Because there is no universal measure of nonprofit impact, we had to devise an alternative way to generate a list of successful organizations. We decided to ask nonprofit leaders themselves in a national survey, inspired by the methodology Jim Collins and Jerry Porras employed to select the companies profiled in *Built to Last*.[3] They conducted a peer survey of seven hundred corporate CEOs to nominate the most "visionary" companies and then used the resulting data and further research to select the eighteen corporations they studied. Similarly, we conducted a national survey of nonprofit CEOs, asking them to nominate organizations that had created "the most significant impact" in their fields. The survey was administered by the Center for the Advancement of Social Entrepreneurship (CASE) at Duke University, with the help of the Aspen Institute Nonprofit Sector and Philanthropy Program. This part of the process involved several smaller steps.

Compiled a List of Nonprofit CEOs

We created a list of 2,790 nonprofit CEOs who led a diverse group of organizations that were broadly representative of the social sector as a whole. We compiled the list according to organization size (budget) and tracked the organizations by NTEE code (a system developed by the National Center for Charitable Statistics to identify nonprofits by issue area) and geography (with representation from all fifty states, as well as Puerto Rico and the District of Columbia). We used the following lists:

Large nonprofits. *The Chronicle of Philanthropy* allowed us to e-mail its 2003 list of the four hundred largest nonprofits ranked by budget size (greater than $50 million).

Medium-size nonprofits. We purchased a randomly generated, diverse sample of two thousand medium-size organizations ($1 million to $50 million budgets) from GuideStar's database of 850,000 American nonprofits.

Small and start-up nonprofits. We compiled a list of about four hundred CEOs of early-stage nonprofits from various sources, including Ashoka, Echoing Green, Draper Richards Foundation, New Profit Inc., Roberts Enterprise Development Fund, Schwab Foundation, Skoll Foundation, Venture Philanthropy Partners, and *Fast Company* "Social Capitalist" award nominees.

Designed and Sent a Survey

In June 2004, we sent these selected CEOs a survey that contained a single question, which was simply worded to increase our response rate. We asked respondents to list "up to five (5) U.S.-based nonprofit organizations that have achieved the most significant impact at the national, international, and/or regional level during the last 30 years, and why." We instructed respondents to "focus your responses on organizations within your field(s) of expertise" and "to refrain from nominating your own organization."

Tallied Responses

Of the 2,790 chief executives we e-mailed, 398 e-mails were undeliverable for various reasons. Of the remaining 2,392 successfully delivered e-mails, we received 512 responses, or a response rate of 21.4 percent. This response rate surpassed baseline criteria required for statistical validity.[4] Responses were also reasonably well distributed by NTEE code and mirrored the general geographical distribution we surveyed.

We then cleaned the data, combining counts for organizations that respondents referred to using different names or acronyms (for instance, National Council of La Raza was sometimes referred to as NCLR or La Raza). We also removed responses in which CEOs voted for their own nonprofit or in which a subsidiary organization voted for its national affiliate. Finally, we combined some NTEE codes and categorized organizations into nine general fields for further analysis: arts and culture; advocacy and civil rights; education; environment; health; housing and economic development; hunger; international relief and development (U.S.-based); and youth development.

Conducted Additional Research to Fill Gaps

Our survey results in the arts category were underrepresented, both in terms of respondents and responses. So we developed a follow-up e-mail survey, which was sent to three hundred additional CEOs of arts organizations, using the same survey method detailed previously. The list of additional arts respondents was evenly distributed between theatres, opera companies, museums, symphonies, dance companies, and other performing arts organizations, and followed similar guidelines for diversity as those mentioned previously.

Analyzed Results and Narrowed Organizations

Once we received and tallied the results of our survey, we pared down the list of nominations according to the basic parameters set out earlier, eliminating those that didn't meet our test for scale of impact (national or international), time frame (founded between 1965 and 1994), geography (U.S.-based), or type of nonprofit (eliminating foundations, membership groups, and so on).

Addressed Questions About the Validity of Survey Data

After analyzing the survey results, narrowing the list of organizations to those that met our criteria, and vetting the results with advisers, we were concerned that the survey data were not robust enough to select a sample of nonprofits for further study. We were worried that the survey may have resulted in nominations of groups with the highest levels of brand awareness, not necessarily those with the highest levels of impact. So we devised an additional step for selecting our final sample.

FIELD-EXPERT INTERVIEWS AND VALIDATION

To help us generate further data for consideration when selecting our final group of high-impact nonprofits, we consulted with experts in various fields of the social sector. We followed the Delphi methodology, a process for structuring communication among experts, often used when there is a large amount of qualitative information that needs to be narrowed or synthesized.[5] Following is a brief outline of the process we followed.

Selected Fields or Issue Areas

We solicited detailed commentary from six to ten thought-leaders in each of the nine major fields we had already identified.

Selected Field Experts

In selecting our panels of field experts, we aimed to identify individuals who possessed a perspective across the field (funders, journalists, academics, thought-leaders, and intermediaries); who had deep knowledge in a particular issue area; and who were relatively diverse in terms of political orientation, geographical location, race and ethnicity, and other factors. Further, we tried to control for any conflict of interest with organizations under consideration. For a list of our field experts, see Appendix B.

Conducted First-Round Interviews

First, we conducted one-on-one calls with each expert following a predetermined script, which allowed us to solicit a priori responses to our question of which nonprofits in his or her field had significant impact. We then asked the experts to respond to results from the peer survey, provide additional supporting information for certain nominations, or argue why an organization with many votes had not actually achieved significant impact. We synthesized all the information from the first round of phone calls, made it anonymous, and redistributed it to the field experts (within fields) for further consideration.

Conducted Second-Round Group Interviews

On a group conference call for each field panel (or individually for those who couldn't join), we asked the experts to help us narrow the list to a few finalists within each issue area. This allowed them to respond to data generated in the first-round calls and to have an informed discussion and debate.

Results

Our discussions with these experts helped us winnow the list of nonprofits under final consideration, and it deepened our understanding of how to evaluate an organization's impact in a given field. The experts also surfaced additional high-impact nonprofits that did not emerge from the survey, and helped us eliminate groups that surfaced because of brand awareness but lacked substantial, sustained impact.

SELECTING THE FINAL SAMPLE OF TWELVE ORGANIZATIONS

By this point, we had narrowed our list of possible nonprofits for consideration to about thirty-five semifinalists. These groups were recognized as having achieved significant impact at the national or international level by their peers or by experts in their respective fields, and they met our other research criteria. We then compiled additional data from public sources on each organization (such as budget size, issue area, geographical location, age, business model, and substantiated results available from public sources). Next, we worked with our partners at CASE and the Aspen Institute to select a smaller sample of organizations for further case study.

We ultimately picked the twelve organizations profiled in this book on the basis of a variety of considerations. We wanted a sample that included groups from a range of geographical locations within the United States, represented a variety of issues or causes, and had diverse business models and leadership. We wanted the patterns of success that emerged from our research to be applicable to a wide variety of nonprofits. We used these guidelines to select a reasonably diverse group to study:

- **Type of activities and model.** We selected organizations with different models providing a range of programs, including direct service, advocacy, organizing, and policy research.
- **Size of budget.** We deliberately did not select organizations based on the size of their budgets, but rather based on their impact. However, we also made sure the sample was representative in terms of the size of organizations included.
- **Issue area.** To ensure representation of an array of causes, we aimed to include no more than two nonprofits from any field out of the nine we had identified. After careful consideration, we decided to exclude the U.S.-based international relief and development category, just as we had initially excluded organizations founded abroad. Because our peer survey did not include international respondents, we determined that it was biased toward the United States, and we didn't have the resources to conduct further research on a global scale.
- **Geographical distribution.** Although most finalist organizations tended to be based in large East Coast cities, the final sample included a reasonably diverse geographical representation.
- **Leadership.** We kept an eye on the balance of the organizations' leadership in terms of gender, race, and ethnicity, but we didn't let this factor drive our decision making or let it outweigh other important criteria.
- **Representative sample.** All things being equal, in some cases we chose one organization over another because we believed that it would provide a more interesting case study or because it would make for a more robust, representative sample.

A note on exclusions: Because of the way in which we defined the parameters for our research, particularly the time period, we noticed that certain groups were left out of consideration. For example, many of the highly ranked African American–led organizations or civil rights groups, such as the NAACP Legal Defense Fund, were excluded from consideration because they were founded before 1965. At the same time, a number of younger organizations that are Internet based were left out, because most of these were founded after 1995 (MoveOn, VolunteerMatch, and others).

Resolving the Dilemma of Comparability

As we analyzed our peer survey data and vetted nominations with field experts, we also considered creating a set of less successful, or "B-case," organizations with which to compare our top-ranked "A-case" groups. This so-called matched-pair methodology was employed by the authors of *Built to Last* and *Good to Great*.[6] A match was made if two companies operated in the same industries, had similar missions, and were of similar ages. The key metric used to differentiate them was exceptional cumulative stock returns over a sustained period of time.[7]

However, we encountered multiple obstacles in applying a matched-pair methodology to the social sector, despite a concerted effort. First, we found few instances in which a pair of organizations constituted a match—doing similar things at the national level, founded around the same time, and operating in the same issue area. In the rare instances when we did find a reasonable match, there was insufficient evidence to indicate that one was "good" and the other "great," because of the lack of universal measures to gauge relative performance across a variety of business models or issue areas.

And because there is a lack of high-quality public information available in the nonprofit sector, unlike in the for-profit sector, we knew we would have to rely on the participation of all the organizations in our research. Our concern was that any nonprofit selected as a B case in our study would have a disincentive to share information: it would worry about being seen as "less great" by funders and other important stakeholders. Without equal information, we couldn't adequately compare the two groups. Therefore, we did not pursue the matched-pair approach in our research.

Phase 3: Case Study Research and Analysis

In the next phase of our research, we conducted extensive case study research on the twelve organizations over a year and a half. We followed a more detailed process within this phase to gather data about each nonprofit before comparing it to its peers within the larger sample. All interviews with organizational leaders, as well as all fundamental analyses, were conducted by one or both of us. The bulk of the background research, some analyses, and administrative tasks were completed by graduate student teams of MBAs and PhDs who received ongoing supervision from us.[8]

COMPILED INFORMATION FOR A CASE HISTORY

We first conducted background research on each of the twelve organizations, referring to publicly available material, such as books, Web sites, annual reports, published case studies, GuideStar information, media coverage, and other secondary sources. From this, we created an internal case history of about fifteen to thirty pages in length, with high-level overviews of the organization's history, programs, leadership, and financial progress to date. This grounded us in the facts of each case before we visited to conduct interviews, and saved us from asking obvious questions.

CONDUCTED SITE VISITS AND FORMAL INTERVIEWS

We then visited each of the twelve organizations, interviewing on average ten senior leaders, board members, and staff members per organization. In addition, we observed the organization and attended special events, or visited local program sites when possible. We used a broad questionnaire to guide our interview process, touching on such subjects as strategy, organization, development and fundraising, leadership, governance, program administration, and marketing; we also asked open-ended questions. For a detailed list of interview guidelines and questions, see Appendix C.

COLLECTED ADDITIONAL INTERNAL DATA

Following our site visits, we asked each organization to send us internal data and information, including annual reports (or budget information) dating back to the founding year; organizational charts; salary and compensation information; evaluation reports; and any other internal data that were relevant to our research. We analyzed the data, looked for interesting patterns, and compared them to available benchmarking data for nonprofits.

- **Financial data.** We analyzed budget growth from the founding to present, and calculated a compound annual growth rate (CAGR) for each organization. We also looked for high-level patterns around sources or uses of funding, or evidence of a financial crisis within an organization. For basic metrics and ratios, we relied on publicly available information from GuideStar and Charity Navigator.
- **Organizational data.** We examined organizational charts and analyzed such things as compensation data, turnover, and tenure, comparing the information to national benchmarks for nonprofits. We also looked at the organization's structure and any linkages between structure and funding patterns, issue areas, or strategies.

CREATED CASE SUMMARIES

After we had visited each organization, we wrote up detailed case summaries in which we synthesized interviews, field notes, and other data, grouping them according to overarching themes. We tried to analyze all the data for an organization within each case, before beginning to look for overarching patterns across the cases. At the end of this process, once we had written a first draft of the book, we fact-checked all data, information, and quotations with each organization.

PHASE 4: FINAL ANALYSIS AND SYNTHESIS OF RESEARCH FINDINGS

After compiling our notes by case, we then stepped back and looked at all the data as a whole, coding them by subjects and themes and analyzing them to look for patterns across the sample. As patterns emerged, we engaged in an iterative process, testing themes against the data, referring back to our conversations with field experts, and drawing on our knowledge of nonprofit management practices and literature. We also used internal data either to substantiate or to refute the qualitative data from interviews, and we performed several additional analyses on these internal data as well.

We developed a "significance" test for the unifying patterns that revealed themselves during this phase of research. The level at which these practices applied within the organizations varied, but a significant majority (ten out of twelve) had to embody the practice at a basic level for it to constitute a "pattern." Further, we made note of where patterns did *not* hold up, or where some initial hypotheses fell by the wayside.

As the patterns emerged and became clearer, we field tested our hypotheses through several working sessions with practitioners and thought-leaders. We wanted to confirm that the patterns we saw indeed differentiated these nonprofits from merely average organizations *and in some way helped explain how they had achieved such substantial and sustained impact*. We also looked for new insights and deliberately sought to avoid making statements of the obvious. Where our findings either confirmed or repudiated existing research or conventional wisdom, we made note. This iterative process helped refine our thinking and often led us to go back to collect more data or to test emerging hypotheses with the organizations themselves. These patterns, over time, eventually became the six practices that we present in this book.

FIELD EXPERTS

Note: Titles and organizations reflect experts' positions when interviewed in 2004–05.

Advocacy and Civil Rights

Elizabeth Boris, project director, the Urban Institute

Dave Brady, deputy director, Hoover Institution, Stanford University

John Bridgeland, USA Freedom Corps director, George W. Bush administration

Ramona Edelin, vice chair, Black Leadership Forum

Pablo Eisenberg, founder, Center for Community Change

Tessie Guillermo, president and CEO, Community Technology Foundation of California

Miles Rapoport, president, Demos

Andrew Rich, author of *Think Tanks, Public Policy, and the Politics of Expertise*

Urvashi Vaid, deputy director, governance and civil society, Ford Foundation

Arts and Culture

Maxwell Anderson, PhD, principal, AEA Consulting

John Killacky, program officer for arts and culture, San Francisco Foundation

Catherine Maciariello, program officer for arts, Andrew W. Mellon Foundation

Ed Martenson, senior adviser for education, National Arts Strategies

Kevin McCarthy, PhD, senior social scientist, RAND Corporation

Sam Miller, former executive director of the New England Foundation for the Arts

Holly Sidford, associate, AEA Consulting

Andrew Taylor, director, Bolz Center for Arts Administration, University of Wisconsin–Madison School of Business

Education

Amy Gerstein, executive director, Noyce Foundation

Kevin Hall, chief operating officer, Broad Foundation

Diane Ravitch, former assistant secretary of education (under George H. W. Bush)

Jim Shelton, program director for education, Bill and Melinda Gates Foundation

Ted Sizer, founder and chairman, Coalition of Essential Schools

Kim Smith, cofounder and CEO, New Schools Venture Fund

Environment

Richard Ayres, cofounder, Natural Resources Defense Council

Hooper Brooks, program officer for environment, Surdna Foundation

Dan Esty, dean, Yale School of Forestry and Environmental Studies

David Roe, former senior attorney, Environmental Defense Fund

Phillip Shabecoff, former environmental correspondent, the *New York Times*

Jonathan Wiener, professor, schools of law and public policy studies, Duke University

Health

Fatima Angeles, program officer, California Wellness Foundation

Nancy Barrand, senior program officer, Robert Wood Johnson Foundation

Barbara Brenner, executive director, Breast Cancer Action Network

Tom David, consultant (formerly with California Wellness Foundation)

Shaheen Kassim-Lakha, program officer, Uni-Health Foundation

Larry Levitt, vice president, Kaiser Family Foundation

Mary Pittman, executive director, Health Research and Education Trust

Diane Rowland, executive vice president, Kaiser Family Foundation

Anne Schwartz, vice president, Grantmakers in Health

Anthony So, professor, Sanford Institute for Public Policy, Duke University

Housing and Economic Development

Bill Kelly, former executive assistant to the secretary of the U.S. Department of Housing and Urban Development (HUD)

Ellen Lazar, senior vice president, housing and community initiatives, Fannie Mae Foundation

Andrea Levere, president, Corporation for Enterprise Development

George McCarthy, program officer for community development, Ford Foundation

Kirsten Moy, director, Economic Opportunities Program, The Aspen Institute

Nicolas Retsinas, director, Joint Center for Housing Studies, Harvard University; board member, Habitat for Humanity International

Hunger

Joel Berg, executive director, New York City Coalition Against Hunger

Larry Brown, PhD, director, Center on Hunger and Poverty, Brandeis University

Robert Egger, executive director and founder, D.C. Central Kitchen

Terry Langston, director of programs, Public Welfare Foundation

Lynn Phares, consultant and former president, ConAgra Foods Feeding Children Better Foundation; board member, America's Second Harvest—The Nation's Food Bank Network (now Feeding America)

John E. Riggan, chairman and CEO, TCC Group

International Relief and Development

Susan Davis, board chair, Grameen Foundation USA

Sushmita Ghosh, president, Ashoka; founder, Changemakers.net

Jody Olsen, deputy director, U.S. Peace Corps

Note: We eliminated this category because peer survey participants and experts represented only U.S.-based organizations.

Youth Development

Bob Granger, PhD, president, William T. Grant Foundation
Jim Kielsmeier, founder and president, National Youth Leadership Council
Gregg Petersmeyer, chief architect, President's Summit on Volunteerism
Karen Pittman, executive director, Forum for Youth Investment
Marguerite Sallee, president and CEO, America's Promise
Wendy Wheeler, founder and president, Innovation Center for Youth and Community Development

Case Study Research Guidelines and Questions

Following is a list of general questions and areas of inquiry that were used to guide our interviews with CEOs and other senior leaders in each of the organizations. We tailored specific questions to interviewees' areas of expertise.

Executive Director Interview Guide

1. When you first founded or joined your organization, what was your big vision? How close to realizing that are you today?
2. What do you see as your organization's most significant *outcomes or impact?*
3. What are your goals for scaling out your impact further in the next five to ten years?
4. What would you say are the top five factors that have contributed to your organization's success at scaling out its impact to such a significant level?
5. Considering the factors that you listed above, how would you rank those factors?
6. How did your organization make key decisions around growth and scaling impact?
7. How did your organization manage the need to raise operating funds year to year while continuing to pursue your long-term vision and make investments for the future?
8. Please describe an instance in which your organization tried to advance its impact but failed.
9. What would you say are the primary factors that distinguish your organization from others?

10. How would you characterize your own leadership style, and what do you see as your strengths and weaknesses, both at founding and currently (if different)?

11. Are there any questions you'd wished we asked, but didn't?

Specific Areas of Organizational Inquiry

I. MISSION, VISION, STRATEGY: What does the organization do, and how does it do it?

   A. Mission and Vision Statements: What are they?
   B. Founding History: Who started the organization and why?
   C. Business Model: What is the organization's business model?
   D. Strategy: How does the organization execute its strengths and weaknesses?
   E. Customers/Stakeholders: Who is the target market the organization aims to serve?

II. IMPACT, OUTCOMES: How does this organization think about its own impact?

   A. General: What is the organization's "theory of change"?
   B. Measurement/Evaluation: How does the organization measure the impact it is having?

III. ORGANIZATION, STRUCTURE: How is the nonprofit organized?

   A. Sites/Affiliates: What is the overall size/scope of the organization?
   B. Structure: What is the current organizational structure?
   C. Growth: Was the original model designed "to scale" or was this an afterthought?
   D. Staff/HR: How many staff work for the organization, and where are they based?
      1. What are salary ranges, turnover rates, general policies?
   E. Culture: How does the organization characterize and/or manage its culture?

IV. LEADERSHIP: What role has leadership played in this organization?

    A. Founder/Executive: How many executives has the organization had?

    B. Senior Management: What are important management positions, and turnover?

    C. Governance: How many board members does the organization have? What is the board's role?

V. BUDGET, FINANCING: How does the organization support its work?

    A. Budget: How has the organization grown financially— inflection points?

    B. Sources of Funding: How does the organization support its activities?

VI. PROGRAM, OPERATIONS: What does the organization do?

    A. Activities/Programs: What are the most important program areas?

    B. Operations/Program: Are there any critical processes?

    C. Systems/Information Technology: How deliberate is this organization about its systems and processes?

VII. MARKETING, PR

    A. Marketing: To whom do they communicate? How and through what channels?

    B. Media/Communications: How deliberate is the organization about its PR/communications strategy?

ORIGINAL RESEARCH INTERVIEW LIST

Note: Interviewees are identified here by their organizational titles as of 2006, when we completed the first edition of *Forces for Good*.

Center on Budget and Policy Priorities

Joel Friedman, senior fellow, Aug. 12, 2005
Kathryn Greenberg, director, development and external affairs, Aug. 30, 2005
Robert Greenstein, founder and executive director, Aug. 5, 2005
Henry Griggs, director, State Fiscal Project, Aug. 16, 2005
Nick Johnson, director, communications, Sept. 8, 2005
Richard Kogan, senior fellow, Aug. 12, 2005
Iris J. Lav, deputy director, Aug. 8, 2005; Nov. 28, 2006
Ellen Nissenbaum, legislative affairs director, Aug. 30, 2005
Sharon Parrot, director, welfare reform and income support, Aug. 16, 2005
Donna Cohan Ross, director, outreach, Jan. 11, 2006
Isaac Shapiro, associate director, Aug. 16, 2005
Susan Steinmetz, associate director, Aug. 23, 2005

City Year

Jim Balfanz, chief operating officer, Aug. 11, 2005
Michael Brown, cofounder, president, June 8, 2005
AnnMaura Connolly, senior vice president, Mar. 23, 2006
Alison Franklin, director, communications, June 8, 2005
David Gergen, board member, June 9, 2005

Ilene Jacobs, board member, Aug. 11, 2005
Hubie Jones, entrepreneur in residence, June 10, 2005
Alan Khazei, cofounder and former CEO, June 10, 2005
Julie Marcus, director, communications, June 8, 2005
Ted Marquis, director, Care Force, June 8, 2005
Mithra Irani Ramaley, coexecutive director, City Year New York, Aug. 10, 2005
Charlie Rose, vice president and dean, June 9, 2005
Nancy Routh, vice president, development, June 8, 2005
Stephen Spaloss, office of the dean, June 8, 2005
Steph Wu, senior vice president, people and programs, June 9, 2005

Note: We also interviewed nine additional executive directors or coexecutive directors of local City Year sites.

Environmental Defense Fund

Peter Accinno, vice president, finance and administration, Oct. 21, 2005
Marcia Aronoff, vice president, programs, Aug. 24, 2005
Michael Bean, senior attorney, Aug. 25, 2005
Dan Dudek, chief economist, climate and air, Aug. 25, 2005
Peter Goldmark, program director, climate and air, Oct. 20, 2005
Cynthia Hampton, vice president, marketing and communications, Oct. 17, 2005
Paula Hayes, vice president, development, Oct. 20, 2005
Fred Krupp, president, Oct. 21, 2005
Annie Petsonk, international council, climate and air, Aug. 26, 2005
Joel Plagenz, associate director, organizational communications, Oct. 17, 2005
Jane Preyer, regional director, North Carolina office, Aug. 25, 2005
Gwen Ruta, program director, alliances, Aug. 25, 2005
David Yarnold, executive vice president, Aug. 24, 2005

Exploratorium

Dennis Bartels, executive director, June 20, 2006
Ann Bowers, board member, Jan. 9, 2006
William Bowes Jr., chairman, board of directors, Jan. 10, 2006
K. C. Cole, science writer, *The Los Angeles Times,* Jan. 18, 2006
Goéry Delacôte, PhD, former executive director, Jan. 16, 2006

Alan Friedman, PhD, director, New York Hall of Science, Jan. 9, 2006
Van Kasper, chairman emeritus and board member, Jan. 10, 2006
Debra Menaker, chief financial officer, Jan. 9, 2006
Gordon Moore, advisory council member, Jan. 16, 2006
Pat Murphy, manager, learning tools, Jan. 18, 2006
Christina Orth, chief of staff, Jan. 18, 2006
Wolfgang (Pief) Panofsky, PhD, director emeritus, board of directors, Jan. 10, 2006
Peter Richards, senior artist, Jan. 10, 2006
Virginia (Ginny) Rubin, director, development and marketing, Jan. 18, 2006
Robert Semper, PhD, director, Center for Learning and Teaching, Jan. 9, 2006

Feeding America (formerly America's Second Harvest— The Nation's Food Bank Network)
Alice Archabal, vice president, Philanthropy Chicago, Nov. 30, 2005
Phil Ash, executive director, San Francisco Food Bank, Dec. 21, 2005
Al Brislain, senior vice president, member services, Nov. 30, 2005
Ertharin Cousin, chief operating officer, Nov. 29, 2005
Jaynee Day, executive director, Nashville Food Bank, Nov. 28, 2005
Bob Forney, CEO, Nov. 29, 2005
Brian Green, president and CEO, Houston Food Bank, Dec. 8, 2005
Melanie Nowacki, national office staff, Nov. 29, 2005
Doug O'Brien, vice president, public policy and research, Dec. 7, 2006
David Prendergast, senior vice president, technology and planning, Nov. 29, 2005
Jan Pruitt, executive director, North Texas Food Bank, Nov. 28, 2005
Eleanor Thompson, director, government relations and public policy, June 30, 2006
Phil Zepeda, vice president, communications, Nov. 30, 2005

Habitat for Humanity International
Dennis Bender, former senior vice president, communications, Apr. 6, 2006

Pam Campbell, education program director, church relations, Apr. 12, 2006

Mike Carscaddon, executive vice president, international, Apr. 13, 2006

Sybil Carter, director, cash sponsors, Apr. 25, 2006

John Cerniglia, senior director, campaigns, Apr. 11, 2006

Jill Claflin, senior director, communications, Apr. 11, 2006

Chris Clarke, senior vice president, communications, Apr. 13, 2006

Tim Daugherty, senior director, direct marketing, Apr. 13, 2006

Rendell Day, director, employee relations, global support, Apr. 12, 2006

Millard Fuller, founder and former CEO, Apr. 11, 2006

Tom Jones, director, advocacy, Apr. 18, 2006

Paul Leonard, former interim CEO and board member, Apr. 14, 2005

Clive Rainey, director, community relations, Apr. 12, 2006

Stephen Seidel, director, urban programs, Apr. 12, 2006

David Williams, former chief operating officer, Apr. 14, 2006

The Heritage Foundation

Stuart Butler, vice president, domestic and economic policy studies, Aug. 29, 2005

Becky Norton Dunlop, vice president, external relations, Apr. 25, 2006

Edwin Feulner, president, Aug. 31, 2005

Rebecca Hagelin, vice president, communications and marketing, Apr. 25, 2006

Kim Holmes, vice president, Davis Institute for International Studies, Aug. 22, 2005

Ted E. Schelenski, vice president, finance and operations, Apr. 25, 2006

Phil Truluck, executive vice president, Aug. 29, 2005

National Council of La Raza

Gerald Borenstein, vice president and chief financial officer, Aug. 15, 2005

Marco Davis, director, leadership development, Aug. 17, 2005

Tom Espinoza, CEO of the Raza Development Fund, Aug. 15, 2005
Charles Kamasaki, senior vice president, ORAL, Aug. 18, 2005
Emily Gantz McKay, former senior vice president, Sept. 15, 2005
Cecilia Muñoz, vice president, ORAL, Aug. 17, 2005
Janet Murguía, president and CEO, Sept. 12, 2005
Sonia Perez, vice president, Sept. 12, 2005
Carlos Ugarte, deputy vice president, Institute for Hispanic Health, Aug. 15, 2005
Delia de la Vara, vice president, Strategic Communications Group, Aug. 17, 2005
Raul Yzaguirre, former president and CEO of the National Council of La Raza, Aug. 18, 2005

Self-Help

Mike Calhoun, president, Center for Responsible Lending, Aug. 30, 2006
Randy Chambers, chief financial officer, Nov. 16, 2005
Martin Eakes, founder and CEO, Nov. 14, 2006
Armeer Kenchen, director, staff, Nov. 14, 2005
Toni Lipscomb, president, Self-Help Credit Union, Nov. 14, 2005
Mary Mountcastle, former president, Center for Community Self-Help, Nov. 14, 2005
Bob Schall, president, Self-Help Ventures Fund, Nov. 14, 2005
Eric Stein, chief operating officer, Nov. 14, 2005; June 27 and Dec. 7, 2006

Share Our Strength

Hadley Boyd, director, community investment programs, June 23, 2005
John Gillespie, interim chief financial officer, June 20, 2005
Maria Gomez, board member, July 5, 2005
Ashley Graham, director, leadership, Aug. 31, 2005
Hannah Isles, corporate public relations manager, Aug. 31, 2005
Mike McCurry, board member, Aug. 22, 2005
Pat Nicklin, managing director, June 21, 2005
Chuck Scofield, director, development, Aug. 22, 2005
Bill Shore, founder and executive director, June 21, 2005
Debbie Shore, cofounder and associate director, June 22, 2005

Teach For America

Elissa Clapp, vice president, recruitment and selection, July 12, 2005

Aimee Eubanks, senior vice president, human assets, July 12, 2005

Kevin Huffman, senior vice president, growth, strategy, and development, July 11, 2005

Wendy Kopp, president and founder, July 11, 2005

Daniel Oscar, vice president, program design, July 11, 2005

Abigail Smith, vice president, research and public policy, Aug. 23, 2005

Jonathan Travers, vice president, finance and administration, July 12, 2005

YouthBuild USA

John Bell, vice president, leadership development, Sept. 28, 2005

Charles Clark, vice president, asset development, Aug. 10, 2005

Tim Cross, chief operating officer, Sept. 27, 2005

Bob Curvin, funder (formerly with Ford Foundation), Aug. 11, 2005

Suzanne Fitzgerald, president, YouthBuild Affiliates Network, Sept. 20, 2005

Adonija Hill, national alumni council, Oct. 4, 2005

Cliff Johnson, former board chair (interview date not recorded)

Leroy Looper, board chair emeritus, Sept. 26, 2005

B. J. Rudman, vice president, finance and administration, Sept. 15, 2005

Dorothy Stoneman, founder and president, Sept. 6, 2005

UPDATED ORGANIZATION PROFILES

THE CENTER ON BUDGET AND POLICY PRIORITIES

The Center on Budget and Policy Priorities (www.cbpp.org)
820 First Street NE, Suite 510
Washington, DC 20002
Telephone: (202) 408-1080

PURPOSE

The Center on Budget and Policy Priorities (the Center or CBPP) is one of the nation's premier policy organizations working at the federal and state levels on fiscal policy and public programs that affect low- and moderate-income families and individuals. The Center conducts research and analysis to inform public debates over proposed budget and tax policies and to help ensure that the needs of low-income families and individuals are considered in these debates.

PROGRAMS

The Center conducts and disseminates research and develops policy proposals in the following areas: federal budget, federal tax, food assistance, health policies, low-income immigrants, earned income tax credit (EITC) and other tax credits for low-income families, labor market policies, low-income housing, poverty/income, Social Security and retirement income, state fiscal policies, unemployment insurance, and welfare reform/TANF. The Center provides information and technical assistance to policymakers and to state and federal nonprofit policy organizations, conducts an outreach campaign to help eligible working families receive refundable tax credits, and provides information on a regular basis to the media.

Participants and/or Recipients

The Center's materials and research are used by policymakers across the political spectrum, nonprofit organizations, and journalists from a variety of media outlets. In particular, the Center has helped build the State Fiscal Analysis Initiative, a network of state policy institutes that now exist in more than half the states.

Impact

Over the past several decades, the Center has gained a reputation for producing materials that are balanced, authoritative, accessible, and responsive to issues currently before the country. It has contributed to significant policy gains for low-income families in areas ranging from the EITC to food stamps to health programs, and has been at the forefront of advancing fiscally responsible budget and tax policies at the national and state levels.

Organization

Although the Center's work is now conducted at local, state, national, and international levels in partnership with numerous nonprofits, its only office is in Washington, D.C. The organization has a sixteen-member board of directors, and Robert Greenstein is the founder and executive director. There are currently about 120 staff members employed at the Center.

REVENUE/EXPENSES

In 2010, the Center's revenues totaled approximately $27 million. Approximately 69 percent of the revenue came from major foundations; 26 percent from family foundations, donor-advised funds, and major donors; and 5 percent from other sources. In 2010, expenses totaled $26.5 million; approximately 92 percent of this was directed toward program and policy areas. Included in these expenses were about $7 million in grants the Center provided to build the capacity of nonprofit organizations in the states and in developing countries that work on budget priorities and low-income issues. The Center normally expends about 5 percent on general and administrative costs and 3 percent on fundraising.

HISTORY

The Center was founded in 1981 to analyze federal budget priorities and develop policy options, with particular emphasis on the impact of various budget choices on low-income Americans. Its work has broadened considerably since then. Most notably, the Center initiated extensive new work on budget priorities and low-income programs at the state level during the early 1990s in response to the devolution of responsibility to the state level. The Center now provides information and technical assistance to state nonprofit organizations and government officials on issues ranging from state budget priorities and revenue structures to the design and implementation of low-income programs. Another example of the Center's expansion into new policy areas is the International Budget Partnership (IBP). The Center established IBP in 1997 to help civil society organizations in emerging democracies and developing countries conduct budget analysis aimed at making these countries' budget systems more open and more responsive to the needs of society.

CITY YEAR

City Year (www.cityyear.org)
287 Columbus Avenue
Boston, MA 02116
Telephone: (617) 927-2500

Purpose

City Year is an education-focused nonprofit organization founded in 1988, which partners with public schools to help keep students in school and on track to graduate. This innovative public-private partnership brings together teams of young AmeriCorps members who commit to a year of full-time service in schools. Corps members support students by focusing on attendance, behavior, and academic performance through in-class tutoring, mentoring, and after-school programs.

Programs

In 2009, City Year CEO and cofounder Michael Brown announced In School & On Track: A National Challenge, a campaign to address the nation's high school dropout crisis and to turn around low-performing schools by scaling City Year programs nationwide. City Year corps members are laser focused on this work, implementing its Whole School, Whole Child model in classrooms in twenty-one U.S. cities and through two international affiliates. The City Year corps is a ten-month program that unites diverse teams of young people ages seventeen to twenty-four for a year of full-time service in high-need schools. City Year also operates Care Force, a revenue-generating division that engages corporate partners and their employees in high-impact community service events that improve youth- and family-focused educational, recreational, and residential facilities.

Participants and/or Recipients

Since its inception in 1988, City Year's 15,100 corps members have served more than 1,225,000 children and completed more than twenty-six million hours of service. In 2011, City Year deployed its largest corps ever—two thousand members strong—who will work in 187 high-need schools, impacting 110,000 students through their service as tutors, mentors, and role models.

Impact

From a fifty-person summer pilot program in 1988, City Year has grown to twenty-one U.S. sites and international affiliates in

London and Johannesburg. City Year has also played an influential role in advocating for national service policy in the United States, including the formation of AmeriCorps and the passage of the Edward M. Kennedy Serve America Act. In 2010, 88 percent of third- through fifth-grade students tutored by City Year improved raw literacy scores. As a result of City Year's attendance support initiatives, over half of sixth- through ninth-grade students who were off track in attendance were back on track in 2010. Among ninth graders working with corps members, 90 percent agreed that City Year helped them understand the class content better.

ORGANIZATION

City Year's leadership includes corps alumni in addition to professionals from various sectors. City Year has a twenty-nine-member board of trustees and a thirteen-person senior leadership team. Cofounder Michael Brown became CEO in 2006; cofounder Alan Khazei was CEO during the period when original research for this book was conducted.

REVENUE/EXPENSES

City Year finished FY2011 with total operating revenue of just over $79 million. Of this operating revenue, 57 percent was generated by contributions and private grants, and 27 percent came from federal grants through the Corporation for National and Community Service; contributions from private grants increased by 40 percent from the previous year. City Year has earned a four-star rating (the highest rating offered) from Charity Navigator for six consecutive years, for its ability to efficiently manage and grow its finances. Charity Navigator ranks City Year in the top 4 percent of all nonprofits for sound fiscal management.

HISTORY

City Year was founded in 1988 by Michael Brown and Alan Khazei, then roommates at Harvard Law School, who felt strongly that young people in service could be a powerful resource for addressing our nation's most pressing issues. With fifty corps members and five founding sponsors, City Year piloted its first eight-week program in Boston. In 1990, City Year's first full-year corps launched Camp City Year and organized the first Serve-a-thon. In 1993, City Year opened its first expansion site in Rhode Island. In 1994, four more sites were opened; and in 1995, City Year Columbus hosted the organization's first annual "convention of idealism," called "cyzygy." More sites were opened over the next ten years, and in 2004, the City Year Alumni Association and the Web site www.cityyearalumni.org were launched. In 2005, City Year opened its first international site in Johannesburg, South Africa; City Year London launched in 2010.

ENVIRONMENTAL DEFENSE FUND

Environmental Defense Fund (www.edf.org)
257 Park Avenue South
New York, NY 10010
Telephone: (212) 505-2100

PURPOSE

Environmental Defense Fund's mission is to preserve the natural systems on which all life depends. Guided by science and economics, Environmental Defense Fund (EDF) finds practical and lasting solutions to the most serious environmental problems.

PROGRAMS

To achieve its program goals (in the areas of climate and energy; health; land, water, and wildlife; and oceans), EDF brings together experts in science, law, and economics to tackle complex environmental issues. In addition to research, advocacy, partnerships, and litigation, EDF produces reports, print and e-mail newsletters, fact sheets, and educational materials on "green" behavior and business practices that can help sustain and improve our environment. It has also created several Web sites to provide information on its activities, with recommendations on how to protect the environment.

PARTICIPANTS AND/OR RECIPIENTS

As of 2011, EDF represented more than seven hundred thousand members. Since 1967, it has linked science, economics, law, and innovative private sector partnerships to create breakthrough solutions to the most serious environmental problems. EDF maintains a five-hundred-thousand-member Action Network, which alerts an online community of activists to send e-mails and faxes to legislators and other policymakers.

IMPACT

Recent accomplishments include working with FedEx to develop the next generation of clean trucks that emit 96 percent less soot and increase fuel economy by 50 percent; working with landowners and government officials to protect four million acres of wildlife habitat; rebuilding severely depleted fish populations in the Gulf of Mexico and elsewhere through a new approach to fishery management, called catch shares; and cosponsoring the legislation that led California to adopt America's first economy-wide cap on greenhouse gas emissions.

ORGANIZATION

EDF has a staff of 350 people, strategically located in offices around the country. In total, there are eight regional offices in addition to the headquarters in New York City and offices in China and Mexico. EDF has a thirty-eight-member board of trustees and four honorary trustees. Fred Krupp is president.

REVENUE/EXPENSES

Unrestricted operating support and revenue of $101.4 million was used for current operations during FY2010. Members contributed $51.4 million, representing 51 percent of the total. Foundation grants totaled $42.0 million, or 41 percent of the total. Bequests of $2.4 million from members of the Osprey Legacy Society accounted for 2 percent of the total; government and other grants provided 3 percent; and investment income and other revenue accounted for the remaining 3 percent. EDF receives less than 1 percent of its financial support from corporate donors; to ensure independence and public credibility, it does not accept payments from corporate partners. Expenditures totaled $100.4 million in FY2010. Program services expenditures of $83.5 million accounted for 83 percent of total operating expenses, with almost all devoted to EDF's four priority areas—climate, ecosystems, health, and oceans. Management and administration expenditures made up 6 percent of the total, 10 percent went toward the fundraising needed to generate current income and support for future years, and 1 percent was spent on the acquisition of new members.

History

More than forty years ago, EDF was started when four scientists on Long Island set out to halt the use of DDT (dichlorodiphenyltrichloroethane), the pesticide Rachel Carson warned of in *Silent Spring*. Their efforts led to a nationwide ban on DDT and the birth of modern environmental law. Soon EDF began to hire economists, engineers, and computer analysts to find ways to help the environment without harming the economy. In the process, it became one of America's most influential environmental advocacy groups. From the beginning, EDF has made a commitment not only to oppose ill-conceived policies but also to propose alternatives. The organization still goes to court when necessary, but increasingly it works directly with business, government, and community groups, forging solutions that make sense for all.

Exploratorium

Exploratorium (www.exploratorium.edu)
3601 Lyon Street
San Francisco, CA 94123
Telephone: (415) 563-7337

Purpose

The Exploratorium is a museum of science, art, and human perception founded in 1969. The Exploratorium's mission is to create a culture of learning through innovative environments, programs, and tools that help people nurture their curiosity about the world around them.

Programs

The Exploratorium offers exhibitions and public programs, professional development for educators, and workshops for families. It also conducts museum research and evaluation, maintains a Web site with eighteen thousand pages of original content, produces webcasts, and distributes Exploratorium-developed publications. The Center for Museum Partnerships supports a network of museums and science centers dedicated to exhibit-based teaching. The Exploratorium also serves museums worldwide through exhibit sales, rentals, and consulting.

Participants and/or Recipients

Of the 560,000 people who annually visit the Exploratorium in San Francisco, 70 percent of visitors are adults and 30 percent are children; 61 percent are from the Bay Area, 30 percent are from the rest of California, 6 percent are from other states, and 3 percent are from outside the United States. Every year, approximately 180 million people visit Exploratorium exhibits at science centers and other locations, nationally and internationally.

Impact

Each year, 97,000 students and teachers visit the Exploratorium on school field trips; 12,500 individuals and families are Exploratorium members. In 2006, 41,000 visitors attended on Free Wednesdays (the first Wednesday of every month). Since 1995, more than sixty-four hundred educators from forty-eight states and eleven countries have participated in Exploratorium workshops. Children's Educational Outreach offers free workshops to thirty-five hundred underserved children and families, and the Explainer Program hires and trains a diverse group of up to 120 high school students each year. The Exploratorium has 650 original interactive exhibits, displays, and artworks, with 400 currently on view; public programs include lectures, performances, live webcasts, art, and film. Twelve million Web visitors annually access www.exploratorium.edu, which has eighteen thousand pages of original content; up to seventy-five live webcasts, podcasts, and videos originate each year from the Exploratorium and remote locations; twenty-five thousand copies of Exploratorium-developed publications were sold in 2006–07, with eighteen titles in print. More than twenty-five hundred exhibits have been installed at two hundred science centers, museums, universities, and other organizations worldwide.

ORGANIZATION

The Exploratorium has a twenty-eight-member board of directors and a seventeen-member advisory council. Dr. Dennis M. Bartels was named executive director in 2006; Virginia Carollo Rubin was acting director during the period that the original research for this book was conducted.

REVENUE/EXPENSES

In FY2011, the Exploratorium reported total revenues of approximately $56 million and total expenses of approximately $36 million. The majority of expenses were incurred for program services, with the remainder going to support services.

HISTORY

The Exploratorium was founded in 1969 by noted physicist and educator Dr. Frank Oppenheimer, who devoted his efforts to it until his death in 1985. Oppenheimer's vision was to create a collection of experiments that would make natural phenomena accessible and understandable to everyone. Oppenheimer eventually found a home for his museum in San Francisco, at the Palace of Fine Arts, which was a vacant remnant of the Panama-Pacific International Exposition of 1915. The museum's doors opened in 1969, with just a few dozen exhibits—most of which were being borrowed. The Exploratorium grew rapidly, and in 1980, cramped by its growing collection of exhibits, the museum built a mezzanine within the exhibition hall. Oppenheimer died in 1985, and from 1991 until 2005, the museum was led by renowned French scientist and educator Dr. Goéry Delacôte. During his tenure, Delacôte focused on creating a "networked" Exploratorium, bringing the Exploratorium to the world and the world to the Exploratorium.

FEEDING AMERICA

Feeding America (www.feedingamerica.org)
35 E. Wacker Drive, #2000
Chicago, IL 60601
Telephone: (312) 263-2303; (800) 771-2303

PURPOSE

Feeding America provides low-income individuals and families with the fuel to survive and even thrive. The nation's largest domestic hunger-relief charity, Feeding America network members supplied food to more than thirty-seven million Americans in 2010, including fourteen million children and three million seniors. Serving the entire United States, more than two hundred member food banks provide food and groceries to more than 5.7 million people each week.

PROGRAMS

Feeding America itself maintains several programs:

- **After-school snack program**—provides snacks to children through a variety of existing community locations where children congregate during after-school hours
- **BackPack Program**—provides food to at-risk children on weekends and out-of-school periods
- **Disaster relief**—provides relief supplies to emergency feeding centers serving disaster victims
- **National Produce Program**—offers services built around securing and distributing fresh produce throughout the Feeding America network

- **Kids Cafe**—provides free meals and snacks to low-income children through a variety of existing community locations where children congregate, such as Boys and Girls Clubs, churches, or public schools
- **Relief Fleet**—works to lower transportation costs by soliciting free or deeply discounted freight for donated loads for all network members
- **School Pantry Program**—operates from school sites to provide food to children and families for them to prepare and consume at home
- **Summer Food Program**—provides nutritious, healthy meals; food packages; vouchers; and snacks to children at risk of hunger in the summer months when school is not in session

PARTICIPANTS AND/OR RECIPIENTS

According to Feeding America's study *Hunger in America 2010*, the nationality or ethnic breakdown of the clients served that year was 40 percent non-Hispanic white; 34 percent non-Hispanic black; 21 percent Latino or Hispanic; and 6 percent American Indian, Alaskan Native, Asian, Native Hawaiian, or other Pacific Islander.

IMPACT

In 2010, the Feeding America network provided emergency food assistance to more than thirty-seven million Americans, including more than fourteen million children and three million seniors. In 2010, the Feeding America network distributed more than three billion pounds of food and grocery products. The percentages of food streams shift and change from year to year. Here is how food streams broke down for FY2010:

- Purchased food: 17%
- Manufacturing: 21%
- Retailers: 19%
- Produce: 15%
- Federal commodities: 28%

Feeding America has also played an important role in influencing public policies and programs, such as the Temporary Emergency Food Assistance Program, the Supplemental Nutrition Assistance Program (SNAP, formerly known as Food Stamps), and most other federal nutrition programs.

ORGANIZATION

The Feeding America network of food banks provides food and groceries to approximately sixty-one thousand local charitable agencies, including food pantries, soup kitchens, emergency shelters, after-school programs, Kids Cafes, and BackPack Programs. The organization has a twenty-one person board of directors. Vicki Escarra became president and CEO in 2006.

REVENUE/EXPENSES

Of the three billion pounds of food and grocery products that the Feeding America network has distributed, the vast majority has come from donations. Although the organization was aided by the federal government during the 1970s, federal funding was discontinued by 1982, and Feeding America increased its pursuit of alternative sources of financial support. In FY2011, total cash revenues were $98 million. In-kind donations of food, grocery products, and services exceeded $1.1 billion. Charity Navigator gives Feeding America a 98 percent efficiency rating.

HISTORY

The concept of food banking began in the late 1960s in Phoenix, Arizona, when John Van Hengel, a retired businessman, volunteered at a local soup kitchen. He solicited donations of food products that might otherwise go to waste, and soon was generating more food than the soup kitchen could handle. So he set up a warehouse where he could store the donated products and distribute them to charities feeding hungry people. By 1976, the federal government had given Van Hengel's food bank a grant to assist in developing other food banks throughout the nation. By 1979, this federally funded effort had expanded to include the solicitation of food donations and was incorporated formally as Second Harvest, which soon became the clearinghouse for large donations from national corporations. (In 1999, the name of the organization was officially changed from Second Harvest to America's Second Harvest—The Nation's Food Bank Network. In 2008, the name was again changed to Feeding America.) With many major cities developing food banks by the mid-1980s, network expansion slowed, and Feeding America's focus shifted to improving existing programs. Professionalism and efficiency of food bank operations improved dramatically, resulting in the network's distributing a much greater amount of food and grocery products.

HABITAT FOR HUMANITY

270 Peachtree Street NW, Suite 1300 (www.habitat.org)
Atlanta, GA 30303
Telephone: (404) 962-3400

PURPOSE

Habitat for Humanity International (Habitat, Habitat for Humanity, HFHI) is a global nonprofit Christian housing organization that seeks to put God's love into action by bringing people together to build homes, communities, and hope.

PROGRAMS

Habitat helps eliminate poverty housing around the world by constructing, rehabilitating, and repairing homes; advocating for fair and just housing policies; and providing training to help families improve their shelter conditions. Habitat's Neighborhood Revitalization Initiative helps improve the quality of life in U.S. neighborhoods through local community planning partnerships and by expanding housing services. Habitat also has innovative housing finance programs with microfinance institutions to help provide home improvement opportunities in developing countries. The organization has disaster response programs that focus on preparedness, mitigation, and recovery. Typically, Habitat's houses are built with the help of volunteer labor, and

Habitat has several programs to involve youth, women, professional homebuilders, and even recreational vehicle owners in the work. The organization has short-term and long-term volunteer opportunities in the United States and around the world.

PARTICIPANTS AND/OR RECIPIENTS

According to Habitat, millions around the world support its mission and contribute to its work. Annually, an estimated eight hundred thousand to nearly one million people volunteer with Habitat.

IMPACT

Helping a family improve their housing conditions somewhere in the world every seven minutes, Habitat serves more than seventy-five thousand families a year through its various programs. Habitat dedicated its 500,000th home built, rehabilitated, repaired, or improved worldwide in Maai Mahiu, Kenya, in October 2011, and raised the walls on its 500,001st house the same day in Paterson, New Jersey. Currently, more than 2.5 million people in communities worldwide live in housing they built or improved with Habitat's help.

ORGANIZATION

Habitat for Humanity is a global home-building movement made up of local affiliates, state support organizations, Habitat Resource Centers, and national organizations and branches in nearly eighty countries. Affiliates—about fifteen hundred in the United States—vary in size and character, but they all undergo a lengthy affiliation process consisting of more than seventy steps, including establishing committees and a board of directors, fundraising, and gaining local community support. Each U.S. affiliate coordinates all aspects of Habitat home building in its local area: fundraising, building-site selection, partner family selection and support, home improvement intervention, and mortgage servicing.

Habitat for Humanity International has a twenty-two-member board of directors. Jonathan Reckford is CEO. The organization's administrative headquarters office is in Atlanta, and its operational headquarters office is in Americus, the city in south-west Georgia where Habitat was founded. Habitat has area offices in San Jose, Costa Rica; Bangkok, Thailand; Bratislava, Slovakia; and Pretoria, South Africa.

Revenue/Expenses

Total revenue for Habitat for Humanity International in FY2011 was slightly over $287 million. Support comes in the form of contributions from individuals (cash, stock gifts, estate gifts, and an annuity program), corporations (both cash and donated assets and services), foundations and other organizations, as well as tithe funds collected from U.S. affiliates that are used to support the work of affiliates in other countries. Tithes from U.S. affiliates totaled nearly $13.2 million in FY2011. In FY2011, Habitat spent a total of approximately $268.5 million on programs, representing 84 percent of total expenses. Program expenses in FY2011 included costs for programs that directly benefit affiliates and national organizations; 12 percent of FY2011 expenses went to fundraising and 4 percent to management and general expenses. For each dollar spent at Habitat for Humanity, 81 cents goes to program-related activities.

History

The Habitat for Humanity concept was conceived at Koinonia Farm, a small, interracial Christian farming community founded in 1942 outside Americus, Georgia, by farmer and biblical scholar Clarence Jordan and a small group of friends. In the 1960s, Millard and Linda Fuller left a successful business and affluent lifestyle in Montgomery to begin a new life of Christian service and, with Jordan, developed the concept of "partnership housing." This model called for those in need of adequate, affordable housing to work side by side with volunteers to build simple, decent houses. The houses were built with no profit added and no interest charged, and homeowner repayments went into a revolving Fund for Humanity. After proving the self-help housing model in the American South and in Africa, the Fullers formally founded Habitat for Humanity in 1976. The involvement of Jimmy Carter, former president and Nobel Peace Prize laureate, helped transform

Habitat from a small nonprofit to an internationally known organization with enormous impact and fundraising capabilities.

THE HERITAGE FOUNDATION

The Heritage Foundation (www.heritage.org)
214 Massachusetts Avenue NE
Washington, DC 20002-4999
Telephone: (202) 546-4400

PURPOSE

Founded in 1973, The Heritage Foundation (Heritage) is a research and educational institute—a think tank—whose mission is to formulate and promote conservative public policies based on the principles of free enterprise, limited government, individual freedom, traditional American values, and a strong national defense. The organization's vision is to build an America where freedom, opportunity, prosperity, and civil society flourish.

PROGRAMS

Heritage conducts research and publishes policy papers on important social and economic domestic and international issues, such as health care, education, crime, Social Security, taxes, national security, politics, and government regulation. It also organizes issue working groups and convenes lectures and panel discussions. Heritage frequently briefs the media and national, state, and local policymakers on important domestic and foreign issues. The popular Heritage Young Leaders Program is intended to introduce bright, innovative undergraduate and graduate students to the policymaking process and encourage them to become active and effective participants in public affairs.

PARTICIPANTS AND/OR RECIPIENTS

Heritage engages policymakers at local, state, and federal levels, as well as the nation as a whole, through its media briefings and communication network.

Impact

The Heritage Foundation is known for the wide-ranging and influential nature of its work. Its 1981 book of policy analysis, *Mandate for Leadership*, revolutionized the character of public policy advice giving. At over one thousand pages, it offered specific recommendations on policy, budget, and administrative action for all Cabinet departments and many agencies to be staffed by political appointees in the incoming conservative administration of President Ronald Reagan. Internationally and in partnership with *The Wall Street Journal*, Heritage publishes the annual Index of Economic Freedom, which measures the level of economic freedom in each of more than 180 countries. In domestic policy, Heritage is a proponent of supply-side economics, which holds that reductions in the marginal rate of taxation can spur economic growth. In 1994, Heritage advised Newt Gingrich and other conservatives on the development of the "Contract with America," which was credited with helping produce a conservative majority in Congress. The result is that many consider Heritage the most influential think tank in the United States.

Organization

Headquartered in Washington, D.C., Heritage employs more than 250 staff members. There are twelve senior managers who work under Edwin J. Feulner, president, and Phillip N. Truluck, executive vice president. Centers of policy analysis include the Allison Center for Foreign Policy Studies, the Asian Studies Center, the Center for Policy Innovation, the Center for Data Analysis, the Center for Health Policy Studies, the Center for International Trade and Economics, the Meese Center for Legal and Judicial Studies, the Davis Institute for International Studies, the DeVos Center for Religion and Civil Society, the Roe Institute for Economic Policy Studies, the Simon Center for Principles and Politics, and the Thatcher Center for Freedom. The Heritage Foundation also makes use of supporting departments, such as external relations, finance and operations, development, communications, and information technology. In 2010, Heritage created a 501(c)(4) sister organization, known as Heritage Action, to lobby members of Congress to advance their mission to promote conservative public policy. Heritage has a twenty-three-member board of trustees and three honorary trustees.

Revenue/Expenses

Heritage reported total revenues of more than $81 million in 2010, over two-thirds of which came from individual contributors. Heritage's initial funding came from Joseph Coors of the Adolph Coors Company. Other wealthy philanthropists have been generous Heritage donors as well. With 710,000 individual donors, however, Heritage enjoys the broadest base of support of all think tanks and accepts no government funding. Heritage uses mail, telemarketing, one-on-one meetings, planned giving, grant proposals, publication sales, and Internet appeals to raise funds. In 2010, Heritage reported total expenses of approximately $80.5 million, of which about $61 million was devoted to program expenses.

History

Heritage was founded in 1973, with conservative activist Paul Weyrich as its first leader. Since 1977, Heritage's president has been Edwin J. Feulner, PhD, former staff director of the House Republican Study Committee and a former staff assistant to Congressman Phil Crane (R-IL). Under Feulner's leadership, Heritage has come to be known for the wide-ranging and influential nature of its work. Unlike traditional think tanks, which tend to house scholars and politicians-in-exile who produce large books, Heritage tends to employ public policy analysts who produce comparatively short policy papers intended to pass what Heritage calls "the briefcase test" for busy politicians to read on the run. Heritage also pioneered the "marketing" of policy ideas through astute packaging and public relations, now a staple feature of Washington think-tank activity.

National Council of La Raza

National Council of La Raza (www.nclr.org)
1126 Sixteenth Street NW, 6th floor
Washington, DC 20036
Telephone: (202) 785-1670

Purpose

The National Council of La Raza (NCLR)—the largest national Hispanic civil rights and advocacy organization in the United States—works to improve opportunities for Hispanic Americans.

Programs

NCLR works through two primary, complementary approaches. First, NCLR provides organizational assistance in management, governance, program operations, and resource development to Hispanic community-based organizations nationwide, especially those that serve low-income and disadvantaged Hispanics. Second, NCLR conducts applied research, policy analysis, and advocacy, increasing policymaker and public understanding of Hispanic needs and encouraging the adoption of programs and policies that equitably serve Hispanics. NCLR strengthens these efforts with public information, media activities, and collaboration.

Participants and/or Recipients

NCLR serves all Hispanic subgroups in all regions of the country and has operations in Atlanta, Chicago, Los Angeles, New York, Phoenix, Sacramento, San Antonio, and San Juan, Puerto Rico. Through its network of nearly three hundred affiliated community-based organizations, NCLR reaches millions of Hispanics each year in forty-one states, Puerto Rico, and the District of Columbia.

Impact

NCLR conducts research, policy analysis, and advocacy, and provides capacity-building assistance to its affiliates working at the state and local levels. NCLR shaped the Immigration Reform and Control Act of 1986, which legalized the status of nearly three million previously undocumented workers; the Immigration Act of 1990; and legislation over the 1997–2009 period restoring benefits to millions of low-income legal immigrants. The organization helped preserve and expand the Voting Rights Act in 1992, and again in 2006; catalyzed a 1990 executive order on Hispanic Educational Excellence, which helped reduce Latino underrepresentation in college preparation; and helped shape the expansion of the Earned Income Tax Credit in 1992 and the establishment of a partially refundable child tax credit in 2001, lifting millions of Hispanics out of poverty. NCLR and its network of affiliates operate the largest Latino-focused home ownership and alternative–charter school networks in the country. The organization's subsidiary, the Raza Development Fund, is the largest Hispanic community development bank in the United States. NCLR sponsors the American Latino Media Arts (ALMA) Awards, the only prime-time network television awards recognizing Hispanics' contributions in film, television, and other media.

ORGANIZATION

NCLR is governed by a board of directors, which includes about twenty-five members who are representative of all geographical regions of the United States and all Hispanic subgroups. The organization also receives guidance from a corporate board of advisers, which includes senior executives from thirty major corporations and their liaison staff, and from the affiliate council, which includes twelve affiliated community-based organization executive directors and other senior executive staff members, elected from all regions of the country.

REVENUE/EXPENSES

In 2010, NCLR reported total consolidated revenues of $47 million. General support from individual and affiliate organization members, special events registrations and sponsorships, and other revenue totaled $14.9 million; corporate and foundation grants totaled $23 million; and $9.4 million came from government entities.

NCLR's balance sheet includes assets and liabilities of the Raza Development Fund, a subsidiary corporation, and the assets, liabilities, revenues, and expenses of the Strategic Investment Fund for La Raza, a support corporation created to house NCLR's endowment, which had grown to $35 million by 2010. In 2010, NCLR reported total expenses of $46 million, of which investments in program services totaled $39 million, or 85 percent, excluding fundraising. The two biggest program activity expenses were public policy ($6 million) and community development ($7.9 million).

HISTORY

Originally the Southwest Council of La Raza, NCLR was founded in 1968 by three key individuals—Herman Gallegos, Julian Samora, and Ernesto Galarza—in the wake of the civil rights movement, to provide grassroots programs and services to a growing Latino community and to advocate for their civil rights. NCLR helped launch and support seven barrio organizations in three southwestern states as its first "affiliates." In 1974, Raul Yzaguirre joined NCLR as director. (His title later shifted to president and CEO.) In the late 1970s, NCLR formally revised its mission to serve all Hispanics—not just Mexican Americans—and established a policy analysis and advocacy capacity to complement its program work. Yzaguirre left NCLR in 2005, and was replaced by Janet Murguía, who had joined NCLR the previous year as chief operating officer.

SELF-HELP

Self-Help (www.self-help.org; www.responsiblelending.org)
P.O. Box 3619
Durham, NC 27702
Telephone: (919) 956-4400; (800) 476-7428

PURPOSE

Self-Help's work is based on the belief that ownership allows people to improve their economic position. Owning assets, such as a home, can enable a family to send a child to college, start a business, or weather a financial crisis. In its work as a lender, Self-Help acts as a laboratory for economic development—experimenting to find out what works and advocating for change in the public and private sectors.

Programs

Self-Help has several major programs that serve the organization's purpose. The Center for Community Self-Help is a nonprofit 501(c)(3) organization that develops and coordinates Self-Help's programs, raises resources, and advocates for economic opportunity. Self-Help includes two credit unions. Self-Help Credit Union is a federally insured credit union chartered in North Carolina; it raises market rate deposits from members in order to make commercial and home loans. Self-Help Federal Credit Union was chartered in 2008 to build a network of branches throughout California serving the state's working-class families. Traditionally, credit union membership has focused on nonprofit and religious organizations and other socially responsible individuals and institutions. More recently, Self-Help has merged with retail credit unions in North Carolina and California in order to enhance its ability to provide a full range of retail financial services to working-class families. Self-Help Ventures Fund is a nonprofit 501(c)(3) organization that concentrates its lending on higher-risk, unconventional, and high-impact business loans. It is funded with loans and grants from foundations, religious organizations, corporations, and government sources. It manages Self-Help's home loan secondary market programs, real estate development, and higher-risk business loans. The Center for Responsible Lending (CRL) is a national nonprofit, nonpartisan research and policy affiliate, and its own 501(c)(3). CRL is dedicated to protecting home ownership and family wealth by working to eliminate abusive financial practices.

Participants and/or Recipients

In 2010, even with the housing crisis still crippling mortgage lending, Self-Help closed 216 direct home loans worth $18.2 million, with 28 percent going to female-headed households, 86 percent to minorities, and 33 percent to rural families. In 2010, Self-Help

closed 347 home, community facility, and small business loans totaling over $100 million. (With essentially no demand for purchases
from conventional lenders, Self-Help's secondary market program
was considerably less active, and Self-Help shifted focus to helping
troubled borrowers.) The impact of Self-Help Credit Union's work
continued to increase significantly as, combined, both credit unions
now operate more than twenty-five retail branches serving seventy-
three thousand members. Self-Help Federal Credit Union also has
launched a pilot credit union concept, the Micro Branch, designed
specifically around the needs of families living paycheck to paycheck.

Impact

Since Self-Help's start in 1980, it has provided $6 billion in financ-
ing to more than seventy thousand small businesses, nonprofits,
and homebuyers across the United States. Self-Help reaches out
to female, rural, and minority borrowers all over North Carolina,
and now in Washington, D.C., and other states, to help them
build wealth through ownership of a home or business. Self-Help
headed a coalition to pass the country's first anti–predatory lending law in 1999. Subsequent work to curtail predatory lending has
saved families more than $4 billion annually.

Organization

Headquartered in Durham, North Carolina, Self-Help works in
the areas of home lending, retail credit union financial services,
secondary market financing, small business lending, real estate
development, community facilities lending, and policy and advocacy. Self-Help operates thirty regional offices and credit union
branches across North Carolina and California, as well as in
Washington, D.C. Martin Eakes is the founder and CEO. Self-
Help's five boards have fifty-three members, including nineteen
women and eighteen people of color.

Revenue/Assets

In 2010, Self-Help reported total gross revenues of approximately
$107 million, the majority of which came from interest on loans

and securities. Although Self-Help's losses have increased due to the severity of the housing crisis and its devastating economic impact in the communities that Self-Help serves, Self-Help's net worth in 2010 was $327 million, with assets of $1.5 billion.

HISTORY

In the late 1970s, Martin Eakes and his then-girlfriend (now wife), Bonnie Wright, planted the seeds for Self-Help when they started providing business and technical assistance to help displaced blue-collar workers create worker-owned cooperatives. But the greatest barrier that the organization came across was access to capital. The founders solved this by starting their own lending institutions in 1984, the Self-Help Credit Union and a complementary organization, the Self-Help Ventures Fund, with $77 raised at a bake sale. As the Credit Union and Ventures Fund grew, Self-Help's activities in financing grew much more rapidly than its technical assistance programs. Self-Help's entrepreneurial spirit never subsided, and it expanded into many new areas, such as loans and counseling to child-care providers. Self-Help also provides technical assistance to key partners, helping create the Minority Support Center and working with Latino leaders to open a Latino-focused credit union. Self-Help also created the nation's largest secondary market program for low-income borrowers; in 1998, the Ford Foundation and Fannie Mae partnered with Self-Help to provide $2 billion in loans to low-income borrowers.

SHARE OUR STRENGTH

Share Our Strength (www.strength.org)
1730 M Street NW, Suite 700
Washington, DC 20036
Telephone: (202) 393-2925; (800) 969-4767

PURPOSE

Share Our Strength, a national nonprofit, is ending childhood hunger in America by connecting children with the nutritious food they need to lead healthy, active lives. Through its No Kid Hungry campaign to end childhood hunger in America by 2015, Share Our Strength ensures that children in need are enrolled in effective federal nutrition programs; invests in community organizations fighting hunger; teaches families how to cook healthy, affordable meals; and builds public-private partnerships to end childhood hunger, at the state and city levels. The organization raises funds in innovative ways, from holding volunteer-led special events across the country to implementing creative online donation drives and developing corporate partnerships and cause-related marketing ventures that support No Kid Hungry.

PROGRAMS

Share Our Strength runs a number of fundraising programs to raise money for hunger relief. Its Taste of the Nation is the country's largest and finest culinary benefit, where thousands of the best chefs and restaurants donate their time, talent, and products at nearly forty events across the country to support No Kid Hungry. The Great American Bake Sale is a national effort that encourages Americans to host bake sales in their communities to help end childhood hunger by 2015. Share Our Strength's Dine Out for No Kid Hungry is a national event that brings together thousands of restaurants and millions of consumers to raise funds each September through a variety of creative tactics; all funds support No Kid Hungry.

Share Our Strength also runs various local and state programs. Its state and city-based No Kid Hungry campaigns bring together public officials, private funders, and nonprofit organizations to create a measurable action plan to ensure that at-risk children in that state or city get the food they need. These campaigns also fund local antihunger organizations across the country. Cooking Matters empowers families at risk of hunger with the skills, knowledge, and confidence to make affordable, healthy meals. Community Investments provides grants nationally to help nonprofits build access to federal nutrition programs, including school breakfast, summer meals, afterschool snacks and meals, SNAP (food stamps), and WIC. The No Kid Hungry Pledge mobilizes individuals nationally in the fight to end childhood hunger.

PARTICIPANTS AND/OR RECIPIENTS

Participants include chefs, restaurants, individual citizens, and corporations. Recipients include impoverished and hungry individuals in the United States and selected countries abroad.

IMPACT

Share Our Strength has established No Kid Hungry campaigns in eighteen states, catalyzing public-private partnerships to feed children at risk of hunger, and in 2011 instituted a No Kid Hungry Allies program to expand its efforts to more communities across the country. Since 2010, the organization also granted nearly $7 million to more than four hundred organizations across the country. Overall, through its range of fundraising activities, Share Our Strength has raised more than $300 million since 1984 to fight hunger. Share Our Strength's Cooking Matters program reached nearly twelve thousand participants through 1,020 courses in 2010, with a graduation rate of 86 percent. Since 1993, Cooking Matters staff and thousands of volunteer instructors have conducted more than sixty-two hundred courses, helping more than seventy-four thousand families across the country learn how to eat better for less.

ORGANIZATION

Share Our Strength fights hunger on state, local, and national levels. It has a twenty-member board of directors. Bill Shore is founder and CEO.

REVENUE/EXPENSES

In 2010, Share Our Strength reported total revenues of $36.7 million, including those from Community Wealth Ventures. The majority of Share Our Strength's revenues come from corporate sponsorships and partners, followed by special events and consulting work. In addition, revenues are generated from foundations, online fundraising, and individual donors. In 2010, total assets were $11.7 million. Share Our Strength reported total expenses of

$31.1 million, including those from Community Wealth Ventures. Share Our Strength's biggest costs are incurred through its anti-hunger and antipoverty initiatives, and in fundraising activities.

HISTORY

Share Our Strength was established in 1984 by Bill Shore and his sister, Debbie Shore, who started the organization with the belief that everyone has a strength to share in the global fight against hunger and poverty, and that in these shared strengths lie sustainable solutions. By tapping the creative talents of chefs, restaurateurs, and food-service professionals, they transformed their love of food into a powerful force in the fight against hunger. In its first few years, Share Our Strength collected funds from restaurants nationwide and then distributed the funds to antihunger programs in the United States and overseas. In 1988, Share Our Strength pioneered the largest nationwide culinary benefit, Taste of the Nation, which now spans more than forty cities across North America, involves thousands of chefs and restaurateurs, and has raised more than $75 million. After establishing Taste of the Nation, Share Our Strength founded additional programs and projects, including Great American Bake Sale (2003), Dine Out for No Kid Hungry (2008), and the No Kid Hungry Campaign to end childhood hunger in America (2009). In 1997, Share Our Strength created Community Wealth Ventures (CWV) as a for-profit subsidiary. CWV is a social enterprise consulting firm that helps nonprofit organizations become more self-sustaining by generating revenue through business ventures and corporate partnerships. In addition, CWV helps corporations improve their bottom line through the design and implementation of community investment strategies.

TEACH FOR AMERICA

Teach For America (www.teachforamerica.org)
315 West Thirty-sixth Street, 8th floor
New York, NY 10018
Telephone: (212) 279-2080

PURPOSE

Teach For America's mission is to build a movement of leaders who are working to ensure that all children have access to an excellent education.

PROGRAMS

Teach For America is a national nonprofit that works in partnership with communities to expand educational opportunities for children growing up in poverty. Founded in 1990, Teach For America recruits and trains a diverse corps of outstanding recent college graduates and professionals to commit two years to teach in high-need urban and rural schools and become lifelong leaders in the effort to expand education opportunity.

PARTICIPANTS AND/OR RECIPIENTS

Teach For America corps members have an average GPA of 3.6, and 99 percent held leadership positions before joining the program. Thirty-five percent of the 2011 corps were people of color, and 31 percent were Pell Grant recipients. Today, nine thousand corps members are teaching in forty-three regions across the country. Teach For America places corps members in regions most profoundly affected by the gap in educational outcomes. More than 80 percent of the students reached qualify for free or reduced-price lunches, and the overwhelming majority of students (90 percent) are African American or Latino.

IMPACT

In 2011, more than six hundred thousand students are being taught by Teach For America corps members, and more than three million students have been impacted since the organization's inception. A growing body of independent studies, including 2011 analyses by the states of Louisiana and Tennessee, show that corps members have a positive impact on student achievement even when compared with veteran teachers in their schools. Furthermore, Teach For America alumni are exerting real leadership in communities across the country; two-thirds of twenty-four thousand alumni are working full-time in education, and half of those who have left the field have jobs that relate to schools or low-income communities. Alumni are winning the highest accolades teachers can win, and more than five hundred are running schools as principals; alumni are also assuming district leadership roles, including as superintendents in New Orleans, Newark, and Washington, D.C. Other alumni have launched pioneering education reform initiatives, such as KIPP and the New Teacher Project.

Organization

Teach For America is headquartered in New York City. Its organizational structure comprises forty-three regional offices, nine summer institutes, and national teams that support efforts across all its regions and teams. The regional offices focus on supporting the corps in the specific geographical areas in which it operates. National teams support the efforts of existing regions within key areas of focus and strategically manage the development of new regional sites. Teach For America has a thirty-six-member national board of directors and twenty-four regional board chairs. A ten-person leadership team includes Wendy Kopp, CEO and founder, and Matt Kramer, president.

Revenue/Expenses

Teach For America reported revenue of approximately $277 million in 2010. More than 80 percent of the organization's revenue comes from supporters in the forty-three regions where its corps members teach, and 70 percent of its funds come from private foundations, corporations, and individual donors. On a national level, Teach For America is supported by contributions from corporations, foundations, and individuals, as well as by public funds from the federal government. In 2010, Teach For America's estimated expenses totaled approximately $177 million. The majority of Teach For America's expenses (74 percent) can be attributed to the recruitment, selection, training, and professional development of corps members. Other significant costs include alumni programming, management, and fundraising.

HISTORY

Wendy Kopp proposed the creation of Teach For America in her Princeton University undergraduate thesis. She was convinced that many in her generation were searching for a way to assume a significant responsibility that would make a real difference in the world, and that top college students would choose teaching over more lucrative opportunities. As a twenty-one-year-old, Kopp raised $2.5 million of start-up funding, hired a skeleton staff, and launched a grassroots recruitment campaign. During Teach For America's first year in 1990, five hundred men and women began teaching in six low-income communities across the country. Since then, more than thirty thousand individuals have joined. In 2011, nearly forty-eight thousand individuals applied for five thousand teaching positions with the organization. In the past twenty years, Teach For America has been recognized for building a pipeline of leaders committed to educational equity and excellence.

YOUTHBUILD USA

YouthBuild USA (www.youthbuild.org)
58 Day Street
Somerville, MA 02144
Telephone: (617) 623-9900

PURPOSE

YouthBuild USA's mission is to unleash the positive energy of low-income young adults to rebuild their communities and their own lives, breaking the cycle of poverty with a commitment to work, education, responsibility, and family.

PROGRAM

In YouthBuild programs, low-income young people ages sixteen to twenty-four enroll full-time for six to twenty-four months, working toward their GEDs or high school diplomas while learning job skills by building affordable housing in their communities. YouthBuild places a strong emphasis on leadership development, community service, and the creation of a community of adults and youth committed to one another's success. Students may earn an AmeriCorps education award for their service building affordable housing. Follow-up support is provided to graduates to promote job and college placement and success.

PARTICIPANTS AND/OR RECIPIENTS

In 2010, 71 percent of YouthBuild students were men, and 29 percent were women; 31 percent were parents. They were 53 percent African American, 22 percent white, 20 percent Latino, 3 percent Native American, and 2 percent Asian American. All of the beneficiaries of the affordable housing were low-income individuals or families.

IMPACT

In the United States, since 1992 more than 110,000 YouthBuild students have produced over twenty-one thousand units of affordable, increasingly green housing. In 2010, there were 273 YouthBuild urban and rural programs engaging approximately ten thousand young adults.

Among participants, 94 percent entered the program without their GED or diploma, 32 percent were court-involved, and 45 percent received public assistance prior to joining YouthBuild. In spite of these overwhelming odds, 78 percent completed the program, and 60 percent went on to college or jobs averaging $9.20/hour. In seven pilot sites providing additional resources to build a bridge to postsecondary education, 43 percent went on to college, and 59 percent continued in college for a second year.

Since 2001, YouthBuild International has built partnerships in fourteen other countries that are now sponsoring fifty-six YouthBuild programs. In Mexico and South Africa, the governments have chosen to scale up YouthBuild.

ORGANIZATION

Local YouthBuild programs are small, supportive mini-communities operated by independent community-based and faith-based organizations; some are operated by local public agencies. More than ninety YouthBuild programs have become diploma-granting alternative schools.

YouthBuild USA is the nonprofit agency that serves as national intermediary and support center for YouthBuild programs nationwide. In this role, YouthBuild orchestrates advocacy for public funding, guidance and quality assurance in program implementation, leadership opportunities for youth and staff, research to understand best practices, and grants to YouthBuild affiliates. Through an open competitive process, YouthBuild USA was selected by the U.S. Department of Labor as its sole provider of training and technical assistance to its local YouthBuild grantees. YouthBuild USA also manages a voluntary national network of affiliates that is democratically managed through a process that provides equal participation to directors, students, and graduates in the development of policy governing the network.

The National YouthBuild Coalition, sponsored by YouthBuild USA, includes close to one thousand local and national organizations that advocate for federal funding for YouthBuild programs.

YouthBuild International is a division of YouthBuild USA that works through in-country partnerships to assist NGOs and governments to adapt the YouthBuild program to their realities.

REVENUE/EXPENSES

Each YouthBuild program secures its own funding, generally a mix of government (federal, state, and local) and private support. Federal support for YouthBuild in the United States was authorized under Subtitle D of Title IV of the Cranston-Gonzalez National Affordable Housing Act in 1992, thanks to bipartisan support in both houses of Congress. It was administered by the U.S. Department of Housing and Urban Development (HUD) until 2006, when it was transferred by Congress to the U.S. Department of Labor (DOL). DOL and HUD have awarded local YouthBuild grants totaling more than $1.0 billion since 1992.

YouthBuild USA has received major private support from multiple foundations. It has received major public grants and contracts from HUD, DOL, the U.S. Department of Health and Human Services, the U.S. Department of Justice, the U.S.

Department of Energy, the U.S. Department of Agriculture, USAID, and the Corporation for National and Community Service. In 2010, YouthBuild USA reported total revenues of approximately $26.5 million, of which approximately $11 million were regranted to local YouthBuild programs.

The average cost per student per year is about $22,000, including stipends for work performed. This is less than other full-time options for unemployed young adults, such as Job Corps, the military, prison, and many colleges.

HISTORY

In 1978, Dorothy Stoneman, CEO and founder of YouthBuild USA, asked neighborhood teens in East Harlem how they would improve their community if they had adults supporting them. The students answered, "We'd rebuild the houses. We'd take empty buildings back from drug dealers and eliminate crime." Together Stoneman and the teens formed the Youth Action Program and renovated the first YouthBuild building. They replicated the program in five locations in New York City during the 1980s. In 1990, YouthBuild USA was founded to orchestrate the national replication. By the early 1990s, the program had been replicated in eleven cities nationwide and had been authorized as a federal program administered by HUD; in 2006, it was moved to the DOL. In 2001, YouthBuild International was born when representatives of South Africa asked YouthBuild USA to assist in the development of YouthBuild programs in that country. Since its inception in 1978, tens of thousands of people have contributed to the YouthBuild movement, which has been called "a wellspring of human reclamation" by the *New York Times*.

APPENDIX F

RESEARCH METHODOLOGY AND SOURCES FOR NEW MATERIAL

INTERVIEW LIST OF LEADERS FROM THE TWELVE HIGH-IMPACT NONPROFITS FOR NEW MATERIAL

In 2011, we interviewed the following leaders from the twelve non-profits featured in the first edition of *Forces for Good* for the new content contained in Chapters Ten and Eleven.

Center for Budget and Policy Priorities
Robert Greenstein, founder and executive director, July 15, 2011
Susan Steinmetz, associate director, July 15, 2011

City Year
Michael Brown, cofounder and CEO, July 25, 2011

Environmental Defense Fund
Fred Krupp, president, July 27, 2011

Exploratorium
Dennis Bartels, executive director, Aug. 8, 2011
Robert Semper, director, July 28, 2011

Feeding America
Vicki Escarra, CEO, Nov. 29, 2011
Janet Gibbs, chief financial officer, Aug. 23, 2011

Habitat for Humanity International
Jonathan Reckford, CEO, July 8, 2011

The Heritage Foundation
Edwin Feulner, president, July 12, 2011
Phil Truluck, executive vice president, July 12, 2011

National Council of La Raza
Charles Kamasaki, senior vice president, July 18, 2011
Janet Murguía, president and CEO, July 18, 2011

Self-Help
Randy Chambers, president, Self-Help Credit Union, July 14, 2011

Share Our Strength
Bill Shore, founder and executive director, Aug. 10, 2011

Teach For America
Wendy Kopp, founder and CEO, July 15, 2011

YouthBuild USA
Tim Cross, president of YouthBuild International, July 17, 2011
Dorothy Stoneman, founder and president, July 26, 2011

CHAPTER TWELVE RESEARCH PROCESS

In writing this chapter on local and smaller nonprofits for the updated edition of *Forces for Good,* we set out to answer the following questions:

Can the six practices be executed by local and regional groups with smaller budgets—or are they only applicable to large organizations operating at national or global scale? And if so, What's different about the way the six practices are applied by local and smaller organizations?

For us to answer these questions, our first task was to identify a set of local and smaller nonprofits for further study; to do so, we followed this process:

- We asked national thought-leaders and local field experts from across the United States and Canada to nominate local and smaller organizations operating on budgets of $5 million or less that they perceived to be high impact and had observed using some or all of the six practices. We also looked through our notes from the various workshops, lectures, trainings, and consulting engagements we had led over the past five years for examples of local nonprofits using the six practices. These efforts surfaced several dozen nominees that appeared to us to have potential for further study.

- We segmented this list of nominated groups based on demonstrated impact, as illustrated either on the nomination form or on their Web sites, as well as by other factors, such as issue or cause and geographical location. We then culled that list down to a group of thirteen organizations that were diverse and representative of various locales in the United States and Canada and were working across different issue areas (such as antipoverty, affordable housing, environment, and the arts).
- As we segmented the list and narrowed it down to thirteen organizations for further study, we also sharpened our definition of "local and small" to encompass three types of nonprofits:
    1. Independent (single-site) local nonprofits focused on serving one particular geographical area
    2. Local affiliates of national networks focused on one specific community or region (despite belonging to a national umbrella group)
    3. Smaller organizations that have expanded nationally, but operate on budgets of $5 million or less (whether they are in an earlier stage of scaling up or have reached full scale and operate on less)

In the next phase of our research, we contacted the leaders of each of the thirteen nonprofits that we had selected for further study, conducted telephone interviews with them, and gathered additional background data on how they were applying some or all of the six practices. These telephone interviews were guided by us and conducted by our research associate, Scott Brown.

Once we had spoken with leaders from the thirteen organizations, we worked in collaboration with Scott to cull through the interview notes, analyze the collected data, synthesize our findings, and write them up. Although not all of the organizations that we interviewed are profiled in the narrative of Chapter Twelve, we include in the next section the complete list of organizations we studied, because the interviews helped inform our thinking and advance our understanding of how local nonprofits apply the concepts in *Forces for Good*. There just wasn't enough space to include all of their stories in this edition.

INTERVIEWEES AND LEADERS CONTACTED FROM LOCAL AND SMALLER NONPROFIT ORGANIZATIONS

A Home Within

Anne Marie Burgoyne, portfolio director, Draper Richards Foundation, May 20, 2011

Toni Heineman, executive director, June 14 and July 22, 2011

Avenida Guadalupe

Oscar Ramirez, president and CEO, June 22 and June 24, 2011

Jose Velasquez, vice president, affiliate member services, May 20, 2011

Federation of Appalachian Housing Enterprises

Jim King, president and CEO, June 20 and Sept. 16, 2011

Linda Skelton, communications and public affairs consultant, NeighborWorks America, May 20, 2011

Georgia Justice Project

Doug Ammar, executive director, June 5, Sept. 1, and Sept. 16, 2011

Joseph Iarocci, president, Mission-Driven Partners, May 31, 2011

Little Theatre on the Square

Annie Hernandez, program officer, Lumpkin Family Foundation, May 23, 2011

John Stephens, executive director, June 30 and Sept. 16, 2011

Live Local Alberta

Jessie Radies, founder and CEO, July 2 and Aug. 17, 2011

Meet Each Need with Dignity

Marianne Haver Hill, president and CEO, June 16, Aug. 15, and Aug. 30, 2011

The Mission Continues

Anne Marie Burgoyne, portfolio director, Draper Richards Foundation, May 20, 2011

Eric Greitens, CEO, June 23 and Aug. 5, 2011

NeighborWorks Montana

Sheila Rice, executive director, June 13, June 17, and June 20, 2011

Linda Skelton, communications and public affairs consultant, NeighborWorks America, May 22, 2011

Nonprofit Energy Alliance

Chuck Bean, executive director, Nonprofit Roundtable of Greater Washington, June 5, 2011

Hope Gleicher, director, Nonprofit Montgomery, May 20, 2011

Suzan Jenkins, CEO, Arts and Humanities Council of Montgomery County, June 17, 2011

Partnership to End Poverty

Scott Cooper, executive director, June 15, June 20, and Sept. 15, 2011

Jim Schell, executive director, Central Oregon Partnership, May 17, 2011

RYASAP

Bob Francis, executive director, July 28 and Aug. 1, 2011

Emily Tow Jackson, executive director, The Tow Foundation, May 18, 2011

SafeKids Canada

Pamela Fuselli, executive director, May 12, June 14, and June 15, 2011

PREFACE TO THE FIRST EDITION

It was a chilly spring day in 2003 when Leslie Crutchfield was preparing to welcome a new cohort of social entrepreneurs to the Arlington, Virginia, offices of the global nonprofit Ashoka. For two years, Leslie had led the North America division of this global fellowship, which provides intensive support to public innovators from around the world. She knew that the group was hungry for advice on how to create large-scale social change—but she also knew that she didn't have all the answers.

When she had searched for information to give the social entrepreneurs, she couldn't find many materials that were specific to the unique challenges they faced. Sure, there were plenty of how-to publications about nonprofit management, fundraising, and board development. And she had shelves full of books written about for-profit companies and what makes great businesses great. But there were few rigorous studies of extraordinary nonprofits or of how the best groups achieve real results. So Leslie found herself cobbling together a hodgepodge of how-to manuals, case studies, and copies of renowned business management books. *We need to do better than this*, she thought.

At that moment, the idea for this book was born.

Leslie called up her longtime mentor Greg Dees, an expert in the field and founder of the Center for the Advancement of Social Entrepreneurship (CASE) at Duke University's Fuqua School of Business. He recognized the need for a book like this and offered to have CASE sponsor the research.

Around the same time, Heather McLeod Grant was consulting with philanthropists and nonprofits in the San Francisco Bay

Area, including the Stanford Center for Social Innovation and the Omidyar Network. She experienced firsthand the huge knowledge gap in the sector—particularly with respect to creating social impact—and she shared Leslie's frustration with how little empirical research existed. Management books just didn't go far enough. Countless entrepreneurs were reinventing the wheel, starting new nonprofits without understanding what had been tried before or what really works.

So when Leslie approached her with the idea for this project, Heather jumped at the opportunity. As friends and former colleagues who had cofounded a magazine for social entrepreneurs in the mid-1990s, *Who Cares: The Tool Kit for Social Change,* the two of us decided to lock arms once again to tackle this ambitious project.

What we discovered in the process of researching and writing *Forces for Good* has both surprised and inspired us. The twelve organizations we've studied over the past few years are truly extraordinary, and we feel privileged to have learned from them. We're delighted to share their secrets to success with you and hope you will be as inspired as we were.

ENDNOTES

Note: In researching each of the organizations featured in this book, we conducted numerous interviews and analyzed data from both internal and publicly available sources. (See Appendix D, "Key Stakeholders Interview List," for names of interviewees.) Unless otherwise noted, all quotes come from original research.

FOREWORD TO THE REVISED AND UPDATED EDITION

1. "Oops. Who's Excellent Now?" *Business Week,* Nov. 5, 1984, pp. 76–88.
2. In 2010, CASE published a more academic collection of papers on scaling social impact, and my colleague Paul Bloom has a book for practitioners in the works that presents a new framework for scaling impact that is complementary to the six practices.

INTRODUCTION TO THE REVISED AND UPDATED EDITION

1. Matthew Bishop coined the term "philanthrocapitalism" and writes about these new funders in his book with Michael Green, *Philanthrocapitalism: How Giving Can Save the World.* New York: Bloomsbury Press, 2009.
2. Nonprofit Research Collaborative. "Late Fall 2011 Nonprofit Fundraising Survey." Available on the GuideStar official Web site, Dec. 16, 2011, www2.guidestar.org/rxg/news/publications/nonprofits-and-economy-late-fall-2011.aspx.
3. Crutchfield, L. R., Kania, J. V., and Kramer, M. R. *Do More Than Give: The Six Practices of Donors Who Change the World.* San Francisco: Jossey-Bass, 2010.

Kania, J., and Kramer, M. "Collective Impact: Large-Scale Change Requires Cross-Sector Coordination." *Stanford Social Innovation Review,* Winter 2011, pp. 36–41.

4. According to the National Center for Charitable Statistics in the Urban Institute's publication Wing, K. T., Roeger, K. L., and Pollak, T. H., *The Nonprofit Sector in Brief: Public Charities, Giving, and Volunteering 2010.* Washington, D.C.: Urban Institute, 2010, pp. 2–3. Available at http://www.urban.org/uploadedpdf/412209-nonprof-public-charities.pdf.

5. Kania and Kramer, 2011, p. 38.

INTRODUCTION TO THE FIRST EDITION

1. According to the National Center for Charitable Statistics at the Urban Institute, total expenditures for all reporting 501(c)(3) public charities in 2004 were more than $1 trillion. Reporting organizations accounted for approximately $1.4 trillion in revenue and $3 trillion in assets in 2004. These amounts do not include spending either by "non-reporting" public charities (such as very small nonprofits and many religious congregations, which are not required by law to file annual 990 tax returns with the IRS) or by private foundations. It also does not reflect the value of volunteer time. *Source:* National Center for Charitable Statistics, The Urban Institute. "The Nonprofit Sector in Brief: Facts and Figures from the Nonprofit Almanac 2007." Available at: www.urban.org/UploadedPDF/311373_nonprofit_sector.pdf.

2. Silverman, L., Lowell, S., and Taliento, L. "Nonprofit Management: The Gift That Keeps on Giving." *McKinsey Quarterly,* 2001, no. 1, p. 147.

3. Salamon, L., Helmut, K., Anheier, R., List, S., Toepler, S., Wojciech, S., and Associates. *Global Civil Society: Dimensions of the Nonprofit Sector.* Baltimore, Md.: Johns Hopkins University Center for Civil Society Studies, 1999, p. 4.

4. Salamon and others, 1999.

5. "The State of Foundation Giving, 2006." Excerpted from the 2006 edition of *Foundation Yearbook.* Available on the Foundation Center Web site, www.foundationcenter.org.

6. Havens, J. J., and Schervish, P. *Millionaires and the Millennium: New Estimates of the Forthcoming Wealth Transfer and the Prospects for a Golden Age of Philanthropy.* Boston: Social Welfare Research Institute, Boston College, 1999.

7. A select group of social entrepreneurs participates in World Economic Forum gatherings at the invitation of Klaus Schwab. Schwab is the president and founder of the World Economic Forum in Geneva, Switzerland; he and his wife, Hilde, established the Schwab Foundation for Social Entrepreneurship in 1998.
8. Letts, C. W., Grossman, A., and Ryan, W. P. *High Performance Nonprofit Organizations.* Hoboken, N.J.: Wiley, 1999.
9. Letts, Grossman, and Ryan, 1999.

CHAPTER ONE

1. All facts and quotations presented in this case were taken from interviews with Teach For America staff or from internal or publicly available organizational information.
2. Sellers, P. "Schooling Corporate Giants on Recruiting." *Fortune,* Nov. 27, 2006, p. 87; 2010 statistics provided by Wendy Kopp, CEO of Teach For America, in a telephone interview with the authors, July 15, 2011.
3. All facts and quotations presented in this case were taken from interviews with Habitat for Humanity staff or from internal or publicly available organizational information. Citation refers to the *Chronicle of Philanthropy* list from 2004.
4. All facts and quotations presented in this case were taken from interviews with Environmental Defense Fund staff or from internal or publicly available organizational information.
5. Drayton, W. "What Is a Social Entrepreneur?" 2007. Available on the Ashoka Web site, www.ashoka.org.
6. Dees, J. G. "The Meaning of 'Social Entrepreneurship.'" White paper. Center for Advancement of Social Entrepreneurship, Duke University Fuqua School of Business, May 30, 2001. Available on the Fuqua School of Business Web site: www.fuqua.duke.edu/centers/case/documents/dees_sedef.pdf.
7. Collins, J. *Good to Great and the Social Sectors.* New York: HarperCollins, 2004. Collins writes about the confusion between inputs and outputs in the social sector, because in business, "money is both an input (a resource for achieving greatness) *and* an output (a measure of greatness). In the social sectors, money is *only* an input, and not a measure of greatness" (p. 5).
8. Collins, J. C., and Porras, J. I. *Built to Last: Successful Habits of Visionary Companies.* New York: HarperBusiness, 1997.

CHAPTER TWO

1. All facts and quotations presented in this case were taken from interviews with Self-Help staff or from internal or publicly available organizational information.
2. Smucker, B. *The Nonprofit Lobbying Guide.* Washington, D.C.: INDEPENDENT SECTOR, 1999.
3. All facts and quotations presented in this case were taken from interviews with National Council of La Raza staff or from internal or publicly available organizational information.
4. Letts, C. W., Grossman, A., and Ryan, W. P. *High Performance Nonprofit Organizations.* Hoboken, N.J.: Wiley, 1999, p. 77.
5. All facts and quotations presented in this case were taken from interviews with Feeding America staff or from internal or publicly available organizational information.
6. All facts and quotations presented in this case were taken from interviews with Environmental Defense Fund staff or from internal or publicly available organizational information.
7. Interview with Bob Greenstein, Center on Budget and Policy Priorities.
8. Brown, M. "National Service or Bust: Action Tanking, the Social Entrepreneur's Trap, and a Promising Pathway to a New Progressive Era." Paper presented at the New Profit Inc. Gathering of Leaders, New Paltz, N.Y., Feb. 2006.
9. These observations align closely with the findings of the Aspen Institute study "Effective Nonprofit Advocacy," conducted by independent researcher Susan Rees. The 1997 working paper detailed the key success factors of nonprofit advocacy organizations that members of Congress and executive branch officials ranked as the most influential. Available on the Aspen Institute Nonprofit Sector Research Fund Web site, www.nonprofitresearch.org/usr_doc/15896.pdf.
10. Gantz McKay, E. *The National Council of La Raza: The First Twenty-Five Years.* Washington, D.C.: National Council of La Raza, 1993.

CHAPTER THREE

1. All facts and quotations presented in this case were taken from interviews with Environmental Defense staff or from internal or publicly available organizational information. In addition to case studies cited in other notes for this chapter, we drew on the following as background: Plambeck, E., and Hoyt, D. "FedEx and Environmental

Defense: Building a Hybrid Delivery Fleet," Stanford GSB Case SI-82, Jan. 2006.

2. Krupp, F. "New Environmentalism Factors in Economic Needs." *Wall Street Journal*, Nov. 20, 1986, p. 34.

3. Sale, K. "The Forest for the Trees: Can Today's Environmentalists Tell the Difference?" *Mother Jones*, 1986, *11*(8), 25–33.

4. Reinhardt, F. "Environmental Defense." Harvard Business School Case 9-703-029. Boston: Harvard Business School Publishing, 2003; citing the "Final Report" of the McDonald's Corporation and Environmental Defense Fund Waste Reduction Task Force, Apr. 1991. These data were verified in other internal documents from the Environmental Defense Fund.

5. "A Cleaner Road Ahead." *Solutions* [Environmental Defense Fund newsletter], July-Aug. 2003, *34*(4), 1–2.

6. Vascellaro, J. "Green Groups See Potent Tool in Economics." *Wall Street Journal*, Aug. 23, 2005, published on Web site.

7. Dees, J. G. "Enterprising Nonprofits." In *Harvard Business Review on Nonprofits*. Boston: Harvard Business School Press, 1999, p. 139.

8. Sagawa, S., and Segal, E. *Common Interest, Common Good: Creating Value Through Business and Social Sector Partnerships*. Boston: Harvard Business School Press, 2000, p. 3.

9. All facts and quotations presented in this case were taken from interviews with Self-Help staff or from internal or publicly available organizational information.

10. Sagawa and Segal, 2000.

11. Sagawa and Segal, 2000.
Austin, J. *The Collaboration Challenge: How Nonprofits and Businesses Succeed Through Strategic Alliances*. San Francisco: Jossey-Bass, 2000.

12. Austin, 2000.

13. Sagawa and Segal, 2000, pp. 20–21.

14. Sagawa and Segal, 2000, p. 19.

15. All facts and quotations presented in this case were taken from interviews with Feeding America staff or from internal or publicly available organizational information.

16. All facts and quotations presented in this case were taken from interviews with City Year staff or from internal or publicly available organizational information. In addition to case studies cited in other notes for this chapter, we drew on "City Year: Timberland and Community Involvement," Harvard Business School Case 9-396-196. Boston: Harvard Business School Publishing, 1996; and Dees, J. G., and Jaan, E., "City Year Enterprise," Harvard

Business School Case 9-396-196. Boston: Harvard Business School Publishing, 1996.

17. Reported in the case study "City Year: National Expansion Strategy (A)." Harvard Business School Case 0-496-001. Boston: Harvard Business School Publishing, 1995.

18. All facts and quotations presented in this case were taken from interviews with Share Our Strength staff or from internal or publicly available organizational information. Also used as case study background: Grier, S., Culp, C. D., and Stivers, M. "Share Our Strength and American Express: Development Marketing Alliances," (A) "Taste of the Nation Sponsorship," M-289A, and (B) "Charge Against Hunger and Dine Across America," M-289A, Stanford University Graduate School of Business, Oct. 1997.

19. Austin, J., and Pearson, M. "Community Wealth Ventures, Inc." Harvard Business School Case 399-023. Boston: Harvard Business School Publishing, 1998.

20. Quoted in *Columbus Dispatch*, Sept. 12, 1996.

21. Quoted in Austin and Pearson, 1998, p. 3.

22. Shore, W. *The Cathedral Within: Transforming Your Life by Giving Something Back.* New York: Random House, 1999. Excerpt quoted in "Creating Community Wealth" brochure from organization, p. 1.

23. Quoted in Austin and Pearson, 1998. Quotation taken from executive summary of a symposium sponsored by Share Our Strength and Pfizer, Inc., Feb. 25, 1997.

24. Community Wealth Ventures. *Powering Social Change: Lessons on Community Wealth Generation for Nonprofit Sustainability.* Washington, D.C.: Community Wealth Ventures, 2003. Available at: www .communitywealth.com/pdf-doc/Powering%20Social%20Change.pdf.

25. Quoted in Flint, J., "Strange Bed Partners," *Forbes.com*, Nov. 24, 2003.

CHAPTER FOUR

1. All facts and quotations presented in this case were taken from interviews with Habitat for Humanity International staff or from internal or publicly available organizational information.

2. In 2002, Habitat retained Interbrand to assess the value of its brand. The company determined that Habitat's brand was worth $3.1 billion, in the same league as Starbucks.

3. This figure is based on our analysis of the compound annual growth rate of revenue over twenty years.

4. Hanlon, P. *Primal Branding: Create Zealots for Your Brand, Your Company, and Your Future.* New York. Simon & Schuster, 2006.

5. Podolny, J. "Social Networks as Ends Rather Than Means." Paper presented at the Skoll World Forum, Said Business School, Oxford, Mar. 2005. Later published in *Stanford Social Innovation Review* as "Networks for Good Works," Winter 2007.

6. All facts and quotations presented in this case were taken from interviews with City Year staff or from internal or publicly available organizational information.

7. All facts and quotations presented in this case were taken from interviews with Teach For America staff or from internal or publicly available organizational information.

8. Khazei, A. [CEO, City Year]. "Nineteen Tips for Being a Social Entrepreneur." Internal document.

9. Written responses to fact-checking questions via e-mail from David Yarnold, executive vice president of Environmental Defense Fund.

10. "Building Sustainable Networks." Internal working paper for Building Sustainable Networks group hosted by the Leadership Learning Community: www.leadershiplearning.org. More information available at the wiki: http://sunset.pbwiki.com/.

11. "Effective Alumni Engagement: Key Themes and Promising Practices." Internal study published by Omidyar Network; analysis by McKinsey & Company, 2003.

12. Podolny, 2005.

13. Quoted in "Habitat for Humanity International." Harvard Business School Case 9-694-038. Boston: Harvard Business School Publishing, 1994, p. 7.

14. Quoted in "Ripples." In *Founding Stories*, available at: www.cityyear .org/about/who/foundingstories.cfm.

CHAPTER FIVE

1. All facts and quotations presented in this case were taken from interviews with Exploratorium staff or from internal or publicly available organizational information. Allen, S. *Finding Significance.* San Francisco: Exploratorium, 2004.

2. Semper, R. "Fanning the Flames: The Exploratorium at the Birth of a Science Center Movement." In C. C. Yao (ed.), *Handbook for Small Science Centers.* Lanham, Md.: AltaMira Press, 2006.

3. Semper, 2006.

4. "YouthBuild USA Case Study." Center for the Advancement of Social Entrepreneurship, Fuqua School of Business, Duke University, Dec. 2003. Other facts and quotations presented in this case were

taken from interviews with YouthBuild USA staff or from internal or publicly available organizational information.

5. "YouthBuild USA Case Study," 2003.

6. All facts and quotations presented in this case were taken from interviews with the Center on Budget and Policy Priorities staff or from internal or publicly available organizational information.

7. McWilliams, R. "The Best and the Worst of Public Interest Groups." *Washington Monthly,* 1988, *20*(2), 19–27.

8. All facts and quotations presented in this case were taken from interviews with Teach For America staff or from internal or publicly available organizational information.

9. Teach For America proposal to the Amazon.com Competition, Apr. 2005.

10. Study evaluating City Year alumni engagement conducted by Policy Studies Associates for City Year.

11. Husock, H., written for Moore, M. "The AmeriCorps Budget Crisis of 2003 (Sequel): Why the National Service Movement Faced Cutbacks and How It Responded," HKS Case 1740.1. Kennedy School of Government Case Program, Harvard University, 2004.

12. Waldman, S. *The Bill: How the Adventures of Clinton's National Service Bill Reveal What Is Corrupt, Comic, Cynical—and Noble—About Washington.* New York: Viking, 1995.

13. Interview with Shirley Sawaga, March 17, 2006.

14. Husock, 2004.

15. All facts and quotations presented in this case were taken from interviews with Heritage Foundation staff or from internal or publicly available organizational information.

16. Edwards, L. *The Power of Ideas.* Ottawa, Ill.: Jameson Books, 1997.

17. Brafman, O., and Beckstrom, R. *The Starfish and the Spider: The Unstoppable Power of Leaderless Organizations.* New York: Portfolio, 2006.

CHAPTER SIX

1. All facts and quotations presented in this case were taken from interviews with Share Our Strength staff or from internal or publicly available organizational information.

2. Letts, C. W., Grossman, A., and Ryan, W. P. *High Performance Nonprofit Organizations.* Hoboken, N.J.: Wiley, 1999. The authors cite Ronald A. Heifetz, *Leadership Without Easy Answers* (Cambridge, Mass.: Belknap Press of Harvard University, 1994) in their discussion of adaptive capacity in the context of leadership.

3. Govindarajan, V., and Trimble, C. *Ten Rules for Strategic Innovators: From Idea to Execution.* Boston: Harvard Business School Press, 2005.
4. Our thinking in developing the "cycle of adaptation" described in this chapter was informed partly by the Plan-Do-Check-Act (PDCA) Cycle, also known as the Deming Cycle, which is an iterative four-step quality control process. PDCA was made popular by Dr. W. Edwards Deming, the father of modern quality control. Kolb's Learning Cycle is a similar model developed by Dr. David Kolb to explain the four stages of experiential adult learning: Experience, Observe and Reflect, Form Concept, and Test in New Situations. The model originated from research on individuals, but has applications for organizations as well.
5. All facts and quotations presented in this case were taken from interviews with Feeding America staff or from internal or publicly available organizational information.
6. All facts and quotations presented in this case were taken from interviews with Self-Help staff or from internal or publicly available organizational information.
7. All facts and quotations presented in this case were taken from interviews with Exploratorium staff or from internal or publicly available organizational information.
8. All facts and quotations presented in this case were taken from interviews with Teach For America staff or from internal or publicly available organizational information.
9. Teach For America proposal to the Amazon.com Competition, Apr. 2005.
10. All facts and quotations presented in this case were taken from interviews with Heritage Foundation staff or from internal or publicly available organizational information.
11. Sellers, P. "Schooling Corporate Giants on Recruiting." *Fortune*, Nov. 27, 2006, p. 87.
12. Kopp, W. *One Day, All Children . . . : The Unlikely Triumph of Teach For America, and What I Learned Along the Way.* New York: Perseus Books, 2001.

Chapter Seven

1. All facts and quotations presented in this case were taken from interviews with Heritage Foundation staff or from internal or publicly available organizational information.
2. Edwards, L. *The Power of Ideas.* Ottawa, Ill.: Jameson Books, 1997, p. 90.
3. Light, P. C. "Reshaping Social Entrepreneurship." *Stanford Social Innovation Review*, 2006, 4(3), 46–51.

4. Heifetz, R. A., Kania, J. V., and Kramer, M. R. "Leading Boldly." *Stanford Social Innovation Review,* Winter 2004, pp. 21–31. In the first edition of *Forces for Good,* we referenced a report by Betsy Hubbard on the field of nonprofit leadership development, in which she wrote, "A more collective orientation to leadership is often considered especially appropriate for complex, messy situations that lack clear answers or even clearly defined problems. In such situations, a top-down model of leadership—a traditional approach in which a single leader operates primarily from his or her own perspective, experience, and judgment—is unlikely to prove successful." Hubbard, B. *Investing in Leadership: Vol. 1. A Grantmaker's Framework for Understanding Nonprofit Leadership Development.* Washington, D.C.: Grantmakers for Effective Organizations, 2005, p. 11.
5. Markus, G. *Building Leadership: Findings from a Longitudinal Evaluation of the Kellogg National Fellowship Program.* Battle Creek, Mich.: W. K. Kellogg Foundation, 2001. Cited in Hubbard, 2005, p. 11.
6. Collins, J. *Good to Great: Why Some Companies Make the Leap . . . and Others Don't.* New York: HarperBusiness, 2001, p. 21.
7. Collins, 2001, p. 27.
8. Kopp, W. *One Day, All Children . . . : The Unlikely Triumph of Teach For America, and What I Learned Along the Way.* New York: Perseus Books, 2001.
9. Bennis, W., and Nanus, B. *Leaders: Strategies for Taking Charge.* New York: HarperBusiness, 1997.
10. All facts and quotations presented in this case were taken from interviews with National Council of La Raza staff or from internal or publicly available organizational information.
11. NCLR tenure data were taken from interviews and original research in 2005.
12. All facts and quotations presented in this case were taken from interviews with Exploratorium staff or from internal or publicly available organizational information.
13. Bell, J., Moyers, R., and Wolfred, T. *Daring to Lead 2006: A National Study of Nonprofit Executive Leadership.* (A joint project of CompassPoint Nonprofit Services and the Meyer Foundation.) San Francisco: CompassPoint, 2006, pp. 3, 6.
14. Bell, Moyers, and Wolfred, 2006, p. 17.
15. Interviews with Millard Fuller and other Habitat staff.
16. Collins, 2001.
17. Bell, Moyers, and Wolfred, 2006, p. 9.
18. Tierney, T. J. *The Nonprofit Sector's Leadership Deficit.* San Francisco: Bridgespan Group, Feb. 2006, p. 17.

19. Van Velsor, E., and McCauley, C. "Our View of Leadership Development." In *The Center for Creative Leadership Handbook of Leadership Development.* (2nd ed.). San Francisco: Jossey-Bass, 2004. Cited in Hubbard, 2005, p. 11.

Chapter Eight

1. This story and most narrative background were taken from Kopp, W., *One Day, All Children . . . : The Unlikely Triumph of Teach For America, and What I Learned Along the Way.* New York: Perseus Books, 2001.
2. Foster, W. "How Nonprofits Get Really Big." *Stanford Social Innovation Review,* 2007, *5*(2), 46–55. (*Note:* This exact quotation was taken from an earlier internal draft of the paper and does not appear in the published version.)
3. See "Capital Markets" in the Chapter Three section of the Additional Resources, including Emerson, Miller, Foster, and others.
4. Letts, C. W., Ryan, W. P., and Grossman, A. "Virtuous Capital: What Foundations Can Learn from Venture Capitalists." In *Harvard Business Review on Nonprofits.* Boston: Harvard Business School Press, 1999, p. 91.
5. Collins, J. *Good to Great: Why Some Companies Make the Leap . . . and Others Don't.* New York: HarperBusiness, 2001.
6. Bell, J., Moyers, R., and Wolfred, T. *Daring to Lead 2006: A National Study of Nonprofit Executive Leadership.* (A joint project of CompassPoint Nonprofit Services and the Meyer Foundation.) San Francisco: CompassPoint, 2006.
7. Based on our analysis of organizations' current sources of revenue. The idea of looking at the concentration of funding in one source came from William Foster's paper, cited in note 2.
8. *The City Year Challenge: Strengthening Our Capacities to Serve.* Internal document.
9. GuideStar ratings were taken from GuideStar reports on the organizations in our sample. Stars are assigned on the basis of organizational "efficiency," with 4 being the highest rating and 0 the lowest, determined by such measures as the ratio of spending on administration to spending on programs. For more details, see www.guidestar.org. Charity Navigator uses a similar rating system. Nonprofit data analyzed by these sites are taken from IRS form 990s, which nonprofits are required to file for tax purposes.
10. Lowell, S., Trelstad, B., and Meehan, B. "The Ratings Game." *Stanford Social Innovation Review,* 2005, *3*(2), 39–45.

CHAPTER NINE

1. All facts and quotations presented in this case were taken from interviews with Self-Help staff or from internal or publicly available organizational information.
2. Drayton, W. "What Is a Social Entrepreneur?" 2007. Available on the Ashoka Web site, www.ashoka.org.

CHAPTER TEN

1. "Oops. Who's Excellent Now?" *Business Week,* Nov. 5, 1984, pp. 76–88.
2. In a telephone interview with us on July 8, 2011, Jonathan Reckford, CEO of Habitat for Humanity International, conveyed that Habitat had grown globally to $2 billion; we were unable to obtain a current annual report to be able to give specific figures for the global affiliate network at the time of this writing.

CHAPTER TWELVE

1. Portions of Will's story are excerpted from the Georgia Justice Project's official Web site, www.gjp.org/http%3A/%252Fwww.gjp .org/client; other details about GJP were provided in interviews and e-mail exchanges with CEO Doug Ammar.
2. Crutchfield, L. R., Kania, J. V., and Kramer, M. R. *Do More Than Give: The Six Practices of Donors Who Change the World.* San Francisco: Jossey-Bass, 2010.
3. From Taproot Foundation internal document archives.

APPENDIX A

1. Eisenhardt, K. "Building Theories from Case Study Research." *Academy of Management Review,* 1989, *14*(4), 532.
2. Lowell, S., Trelstad, B., and Meehan, B. "The Ratings Game." *Stanford Social Innovation Review,* 2005, *3*(2), 39–45.
3. Collins, J., and Porras, J. I. *Built to Last: Successful Habits of Visionary Companies.* New York: HarperBusiness, 1997.
   Collins, J. *Good to Great: Why Some Companies Make the Leap . . . and Others Don't.* New York: HarperBusiness, 2001.
4. Using as our population the 53,583 nonprofit 501(c)(3) organizations listed in the GuideStar database with total incomes above $1 million, and assuming a confidence level of 95 percent and a

confidence interval of ± 5 percent, we needed 383 responses to have a statistically significant response. From Salant, P., and Dillman, D. A. *How to Conduct Your Own Survey.* Hoboken, N.J.: Wiley, 1994.

5. For more information on the Delphi methodology, see www.iit .edu/~delphi.html.
6. Collins and Porras, 1997; Collins, 2001.
7. Collins and Porras, 1997, p. 5.
8. See the Acknowledgments for a listing of all team member names.

ADDITIONAL RESOURCES

INTRODUCTION

Austin, J. E., and Backman, E. V. "Overview of the Nonprofit Sector." Harvard Business School Teaching Note 399-027. Boston: Harvard Business School Publishing, Aug. 13, 1998.

The Bridgespan Group. "Knowledge Sharing in the Social Sector." Available at www.bridgespan.org. Feb. 2003.

Drayton, W. "The Citizen Sector: Becoming as Entrepreneurial and Competitive as Business." *California Management Review*, 2002, *44*(3), 120–132.

Fulton, K., and Blau, A. "Trends in Twenty-First Century Philanthropy." Working paper. Global Business Network, June 2003. Available at: www.gbn.org.

Salamon, L. "The Rise of the Nonprofit Sector." *Foreign Affairs*, July–Aug. 1994, *73*(4), 109–122.

Wolpert, J. *Patterns of Generosity in America: Who's Holding the Safety Net?* New York: Twentieth Century Fund, 1993.

CHAPTER ONE

Social Entrepreneurship and Social Enterprise

Alvord, S. H., Brown, L. D., and Letts, C. W. "Social Entrepreneurship and Societal Transformation." *Journal of Applied Behavioral Science*, 2004, *40*(3), 260–282.

Bornstein, D. *How to Change the World: Social Entrepreneurs and the Power of New Ideas.* London: Penguin Books, 2005. (Originally published by Oxford University Press, 2004.)

The Bridgespan Group. "Growth of Youth-Serving Organizations." White paper commissioned by the Edna McConnell Clark Foundation, Mar. 2005. Available at: www.bridgespan.org.

Community Wealth Ventures. *Venture Philanthropy 2000: Landscape and Expectations.* Washington, D.C.: Venture Philanthropy Partners, 2000.

Community Wealth Ventures. *High Engagement Philanthropy: A Bridge to a More Effective Social Sector.* Washington, D.C.: Venture Philanthropy Partners, 2004.

Dees, J. G. "Note on Starting a Nonprofit Venture." Harvard Business School Case 9-391-096. Boston: Harvard Business School Press, 1992.

Drayton, B. "Social Entrepreneurs: Creating a Competitive and Entrepreneurial Citizen Sector." Available on the Ashoka Changemakers Library Web site, www.changemakers.net.

Emerson, J., and Twersky, F. (eds.). *New Social Entrepreneurs: The Success, Challenge, and Lessons of Non-Profit Enterprise Creation: A Progress Report on the Planning and Start-up of Non-Profit Businesses.* San Francisco: Roberts Foundation Homeless Economic Development Fund, 1996.

Grossman, A., and Rangan, K. V. Social Enterprise Series No. 8: "Managing Multi-Site Nonprofits." Harvard Business School Working Paper Series, No. 99-095. Boston: Harvard Business School Press, 1999.

Kanter, R. M. "Even Bigger Change: A Framework for Getting Started at Changing the World." Harvard Business School Teaching Note 9-305-099. Boston: Harvard Business School Publishing, Mar. 29, 2005.

Moy, K. S., and Ratliff, G. "New Pathways to Scale for Community Development Finance." *Profitwise,* Dec. 2004, pp. 2–23.

Skloot, E. *The Nonprofit Entrepreneur: Creating Ventures to Earn Income.* New York: Foundation Center, 1988.

Scale

Bradach, J. "Going to Scale." *Stanford Social Innovation Review,* 2003, *1*(1), 19–25.

Dees, G. J., Emerson, J., and Economy, P. *Enterprising Nonprofits: A Toolkit for Social Entrepreneurs.* Hoboken, N.J.: Wiley, 2001.

Taylor, M. A., Dees, G. J., and Emerson, J. "The Question of Scale: Finding an Appropriate Strategy for Building on Your Success." In G. J. Dees, J. Emerson, and P. Economy (eds.), *Strategic Tools for Social Entrepreneurs: Enhancing the Performance of Your Enterprising Nonprofit.* Hoboken, N.J.: Wiley, 2002.

Wei-Skillern, J., and Anderson, B. B. Social Enterprise Series No. 27: "Nonprofit Geographic Expansion: Branches, Affiliates, or Both?" Working Paper No. 04-011. Boston: Harvard Business School Press, 2003.

Measuring Impact

Colby, S., Stone, N., and Carttar, P. "Zeroing in on Impact." *Stanford Social Innovation Review,* 2004, *2*(3), 24–33.

Kanter, R., and Summers, D. "Doing Well While Doing Good: Dilemmas of Performance Measurement in Nonprofit Organizations and the Need for a Multiple-Constituency Approach." In W. Powell and R. Steinberg (eds.), *The Nonprofit Sector: A Research Handbook.* (2nd ed.) New Haven, Conn.: Yale University Press, 2006.

Kaplan, E. "Strategic Performance Measurement and Management in Nonprofit Organizations." *Nonprofit Management and Leadership,* 2001, *11*(3), 353–370.

Lowell, S., Trelstad, B., and Meehan, B. "The Ratings Game." *Stanford Social Innovation Review,* 2005, *3*(2), 39–45.

Sawhill, J. C., and Williamson, D. "Mission Impossible? Measuring Success in Nonprofit Organizations." *Nonprofit Management and Leadership,* 1999, *11*(3), 371–386.

General Sources

Osborne, D., and Gaebler, T. *Reinventing Government: How the Entrepreneurial Spirit Is Transforming the Public Sector.* Reading, Mass.: Addison-Wesley, 1992.

Oster, S. *Strategic Management for Nonprofit Organizations.* Oxford: Oxford University Press, 1995.

Peters, J. P., and Waterman, R. H. *In Search of Excellence.* New York: HarperCollins, 1982.

Salamon, L. M. (ed.). *The State of Nonprofit America.* Washington D.C.: Brookings Institution Press, 2002.

Schorr, L. B. *Common Purpose: Strengthening Families and Neighborhoods to Rebuild America.* New York: Doubleday, 1997.

CHAPTER TWO

Jenkins, C. "Nonprofit Organizations and Policy Advocacy." In W. Powell and R. Steinberg (eds.), *The Nonprofit Sector: A Research Handbook.* (2nd ed.) New Haven, Conn.: Yale University Press, 2006.

Rich, A. *Think Tanks, Public Policy, and the Politics of Expertise.* Cambridge: Cambridge University Press, 2005.

Rich, A. "War of Ideas." *Stanford Social Innovation Review,* 2005, *3*(1), 18–25.

Sagawa, S. "Fulfilling the Promise: Social Entrepreneurs and Action Tanking in a New Era of Entrepreneurship." Unpublished working paper developed for New Profit Inc., Feb. 2006.

Smucker, B. *The Nonprofit Lobbying Guide.* Washington, D.C.: INDEPENDENT SECTOR, 1999.

CHAPTER THREE

Dees, J. G. "Enterprising Nonprofits." *Harvard Business Review,* Jan.–Feb. 1998. Reprinted in *Harvard Business Review on Nonprofits.* Boston: Harvard Business School Press, 1999, pp. 135–166.

Dees, J. G., Emerson, J., and Economy, P. *Strategic Tools for Social Entrepreneurs: Enhancing the Performance of Your Enterprising Nonprofit.* Hoboken, N.J.: Wiley, 2002.

Galaskiewicz, J., and Sinclair, C. M. "Collaboration Between Corporations and Nonprofit Organizations." In W. Powell and R. Steinberg (eds.), *The Nonprofit Sector: A Research Handbook.* (2nd ed.) New Haven, Conn.: Yale University Press, 2006.

"How Nonprofits, For-Profits and Government Are Pushing Sector Boundaries: Key Issues for Research, Policy and Practice." *Snapshots: Research Highlights from the Nonprofit Sector Research Fund,* a publication of the Aspen Institute, May–June 2003, pp. 1–3.

Prahalad, C. K. *The Fortune at the Bottom of the Pyramid: Eradicating Poverty Through Profits.* Upper Saddle River, N.J.: Pearson Education/ Wharton, 2006.

Skloot, E. "Enterprise and Commerce in Nonprofit Organizations." In W. Powell and R. Steinberg (eds.), *The Nonprofit Sector: A Research Handbook.* (2nd ed.) New Haven, Conn.: Yale University Press, 2006.

CHAPTER FOUR

Andreason, A. "Profits for Nonprofits: Finding a Corporate Partner." *Harvard Business Review,* Nov.–Dec. 1996. Reprinted in *Harvard Business Review on Nonprofits.* Boston: Harvard Business School Press, 1999, pp. 111–133.

Davis, G. F., McAdam, D., Scott, W. R., and Zald, M. N. (eds.). *Social Movements and Organization Theory.* New York: Cambridge University Press, 2005.

Fine, A. *Momentum: Igniting Social Change in the Connected Age.* San Francisco: Jossey-Bass, 2006.

Gladwell, M. *The Tipping Point: How Little Things Can Make a Big Difference.* Boston: Little, Brown, 2000.

Kotler, P., and Andreasen, A. *Strategic Marketing for Nonprofit Organizations.* Upper Saddle River, N.J.: Prentice Hall, 2003.

Sirianni, C., and Friedlan, L. *Civic Innovation in America: Community Empowerment, Public Policy, and the Movement for Civic Renewal.* Berkeley: University of California Press, 2001.

CHAPTER FIVE

Barabasi, A. *Linked: How Everything Is Connected to Everything Else and What It Means for Business, Science, and Everyday Life.* New York: Penguin Group, 2003.

Brandenburger, A., and Nalebuff, B. *Co-opetition.* New York: Currency Doubleday, 1996.

Davis, G. F., McAdam, D., Scott, W. R., and Zald, M. N. (eds.). *Social Movements and Organization Theory.* New York: Cambridge University Press, 2005.

Gibson, C. "Citizens at the Center: A New Approach to Civic Engagement." A report commissioned by the Case Foundation, 2006. Available at: www.casefoundation.org/spotlight/ civic_engagement/summary.

O'Flanagan, M., and Taliento, L. "Ensuring That Bigger Is Better." *McKinsey Quarterly,* 2004, no. 2. Available at www.mckinseyquarterly .com/article_abstract.aspx?ar=1419&L2=33&L3=95.

Zald, M. "Making Change: Why Does the Social Sector Need Social Movements?" *Stanford Social Innovation Review,* 2004, 2(2), 25–34.

CHAPTER SIX

Christensen, C. *The Innovator's Dilemma.* Boston: Harvard Business School Press, 1997.

Harvard Business Review on Knowledge Management. Boston: Harvard Business School Press, 1987.

Kim, W. C., and Mauborgne, R. *Blue Ocean Strategy: How to Create Uncontested Market Space and Make Competition Irrelevant.* Boston: Harvard Business School Press, 2005.

Kotter, J. P., and Heskett, J. L. *Corporate Culture and Performance.* New York: Macmillan, 1992.

Light, P. C. *Sustaining Innovation: Creating Nonprofit and Government Organizations That Innovate Naturally.* San Francisco: Jossey-Bass, 1998.

Schein, E. *Organizational Culture and Leadership.* (2nd ed.). San Francisco: Jossey-Bass, 1992.

Senge, P. M. *The Fifth Discipline: The Art and Practice of the Learning Organization.* New York: Currency, 1990.

CHAPTER SEVEN

Carver, J. *Boards That Make a Difference: A New Design for Leadership in Nonprofit and Public Organizations.* (2nd ed.). San Francisco: Jossey-Bass, 2006.

Chait, R. P., Ryan, W. P., and Taylor, B. E. *Governance as Leadership: Reframing the Work of Nonprofit Boards.* Hoboken, N.J.: Wiley, 2005.

Chrislip, D. *Collaborative Leadership: How Citizens and Civic Leaders Can Make a Difference.* San Francisco: Jossey-Bass, 1994.

Crosby, B. C., and Bryson, J. *Leadership for the Common Good: Tackling Public Problems in a Shared-Power World.* (2nd ed.). San Francisco: Jossey-Bass, 2005.

Enright, K. *Investing in Leadership: Vol. 2. Inspiration and Ideas from Philanthropy's Latest Frontier.* Washington, D.C.: Grantmakers for Effective Organizations, 2005.

Henton, D., Melville, J., and Walesh, K. *Grassroots Leaders for a New Economy.* San Francisco: Jossey-Bass, 1997.

Hesselbein, F., Goldsmith, M., Beckhard, R., and Schubert, R. F. (eds.). *The Leader of the Future.* San Francisco: Jossey-Bass, 1996.

Raelin, J. *Creating Leaderful Organizations: How to Bring Out Leadership in Everyone.* San Francisco: Berrett-Koehler, 2003.

CHAPTER EIGHT

Human Resources

Pynes, J. *Human Resource Management for Public and Nonprofit Organizations.* San Francisco: Jossey-Bass, 1999.

Tierney, T. J. "The Nonprofit Sector's Leadership Deficit." San Francisco: Bridgespan Group, Feb. 2006. Available at: www.bridgespan.org/nonprofit-leadership-deficit.aspx?resource=Articles.

Social Capital Markets

Emerson, J. "The U.S. Nonprofit Capital Market: An Introductory Overview of Developmental Stages, Investors and Funding Instruments." 2000. Includes contributions by J. G. Dees and C. W. Letts. Available on the Roberts Enterprise Development Fund Web site, www.redf.org.

Grossman, A. Social Enterprise Series No. 12: "Philanthropic Social Capital Markets Performance Driven Philanthropy." Harvard Business School Working Paper Series, No. 00-002. Boston: Harvard Business School Publishing, 1999.

Meehan, W., Kilmer, D., and O'Flanagan, M. "Investing in Society: Why We Need a More Efficient Social Capital Market and How We Can Get There." *Stanford Social Innovation Review,* Spring 2004, pp. 35–43.

Miller, C. "Hidden in Plain Sight: Understanding Nonprofit Capital Structure." *Nonprofit Quarterly,* Spring 2003, pp. 1–8.

Young, D. R., Bania, N., and Bailey, D. "Structure and Accountability: A Study of National Nonprofit Associations." *Nonprofit Management and Leadership,* 1996, *6*(4), 347–365.

Systems, Capacity Building

For numerous reports on various aspects of organizational capacity building, see the Grantmakers for Effective Organizations Web site, www.geofunders.org.

ACKNOWLEDGMENTS

Like any endeavor that requires great effort, this book—both the original and updated edition—is the result of the combined contributions of many individuals and institutions.

We are deeply grateful to Greg Dees for his contribution of the Foreword to this revised and updated edition of *Forces for Good*. For nearly two decades, we have both been privileged to know Greg; he has at various times been our adviser, mentor, professor, colleague, and, always, friend. Greg is on the faculty at Duke University's Fuqua School of Business and is the founding director of the Center for the Advancement of Social Entrepreneurship (CASE). Without Greg's leadership and thought-partnership, *Forces for Good* would not have come to fruition in its current form. Beth Anderson, who served as managing director of CASE when we conducted the research for the first edition, was also a true partner in this project, providing intellectual guidance, project management, and moral support. At every initial phase, both Greg and Beth pushed our thinking and provided critical in-kind assistance. CASE also created a two-year research fellowship for Heather to join Leslie as coauthor of the book.

Producing this revised and updated edition of *Forces for Good* has involved a new cadre of characters, who have expanded our circle of publishing partners. Alison Hankey, our new editor at Jossey-Bass/John Wiley and Sons, approached us with the idea of writing this updated edition and fearlessly shepherded it through the publishing process. We thank Alan Shrader as well, who helped polish and organize the new manuscript; and our research associate, Scott Brown, who tirelessly assisted us with interviews and with writing and fact-checking the new material. Alison, Alan, and Scott each went the extra mile for us on deadline, for which we are grateful.

We extend deep respect and appreciation to our colleagues Katherine Fulton of Monitor Institute and John Kania and Mark Kramer of FSG for enthusiastically supporting us when we took on writing this new edition. Katherine, John, and Mark's thought-partnership has pushed our thinking and deepened our understanding of how social change is accomplished, and we feel truly privileged to work with them at their respective strategy consulting firms.

The original material from *Forces for Good* would not exist without the intellectual and institutional support of Alan Abramson and the Aspen Institute's Philanthropy and Social Innovation Program, who helped sponsor the initial research. When others questioned whether a book like this could, or should, be written, Alan unhesitatingly offered both time and funding, and had the Aspen Institute act as our fiscal agent; Alan has since joined the faculty at George Mason University. Similarly, Jenny Shilling Stein, executive director of the Draper Richards Foundation, backed the original research project, funding it and acting as a fiscal agent.

To Jim Collins, we owe our respect and gratitude. His books about great businesses inspired this book about great nonprofits—and he wholeheartedly encouraged the idea from the outset. He also provided valuable guidance early on, as we wrestled with the challenge of developing a rigorous methodology for selecting and studying the twelve great social sector organizations featured in the first edition, and he has continued to be a trusted adviser over the years.

We thank Jean and Steve Case of The Case Foundation and their former colleague, Ben Binswanger; Steve generously contributed the Foreword to the first edition of *Forces for Good* in addition to funding the original research. We also thank our other generous financial supporters of the initial research, including leaders from the United Nations Foundation, particularly Kathy Calvin; Rockefeller Brothers Fund and Stephen Heintz; the Surdna Foundation and Ed Skloot and Vince Stehle; the Skoll Foundation and Dan Crisafulli, Lance Henderson, and Sally Osberg; Fannie Mae Foundation and Kil Huh and Ellen Lazar; Ewing Marion Kauffman Foundation and Munro Richardson; the Fitzie Foundation and Gregg Petersmeyer; the Goldhirsh

Foundation and Phil Cutter; and Steve and Roberta Denning. Of special note is Draper Richards Foundation partner Christy Chin, whose commitment to field building has been an inspiration.

Other institutional supporters of the first edition deserve special recognition. Mario Morino, of the Morino Institute and Venture Philanthropy Partners, has been a friend and adviser for years; he and Cheryl Collins provided our very first research grant, along with office space for Leslie. Stanford University's Center for Social Innovation (CSI) provided financial and in-kind support. Kriss Deiglmeier, the executive director, arranged for office space for Heather; and CSI underwrote the valuable time of two graduate research assistants. The staff of the *Stanford Social Innovation Review* provided editorial encouragement.

A host of formal and informal advisers also contributed in meaningful ways to the first edition—from guiding our original research to providing feedback at briefing sessions to reading early drafts of our first-edition manuscript. Brian Trelstad of the Acumen Fund, and a longtime friend and colleague, provided much early intellectual guidance, as did Bill Meehan of McKinsey & Company. Christine Letts of Harvard University provided highly constructive feedback, and her publications have strongly influenced our thinking.

We are also indebted to our teams of graduate student research assistants, who joined us to help with our initial research through their respective universities. These able assistants included Jessica Thomas and Adrian Cighi, then at Duke University's Fuqua School of Business; Brooke Ricalde and Rand Quinn from Stanford University; Christy Gibb and Sarah Lucas from Harvard Business School; and Jennifer Kyne from the Yale School of Management. We also thank researchers Elizabeth Ayala, Annabel Kandiah, Maxime Ko, and Jessica Droste Yagan.

The leaders of the twelve national nonprofits profiled in this book also deserve our appreciation and gratitude for their participation in both the initial and updated research. The CEOs and their senior management teams invited us into their institutions and allowed us to study their "secrets to success." Every one of the organizations profiled in this book was responsive to our many research requests; they generously shared staff time and volumes of internal and sometimes sensitive documents. Of particular note are Alison Franklin, former director of communications at City Year; Charles Kamasaki, senior vice president at NCLR; Mary Mountcastle, senior associate at Self-Help; and David Yarnold, former executive vice president at Environmental Defense Fund. (David now leads the National Audubon Society.) These individuals went out of their way to respond to our queries and engage with us as thought-partners as our research progressed.

In the execution of our research for the first edition, we relied on a wide circle of institutions and individuals. The *Chronicle of Philanthropy* and a number of early-stage nonprofit funders donated lists for our peer survey (see Appendix A for details). Individual field experts generously shared their time and insights to help us select a sample of twelve truly high-impact nonprofits. They are too numerous to list here, but all are credited by name in Appendix B.

To conduct the research for the new material included in this expanded edition, we also relied on the generosity of dozens of leaders of smaller and local organizations across the United States and Canada, who agreed to share their stories and materials with us for a chance at inclusion in the book. (A complete list is included in Appendix F.) We also appreciate the many colleagues and friends, too numerous to list here, who responded when we reached out to them for nominations of local groups to study.

This endeavor began with intensive research and ended with two editions of a book. To help us get it there, we are indebted to our literary agent, Rafe Sagalyn, who has been a constant source of guidance. We also extend our gratitude to our editor of the first edition, Allison Brunner, who championed the initial project. And as we entered into the writing stage the first time around, we were aided by our freelance editor, Mickey Butts, who helped us structure our outline, sharpen our thinking, and refine our prose—just as Alan Shrader did this time.

This book was improved by the many friends and colleagues who agreed to review early drafts of our first edition. In addition to a number of the advisers already mentioned, we are also grateful to Shirley Sagawa, Tony Deifell, Betsy Fader, Alana Conner, and Margaret Hutton Griffin, who each provided feedback at critical junctures. Others who helped stimulate our thinking include Bill Drayton, Sushmita Ghosh, Anamaria Schindler, Diana Wells, and

Susan Davis of Ashoka, as well as Julien Phillips, Dick Cavanaugh, Don Clifford, Alan Grossman, Cheryl Dorsey, Jed Emerson, and David Bornstein.

We also want to thank our personal friends, who were there for us throughout the long four-year journey of researching, writing, and launching the original edition—and the more recent update. To Susan Glasser and Peter Baker, we offer our special appreciation for their literary camaraderie, and for hosting Heather (and family) several times at their home in Washington, D.C. Thanks to the Baxter family for hosting Leslie and her daughter in their Bay Area home. To Jan Brown, Andy Cohen, and Leonora Zilkha, thanks are in order for hosting us in their New York City abodes. To Katie and Will Procter, a special thanks for sharing their nanny in New York. And to our many other friends and colleagues in the nonprofit field, we appreciate your listening to our stories over dinner, sympathizing when we agonized about deadlines, and contributing your ideas to our search for a winning title.

Finally, we owe our deepest gratitude to our families. In particular, we are grateful for Heather's husband, Elliott Grant, and Leslie's husband, Anthony Macintyre, who both read and reread multiple drafts of the original as well as updated chapters, offering critical commentary, helpful advice, and endless encouragement. (Elliott helped with our graphic presentation in both editions of the book!) Our husbands are our true intellectual and emotional partners—and the best dads that two working moms could have taking care of our respective children when we faced unforgiving deadlines and relentless travel demands. We feel blessed to have Anthony and Elliott in our lives.

To our extended families, especially both sets of parents, Pam and Jim Crutchfield and Ruthie and Al McLeod, we owe our deep appreciation for their lifelong love, inspiration, and encouragement. We thank them as well for the child-care safety net they've provided, as we've juggled being first-time authors, first-time moms, and consultants over the past few years.

And to our young children, Heather's Somerset Ellinor Grant and Leslie's Caleigh Crutchfield Macintyre and Quinn Gunn Macintyre, we dedicate this book. We hope that you will go forth into the world and become—in your own unique ways—forces for good.

THE AUTHORS

Leslie R. Crutchfield is a senior adviser with FSG and an author, speaker, and leading authority on scaling social innovation and high-impact philanthropy. Leslie coauthored the first edition of *Forces for Good* (Jossey-Bass, 2007), recognized by *The Economist* on its Best Books of 2007 list. Leslie more recently coauthored with FSG managing directors John Kania and Mark Kramer a book on catalytic philanthropy, *Do More Than Give: The Six Practices of Donors Who Change the World* (Jossey-Bass, 2011), which was inspired by the ideas in *Forces for Good*. FSG is a nonprofit strategy firm cofounded in 1999 as Foundation Strategy Group by Mark Kramer and Michael Porter. Leslie is a former managing director of Ashoka, and she cofounded a social enterprise in the 1990s. Leslie frequently lectures and has published articles in *Fortune, Forbes, Harvard Business Review Online,* the *Chronicle of Philanthropy,* and *Stanford Social Innovation Review.* Leslie serves on the board of the SEED Foundation and was a Crossroads volunteer in Africa. She holds an MBA and an AB from Harvard University, and resides in the Washington, D.C., area with her family. She can be reached via e-mail: leslie.crutchfield@fsg.org.

Heather McLeod Grant is a senior consultant with the Monitor Institute and an author, speaker, and adviser to high-impact non-profits. Her work at Monitor focuses on scaling social innovations and impact, working through networks, and transforming legacy nonprofit organizations. Heather coauthored the first edition of *Forces for Good* (Jossey-Bass, 2007), recognized by *The Economist* on its Best Books of 2007 list. In addition, she has recently published the following articles: "Working Wikily: Social Change with a Network Mindset," "Transformer: How to Build a Network to Change a System," and "Breaking New Ground: Using the Internet to Scale"; her work has been published in numerous industry publications, including *Stanford Social Innovation Review.* Heather is a former McKinsey & Company consultant and a cofounder of *Who Cares,* a national magazine for young social entrepreneurs published from 1993 to 1999. She lectures at Stanford, speaks at industry conferences, and serves on several advisory boards, including at her daughter's school. She holds an MBA from Stanford University and an AB from Harvard University, and resides in the Bay Area with her husband and daughter. She can be reached via e-mail: heather_grant@monitor.com.

INDEX

A

Academics, six practices' applicability to, 21–22

ACORN, 52

Adaptation, 149–173; adaptive capacity and, 152–153; benchmarking and, 167–168; checklist for, 244; cycle of, 151–153, 164–172, 405 n. 4; deepened practice of, over time, 282–284; drivers of, 153–156; embracing change and, 258–259; environmental listening step in, 165, 173, 315–316; evaluate-and-learn step in, 167–168, 173, 316; experiment-and-innovate step in, 165–166, 173, 316; "Free Spirit" approaches to, 157–160, 164, 170–171; implementing, in other organizations, 243, 244; leveraging, 236–237; of local and small nonprofits, 292, 315–316; "MBA" approaches to, 157, 161–164, 171–172; organizational culture and styles of, 156–164, 170–173; overview of, 38; planning and, 161, 162–164, 169, 170–173; program modification step in, 168–169, 173, 316; resources on, 415; steps in, 164–172, 173; summary of, 172–173; winnowing process in, 170–173

Advertising, affiliated, 291–292

Advocacy, defined, 49–50. See also Policy advocacy

Advocacy experts, 341

Affordable housing nonprofits. See Federation of Appalachian Housing Enterprises; Habitat for Humanity; Self-Help; YouthBuild USA

Alcoholics Anonymous, 146, 147

Alumni: engagement of, 120; leadership development with, 120, 137–138, 139, 383–384

America Online (AOL), 16

American Association of Retired Persons (AARP), 48

American Express, 86, 90–91, 118, 150

American Red Cross, 43

America's Second Harvest—The Nation's Food Bank Network. See Feeding America

AmeriCorps: City Year and, 31, 68, 104, 141–142, 143, 217, 247, 358, 359; Teach For America funding from, 226; YouthBuild USA and, 386

Amgen, 86

Ammar, D., 296, 297, 298, 392

Andrews, J., 145

Annual conferences and events: community building with, 119–120, 311; income generation from, 68–69, 90; for program planning and improvement, 169

Anti–predatory lending legislation, 47–49, 158, 255, 257, 272

Apache Nation, 146

Appalachian development organization. See Federation of Appalachian Housing Enterprises

Applebee's, 150

Archimedes, 36

Aronoff, M., 198, 350

Arts and culture experts, 341–342

Arts case study organization. See Little Theatre on the Square

Arts organizations, 332

Ashoka, 41, 178, 329, 331

Aspen Institute, 330, 334, 400 n. 9

Atlantic Philanthropies, 225

Avenida Guadalupe, 392

Aviv, D., 116

F

M